Get the eBook FREE!

(PDF, ePub, Kindle, and liveBook all included)

We believe that once you buy a book from us, you should be able to read it in any format we have available. To get electronic versions of this book at no additional cost to you, purchase and then register this book at the Manning website.

Go to https://www.manning.com/freebook and follow the instructions to complete your pBook registration.

That's it!
Thanks from Manning!

Praise for earlier editions of
Unity in Action

Step-by-step examples and clear prose make this the go-to book for Unity!
—Victor M. Perez, Software developer

Everything you need to know about Unity in one single resource.
—Dan Kacenjar, Cornerstone Software

Start creating your own game prototypes in no time.
—David Torrubia Iñigo, Fintonic

The text is clear and concise, and the examples are outstanding.
—Dan Kacenjar, Sr., Wolters Kluwer

All the roadblocks evaporated, and I took my game from concept to build in short order.
—Philip Taffet, SOHOsoft

Joe Hocking wastes none of your time and gets you coding fast.
—Jesse Schell, author of The Art of Game Design

I've wanted to program in Unity for a long time, and this book has given me the confidence to do so.
—Robin Dewson, Schroders

Gets you up and running in no time.
—Sergio Arbeo, codecantor

Unity in Action, Third Edition

MULTIPLATFORM GAME DEVELOPMENT IN C#

JOSEPH HOCKING

FOREWORD BY JESSE SCHELL

MANNING

SHELTER ISLAND

For online information and ordering of this and other Manning books, please visit
www.manning.com. The publisher offers discounts on this book when ordered in quantity.
For more information, please contact

    Special Sales Department
    Manning Publications Co.
    20 Baldwin Road
    PO Box 761
    Shelter Island, NY 11964
    Email: orders@manning.com

The author and publisher have made every effort to ensure that the information in this book
was correct at press time. The author and publisher do not assume and hereby disclaim any
liability to any party for any loss, damage, or disruption caused by errors or omissions, whether
such errors or omissions result from negligence, accident, or any other cause, or from any usage
of the information herein.

Manning Publications Co. 20 Baldwin Road PO Box 761 Shelter Island, NY 11964	Development editor: Becky Whitney Review editor: Mihaela Batinić Production editor: Deirdre S. Hiam Copy editor: Sharon Wilkey Proofreader: Jason Everett Typesetter: Gordan Salinovic Cover designer: Marija Tudor

ISBN 9781617299339

Printed in the United States of America

brief contents

PART 1 FIRST STEPS 1

    1 ▪ Getting to know Unity 3

    2 ▪ Building a demo that puts you in 3D space 23

    3 ▪ Adding enemies and projectiles to the 3D game 50

    4 ▪ Developing graphics for your game 75

PART 2 GETTING COMFORTABLE 101

    5 ▪ Building a Memory game using Unity's 2D functionality 103

    6 ▪ Creating a basic 2D platformer 128

    7 ▪ Putting a GUI onto a game 147

    8 ▪ Creating a third-person 3D game: Player movement and animation 171

    9 ▪ Adding interactive devices and items within the game 200

PART 3 STRONG FINISH 227

    10 ▪ Connecting your game to the internet   229
    11 ▪ Playing audio: Sound effects and music   257
    12 ▪ Putting the parts together into a complete game   282
    13 ▪ Deploying your game to players' devices   314

contents

foreword *xv*
preface *xvii*
acknowledgments *xix*
about this book *xxi*
about the author *xxv*
about the cover illustration *xxvi*

PART 1 FIRST STEPS 1

1 Getting to know Unity *3*

1.1 Why is Unity so great? 4

Unity's strengths and advantages *4* ▪ *Downsides to be aware of* *6*
Example games built with Unity *7*

1.2 How to use Unity 10

Scene view, Game view, and the Toolbar *12* ▪ *The mouse and*
keyboard *14* ▪ *The Hierarchy view and the Inspector panel* *15*
The Project and Console tabs *16*

1.3 Getting up and running with Unity programming 16

Running code in Unity: Script components *17* ▪ *Using Visual*
Studio, the included IDE *18* ▪ *Printing to the console: Hello*
World! *19*

2 Building a demo that puts you in 3D space 23

2.1 Before you start . . . 24

Planning the project 24 ▪ Understanding 3D coordinate space 25

2.2 Begin the project: Place objects in the scene 27

The scenery: Floor, outer walls, and inner walls 28 ▪ Lights and cameras 30 ▪ The player's collider and viewpoint 32

2.3 Make things move: A script that applies transforms 33

Visualizing how movement is programmed 33 ▪ Writing code to implement the diagram 34 ▪ Understanding local vs. global coordinate space 35

2.4 Script component for looking around: MouseLook 37

Horizontal rotation that tracks mouse movement 38 ▪ Vertical rotation with limits 39 ▪ Horizontal and vertical rotation at the same time 41

2.5 Keyboard input component: First-person controls 44

Responding to keypresses 44 ▪ Setting a rate of movement independent of the computer's speed 45 ▪ Moving the CharacterController for collision detection 46 ▪ Adjusting components for walking instead of flying 47

3 Adding enemies and projectiles to the 3D game 50

3.1 Shooting via raycasts 51

What is raycasting? 51 ▪ Using the ScreenPointToRay command for shooting 52 ▪ Adding visual indicators for aiming and hits 54

3.2 Scripting reactive targets 57

Determining what was hit 57 ▪ Alerting the target that it was hit 58

3.3 Basic wandering AI 60

Diagramming how basic AI works 60 ▪ "Seeing" obstacles with a raycast 61 ▪ Tracking the character's state 62

3.4 Spawning enemy prefabs 64

What is a prefab? 64 ▪ Creating the enemy prefab 65 Instantiating from an invisible SceneController 65

3.5 Shooting by instantiating objects 68

Creating the projectile prefab 68 ▪ Shooting the projectile and colliding with a target 70 ▪ Damaging the player 73

4 Developing graphics for your game   75

4.1 Understanding art assets   76

4.2 Building basic 3D scenery: Whiteboxing   78

*Whiteboxing explained   79 • Drawing a floor plan for the
level   79 • Laying out primitives according to the plan   80*

4.3 Texturing the scene with 2D images   82

*Choosing a file format   83 • Importing an image file   84
Applying the image   85*

4.4 Generating sky visuals by using texture images   87

What is a skybox?   87 • Creating a new skybox material   88

4.5 Working with custom 3D models   90

*Which file format to choose?   91 • Exporting and importing the
model   92*

4.6 Creating effects by using particle systems   95

*Adjusting parameters on the default effect   96 • Applying a new
texture for fire   98 • Attaching particle effects to 3D objects   99*

PART 2 GETTING COMFORTABLE 101

5 Building a Memory game using Unity's 2D functionality   103

5.1 Setting up everything for 2D graphics   104

*Preparing the project   105 • Displaying 2D images (aka
sprites)   107 • Switching the camera to 2D mode   108*

5.2 Building a card object and making it react to clicks   110

*Building the object out of sprites   110 • Mouse input code   111
Revealing the card on a click   112*

5.3 Displaying the various card images   113

*Loading images programmatically   113 • Setting the image from
an invisible SceneController   114 • Instantiating a grid of
cards   116 • Shuffling the cards   118*

5.4 Making and scoring matches   119

*Storing and comparing revealed cards   120 • Hiding mismatched
cards   120 • Text display for the score   121*

5.5 Restart button   123

*Programming a UIButton component by using SendMessage   124
Calling LoadScene from SceneController   126*

6 Creating a basic 2D platformer   128

6.1 Setting up the graphics   129

Placing the scenery   129 ▪ *Importing sprite sheets   130*

6.2 Moving the player left and right   132

Writing keyboard controls   133 ▪ *Colliding with the block   134*

6.3 Playing the sprite's animation   134

Explaining the Mecanim animation system   134 ▪ *Triggering animations from code   136*

6.4 Adding the ability to jump   137

Falling from gravity   137 ▪ *Applying an upward impulse   138 Detecting the ground   139*

6.5 Additional features for a platform game   140

Unusual floors: Slopes and one-way platforms   140 ▪ *Implementing moving platforms   142* ▪ *Camera control   145*

7 Putting a GUI onto a game   147

7.1 Before you start writing code . . .   149

Immediate mode GUI or advanced 2D interface?   149 ▪ *Planning the layout   150* ▪ *Importing UI images   151*

7.2 Setting up the GUI display   151

Creating a canvas for the interface   151 ▪ *Buttons, images, and text labels   153* ▪ *Controlling the position of UI elements   156*

7.3 Programming interactivity in the UI   157

Programming an invisible UIController   158 ▪ *Creating a pop-up window   160* ▪ *Setting values using sliders and input fields   163*

7.4 Updating the game by responding to events   166

Integrating an event system   166 ▪ *Broadcasting and listening for events from the scene   167* ▪ *Broadcasting and listening for events from the HUD   168*

8 Creating a third-person 3D game: Player movement and animation   171

8.1 Adjusting the camera view for third-person   173

Importing a character to look at   174 ▪ *Adding shadows to the scene   175* ▪ *Orbiting the camera around the player character   177*

8.2 Programming camera-relative movement controls   180

Rotating the character to face movement direction   180 ▪ *Moving forward in that direction   183*

8.3 Implementing the jump action 184

Applying vertical speed and acceleration 185 • Modifying the ground detection to handle edges and slopes 186

8.4 Setting up animations on the player character 190

Defining animation clips in the imported model 192 • Creating the animator controller for these animations 194 • Writing code that operates the animator 197

9 *Adding interactive devices and items within the game* 200

9.1 Creating doors and other devices 201

Doors that open and close on a keypress 201 • Checking distance and facing before opening the door 203 • Operating a color-changing monitor 205

9.2 Interacting with objects by bumping into them 206

Colliding with physics-enabled obstacles 206 • Operating the door with a trigger object 207 • Collecting items scattered around the level 210

9.3 Managing inventory data and game state 212

Setting up player and inventory managers 212 • Programming the game managers 214 • Storing inventory in a collection object: List vs. Dictionary 217

9.4 Inventory UI for using and equipping items 220

Displaying inventory items in the UI 220 • Equipping a key to use on locked doors 223 • Restoring the player's health by consuming health packs 224

PART 3 STRONG FINISH 227

10 *Connecting your game to the internet* 229

10.1 Creating an outdoor scene 231

Generating sky visuals by using a skybox 231 • Setting up an atmosphere that's controlled by code 232

10.2 Downloading weather data from an internet service 235

Requesting HTTP data using coroutines 238 • Parsing XML 242 • Parsing JSON 243 • Affecting the scene based on weather data 246

10.3 Adding a networked billboard 247

Loading images from the internet 247 • Displaying images on the billboard 250 • Caching the downloaded image for reuse 251

10.4   Posting data to a web server   253

    Tracking current weather: Sending post requests   254 ▪ *Server-side code in PHP   255*

11 **Playing audio: Sound effects and music   257**

11.1   Importing sound effects   258

    Supported file formats   258 ▪ *Importing audio files   260*

11.2   Playing sound effects   261

    Explaining what's involved: Audio clip vs. source vs. listener   261 Assigning a looping sound   263 ▪ *Triggering sound effects from code   264*

11.3   Using the audio control interface   265

    Setting up the central AudioManager   265 ▪ *Volume control UI   267* ▪ *Playing UI sounds   271*

11.4   Adding background music   272

    Playing music loops   272 ▪ *Controlling music volume separately   276* ▪ *Fading between songs   278*

12 **Putting the parts together into a complete game   282**

12.1   Building an action RPG by repurposing projects   283

    Assembling assets and code from multiple projects   284 Programming point-and-click controls: Movement and devices   286 Replacing the old GUI with a new interface   292

12.2   Developing the overarching game structure   299

    Controlling mission flow and multiple levels   299 ▪ *Completing a level by reaching the exit   303* ▪ *Losing the level when caught by enemies   305*

12.3   Handling the player's progression through the game   307

    Saving and loading the player's progress   307 ▪ *Beating the game by completing three levels   311*

13 **Deploying your game to players' devices   314**

13.1   Start by building for the desktop: Windows, Mac, and Linux   317

    Building the application   317 ▪ *Adjusting player settings: Setting the game's name and icon   318* ▪ *Platform-dependent compilation   319*

13.2   Building for the web   321

    Building the game embedded in a web page   321 ▪ *Communicating with JavaScript in the browser   322*

13.3   Building for mobile: iOS and Android   325

Setting up the build tools   326 ▪ *Texture compression   331*
Developing plugins   332

13.4   Developing XR (both VR and AR)   341

Supporting virtual reality headsets   341 ▪ *AR Foundation for*
mobile Augmented Reality   342

afterword   349

appendix A   Scene navigation and keyboard shortcuts   353
appendix B   External tools used alongside Unity   356
appendix C   Modeling a bench in Blender   360
appendix D   Online learning resources   369

index   373

foreword

I started programming games in 1982. It wasn't easy. We had no internet. Resources were limited to a handful of mostly terrible books and magazines that offered fascinating but confusing code fragments, and as for game engines—well, there weren't any! Coding games was a massive uphill battle.

How I envy you, reader, holding the power of this book in your hands. The Unity engine has done so much to open game programming up to so many people. Unity has managed to strike an excellent balance by being a powerful, professional game engine that's still affordable and approachable for someone just getting started.

Approachable, that is, with the right guidance. I once spent time in a circus troupe run by a magician. He was kind enough to take me in and helped guide me toward becoming a good performer. "When you stand on a stage," he pronounced, "you make a promise. And that promise is 'I will not waste your time.'"

What I love most about *Unity in Action* is the "action" part. Joe Hocking wastes none of your time and gets you coding fast—and not just nonsense code, but interesting code that you can understand and build from, because he knows you don't just want to read his book, and you don't just want to program his examples—you want to be coding *your own game.*

And with his guidance, you'll be able to do that sooner than you might expect. Follow Joe's steps, but when you feel ready, don't be shy about diverging from his path and breaking out on your own. Skip to what interests you most—try experiments, be bold and brave! You can always return to the text if you get too lost.

But let's not dally in this foreword—the entire future of game development is impatiently waiting for you to begin! Mark this day on your calendar, for today is the day that everything changed. It will be forever remembered as the day you started making games.

JESSE SCHELL
CEO OF SCHELL GAMES
AUTHOR OF *THE ART OF GAME DESIGN*

preface

I've been programming games for quite some time, but started using Unity only relatively recently. Unity didn't exist when I first started developing games; the first version was released in 2005. Right from the start, it had a lot of promise as a game development tool, but it didn't come into its own until several versions later. In particular, platforms like iOS and Android (collectively referred to as *mobile*) didn't emerge until later, and those platforms factor heavily into Unity's growing prominence.

Initially, I viewed Unity as a curiosity, an interesting development tool to keep an eye on but not actually use. During that time, I was programming games for both desktop computers and websites and doing projects for a range of clients. I was using tools like Blitz3D and Adobe Flash, which were great to program in but were limiting in a lot of ways. As those tools started to show their age, I kept looking for better ways to develop games.

I started experimenting with Unity around version 3 and then completely switched to it for my development work at Synapse Games. At first, I worked for Synapse on web games, but we eventually moved over to mobile games. And then we came full circle because Unity enabled us to deploy to the web in addition to mobile, all from one codebase!

I've always seen sharing knowledge as important and have taught game development for several years. A large part of why I do this is the example set by my many mentors and teachers. (Incidentally, you may even have heard of one of my teachers because he was such an inspiring person: Randy Pausch delivered "The Last Lecture" shortly before he passed away in 2008.) I've taught classes at several schools and have always wanted to write a book about game development.

In many ways, what I've written here is the book I wish had existed back when I was first learning Unity. Among Unity's many virtues is a huge treasure trove of learning resources, but those resources tend to take the form of unfocused fragments (like the script reference or isolated tutorials) and require much digging to find what you need. Ideally, I'd have a book that wrapped up everything I needed to know in one place and presented it in a clear and logical manner, so now I'm writing such a book for you. I'm targeting people who already know how to program but who are newcomers to Unity, and possibly new to game development in general. The choice of projects reflects my experience of gaining skills and confidence by doing a variety of freelance projects in rapid succession.

In learning to develop games using Unity, you're setting out on an exciting adventure. For me, learning how to develop games meant putting up with a lot of hassle. You, on the other hand, have the advantage of a single coherent resource to learn from: this book!

acknowledgments

I would like to thank Manning Publications for giving me the opportunity to write this book. The editors I worked with, including Robin de Jongh and especially Dan Maharry, helped me throughout this undertaking, and the book is much stronger for their feedback. Becky Whitney took over as primary editor for this third edition, while Candace West filled that role on the second edition. My sincere thanks also to the many others who worked with me during the development and production of the book: Deirdre Hiam, the project editor; Sharon Wilkey, the copyeditor; Jason Everett, the proofreader; and Mihaela Batinić, the reviewing editor.

My writing benefited from the scrutiny of reviewers every step of the way. Thanks to Aharon Sharim Rani, Alain Couniot, Alain Lompo, Alberto Simões, Bradley Irby, Brent Boylan, Chris Lundberg, Cristian Antonioli, David Moskowitz, Erik Hansson, Francesco Argese, Hilde Van Gysel, James Matlock, Jan Kroken, John Ackley, John Guthrie, Jose San Leandro, Joseph W. White, Justin Calleja, Kent R. Spillner, Krishna Chaitanya Anipindi, Martin Tidman, Max Weinbrown, Nenko Ivanov Tabakov, Nick Keers, Owain Williams, Robert Walsh, Satej Kumar Sahu, Scott Chaussée, and Walter Stoneburner. Special thanks to the notable review work by technical development editor Scott Chaussée and by technical proofreader Christopher Haupt. René van den Berg and Shiloh Morris stepped into those roles for the second edition, while René was technical proofreader on the third edition and Robin Dewson did the tech edit. And I also want to thank Jesse Schell for writing the foreword to my book.

Next, I'd like to recognize the people who've made my experience with Unity a fruitful one. That, of course, starts with Unity Technologies, the company that makes

Unity (the game engine). I am also indebted to the community at the Game Development site on Stack Exchange (https://gamedev.stackexchange.com); while writing the first edition, I visited that QA site almost daily to learn from others and to answer questions. And the biggest push for me to use Unity came from Alex Reeve, my boss at Synapse Games. Similarly, I've picked up tricks and techniques from my coworkers, in both that and every job I've held since, and they all show up in the code I write.

Finally, I want to thank my wife, Virginia, for her support during the time I was writing the book. Until I started working on it, I never really understood how much a book project takes over your life and affects everyone around you. Thank you so much for your love and encouragement.

about this book

Who should read this book

Unity in Action, Third Edition is a book about programming games in Unity. Think of it as an intro to Unity for experienced programmers. The goal of this book is straightforward: to take people who have some programming experience, but no experience with Unity, and teach them how to develop a game by using Unity.

The best way of teaching development is through example projects, with students learning by doing, and that's the approach this book takes. I'll present topics as steps toward building sample games, and you'll be encouraged to build these games in Unity while exploring the book. We'll go through a selection of projects every few chapters, rather than one monolithic project developed over the entire book. (Sometimes other books take the "one monolithic project" approach, but that can make it hard to jump into the middle if the early chapters aren't relevant to you.)

This book has more rigorous programming content than most Unity books (especially beginners' books). Unity is often portrayed as a list of features with no programming required, which is a misleading view that won't teach people what they need to know in order to produce commercial titles. If you don't already know how to program a computer, I suggest going to one of the various "free interactive coding lessons" websites (https://learnprogramming.online, for example) and then coming back to this book after learning how to program.

Don't worry about the exact programming language; C# is used throughout this book, but skills from other languages will transfer quite well. Although the first part of the book takes its time introducing new concepts and will carefully and deliberately step you through developing your first game in Unity, the remaining chapters move a lot faster in order to take you through projects in multiple game genres. The book ends with a chapter describing deployment to various platforms including the web and mobile, but the main thrust of the book doesn't make any reference to the ultimate deployment target because Unity is wonderfully platform-agnostic.

As for other aspects of game development, extensive coverage of art disciplines would water down how much the book can cover and would be largely about software external to Unity (for example, the animation software used). Discussion of art tasks will be limited to aspects specific to Unity or that all game developers should know. (Note, though, that appendix C is about modeling custom objects.)

How this book is organized: A roadmap

Chapter 1 introduces you to Unity, the cross-platform game development environment. You'll learn about the fundamental component system underlying everything in Unity, as well as how to write and execute basic scripts.

Chapter 2 progresses to writing a demo of movement in 3D, covering topics like mouse and keyboard input. Defining and manipulating both 3D positions and rotations are thoroughly explained.

Chapter 3 turns the movement demo into a first-person shooter, teaching you raycasting and basic AI. Raycasting (shooting a line into the scene and seeing what it intersects) is a useful operation for all sorts of games.

Chapter 4 covers importing and creating art assets. This is the one chapter of the book that does not focus on code, because every project needs (basic) models and textures.

Chapter 5 teaches you how to create a 2D puzzle game in Unity. Although Unity started exclusively for 3D graphics, it now has excellent support for 2D graphics.

Chapter 6 expands the 2D game explanations with platform game mechanics. In particular, we'll implement controls, physics, and animation for the player.

Chapter 7 introduces you to the latest GUI functionality in Unity. Every game needs a UI, and the latest versions of Unity feature an improved system for creating UIs.

Chapter 8 shows how to create another movement demo in 3D, seen only from the third-person perspective this time. Implementing third-person controls will demonstrate key 3D math operations, and you'll learn how to work with an animated character.

Chapter 9 goes over how to implement interactive devices and items within your game. The player will have multiple ways of operating these devices, including touching them directly, touching triggers within the game, or pressing a button on the controller.

Chapter 10 covers how to communicate with the internet. You'll learn how to send and receive data by using standard internet technologies, like HTTP requests to get XML or JSON data from a server.

Chapter 11 teaches how to program audio functionality. Unity has great support for both short sound effects and long music tracks; both sorts of audio are crucial for almost all video games.

Chapter 12 walks you through bringing together pieces from different chapters into a single game. In addition, you'll learn how to program point-and-click controls and how to save the player's game.

Chapter 13 goes over building the final app, with deployment to multiple platforms like desktop, web, mobile, and even VR. Unity enables you to create games for every major gaming platform!

Four appendixes provide additional information about scene navigation, external tools, Blender, and learning resources.

About the code

All the source code in the book, whether in code listings or snippets, is in a `fixed-width font like this`, which sets it off from the surrounding text. In most listings, the code is annotated to point out key concepts. The code is formatted so that it fits within the available page space in the book by adding line breaks and using indentation carefully.

The only software required is Unity; this book uses Unity 2020.3.12, which is the current default release as I write this. Certain chapters do occasionally discuss other pieces of software, but those are treated as optional extras and not core to what you're learning.

> **WARNING** Unity projects remember which version of Unity they were created in and will issue a warning if you attempt to open them in a different version. If you see that warning while opening this book's sample downloads, click Continue and ignore it.

The code listings sprinkled throughout the book generally show what to add or change in existing code files; unless it's the first appearance of a given code file, don't replace the entire file with subsequent listings. Although you can download complete working sample projects to refer to, you'll learn best by typing out the code listings and looking at the working samples only for reference. Those downloads are available from the publisher's website (https://www.manning.com/books/unity-in-action-third-edition) and on GitHub (https://github.com/jhocking/uia-3e).

liveBook discussion forum

Purchase of *Unity in Action, Third Edition,* includes free access to liveBook, Manning's online reading platform. Using liveBook's exclusive discussion features, you can attach comments to the book globally or to specific sections or paragraphs. It's a snap to make notes for yourself, ask and answer technical questions, and receive help from the author and other users. To access the forum, go to https://livebook.manning.com/#!/book/unity-in-action-third-edition/discussion. You can also learn more about Manning's forums and the rules of conduct at https://livebook.manning.com/#!/discussion.

Mannings's commitment to our readers is to provide a venue where a meaningful dialogue between individual readers and between readers and the author can take place. It is not a commitment to any specific amount of participation on the part of the author, whose contribution to the forum remains voluntary (and unpaid). We suggest you try asking the author some challenging questions lest his interest stray! The forum and the archives of previous discussions will be accessible from the publisher's website as long as the book is in print.

about the author

JOE HOCKING is a software engineer who specializes in interactive media development. He currently works for Qualcomm, wrote most of the third edition while working for BUNDLAR, and wrote the first edition while at Synapse Games. He has also taught classes at the University of Illinois Chicago, the School of the Art Institute of Chicago, and Columbia College Chicago. He lives in the Chicago suburbs with his wife and two kids. His website is www.newarteest.com.

about the cover illustration

The figure on the cover of *Unity in Action, Third Edition* is captioned "Habit of the Master of Ceremonies of the Grand Signior." The Grand Signior was another name for a sultan of the Ottoman Empire. The illustration is taken from *A Collection of the Dresses of Different Nations, Ancient and Modern* by Thomas Jefferys, published in London between 1757 and 1772. The title page states that these are hand-colored copperplate engravings, heightened with gum arabic. Jefferys (1719–1771) was called "Geographer to King George III." An English cartographer who was the leading map supplier of his day, Jefferys engraved and printed maps for government and other official bodies and produced a wide range of commercial maps and atlases, especially of North America. His work as a mapmaker sparked an interest in local dress customs of the lands he surveyed, which are brilliantly displayed in this four-volume collection.

Fascination with faraway lands and travel for pleasure were relatively new phenomena in the late 18th century, and collections such as this one were popular, introducing the tourist as well as the armchair traveler to the inhabitants of other countries. The diversity of the drawings in Jefferys's volumes speaks vividly of the uniqueness and individuality of the world's nations some 200 years ago. Dress codes have changed since then, and the diversity by region and country, so rich at the time, has faded away. It is now hard to tell the inhabitant of one continent apart from another. Perhaps, trying to view it optimistically, we have traded a cultural and visual diversity for a more varied personal life, or a more varied and interesting intellectual and technical life.

At a time when it is hard to tell one computer book from another, Manning celebrates the inventiveness and initiative of the computer business with book covers based on the rich diversity of regional life of two centuries ago, brought back to life by Jefferys's pictures.

Part 1

First steps

It's time to take your first steps in using Unity. If you don't know anything about Unity, that's okay! I'm going to start by explaining what Unity is, including the fundamentals of how to program games in it. Then we'll walk through a tutorial about developing a simple game in Unity. This first project will teach you several specific game development techniques, as well as give you a good overview of how the process works. Onward to chapter 1!

Getting to know Unity

If you're anything like me, you've had developing a video game on your mind for a long time. But it's a big jump from playing games to making them. Numerous game development tools have appeared over the years, and we're going to discuss one of the most recent and most powerful of these tools.

Unity is a professional-quality game engine used to create video games targeting a variety of platforms. It's not only a professional development tool used daily by thousands of seasoned game developers, but also one of the most accessible modern tools for novice game developers. Until recently, a newcomer to game development would face lots of imposing barriers right from the start, but Unity makes it easy to start learning these skills.

Because you're reading this book, chances are you're curious about computer technology and have either developed games with other tools or built other kinds of software, such as desktop applications or websites. Creating a video game isn't fundamentally different from writing any other kind of software; it's mostly a difference of degree. For example, a video game is a lot more interactive than most websites, and thus involves different sorts of code, but the skills and processes involved in creating both are similar.

If you've already cleared the first hurdle on your path to learning game development, having learned the fundamentals of programming software, then your next step is to pick up some game development tools and translate that programming knowledge into the realm of gaming. Unity is a great choice of game development environment to work with.

A warning about terminology

This book is about programming in Unity and is therefore primarily of interest to coders. Although many other resources discuss different aspects of game development and Unity, in this book programming takes front and center.

Incidentally, note that the word *developer* may have an unfamiliar meaning in the context of game development: *developer* is a synonym for *programmer* in disciplines like web development, but in game development, *developer* often refers to anyone who works on a game, and *programmer* is a specific role within that. Other kinds of game developers are artists and designers, but this book focuses on programming.

To start, go to www.unity.com to learn more about the software. Although Unity's original focus was on 3D games, Unity works great for 2D games as well, and this book covers both. Indeed, even when demonstrated on a 3D project, many topics (saving data, playing audio, and so on) apply to both. Section 1.2 will walk you through installing Unity as a newcomer, but first let's discuss specific reasons to choose this tool.

1.1   *Why is Unity so great?*

Let's take a closer look at that description from the beginning of the chapter: Unity is a professional-quality game engine used to create video games targeting a variety of platforms. That's a fairly straightforward answer to the straightforward question "What is Unity?" But what exactly does that answer mean, and why is Unity so great?

1.1.1   *Unity's strengths and advantages*

Game engines provide a plethora of features that are useful across many games. A game implemented using a particular engine will get all those features, while adding custom art assets and gameplay code specific to that game. Unity has physics simulation, normal maps, screen space ambient occlusion (SSAO), dynamic shadows . . . and the list goes on. Many game engines boast such features, but Unity has two main advantages over similar cutting-edge game development tools: an extremely productive visual workflow and a high degree of cross-platform support.

The visual workflow is a fairly unique design, different from most other game development environments. Whereas other game development tools are often a complicated mishmash of disparate parts that must be wrangled, or perhaps a programming library that requires you to set up your own integrated development environment (IDE), build-chain, and whatnot, the development workflow in Unity is anchored by a sophisticated visual editor.

The editor is used to lay out the scenes in your game and to tie together art assets and code into interactive objects. The beauty of this editor is that it enables professional-quality games to be built quickly and efficiently, giving developers tools to be incredibly productive, while still using an extensive list of the latest technologies in video gaming.

> **NOTE** Most other game development tools that have a central visual editor are also saddled with limited and inflexible scripting support, but Unity doesn't suffer from that disadvantage. Although everything created for Unity ultimately goes through the visual editor, this core interface can be used to link projects to custom code that runs in Unity's game engine. Experienced programmers shouldn't dismiss this development environment, mistaking it for some click-together game creator with limited programming capability!

The editor is especially helpful for doing rapid iteration, honing the game through cycles of prototyping and testing. You can adjust objects in the editor and move things around even while the game is running. Plus, Unity allows you to customize the editor itself by writing scripts that add new features and menus to the interface.

Besides the editor's significant productivity advantages, the other main strength of Unity's tool set is a high degree of cross-platform support. Not only is Unity multiplatform in terms of deployment targets (you can deploy to PC, web, mobile, or consoles), but it's also multiplatform in terms of development tools (you can develop a game on Microsoft Windows or Apple macOS). This platform-agnostic nature is largely because Unity started as Mac-only software and was later ported to Windows. The first version launched in 2005 and initially supported only Mac, but within months Unity had been updated to work on Windows as well.

Successive versions gradually added more deployment platforms, such as a cross-platform web player in 2006, iPhone in 2008, Android in 2010, and even game consoles like Xbox and PlayStation. More recently, Unity has added deployment to WebGL, the new framework for graphics in web browsers, and even has support for extended reality (XR)—both virtual reality (VR) and augmented reality (AR)—platforms like Oculus and VIVE. Few game engines support as many deployment targets as Unity, and none make deploying to multiple platforms so simple.

In addition to these main strengths, a third, more subtle, benefit comes from the modular component system used to construct game objects. In a component system, *components* are mix-and-match packets of functionality, and objects are built up as a collection of components, rather than as a strict hierarchy of classes. A component system is a different (and usually more flexible) approach to object-oriented programming (OOP) that constructs game objects through composition rather than inheritance. Figure 1.1 diagrams an example comparison.

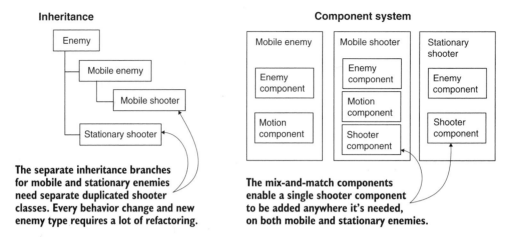

Figure 1.1   Inheritance versus composition

In a component system, objects exist on a flat hierarchy, and different objects have different collections of components. An inheritance structure, in contrast, has different objects on completely different branches of the tree. The component arrangement facilitates rapid prototyping, because you can quickly mix and match components rather than having to refactor the inheritance chain when objects change.

Although you could write code to implement a custom component system if one didn't exist, Unity already has a robust component system, and this system is even integrated with the visual editor. Instead of being able to manipulate components only in code, you can attach and detach components within the visual editor. Meanwhile, you aren't limited to building objects only through composition; you still have the option of using inheritance in your code, including all the best-practice design patterns that have emerged based on inheritance.

1.1.2   *Downsides to be aware of*

Unity has many advantages that make it a great choice for developing games, and I highly recommend it, but I'd be remiss if I didn't mention its weaknesses. In particular, the combination of the visual editor and sophisticated coding, though very effective with Unity's component system, is unusual and can create difficulties. In complex scenes, you can lose track of which objects in the scene have specific components attached. Unity does provide a search feature for finding attached scripts, but it could be more robust; sometimes you still encounter situations requiring you to manually inspect everything in the scene in order to find script linkages. This doesn't happen often, but when it does happen, it can be tedious.

Another disadvantage that can be surprising and frustrating for experienced programmers is that linking in external code libraries can be difficult. Old versions of Unity didn't support external code libraries at all actually, so they had to be manually copied into every project. Now Unity comes with the Package Manager, and libraries (or *packages*) are referenced from a central shared location. These packages work great for optional functionality provided by Unity itself (Unity doesn't automatically include functionality that you don't need in every single project), and future chapters will occasionally have you installing packages for things like advanced font handling. Creating your own packages can be tricky, however, making it awkward to share code among multiple projects. You may find it simpler to just manually copy code between projects and deal with any version mismatches down the road, which is not an ideal trade-off to be making.

> **NOTE** Difficulty working with version-control systems (such as Git or Subversion) used to be a significant weakness of Unity, but more recent versions work fine. You may find out-of-date resources telling you that Unity doesn't work with version control, but newer resources describe which files and folders in a project need to be put in the repository and which don't. To start out, read Unity's documentation (http://mng.bz/BbhD) or look at the .gitignore file maintained by GitHub (http://mng.bz/g7nl).

A third weakness has to do with the sometimes dizzying array of options. Unity offers multiple approaches to some functionalities, and it is not always clear which approach you should use. To a certain extent, that situation is inevitable for a tool under active development, but still results in confusion and discomfort for users. This evolutionary messiness can bewilder even Unity veterans, so newcomers to Unity will definitely face confusion at times. This book highlights such features and offers guidance.

For example, chapter 7 explains how to develop a user interface (UI) for Unity games. Well, Unity actually has *three* UI systems (which are compared at http://mng.bz/r60X) because of successively developed systems that improve on their predecessor. This book covers the second UI system (Unity UI, or uGUI) because it is still preferred over the incomplete third UI system (UI Toolkit), but I wouldn't be surprised if UI Toolkit matures to production-ready within a few years. In the interim, newcomers may have difficulty deciding on a UI approach.

1.1.3 *Example games built with Unity*

You've heard about the pros and cons of Unity, but you might still need convincing that its development tools can give first-rate results. Visit the Unity gallery at https://unity.com/case-study to see a constantly updated list of games and simulations developed using Unity. This section explores a handful of games, showcasing multiple genres and deployment platforms. All game titles are trademarks of their respective game companies, and screenshots are also copyrighted to those companies, with all rights reserved.

DESKTOP (WINDOWS, MAC, LINUX) AND CONSOLE (PLAYSTATION, XBOX, SWITCH)

Because the Unity editor runs on the same platform, deployment to Windows or Mac is often the most straightforward target platform. Meanwhile, console games developed in Unity are often released on PC too, thanks to Unity's easy cross-platform deployment. Here are a couple of examples of desktop and console games in different genres:

- *Fall Guys* (figure 1.2), a chaotic 3D action game developed by Mediatonic (trademarks of Mediatonic Limited)

Figure 1.2   Fall Guys

- *Cuphead* (figure 1.3), a 2D platformer developed by Studio MDHR

Figure 1.3   Cuphead

MOBILE (IOS AND ANDROID)

Unity can also deploy games to mobile platforms like iOS (iPhones and iPads) and Android (phones and tablets). Here are three examples of mobile games in different genres:

- *Monument Valley 2* (figure 1.4), a puzzle game developed by ustwo

Figure 1.4   Monument Valley 2

- *Guns of Boom* (figure 1.5), a first-person shooter developed by Game Insight

Figure 1.5 *Guns of Boom*

- *Animation Throwdown* (figure 1.6), a collectible card game developed by Kongregate

Figure 1.6 *Animation Throwdown*

VIRTUAL REALITY (OCULUS, VIVE, PLAYSTATION VR)

Unity can even deploy to XR platforms, including virtual reality headsets. Here are a couple of examples of VR games in different genres:

- *Beat Saber* (figure 1.7), a rhythm game developed by Beat Games

Figure 1.7 *Beat Saber*

- *I Expect You to Die* (figure 1.8), an escape puzzle game developed by Schell Games

Figure 1.8   *I Expect You to Die*

As you can see from these examples, Unity's strengths can definitely translate into commercial-quality games. But even with Unity's significant advantages over other game development tools, newcomers may misunderstand the involvement of programming in the development process.

Unity is often portrayed as a list of features with no programming required, which is a misleading view that won't teach people what they need to know in order to produce commercial titles. Though it's true that you can click together a fairly elaborate prototype using preexisting components even without a programmer being involved (which is itself a pretty big feat), rigorous programming is required to move beyond an interesting prototype to a polished game ready for release.

1.2   How to use Unity

The previous section talked a lot about the productivity benefits of Unity's visual editor, so let's go over what the interface looks like and how it operates. If you haven't already done so, download the program by going to www.unity.com and clicking Get Started. Here you will see a breakdown of the various subscription plans offered. Everything in this book works in the free version, so select the Individual tab and click the button under the free Personal edition. The paid versions of Unity differ mainly in commercial licensing terms, not in underlying functionality.

The website has separate downloads for new and returning users. The difference is simply that the download for new users will launch into a software wizard that directs users to intro tutorials, whereas the download for returning users goes straight to the main application with no introduction. So even if you are new to Unity, get the download for returning users and skip the intro content (it's redundant with this book, after all).

You'll actually download a lightweight installation manager rather than the main Unity application. This manager application, called *Unity Hub*, exists to simplify the installation and use of multiple versions of Unity simultaneously. As shown in figure 1.9, installing the editor will be the first thing that happens when you launch Unity Hub. Install whichever is the default Recommended Release; this book uses Unity

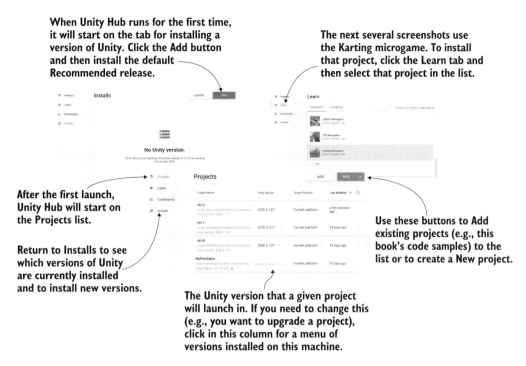

When Unity Hub runs for the first time, it will start on the tab for installing a version of Unity. Click the Add button and then install the default Recommended release.

The next several screenshots use the Karting microgame. To install that project, click the Learn tab and then select that project in the list.

After the first launch, Unity Hub will start on the Projects list.

Return to Installs to see which versions of Unity are currently installed and to install new versions.

Use these buttons to Add existing projects (e.g., this book's code samples) to the list or to create a New project.

The Unity version that a given project will launch in. If you need to change this (e.g., you want to upgrade a project), click in this column for a menu of versions installed on this machine.

Figure 1.9　Unity Hub on first launch versus subsequently

2020.3.12 (the current default release as of this writing). If you later want to install additional versions of Unity (newer versions than the default are available), click Installs on the side menu in Unity Hub.

> **TIP** By the time you read this, newer Unity versions will likely have been released. Advanced features will have changed, and possibly even the look of the interface could be different, but the fundamental concepts covered by this book will still be true. The explanations given in this book will generally still apply to whichever future version of Unity is current.

> **WARNING** Projects remember which version of Unity they were created in and will issue a warning if you attempt to open them in a different version. Sometimes it doesn't matter (for example, ignore the warning if it appears while opening this book's sample downloads), but sometimes you don't want to open a project in the wrong version.

Continuing on from installing the editor, go to the Learn tab to download a first project. Select any project to look around in (you won't be doing much with it anyway) but note that figure 1.10 shows Karting. Unity will download and launch the selected project. You may see a warning message about importing files to set up the new project; realize that the import can take several minutes.

Once the new project is finally loaded, choose Load Scene to dismiss the initial pop-up. If it isn't already open, navigate to Assets/Karting/Scenes/ in the file browser at the bottom of the editor, and double-click MainScene (scene files have the Unity cube icon). You should see a screen similar to figure 1.10.

Scene and Game are tabs for viewing the 3D scene and playing the game, respectively.

The whole top area is the Toolbar. To the left are buttons for looking around and moving objects, and in the middle is the Play button.

The Inspector is on the right side. This displays information about the currently selected object (a list of components mostly).

Hierarchy shows a text list of all objects in the scene, nested according to how they're linked together. Drag objects in the hierarchy to link them.

The Tutorials list appears only in the starter micro-games and won't be here normally.

Project and Console are tabs for viewing all files in the project and messages from the code, respectively.

Navigate folders on the left, and then double-click MainScene.

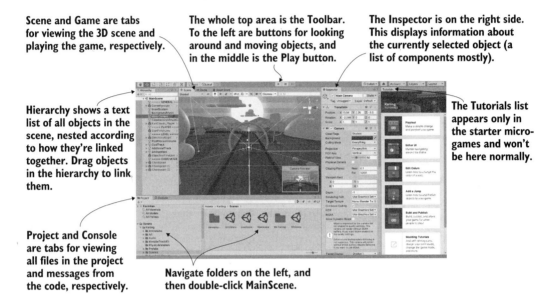

Figure 1.10   Parts of the interface in Unity

The interface in Unity is split into sections: the Scene tab, the Game tab, the Toolbar, the Hierarchy tab, the Inspector, the Project tab, and the Console tab. Each section has a different purpose, but all are crucial to the game-building life cycle:

- You can browse through all the files in the Project tab.
- You can position objects in the current scene by using the Scene tab.
- The Toolbar has controls for working with the scene.
- You can drag and drop object relationships in the Hierarchy tab.
- The Inspector lists information about selected objects, including linked code.
- You can test playing in Game view while watching error output in the Console tab.

This is the default layout in Unity; all of the views are in tabs and can be moved around or resized, docking in different places on the screen. Later, you can play around with customizing the layout, but for now, the default layout is the best way to understand what all the views do.

1.2.1   Scene view, Game view, and the Toolbar

The most prominent part of the interface is the *Scene view* in the middle. This is where you can see what the game world looks like and move objects around. Mesh objects in the scene appear as, well, their mesh (defined in a moment). You can also see other objects in the scene, represented by icons and colored lines: cameras, lights, audio sources, collision regions, and so forth. Note that the view you're seeing here isn't the same as the view in the running game—you're able to look around the scene at will without being constrained to the game's view.

> **DEFINITION**   A *mesh object* is a visual object in space. Visuals in 3D graphics are constructed out of lots of connected lines and shapes—hence the word *mesh*.

The *Game view* isn't a separate part of the screen but rather another tab located right next to Scene (look for tabs at the top left of views). A couple of places in the interface have multiple tabs like this; if you click a different tab, the view is replaced by the new active tab. When the game is running, what you see in this view is the game. It isn't necessary to manually switch tabs every time you run the game, because the view automatically switches to Game when the game starts.

> **TIP**   While the game is running, you can switch back to the Scene view, allowing you to inspect objects in the running scene. This capability is extremely useful for seeing what's going on while the game is running and is a helpful debugging tool that isn't available in most game engines.

Speaking of running the game, that's as simple as clicking the Play button just above the Scene view. That whole top section of the interface is referred to as the *Toolbar,* and Play is located right in the middle. Figure 1.11 breaks apart the full editor interface to show only the Toolbar at the top as well as the Scene/Game tabs right underneath.

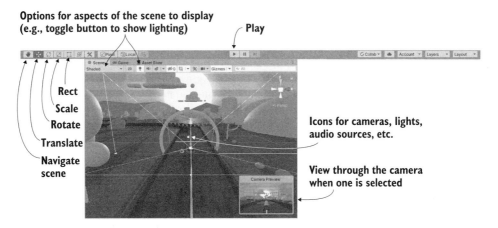

Figure 1.11   Editor screenshot cropped to show Toolbar, Scene, and Game

At the left side of the Toolbar are buttons for scene navigation and transforming objects—to look around the scene and to move objects. I suggest you spend time practicing these, because they are two of the most important activities you'll do in Unity's visual editor. (They're so important that they get their own section following this one.)

The right-hand side of the Toolbar is where you'll find drop-down menus for layouts and layers. As mentioned earlier, the layout of Unity's interface is flexible, so the Layout menu allows you to switch layouts. As for the Layers menu, that's advanced functionality that you can ignore for now (layers are mentioned in future chapters).

1.2.2   *The mouse and keyboard*

Scene navigation is primarily done using the mouse, along with a few modifier keys used to change what the mouse is doing. The three main navigation maneuvers are Move, Orbit, and Zoom. The specific mouse movements vary depending on the mouse you're using and are described in appendix A. The three movements involve clicking and dragging while holding down a combination of Alt (or Option on Mac) and Ctrl (Command on a Mac). Spend a few minutes moving around in the scene to understand what Move, Orbit, and Zoom do.

> **TIP** Although Unity can be used with one- or two-button mice, I highly recommend getting a three-button mouse (and yes, a three-button mouse works fine on a Mac).

Transforming objects is also done through three main maneuvers, and the three scene navigation moves are analogous to the three transforms: Translate, Rotate, and Scale (figure 1.12 demonstrates the transforms on a cube).

Translate   Rotate   Scale

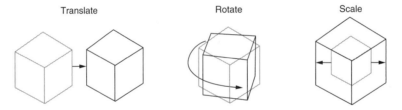

Figure 1.12   Applying the three transforms: Translate, Rotate, and Scale. (The lighter lines are the previous state of the object before it was transformed.)

When you select an object in the scene, you can then move it around (the mathematically accurate technical term is *translate*), rotate it, and scale its size. Relating back to scene navigation maneuvers, Move corresponds to Translate for the camera, Orbit corresponds to Rotate, and Zoom corresponds to Scale. Besides the buttons on the Toolbar, you can switch these functions by pressing W, E, or R on the keyboard. When you activate a transform, you'll notice that a set of color-coded arrows or circles appears over the object in the scene; this is the Transform gizmo, and you can click and drag this gizmo to apply the transformation.

A fourth tool is next to the transform buttons. Called the *Rect tool*, it's designed for use with 2D graphics. This one tool combines movement, rotation, and scaling. Similarly, the fifth button is for a tool that combines movement, rotation, and scaling for

3D objects. Personally, I prefer to manipulate the three transforms separately, but you may find the combined tools more convenient.

Unity has a host of other keyboard shortcuts for speeding up a variety of tasks. Refer to appendix A to learn about them. And with that, on to the remaining sections of the interface!

1.2.3 *The Hierarchy view and the Inspector panel*

Looking at either side of the screen, you'll see the Hierarchy tab on the left and the Inspector tab on the right (see figure 1.13). *Hierarchy* lists the name of every object in the scene and nests the names together according to their hierarchy linkages in the scene. Basically, it's a way of selecting objects by name instead of hunting them down and clicking them within the Scene view. The Hierarchy linkages group objects together visually, like folders, allowing you to move the entire group as one.

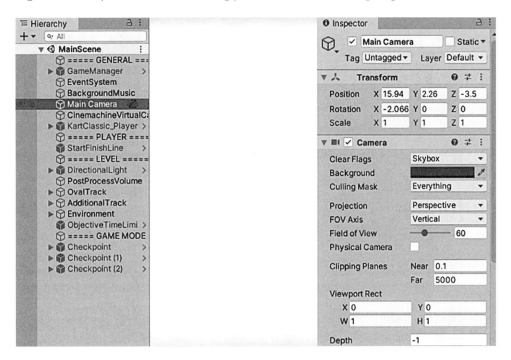

Figure 1.13   Editor screenshot cropped to show the Hierarchy and Inspector tabs

The *Inspector* shows you information about the currently selected object. Select an object, and the Inspector is then filled with information about that object. The information shown is pretty much a list of components, and you can even attach or remove components from objects. All game objects have at least one component, Transform, so you'll always see at least information about positioning and rotation in the Inspector. Often, objects will have several components listed here, including scripts attached to them.

1.2.4   *The Project and Console tabs*

At the bottom of the screen, you'll see Project and Console (see figure 1.14). As with Scene and Game, these aren't two separate portions of the screen, but rather tabs that you can switch between.

Project shows all the assets (art, code, and so on) in the project. Specifically, on the left side of the view is a listing of the project's directories; when you select a directory, the right side of the view shows the individual files in that directory. The directory listing in Project is similar to the list view in Hierarchy, but Hierarchy shows objects in the scene; Project shows files that may not be contained within any specific scene (including scene files—when you save a scene, it shows up in Project!).

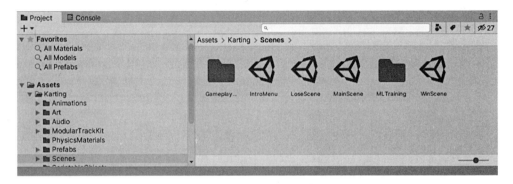

Figure 1.14   Editor screenshot cropped to show the Project and Console tabs

TIP   Project view mirrors the Assets directory on disk, but generally, you shouldn't move or delete files directly by going to the Assets folder in your OS's file explorer. If you do those things within the Project view, Unity will keep in sync with that folder.

The *Console* tab is the place where messages from the code show up. Some of these messages will be debugging output that you placed deliberately, but Unity also emits error messages if it encounters problems in the script you wrote.

1.3   *Getting up and running with Unity programming*

Now let's look at how the process of programming works in Unity. Although art assets can be laid out in the visual editor, you need to write code to control them and make the game interactive. Complex programming in Unity is done using C# as the programming language.

Launch Unity and create a new project: choose New in Unity Hub, or choose File > New Project if Unity is already running. Type a name for the project, leave the default 3D template (future chapters mention 2D), and then choose where you want to save the project. A Unity project is simply a directory full of various asset and settings files, so save the project anywhere on your computer. Click Create, and then Unity will briefly disappear while it sets up the project directory.

Alternatively, you could open the chapter 1 sample project. I strongly recommend you try to follow the upcoming instructions in a new project, and look at the finished sample only afterward to check your work, but it's up to you. Choose Add in Unity Hub to add a downloaded project folder to the list and then click the project in the list.

> **WARNING** If you are opening the book's sample project rather than creating a new project, Unity may emit the following message: `Rebuilding Library because the asset database could not be found!` This refers to the project's Library folder; that folder contains files generated by Unity and used while working, but it is not necessary to distribute those files.

When Unity reappears, you'll be looking at a blank project. Next, let's discuss how programs get executed in Unity.

1.3.1 *Running code in Unity: Script components*

All code execution in Unity starts from code files linked to an object in the scene. Ultimately, this code execution is all part of the component system described earlier; game objects are built up as a collection of components, and that collection can include scripts to execute.

> **NOTE** Unity refers to the code files as *scripts*, using a definition of *script* that's most commonly encountered with JavaScript running in a browser: the code is executed within the Unity game engine, as opposed to compiled code that runs as its own executable. But don't get confused, because many people define the word differently; for example, *scripts* often refer to short, self-contained utility programs. Scripts in Unity are more akin to individual OOP classes, and scripts attached to objects in the scene are object instances.

As you've probably surmised from this description, in Unity, scripts *are* components—not all scripts, mind you, only scripts that inherit from `MonoBehaviour`, the base class for script components. `MonoBehaviour` defines the invisible groundwork for attaching components to game objects, and (as shown in listing 1.1) inheriting from it provides a couple of automatically run methods that you can implement. Those methods include `Start()`, called once when the object becomes active (which is generally as soon as the scene with that object has loaded), and `Update()`, which is called every frame. Your code is run when you put it inside these predefined methods.

> **DEFINITION** A *frame* is a single cycle of the looping game code. Nearly all video games (not only in Unity, but video games in general) are built around a core game loop, where the code executes in a cycle while the game is running. Each cycle includes drawing the screen—hence the name *frame* (like the series of still frames of a movie).

Listing 1.1   Code template for a basic script component

```
using System.Collections;           ◁───┐  Include namespaces for Unity
using System.Collections.Generic;        │  and .NET/Mono classes.
using UnityEngine;

public class HelloWorld : MonoBehaviour {  ◁─── The syntax for inheritance
    void Start() {
        // do something once      ◁─── Put code here that runs once.
    }

    void Update() {                  ┌─ Put code here that
        // do something every frame  ◁┘  runs every frame.
    }
}
```

This is what the file contains when you create a new C# script: the minimal boilerplate code that defines a valid Unity component. Unity has a script template tucked away in the bowels of the application, and when you create a new script, Unity copies that template and renames the class to match the name of the file (which is HelloWorld.cs in my case). Unity also has empty shells for Start() and Update(), because those are the two most common places from which you'll call your custom code.

To create a script, select C# Script from the Create menu, which you access either under the Assets menu (note that Assets and GameObjects both have listings for Create, but they're different menus) or by right-clicking in the Project view. Type in a name for the new script, such as HelloWorld. As explained later in the chapter (see figure 1.16), you'll click and drag this script file onto an object in the scene. Double-click the script, and it'll automatically be opened in another program for editing, as discussed next.

1.3.2   *Using Visual Studio, the included IDE*

Programming isn't done within Unity exactly, but rather code exists as separate files that you point Unity to. Script files can be created within Unity, but you still need to use a text editor or IDE to write all the code within those initially empty files. Unity comes with Microsoft Visual Studio, an IDE for C# (figure 1.15 shows what it looks like). You can visit https://visualstudio.microsoft.com to learn more about this software.

> **NOTE** If Unity opens a different IDE than Visual Studio, you may want to switch the External Tools preference. Go to Preferences > External Tools > External Script Editor to select an IDE.

> **NOTE** Visual Studio organizes files into groupings called a *solution*. Unity automatically generates a solution that has all the script files, so you usually don't need to worry about that.

Various flavors of Visual Studio are available (many programmers prefer Visual Studio Code), or you could use an IDE from a completely different company, like JetBrains Rider. Switching to a different IDE is as simple as going to External Tools in Unity's preferences. I generally use Visual Studio for Mac, but you could use a different IDE

Don't click the Run button within Visual Studio; click Play in Unity to run the code.

Script files open as tabs in the main viewing area. Multiple script files can be open at once.

Solution view shows all script files in the project.

Document Outline may not be showing by default. Select it under View > Other Windows.

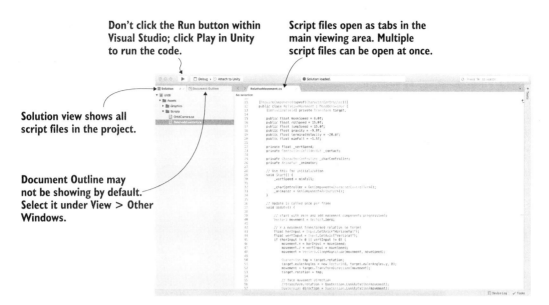

Figure 1.15   Parts of the interface in Visual Studio

and not have any problems following along with this book. Beyond this introductory chapter, I'm not going to talk about the IDE.

Always keep in mind that, although the code is written in Visual Studio, the code isn't run there. The IDE is pretty much a fancy text editor, and the code is run when you click Play within Unity.

1.3.3   *Printing to the console: Hello World!*

All right, you already have an empty script in the project, but you also need an object in the scene to attach the script to. Recall figure 1.1 depicting how a component system works; a script is a component, so it needs to be set as one of the components on an object.

Choose GameObject > Create Empty, and a blank GameObject will appear in the Hierarchy list. Now drag the script from the Project view over to the Hierarchy view and drop it on the empty GameObject. As shown in figure 1.16, Unity will highlight valid places to drop the script, and dropping it on the GameObject will attach the script to that object.

To verify that the script is attached to the object, select the GameObject and look at the Inspector view. You should see two components listed: the Transform component, which is the basic position/rotation/scale component all objects have and which can't be removed, and below that, your script.

> **NOTE**   Eventually, this action of dragging objects from one place and dropping them on other objects will feel routine. A lot of linkages in Unity, not only attaching scripts to objects, are created by dragging things on top of each other.

Click and drag the script from the Project view up to the Hierarchy view and release on the GameObject.

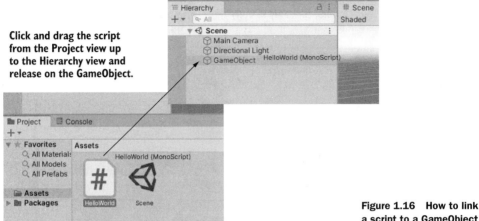

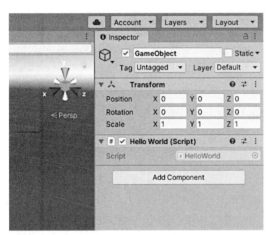

Figure 1.16   How to link a script to a GameObject

When a script is linked to an object, you'll see something like figure 1.17, with the script showing up as a component in the Inspector. Now the script will execute when you play the scene, although nothing is going to happen yet because you haven't written any code. Let's do that next!

Figure 1.17   Linked script being displayed in the Inspector

Double-click the script to open it and get back to listing 1.1. The classic place to start when learning a new programming environment is having it print the text `Hello World!`, so add the line in the following listing inside the `Start()` method.

Listing 1.2   Adding a console message

```
...
void Start() {
    Debug.Log("Hello World!");      ⟵  Add the logging
}                                         command here.
...
```

The `Debug.Log()` command prints a message to the Console view in Unity. Meanwhile, that line goes in the `Start()` method because, as was explained earlier, that method is called as soon as the object becomes active. `Start()` will be called once, as soon as you click Play in the editor. Once you've added the log command, save the script, click Play in Unity, and switch to the Console view. You'll see the message `Hello World!` appear. Congratulations—you've written your first Unity script! Of course, the code will be more elaborate in later chapters, but this is an important first step.

> **WARNING** Always remember to save the file after making adjustments to a script! A pretty common mistake is to adjust the code and then immediately click Play in Unity without saving, resulting in the game still using the code from before you adjusted it.

"Hello World!" steps in brief

Let's reiterate and summarize the steps from the last few pages:

1. Create a new project.
2. Create a new C# script.
3. Create an empty GameObject.
4. Drag the script onto the object.
5. Add the log command to the script.
6. Click Play!

Now it's time to save the scene; this creates a .unity file with the Unity icon. The scene file is a snapshot of everything currently loaded in the game so that you can reload this scene later. Saving this scene may hardly seem worthwhile because it's so simple (a single empty GameObject)—but if you don't save the scene, you'll find it empty again when you come back to the project after quitting Unity.

Errors in the script

To see how Unity indicates errors, purposely put a typo in the `HelloWorld` script. For example, if you type an extra parenthesis symbol, an error message will appear in the Console tab with a red error icon.

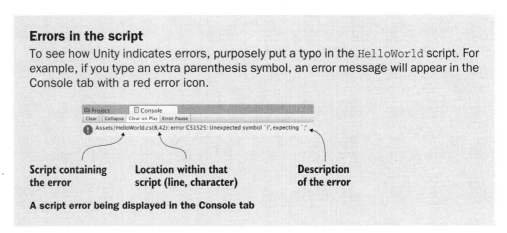

A script error being displayed in the Console tab

Summary

- Unity is a multiplatform development tool.
- Unity's visual editor has several sections that work in concert.
- Scripts are attached to objects as components.
- Code is written inside scripts by using Visual Studio.

Building a demo that
puts you in 3D space

This chapter covers

- Understanding 3D coordinate space
- Putting a player in a scene
- Writing a script that moves objects
- Implementing FPS controls

Chapter 1 concluded with the traditional "Hello World!" introduction to a new programming tool; now it's time to dive into a nontrivial Unity project, a project with interactivity and graphics. You'll put objects into a scene and write code to enable a player to walk around that scene. Basically, it'll be *Doom* without the monsters (something like the depiction in figure 2.1). The visual editor in Unity enables new users to start assembling a 3D prototype right away, without needing to write a lot of boilerplate code first (for things like initializing a 3D view or establishing a rendering loop).

It's tempting to immediately start building the scene in Unity, especially with such a simple (in concept!) project. But it's always a good idea to pause at the beginning and plan out what you're going to do, and this is especially important right now because you're new to the process.

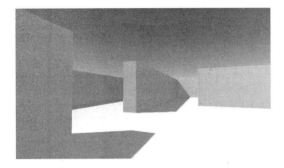

Figure 2.1   Screenshot of the 3D demo (basically, *Doom* without the monsters)

NOTE   Remember, the project for every chapter can be downloaded from the book's website (http://mng.bz/VBY5). First open the project in Unity and then open the main scene (usually just named Scene) to run and inspect. While you're learning, I recommend you type out all the code yourself and use the downloaded sample only for reference.

2.1   *Before you start . . .*

Unity makes it easy for a newcomer to get started, but let's go over a couple of points before you build the complete scene. Even when working with a tool as flexible as Unity, you need to have a sense of the goal you're working toward. You also need to grasp how 3D coordinates operate, or you could get lost as soon as you try to position an object in the scene.

2.1.1   *Planning the project*

Before you start programming anything, you always want to pause and ask yourself, "So what am I building here?" Game design is a huge topic, with many impressively large books focused on how to design a game. Fortunately, for our purposes, you need only a brief outline of this simple demo in mind to develop a basic learning project. These initial projects won't be terribly complex designs anyway, in order to avoid distracting you from learning programming concepts. You can (and should!) worry about higher-level design issues after you've mastered the fundamentals of game development.

For this first project, you'll build a basic first-person shooter (FPS) scene. We will create a room to navigate around, and players will see the world from their character's point of view and can control the character by using the mouse and keyboard. All the interesting complexity of a complete game can be stripped away for now to concentrate on the core mechanics: moving around in a 3D space. Figure 2.2 depicts the road map for this project, laying out the checklist I built in my head:

1. Set up the room: create the floor, outer walls, and inner walls.
2. Place the lights and camera.

3. Create the player object (including attaching the camera on top).

4. Write movement scripts: rotate with the mouse and move with the keyboard.

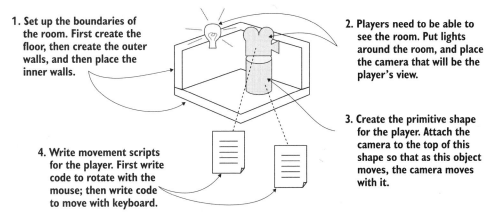

1. Set up the boundaries of the room. First create the floor, then create the outer walls, and then place the inner walls.

2. Players need to be able to see the room. Put lights around the room, and place the camera that will be the player's view.

3. Create the primitive shape for the player. Attach the camera to the top of this shape so that as this object moves, the camera moves with it.

4. Write movement scripts for the player. First write code to rotate with the mouse; then write code to move with keyboard.

Figure 2.2   Road map for the 3D demo

Don't be scared off by everything in this road map! It sounds like a lot of steps in this chapter, but Unity makes them easy. The upcoming sections about movement scripts are so extensive only because we'll be going through every line so that you can understand all the concepts in detail.

This project is a first-person demo in order to keep the art requirements simple; because you can't see yourself, it's fine for "you" to be a cylindrical shape with a camera on top! Now you need to understand how 3D coordinates work so that placing everything in the visual editor will be easy.

2.1.2   *Understanding 3D coordinate space*

If you think about the simple plan we're starting with, it has three aspects: a room, a view, and controls. All of these items rely on you understanding how positions and movements are represented in 3D computer simulations. If you're new to working with 3D graphics, you might not already know this stuff.

It all boils down to numbers that indicate points in space, and the way those numbers correlate to the space is through coordinate axes. If you think back to math class, you've probably seen and used x- and y-axes (see figure 2.3) for assigning coordinates to points on the page. This is referred to as a *Cartesian coordinate system.*

Two axes give you 2D coordinates, with all points in the same plane. Three axes are used to define 3D space. Because the x-axis goes along the page horizontally and the y-axis goes along the page vertically, we now imagine a third axis that sticks straight into and out of the page, perpendicular to both the x- and y-axes. Figure 2.4 depicts the x-, y-, and z-axes for 3D coordinate space. Everything that has a specific position in the scene will have x-, y-, and z-coordinates: the position of the player, the placement of a wall, and so forth.

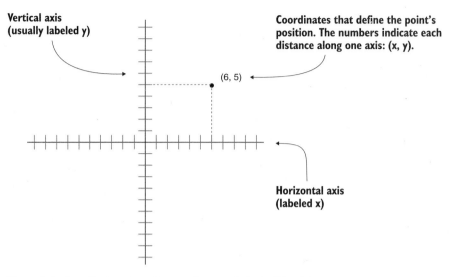

Figure 2.3   Coordinates along the x- and y-axes define a 2D point.

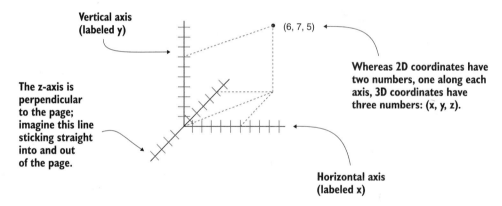

Figure 2.4   Coordinates along the x-, y-, and z-axes define a 3D point.

In Unity's Scene view, you can see these three axes displayed. In the Inspector, you can type in the three numbers required to position an object. You will not only write code to position objects using these three-number coordinates, but also define movements as a distance to move along each axis.

Left-handed vs. right-handed coordinates

The positive and negative direction of each axis is arbitrary, and the coordinates still work no matter in which direction the axes point. You simply need to maintain consistency within a given 3D graphics tool (animation tool, game development tool, and so forth).

But in almost all cases, x goes to the right and y goes up; what differs between different tools is whether z goes into or comes out of the page. These two directions are referred to as *left-handed* or *right-handed*; as this figure shows, if you point your thumb along the x-axis and your index finger along the y-axis, then your middle finger points along the z-axis.

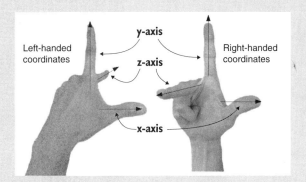

The z-axis points in a different direction on the left hand versus the right hand.

Unity uses a left-handed coordinate system, as do many 3D art applications. Many other tools use right-handed coordinate systems (OpenGL, for example), so don't get confused if you ever see different coordinate directions.

Now that you have a plan in mind for this project and know how coordinates are used to position objects in 3D space, it's time to start building the scene.

2.2 Begin the project: Place objects in the scene

Let's create and place objects in the scene. First, you'll set up all the static scenery—the floor and walls. Then you'll place lights around the scene and position the camera. Lastly, you'll create the object that will be the player, the object to which you'll attach scripts to walk around the scene. Figure 2.5 shows what the editor will look like with everything in place.

Chapter 1 showed how to create a new project in Unity, so you'll do that now. Choose New in Unity Hub (or File > New Project in the editor) and then name your new project in the window that pops up. The scene starts out mostly empty, and the first objects to create are the most obvious ones.

Lights—both directional and point lights are in this scene.

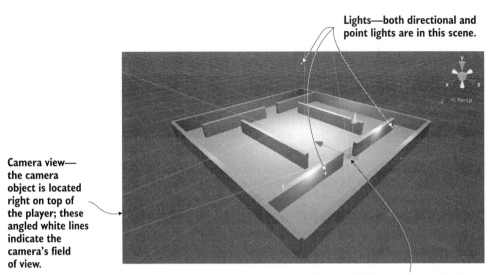

Camera view— the camera object is located right on top of the player; these angled white lines indicate the camera's field of view.

Player—this is a basic capsule object.

Figure 2.5   Scene in the editor with floor, walls, lights, a camera, and the player

2.2.1   *The scenery: Floor, outer walls, and inner walls*

Select the GameObject menu at the top of the screen and then hover over 3D Object to see that drop-down menu. Select Cube to create a new cube object in the scene (later, we'll use other shapes, like Sphere and Capsule). Adjust the position and scale of this object, as well as its name, to make the floor. Figure 2.6 shows which values the floor should be set to in the Inspector (it's a cube only initially, before you stretch it out).

> **NOTE** You can think about the numbers for position in terms of any units you want, as long as you're consistent throughout the scene. The most common choice for units is meters, and that's what I generally choose, but I also use feet sometimes, and I've even seen other people decide that the numbers are inches!

Repeat the same steps to create outer walls for the room. You can create new cubes each time, or you can copy and paste existing objects by using the standard shortcuts. Move, rotate, and scale the walls to form a perimeter around the floor. Experiment with different numbers (for example, 1, 4, 50 for Scale) or use the transform tools introduced in section 1.2.2 (remember that the mathematical term for moving and rotating in 3D space is *transform*).

> **TIP** Recall the navigation controls in chapter 1 to view the scene from different angles or zoom out for a bird's-eye view. If you ever get lost in the scene, press F to reset the view on the currently selected object.

At the top, you can type in a name for the object. For example, call the floor object `Floor`.

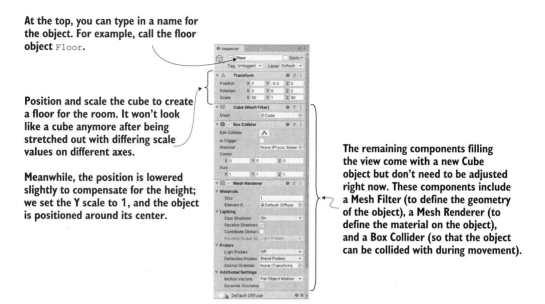

Position and scale the cube to create a floor for the room. It won't look like a cube anymore after being stretched out with differing scale values on different axes.

Meanwhile, the position is lowered slightly to compensate for the height; we set the Y scale to 1, and the object is positioned around its center.

The remaining components filling the view come with a new Cube object but don't need to be adjusted right now. These components include a Mesh Filter (to define the geometry of the object), a Mesh Renderer (to define the material on the object), and a Box Collider (so that the object can be collided with during movement).

Figure 2.6   Inspector view for the floor

Once the outer walls are in place, create inner walls to navigate around. Position the inner walls however you like; the idea is to create hallways and obstacles to walk around once you write code for movement. The exact Transform values that the walls end up with will vary depending on how you rotate and scale the cubes to fit, and on how the objects are linked together in the Hierarchy view. If you need an example to copy working values from, download the sample project and refer to the walls there.

> **TIP**   Drag objects on top of each other in the Hierarchy view to establish linkages. Objects that have accompanying objects attached are referred to as *parents*; objects attached to parent objects are referred to as *children*. When the parent object is moved (or rotated or scaled), the child objects are transformed along with it.

> **DEFINITION**   A *root* object (closely related to the concepts of parent and child objects) is an object at the base of a hierarchy that does not itself have a parent. Thus, all root objects are parents, but not all parents are root objects.

You can also create empty game objects to use for organizing the scene. From the GameObject menu, choose Create Empty. By linking visible objects to a root object, their Hierarchy list can be collapsed. For example, in figure 2.7, the walls are all children of an empty root object (named Building) so that the Hierarchy list will look organized.

> **WARNING**   Before linking any child objects to it, make sure to reset the Transform options (Position and Rotation to 0, 0, 0 and Scale to 1, 1, 1) of the empty root object to avoid any oddities in the position of child objects.

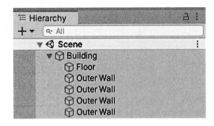

Figure 2.7   The Hierarchy view showing the walls and floor organized under an empty object

---

What is GameObject?

All scene objects are instances of the GameObject class, similar to the way all script components inherit from the MonoBehaviour class. This fact was more explicit with the empty object actually named GameObject, but is still true regardless of whether the object is named Floor, Camera, or Player.

GameObject is really a container for a bunch of components. The main purpose of GameObject is to provide MonoBehaviour something to attach to. What exactly the object is in the scene depends on which components have been added to that Game-Object. Cube objects have a Cube component, Sphere objects have a Sphere component, and so on.

Remember to save the changed scene if you haven't yet. Now the scene has a room in it, but we still need to set up the lighting. Let's take care of that next.

2.2.2   *Lights and cameras*

Typically, you light a 3D scene with a directional light and then a series of point lights. Start with a directional light. The scene probably already has one by default, but if not, create one by choosing GameObject > Light and selecting Directional Light.

Types of lights

You can create several types of light sources, defined by how and where they project light rays. The three main types are point, spot, and directional.

In *point lights*, all the light rays originate from a single point and project out in all directions, like a light bulb in the real world. The light is brighter up close because the light rays are bunched up.

In *spot lights*, all the light rays originate from a single point but project out in only a limited cone. No spot lights are used in the current project, but these lights are commonly used to highlight parts of a level.

In *directional lights*, all the light rays are parallel and project evenly, lighting everything in the scene the same way. This is like the sun in the real world.

The position of a directional light doesn't affect the light cast from it, only the direction the light source is facing, so technically, you could place that light anywhere in the scene. I recommend placing the directional light high above the room so that it intuitively feels like the sun and so that it's out of the way when you're manipulating the rest of the scene. Rotate this light and watch the effect on the room; I recommend rotating it slightly on both the x- and y-axes to get a good effect.

You will see an Intensity setting when you look in the Inspector (see figure 2.8). As the name indicates, that setting controls the brightness of the light. If this were the only light, it'd have to be more intense, but because you'll add a bunch of point lights as well, this directional light can be pretty dim—for example, 0.6 Intensity. This light should also have a slight yellow tinge, like the sun, while the other lights will be white.

Here is where you control the light's brightness, from 0 for completely dark.

The remaining settings don't need to be adjusted right now. These settings include the color of the light, shadows cast by the light, and even a silhouette projection (think of the Bat signal).

Figure 2.8   Directional light settings in the Inspector

As for point lights, create several by using the same menu and place them in dark spots around the room to make sure all the walls are lit. You don't want too many, because performance can degrade if the game has lots of lights. Placing one near each corner should be fine (I suggest raising them to the tops of the walls), plus one placed high above the scene (for example, a Y position of 18) to give variety to the light in the room.

Note that point lights have a Range setting added to the Inspector (see figure 2.9). This controls how far away the light reaches; whereas directional lights cast light evenly throughout the entire scene, point lights are brighter when an object is closer. The point lights closer to the floor should have a range of around 18, but the light placed high up should have a range of around 40 to reach the entire room. Set Intensity to 0.8 for the lights closer to the floor, while the high one is dim extra light to fill the space, at intensity 0.4.

Other than Range, the settings for point lights are the same as for directional lights.

Here is where you control light range, with the same units as position and scale.

(If you see an error about realtime not supported, just ignore it or switch Mode to Mixed.)

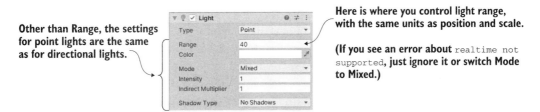

Figure 2.9   Point light settings in the Inspector

The other kind of object needed for the player to see the scene is a camera, but the "empty" scene came with a main camera, so you'll use that. If you ever need to create new cameras (such as for split-screen views in multiplayer games), Camera is another choice in the same GameObject menu, like Cube and Lights. We will position the camera around the top of the player so that the view appears to be through the player's eyes.

2.2.3 *The player's collider and viewpoint*

For this project, a simple primitive shape will do to represent the player. In the GameObject menu (remember, hover over 3D Object to expand the menu), click Capsule. Unity creates a cylindrical shape with rounded ends; this primitive shape will represent the player. Position this object at 1.1 on the y-axis (half the height of the object, plus a bit to avoid overlapping the floor). You can move the object along the x-axis and z-axis wherever you like, as long as it's inside the room and not touching any walls. Name the object `Player`.

In the Inspector, you'll notice that this object has a capsule collider assigned to it. That's a logical default choice for a capsule object, just as cube objects have a box collider by default. But this particular object will be the player and thus needs a slightly different sort of component than most objects. Remove the capsule collider by clicking the menu icon at the top right of that component, shown in figure 2.10; that will display a menu that includes the option Remove Component. The collider is a green mesh surrounding the object, so you'll see the green mesh disappear after deleting the capsule collider.

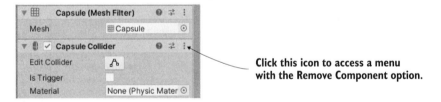

Figure 2.10   Removing a component in the Inspector

Instead of a capsule collider, we're going to assign a *character controller* to this object. At the bottom of the Inspector is a button labeled Add Component; click that button to open a menu of components that you can add. In the Physics section of this menu, you'll find Character Controller; select that option. As the name indicates, this component will allow the object to behave like a character.

You need to complete one last step to set up the player object: attaching the camera. As mentioned previously in section 2.2.1, objects can be dragged onto each other in the Hierarchy view. Drag the camera object onto the player capsule to attach the camera to the player. Now position the camera so that it'll look like the player's eyes (I suggest a Position of 0, 0.5, 0). If necessary, reset the camera's Rotation to 0, 0, 0 (this will be off if you've rotated the capsule).

You've created all the objects needed for this scene. What remains is writing code to move the player object.

2.3   *Make things move: A script that applies transforms*

To have the player walk around the scene, you'll write movement scripts attached to the player. Remember, components are modular bits of functionality that you add to objects, and scripts are a kind of component. Eventually, those scripts will respond to keyboard and mouse input, but first you'll make the player spin in place.

This modest beginning will teach you how to apply transforms in code. Remember that the three transforms are Translate, Rotate, and Scale; spinning an object means changing the rotation. But there's more to know about this task than only "this involves rotation."

2.3.1   *Visualizing how movement is programmed*

Animating an object (such as making it spin) boils down to moving it a small amount every frame, with the frames playing over and over. By themselves, transforms apply instantly, as opposed to visibly moving over time. But applying the transforms over and over causes the object to appear to visibly move, like a series of still drawings in a flipbook. Figure 2.11 illustrates how this works.

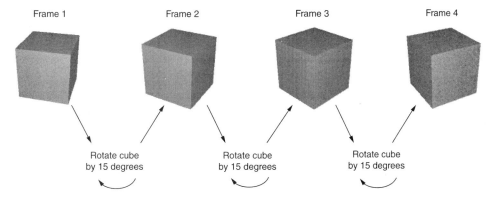

Figure 2.11   The appearance of movement: a cyclical process of transforming between still pictures

Recall that script components have an Update() method that runs every frame. To spin the cube, add code inside Update() that rotates the cube a small amount. This code will run over and over every frame. Sounds pretty simple, right?

2.3.2   *Writing code to implement the diagram*

Now let's put into action the concepts we've just discussed. Create a new C# script (remember, from the Assets menu, open the Create submenu), name it Spin, and write in this code (don't forget to save the file after typing in it!).

Listing 2.1   Making the object spin

```
using System.Collections;
using System.Collections.Generic;        Pull Unity's classes
using UnityEngine;                        into this script.

public class Spin : MonoBehaviour {       Declare a public variable
    public float speed = 3.0f;            for the speed of rotation.

    void Update() {                       Put the Rotate command here
        transform.Rotate(0, speed, 0);    so that it runs every frame.
    }
}
```

To add the script component to the player object, drag the script up from the Project view and drop it onto Player in the Hierarchy view. Now click Play, and you'll see the view spin around; you've written code to make an object move! This code is pretty much the default template for a new script plus two new added lines, so let's examine what those two lines do.

First, we've added the variable for speed toward the top of the class definition (the f after the number tells the computer to treat this as a float value; otherwise, C# treats decimal numbers as a double). The rotation speed is defined as a variable rather than a constant because Unity does something handy with public variables in script components, as described in the following tip.

> **TIP**   Public variables are exposed in the Inspector so that you can adjust the component's values after adding a component to a game object. This is referred to as *serializing* the value, because Unity saves the modified state of the variable.

Figure 2.12 shows what the component in the Inspector looks like when you select the Player object. You can type in a new number, and then the script will use that value instead of the default value defined in the code. This is a handy way to adjust settings for the component on different objects, working within the visual editor instead of hardcoding every value.

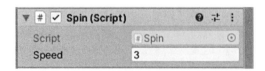

Figure 2.12   The Inspector displaying a public variable declared in the script

The second line to examine from listing 2.1 is the Rotate() method. That's inside Update() so that the command runs every frame. Rotate() is a method of the Transform class, so it's called with dot notation through the transform component of this object (as in most object-oriented languages, this.transform is implied if you type just transform). The transform is rotated by speed degrees every frame, resulting in a smooth spinning movement. But why are the parameters to Rotate() listed as (0, speed, 0) as opposed to, say, (speed, 0, 0)?

Recall that three axes exist in 3D space, labeled x, y, and z. Understanding how these axes relate to positions and movements is fairly intuitive, but these axes can also be used to describe rotations. Aeronautics describes rotations in a similar way, so programmers working with 3D graphics often use a set of terms borrowed from aeronautics: pitch, yaw, and roll. Figure 2.13 illustrates what these terms mean: *pitch* is rotation around the x-axis, *yaw* is rotation around the y-axis, and *roll* is rotation around the z-axis.

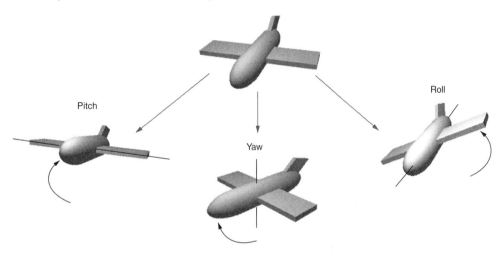

Figure 2.13 Illustration of pitch, yaw, and roll rotation of an aircraft

Given that we can describe rotations around the x-, y-, and z-axes, that means the three parameters for Rotate() are X, Y, and Z rotation. Because we want the player to only spin around sideways, as opposed to tilting up and down, a number should be given for only the Y rotation, and 0 for X and Z rotation.

Hopefully, you can guess what will happen if you change the parameters to (speed, 0, 0) and then play the scene. Try that now! Next, you need to understand one other subtle point about rotations and 3D coordinate axes, embodied in an optional fourth parameter to the Rotate() method.

2.3.3 *Understanding local vs. global coordinate space*

By default, the Rotate() method operates on local coordinates. The other kind of coordinates you could use are global. You tell the method whether to use local or global coordinates by using an optional fourth parameter and writing either `Space.Self` or `Space.World`, like so: `Rotate(0, speed, 0, Space.World)`.

Refer to the explanation about 3D coordinate space in section 2.1.2 and ponder these questions: Where is (0, 0, 0) located? Which direction is the x-axis pointing in? Can the coordinate system itself move around?

It turns out that every single object has its own origin point, as well as its own direction for the three axes, and this coordinate system moves around with the object. This is referred to as *local coordinates*. The overall 3D scene also has its own origin point and its own direction for the three axes, and this coordinate system never moves. This is referred to as *global coordinates*. Therefore, when you specify local or global for the `Rotate()` method, you're telling it whose x-, y-, and z-axes to rotate around (see figure 2.14).

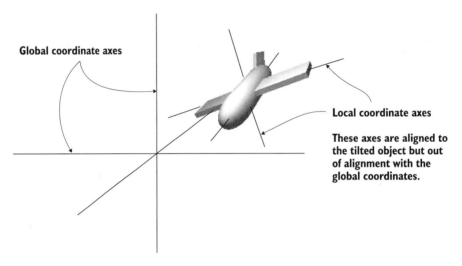

Figure 2.14   Local versus global coordinate axes

If you're new to 3D graphics, this is somewhat of a mind-bending concept. The different axes are depicted in figure 2.14 (notice how "left" to the plane is a different direction than "left" to the world), but the easiest way to understand local and global is through an example.

Select the player object and then tilt it a bit (something like 30 for the X rotation). This will throw off the local coordinates so that local and global rotations look different. Now try running the Spin script both with and without `Space.World` added to the parameters. If it's too hard for you to visualize what's happening, try removing the spin component from the player object and instead spin a tilted cube placed in front of the player. You'll see the object rotating around different axes when you set the command to local or global coordinates.

2.4   *Script component for looking around: MouseLook*

Now you'll make rotation respond to input from the mouse (that is, rotation of the object this script is attached to, which in this case will be the player). You'll do this in several steps, progressively adding new movement abilities to the character. First, the player will rotate only side to side, and then the player will rotate only up and down. Eventually, the player will be able to look around in all directions (rotating horizontally and vertically at the same time), a behavior referred to as *mouse-look*.

Given that we will use three types of rotation behavior (horizontal, vertical, and both), you'll start by writing the framework for supporting all three. Create a new C# script, name it `MouseLook`, and write in this code.

Listing 2.2   `MouseLook` framework with enum for the Rotation setting

```csharp
using System.Collections;
using System.Collections.Generic;
using UnityEngine;

public class MouseLook : MonoBehaviour {        ⟵ Define an enum data structure to associate names with settings.
  public enum RotationAxes {
    MouseXAndY = 0,
    MouseX = 1,
    MouseY = 2
  }
  public RotationAxes axes = RotationAxes.MouseXAndY;    ⟵ Declare a public variable to set in Unity's editor.

  void Update() {
    if (axes == RotationAxes.MouseX) {
      // horizontal rotation here        ⟵ Put code here for horizontal rotation only.
    }
    else if (axes == RotationAxes.MouseY) {
      // vertical rotation here        ⟵ Put code here for vertical rotation only.
    }
    else {
      // both horizontal and vertical rotation here        ⟵ Put code here for both horizontal and vertical rotation.
    }
  }
}
```

Notice that an enum is used to choose horizontal or vertical rotation for the `Mouse-Look` script. Defining an enum data structure allows you to set values by name, rather than typing in numbers and trying to remember what each number means (is 0 horizontal rotation? Is it 1?). If you then declare a public variable typed to that enum, it will display in the Inspector as a drop-down menu (see figure 2.15), which is useful for selecting settings.

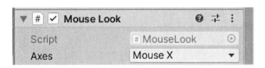

Figure 2.15   The Inspector displays public enum variables as a drop-down menu.

Remove the Spin component (the same way you removed the player's capsule earlier, using the menu at the top right) and attach this new script to the player object instead. Use the Axes drop-down menu in the Inspector to switch the direction of rotation. With the horizontal/vertical rotation setting in place, you can fill in code for each branch of the conditional statement.

> **WARNING**   Make sure to stop the game before changing the menu setting for this axis. Unity allows you to edit the Inspector during the game (to test settings changes) but then reverts the change after you stop the game.

Namespaces

Namespaces are an optional programming construct used to organize the code in a project. Because namespaces are not mandatory, they are omitted from both the script files created by Unity and this book's sample projects. In fact, if you aren't already familiar with namespaces, you may wish to skip this discussion for now.

While this book's sample code doesn't use namespaces, you should strongly consider using them in your own projects, as that will establish clearer organization in a large codebase. Namespaces contain related classes and interfaces, and putting classes into namespaces solves the problem of naming conflicts. Two classes can have the same name if they are in different namespaces.

To put a class into a namespace, enclose it inside curly braces like so:

```
using System.Collections;
using System.Collections.Generic;
using UnityEngine;

namespace UnityInAction {

  public class MouseLook : MonoBehaviour {
    ...
  }
}
```

To then access that class in other code (for example, with the GetComponent statement introduced in the next section), either that other code must also be in the same namespace or you add a statement such as using UnityInAction; to the code. And namespaces don't interfere with script components, so you can still use that class in Unity's editor without trouble.

2.4.1   *Horizontal rotation that tracks mouse movement*

The first and simplest branch is for horizontal rotation. Start by writing the same rotation command you used in listing 2.1 to make the object spin. Don't forget to declare a public variable for the rotation speed; declare the new variable after axes but before Update(), and call the variable sensitivityHor because speed is too generic a name after you have multiple rotations involved. Increase the value of the variable to 9 this time, because that value needs to be bigger for the code written over the next couple of listings. The adjusted code should look like this listing.

Listing 2.3   Horizontal rotation, not yet responding to the mouse

Italicized code was already in script;
it's shown here for reference.

```
...
public RotationAxes axes = RotationAxes.MouseXAndY;     Declare a variable for
public float sensitivityHor = 9.0f;                    the speed of rotation.

void Update() {
  if (axes == RotationAxes.MouseX) {                Put the Rotate command here
    transform.Rotate(0, sensitivityHor, 0);         so that it runs every frame.
  }
...
```

Set the Axes menu of the MouseLook component to horizontal rotation and play the script; the view will spin as before. The next step is to make the rotation react to mouse movement, so let's introduce a new method: Input.GetAxis(). The Input class has a bunch of methods for handling input devices (such as the mouse), and the GetAxis() method returns numbers correlated to the movement of the mouse (positive 1 to −1, depending on the direction of movement). GetAxis() takes the name of the axis desired as a parameter, and the horizontal axis is called Mouse X.

If you multiply the rotation speed by the axis value, the rotation will respond to mouse movement. The speed will scale according to mouse movement, scaling down to zero or even reversing direction. The Rotate command now looks like the following listing.

Listing 2.4   Rotate command adjusted to respond to the mouse

```
...
transform.Rotate(0, Input.GetAxis("Mouse X") * sensitivityHor, 0);

...                                    Note the use of GetAxis() to get mouse input.
```

> **WARNING**   Make sure to type a space in Mouse X. The axis names for this command are defined by Unity, not the axis names from our code. Typing MouseX for this axis is a common mistake.

Click Play and then move the mouse around. As you move the mouse from side to side, the view will rotate from side to side. That's pretty cool! The next step is to rotate vertically instead of horizontally.

2.4.2   *Vertical rotation with limits*

For horizontal rotation, we've been using the Rotate() method, but we'll take a different approach with vertical rotation. Although that method is convenient for applying transforms, it's also kind of inflexible. It's useful only for incrementing the rotation without limit, which was fine for horizontal rotation, but vertical rotation needs limits on how much the view can tilt up or down. This listing shows the vertical rotation code for MouseLook; a detailed explanation of the code will immediately follow.

Listing 2.5   Vertical rotation for `MouseLook`

```
...
public float sensitivityHor = 9.0f;              Declare variables used
public float sensitivityVert = 9.0f;       ◁──┘ for vertical rotation.

public float minimumVert = -45.0f;
public float maximumVert = 45.0f;
                                           Declare a private variable
private float verticalRot = 0;      ◁──┘   for the vertical angle.
                                                        Increment the vertical
void Update() {                                         angle based on the mouse.
  if (axes == RotationAxes.MouseX) {
    transform.Rotate(0, Input.GetAxis("Mouse X") * sensitivityHor, 0);
  }
  else if (axes == RotationAxes.MouseY) {
    verticalRot -= Input.GetAxis("Mouse Y") * sensitivityVert;         ◁──
    verticalRot = Mathf.Clamp(verticalRot, minimumVert, maximumVert);  ◁──
                                           Clamp the vertical angle
    float horizontalRot = transform.localEulerAngles.y;   between minimum and
                                                          maximum limits.
    transform.localEulerAngles = new Vector3(verticalRot, horizontalRot, 0);  ◁──
  }
...                                        Create a new vector from
                                           the stored rotation values.
```

(left margin annotation) Keep the same Y angle (i.e., no horizontal rotation).

Set the Axes menu of the MouseLook component to vertical rotation and play the new script. Now the view won't rotate sideways but will tilt up and down when you move the mouse up and down. The tilt stops at upper and lower limits.

This code introduces several new concepts that need to be explained. First off, we're not using Rotate() this time, so we need a variable in which to store the rotation angle (this variable is called verticalRot here, and remember that vertical rotation goes around the x-axis). The Rotate() method increments the current rotation, whereas this code sets the rotation angle directly. It's the difference between saying "add 5 to the angle" and "set the angle to 30." We do still need to increment the rotation angle, but that's why the code has the -= operator: to subtract a value from the rotation angle, rather than set the angle to that value. By not using Rotate(), we can manipulate the rotation angle in various ways aside from only incrementing it. The rotation value is multiplied by Input.GetAxis(), as in the code for horizontal rotation, except now we ask for Mouse Y because that's the vertical axis of the mouse.

The rotation angle is manipulated further on the next line. We use Mathf.Clamp() to keep the rotation angle between minimum and maximum limits. Those limits are public variables declared earlier in the code, and they ensure that the view can tilt only 45 degrees up or down. The Clamp() method isn't specific to rotation but is generally useful for keeping a number variable between limits. To see what happens, try commenting out the `Clamp()` line; now the tilt doesn't stop at upper and lower limits, allowing you to even rotate completely upside down! Clearly, viewing the world upside down is undesirable, hence the limits.

Because the angles property of `transform` is a `Vector3`, we need to create a new `Vector3` with the rotation angle passed in to the constructor. The `Rotate()` method was automating this process for us, incrementing the rotation angle and then creating a new vector.

> **DEFINITION** A *vector* is multiple numbers stored together as a unit. For example, a `Vector3` is three numbers (labeled x, y, z).

> **WARNING** The reason we need to create a new `Vector3` instead of changing values in the existing vector in the transform is that those values are read-only for transforms. This is a common mistake that can trip you up.

Euler angles vs. quaternion

You're probably wondering why the property is called `localEulerAngles` and not `localRotation`. First, you need to know about quaternions.

Quaternions are another mathematical construct for representing rotations. They're distinct from Euler angles, which is the name for the x-, y-, z-axes approach we've been taking. Remember the whole discussion of pitch, yaw, and roll? Well, that method of representing rotations uses Euler angles. Quaternions are . . . different. It's hard to explain quaternions, because they're an obscure aspect of higher math, involving movement through four dimensions. For a detailed explanation, try "Using Quaternion to Perform 3D Rotations" on the Cprogramming.com website (http://mng.bz/xXOB).

It's a bit easier to explain why quaternions are used to represent rotations: interpolating between rotation values (going through a bunch of in-between values to gradually change from one value to another) looks smoother and more natural when using quaternions.

To return to the initial question, we use `localEulerAngles` because `localRotation` is a quaternion, rather than Euler angles. Unity also provides the Euler angles property to make manipulating rotations easier to understand; the Euler angles property is converted to and from quaternion values automatically. Unity handles the harder math for you behind the scenes, so you don't have to worry about handling it yourself.

One more rotation setting for `MouseLook` needs code: horizontal and vertical rotation at the same time.

2.4.3 *Horizontal and vertical rotation at the same time*

This last chunk of code won't use `Rotate()` either, for the same reason: the vertical rotation angle is clamped between limits after being incremented. That means the horizontal rotation needs to be calculated directly now. Remember, `Rotate()` was automating the process of incrementing the rotation angle, shown here.

Listing 2.6   Horizontal and vertical `MouseLook`

```
...
else {
  verticalRot -= Input.GetAxis("Mouse Y") * sensitivityVert;
  verticalRot = Mathf.Clamp(verticalRot, minimumVert, maximumVert);

  float delta = Input.GetAxis("Mouse X") * sensitivityHor;
  float horizontalRot = transform.localEulerAngles.y + delta;

  transform.localEulerAngles = new Vector3(verticalRot, horizontalRot, 0);
}
...
```

> delta is the amount to change the rotation by.

> Increment the rotation angle by delta.

The first couple of lines, dealing with `verticalRot`, are exactly the same as in listing 2.5. Remember that rotating around the object's x-axis is vertical rotation. Because horizontal rotation is no longer being handled using the `Rotate()` method, that's what the `delta` and `horizontalRot` lines are doing. *Delta* is a common mathematical term for *the amount of change,* so our calculation of delta is the amount that rotation should change. That amount of change is then added to the current rotation angle to get the desired new rotation angle.

Finally, both angles, vertical and horizontal, are used to create a new vector that's assigned to the transform component's angle property.

Disallow physics rotation on the player

Although this doesn't matter quite yet for this project, most modern FPS games use a complex physics simulation affecting everything in the scene. This simulation causes objects to bounce and tumble around. Although this behavior looks and works great for most objects, the player's rotation needs to be solely controlled by the mouse and not affected by the physics simulation.

For that reason, mouse input scripts usually set the `freezeRotation` property on the player's Rigidbody. Add this `Start()` method to the `MouseLook` script:

```
...
void Start() {
    Rigidbody body = GetComponent<Rigidbody>();
    if (body != null) {
        body.freezeRotation = true;
    }
}
```

> This component may not have been added, so check if it exists.

(A `Rigidbody` is an additional component an object can have. The physics simulation acts on `Rigidbody` components and manipulates objects they're attached to.)

In case you've gotten lost on where to make the various changes and additions we've gone over, this listing has the full finished script. Alternatively, download the example project.

Listing 2.7   The finished `MouseLook` script

```
using System.Collections;
using System.Collections.Generic;
using UnityEngine;

public class MouseLook : MonoBehaviour {
  public enum RotationAxes {
    MouseXAndY = 0,
    MouseX = 1,
    MouseY = 2
  }
  public RotationAxes axes = RotationAxes.MouseXAndY;

  public float sensitivityHor = 9.0f;
  public float sensitivityVert = 9.0f;

  public float minimumVert = -45.0f;
  public float maximumVert = 45.0f;

  private float verticalRot = 0;

  void Start() {
    Rigidbody body = GetComponent<Rigidbody>();
    if (body != null) {
        body.freezeRotation = true;
    }
  }

  void Update() {
    if (axes == RotationAxes.MouseX) {
      transform.Rotate(0, Input.GetAxis("Mouse X") * sensitivityHor, 0);
    }
    else if (axes == RotationAxes.MouseY) {
      verticalRot -= Input.GetAxis("Mouse Y") * sensitivityVert;
      verticalRot = Mathf.Clamp(verticalRot, minimumVert, maximumVert);

      float horizontalRot = transform.localEulerAngles.y;

      transform.localEulerAngles = new Vector3(verticalRot, horizontalRot, 0);
    }
    else {
      verticalRot -= Input.GetAxis("Mouse Y") * sensitivityVert;
      verticalRot = Mathf.Clamp(verticalRot, minimumVert, maximumVert);

      float delta = Input.GetAxis("Mouse X") * sensitivityHor;
      float horizontalRot = transform.localEulerAngles.y + delta;

      transform.localEulerAngles = new Vector3(verticalRot, horizontalRot, 0);
    }
  }
}
```

When you set the Axes menu and run the new code, you're able to look around in all directions while moving the mouse. Great! But you're still stuck in one place, looking around as if mounted on a turret. The next step is moving around the scene.

2.5   *Keyboard input component: First-person controls*

Looking around in response to mouse input is an important part of first-person controls, but you're only halfway there. The player also needs to move in response to keyboard input. Let's write a keyboard control component to complement the mouse control component; create a new C# script called FPSInput and attach that to the player (alongside the MouseLook script). For the moment, set the MouseLook component to horizontal rotation only.

> **TIP**   The keyboard and mouse controls explained here are split into separate scripts. You don't have to structure the code this way and could have everything bundled into a single player control script. But a component system (such as the one in Unity) tends to be most flexible and therefore most useful when you have functionality split into several smaller components.

The code you wrote in the previous section affected rotation only, but now we'll change the object's position instead. Refer to listing 2.1; type that into FPSInput, but change Rotate() to Translate(). When you click Play, the view slides up instead of spinning around.

Try changing the parameter values to see how the movement changes (in particular, try swapping the first and second numbers). After experimenting with that for a bit, you can move on to adding keyboard input.

> **Listing 2.8   Spin code from listing 2.1, with a couple of minor changes**

```
using System.Collections;
using System.Collections.Generic;
using UnityEngine;

public class FPSInput : MonoBehaviour {        This will be too fast at first
  public float speed = 6.0f;            ◁────── but will be corrected later.

  void Update() {
    transform.Translate(0, speed, 0);   ◁────── Change Rotate() to Translate().
  }
}
```

2.5.1   *Responding to keypresses*

The code for moving according to keypresses is similar to the code for rotating according to the mouse. The GetAxis() method is used as well and in a similar way. This listing demonstrates how to use it.

> **Listing 2.9   Positional movement responding to keypresses**

```
...
void Update() {
  float deltaX = Input.GetAxis("Horizontal") * speed;    Horizontal and Vertical
  float deltaZ = Input.GetAxis("Vertical") * speed;   ◁── are indirect names for
                                                          keyboard mappings.
```

```
    transform.Translate(deltaX, 0, deltaZ);
  }
...
```

As before, the `GetAxis()` values are multiplied by `speed` to determine the amount of movement. Whereas before, the requested axis was always "Mouse something," now we pass in either `Horizontal` or `Vertical`. These names are abstractions for input settings in Unity; if you look in the Edit menu under Project Settings and then look under Input Manager, you'll find a list of abstract input names and the exact controls mapped to those names. Both the left and right arrow keys and the letters A and D are mapped to `Horizontal`, whereas both the up and down arrow keys and the letters W and S are mapped to `Vertical`.

Note that the movement values are applied to the x- and z-coordinates. As you probably noticed while experimenting with the `Translate()` method, the x-coordinate moves from side to side, and the z-coordinate moves forward and backward.

Put in this new movement code and you should be able to move around by pressing either the arrow keys or W, A, S, and D letter keys, the standard in most FPS games. The movement script is nearly complete, but we have a few more adjustments to go over.

2.5.2 Setting a rate of movement independent of the computer's speed

It's not obvious right now because you've been running the code on only one computer (yours), but if you ran the code on different machines, it'd run at different speeds. That's because some computers can process code and graphics faster than others. Right now, the player would move at different speeds on different computers because the movement code is tied to the computer's speed. That is referred to as *frame-rate dependent*, because the movement code is dependent on the frame rate of the game.

Imagine you run this demo on two computers, one that gets 30 frames per second (fps) and one that gets 60 fps. That means `Update()` would be called twice as often on the second computer, and the same speed value of 6 would be applied every time. At 30 fps, the rate of movement would be 180 units/second, and the movement at 60 fps would be 360 units/second. For most games, movement speed that varies like this would be bad news.

The solution is to adjust the movement code to make it *frame-rate independent*. This speed of movement is not dependent on the frame rate of the game. The way to achieve this is by not applying the same speed value at every frame rate. Instead, scale the speed value higher or lower depending on how quickly the computer runs. This is achieved by multiplying the speed value by another value called `deltaTime`.

> **Listing 2.10 Frame-rate independent movement using `deltaTime`**

```
...
void Update() {
  float deltaX = Input.GetAxis("Horizontal") * speed;
```

```
    float deltaZ = Input.GetAxis("Vertical") * speed;
    transform.Translate(deltaX * Time.deltaTime, 0, deltaZ * Time.deltaTime);
}
...
```

That was a simple change. The Time class has properties and methods that are useful for timing, and one of those properties is deltaTime. We know that *delta* means the amount of change, so that means deltaTime is the amount of change in time. Specifically, deltaTime is the amount of time between frames. The time between frames varies at different frame rates (for example, 30 fps has a deltaTime of 1/30th of a second), so multiplying the speed value by deltaTime will scale the speed value on different computers.

Now the movement speed will be the same on all computers. But the movement script is still not quite done. When you move around the room, you can pass through walls, so we need to adjust the code further to prevent that.

2.5.3 *Moving the CharacterController for collision detection*

Directly changing the object's transform doesn't apply collision detection, so the character will pass through walls. To apply collision detection, what we want to do instead is use CharacterController, a component that makes the object move more like a character in a game, including colliding with walls. Recall that, back when we set up the player, we attached a CharacterController, so now we'll use that component with the movement code in FPSInput.

Listing 2.11 Moving `CharacterController` instead of `Transform`

```
...
private CharacterController charController;           ◁── Variable for referencing
                                                        the CharacterController

void Start() {
    charController = GetComponent<CharacterController>();   ◁── Access other
                                                               components attached
}                                                              to the same object.

void Update() {
    float deltaX = Input.GetAxis("Horizontal") * speed;        Limit diagonal movement
    float deltaZ = Input.GetAxis("Vertical") * speed;          to the same speed as
    Vector3 movement = new Vector3(deltaX, 0, deltaZ);         movement along an axis.
    movement = Vector3.ClampMagnitude(movement, speed);   ◁──
                                                               Transform the movement
                                                               vector from local to
    movement *= Time.deltaTime;                                global coordinates.
    movement = transform.TransformDirection(movement);   ◁──
    charController.Move(movement);                   ◁──
}                                                          Tell the CharacterController
...                                                        to move by that vector.
```

This code excerpt introduces several new concepts. The first concept to point out is the variable for referencing the CharacterController. This variable creates a local reference to the object (code object, that is—not to be confused with scene objects); multiple scripts can have references to this one `CharacterController` instance.

That variable starts out empty, so before you can use the reference, you need to assign an object for it to refer to. This is where `GetComponent()` comes into play; that method returns other components attached to the same GameObject. Rather than passing a parameter inside the parentheses, you use the C# syntax of defining the type inside angle brackets, <>.

Once you have a reference to the `CharacterController`, you can call `Move()` on the controller. Pass in a vector to that method, similar to the way the mouse rotation code used a vector for rotation values. Also, similar to the way rotation values were limited, use `Vector3.ClampMagnitude()` to limit the vector's magnitude to the movement speed. The clamp is used because, otherwise, diagonal movement would have a greater magnitude than movement directly along an axis (picture the sides and hypotenuse of a right triangle).

But there's one tricky aspect to the movement vector here, and it has to do with local versus global, as we discussed earlier for rotations. We'll create the vector with a value to move, say, to the left. That's the *player's* left, though, which may be a completely different direction from the *world's* left—that is, we're talking about left in local space, not global space.

We need to pass a movement vector defined in global space to the `Move()` method, so we're going to need to convert the local space vector into a global space vector. Doing that conversion is complex math, but fortunately for us, Unity takes care of that math for us, and we simply need to call the `TransformDirection()` method in order to, well, transform the direction.

> **DEFINITION** *Transform* in this context means to convert from one coordinate space to another (refer to section 2.3.3 if you don't remember what a coordinate space is). Don't get confused with the other definitions of transform, including both the `Transform` component and the action of moving the object around the scene. It's sort of an overloaded term, because all these meanings refer to the same underlying concept.

Test playing the movement code now. If you haven't done so already, set the `Mouse-Look` component to both horizontal and vertical rotation. You can look around the scene fully and fly around the scene by using keyboard controls. This is pretty great if you want the player to fly around the scene, but what if you want the player walking instead of flying?

2.5.4 Adjusting components for walking instead of flying

Now that collision detection is working, the script can have gravity, and the player will stay down against the floor. Declare a `gravity` variable and use that value for the y-axis.

Listing 2.12   Adding gravity to the movement code

```
...
public float gravity = -9.8f;
...
void Update() {
  ...
  movement = Vector3.ClampMagnitude(movement, speed);

  movement.y = gravity;          ⟵           Use the gravity value
                                             instead of just 0.
  movement *= Time.deltaTime;
  ...
```

Now there's a constant downward force on the player, but it's not always pointed straight down, because the player object can tilt up and down with the mouse. Fortunately, everything we need to fix that is already in place, so we need only to make minor adjustments to the way components are set up on the player. First, set the MouseLook component on the player object to horizontal rotation only. Add the MouseLook component to the camera object, and set that one to vertical rotation only. That's right; you're going to have two objects responding to the mouse!

Because the player object now only rotates horizontally, there's no longer any problem with the downward force of gravity being tilted. The camera object is parented to the player object (remember when we did that in the Hierarchy view?), so even though the camera rotates vertically independently from the player, the camera rotates horizontally along with the player.

Polishing the finished script

Use the RequireComponent attribute to ensure that other components needed by the script are also attached. Sometimes other components are optional (that is, the code says, "If this other component is also attached, then . . . "), but other times you want to make the other components mandatory. Add RequireComponent to the top of the script in order to enforce that dependency, and give the required component as a parameter inside parentheses.

Similarly, if you add the AddComponentMenu attribute to the top of your scripts, that script will be added to the component menu in Unity's editor. Tell the attribute the name of the menu item you want to add, and then the script can be selected when you click Add Component at the bottom of the Inspector. Handy! A script with both attributes added to the top would look something like this:

```
using System.Collections;
using System.Collections.Generic;
using UnityEngine;

[RequireComponent(typeof(CharacterController))]
[AddComponentMenu("Control Script/FPS Input")]
public class FPSInput : MonoBehaviour {
  ...
```

Listing 2.13 shows the full finished script. Along with the small adjustments to the way components are set up on the player, the player can walk around the room. Even with the gravity variable being applied, you can still use this script for flying movement by setting Gravity to 0 in the Inspector.

Listing 2.13 The finished `FPSInput` script

```
using System.Collections;
using System.Collections.Generic;
using UnityEngine;

[RequireComponent(typeof(CharacterController))]
[AddComponentMenu("Control Script/FPS Input")]
public class FPSInput : MonoBehaviour {
  public float speed = 6.0f;
  public float gravity = -9.8f;

  private CharacterController charController;

  void Start() {
    charController = GetComponent<CharacterController>();
  }

  void Update() {
    float deltaX = Input.GetAxis("Horizontal") * speed;
    float deltaZ = Input.GetAxis("Vertical") * speed;
    Vector3 movement = new Vector3(deltaX, 0, deltaZ);
    movement = Vector3.ClampMagnitude(movement, speed);

    movement.y = gravity;

    movement *= Time.deltaTime;
    movement = transform.TransformDirection(movement);
    charController.Move(movement);
  }
}
```

Congratulations on building this 3D project! We covered a lot of ground in this chapter, and now you're well versed in how to code movement in Unity. As exciting as this first demo is, it's still a long way from being a complete game. After all, the project plan described this as a basic FPS scene, and what's a shooter if you can't shoot? So give yourself a well-deserved pat on the back for this chapter's project and then get ready for the next step.

Summary

- 3D coordinate space is defined by x-, y-, and z-axes.
- Objects and lights in a room set the scene.
- The player in a first-person scene is essentially a camera.
- Movement code applies small transforms repeatedly in every frame.
- FPS controls consist of mouse rotation and keyboard movement.

Adding enemies and projectiles to the 3D game

This chapter covers
- Taking aim and firing, both for the player and for enemies
- Detecting and responding to hits
- Making enemies that wander around
- Spawning new objects in the scene

The movement demo from the previous chapter was pretty cool but still not really a game. Let's turn that movement demo into a first-person shooter. If you think about what else we need now, it boils down to the ability to shoot and having things to shoot at.

First, we're going to write scripts that enable the player to shoot objects in the scene. Then, we're going to build enemies to populate the scene, including code to both wander around aimlessly and react to being hit. Finally, we're going to enable the enemies to fight back, emitting fireballs at the player. None of the scripts from chapter 2 need to change; instead, we'll add scripts to the project—scripts that handle the additional features.

I've chosen a first-person shooter for this project for a couple of reasons. One is simply that FPS games are popular: people like shooting games, so let's make a shooting game. A subtler reason has to do with the techniques you'll learn; this project is a great way to learn about several fundamental concepts in 3D simulations. For example, shooting games are a great way to teach raycasting. In a bit, we'll get into the specifics of what that is, but for now, you need to know only that it's a useful concept for many tasks in 3D simulations. Although raycasting is useful in a wide variety of situations, it just so happens that using raycasting makes the most intuitive sense for shooting.

Creating wandering targets to shoot at gives us a great excuse to explore code for computer-controlled characters, as well as to use techniques for sending messages and spawning objects. In fact, this wandering behavior is another place that raycasting is valuable, so we're already going to be looking at a different application of the technique after having first learned about it with shooting. Similarly, the approach to sending messages that's demonstrated in this project is also useful elsewhere. In future chapters, you'll see other applications for these techniques, and even within this one project we'll go over alternative situations.

Ultimately, we'll approach this project one new feature at a time, with the game always playable at every step, but also always feeling like there's a missing part to work on next. This road map breaks the steps into small, understandable changes, with only one new feature added at a time:

1. Write code enabling the player to shoot into the scene.
2. Create static targets that react to being hit.
3. Make the targets wander around.
4. Spawn the wandering targets automatically.
5. Enable the targets/enemies to shoot fireballs at the player.

NOTE This chapter's project assumes you already have a first-person movement demo to build on. We created a movement demo in chapter 2, but if you skipped straight to this chapter, you will need to download the sample files for chapter 2.

3.1 Shooting via raycasts

The first new feature to introduce into the 3D demo is shooting. Looking around and moving are certainly crucial features for a first-person shooter, but it's not a game until players can affect the simulation and apply their skills. Shooting in 3D games can be implemented with a few approaches, and one of the most important approaches is raycasting.

3.1.1 What is raycasting?

As the name indicates, *raycasting* casts a ray into the scene. Clear, right? Well, okay, so what exactly is a ray?

> **DEFINITION** A *ray* is an imaginary or invisible line in the scene that starts at a point of origin and extends out in a specific direction.

In raycasting, you create a ray and then determine what intersects it. Figure 3.1 illustrates the concept. Consider what happens when you fire a bullet from a gun: the bullet starts at the position of the gun and then flies forward in a straight line until it hits something. A ray is analogous to the path of the bullet, and raycasting is analogous to firing the bullet and seeing what it hits.

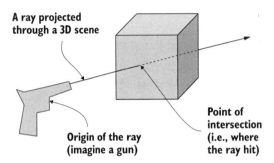

A ray projected through a 3D scene

Origin of the ray (imagine a gun)

Point of intersection (i.e., where the ray hit)

Figure 3.1 A ray is an imaginary line, and raycasting is finding where that line intersects.

As you can imagine, the math behind raycasting often gets complicated. Not only is it tricky to calculate the intersection of a line with a 3D plane, but you need to do that for all polygons of all mesh objects in the scene (remember, a *mesh object* is a 3D visual constructed from lots of connected lines and shapes). Fortunately, Unity handles the difficult math behind raycasting, but you still have to worry about higher-level concerns such as where the ray is being cast from and why.

In this project, the answer to the latter question (why) is to simulate a bullet being fired into the scene. For a first-person shooter, the ray generally starts at the camera position and then extends out through the center of the camera view. In other words, you're checking for objects straight in front of the camera; Unity provides commands to make that task simple. Let's look at these commands.

3.1.2 *Using the ScreenPointToRay command for shooting*

You'll implement shooting by projecting a ray that starts at the camera and extends forward through the center of the view. Unity provides the `ScreenPointToRay()` method to perform this action.

Figure 3.2 illustrates what happens when this method is invoked. It creates a ray that starts at the camera and projects at an angle, passing through the given screen coordinates. Usually, the coordinates of the mouse position are used for *mouse picking* (selecting the object under the mouse), but for first-person shooting, the center of the screen is used. Once you have a ray, it can be passed to the `Physics.Raycast()` method to perform raycasting using that ray.

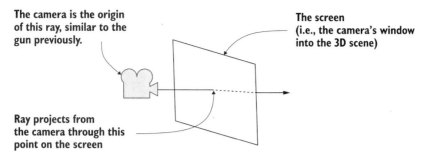

The camera is the origin of this ray, similar to the gun previously.

The screen (i.e., the camera's window into the 3D scene)

Ray projects from the camera through this point on the screen

Figure 3.2 `ScreenPointToRay()` projects a ray from the camera through the given screen coordinates.

Let's write code that uses the methods we just discussed. In Unity, create a new C# script, call it RayShooter, attach that script to the camera (not the player object), and then write the code from this listing in it.

Listing 3.1 RayShooter script to attach to the camera

```
using System.Collections;
using System.Collections.Generic;
using UnityEngine;

public class RayShooter : MonoBehaviour {
  private Camera cam;

  void Start() {
    cam = GetComponent<Camera>();              Access other components
  }                                            attached to the same object.

  void Update() {
    if (Input.GetMouseButtonDown(0)) {         Respond to the left
                                               (first) mouse button.
      Vector3 point = new Vector3(cam.pixelWidth/2, cam.pixelHeight/2, 0);
      Ray ray = cam.ScreenPointToRay(point);
      RaycastHit hit;                          Create the ray at that position
      if (Physics.Raycast(ray, out hit)) {     by using ScreenPointToRay().
        Debug.Log("Hit " + hit.point);
      }                                        The raycast fills a referenced
    }             Retrieve coordinates         variable with information.
  }              where the ray hit.
}
```

The middle of the screen is half its width and height.

You should note several things in this code listing. First, the Camera component is retrieved in Start(), just like the CharacterController in the previous chapter. Then, the rest of the code is put in Update() because it needs to check the mouse repeatedly, as opposed to just one time. The Input.GetMouseButtonDown() method returns true or false, depending on whether the mouse has been clicked, so putting that command in a conditional means the enclosed code runs only when the mouse has been clicked. You want to shoot when the player clicks the mouse—hence the conditional check of the mouse button.

A vector is created to define the screen coordinates for the ray (remember that a vector is several related numbers stored together). The camera's `pixelWidth` and `pixelHeight` values give you the size of the screen, so dividing those values in half gives you the center of the screen. Although screen coordinates are 2D, with only horizontal and vertical components and no depth, a `Vector3` was created because `ScreenPointToRay()` requires that data type (presumably because calculating the ray involves arithmetic on 3D vectors). `ScreenPointToRay()` was called with this set of coordinates, resulting in a `Ray` object (a code object, not a game object; the two can be confused sometimes).

The ray is then passed to the `Raycast()` method, but it's not the only object passed in. There's also a `RaycastHit` data structure; `RaycastHit` is a bundle of information about the intersection of the ray, including where the intersection happened and what object was intersected. The C# syntax `out` ensures that the data structure manipulated within the command is the same object that exists outside the command, as opposed to the objects being separate copies in the different function scopes.

With those parameters in place, the `Physics.Raycast()` method can do its work. This method checks for intersections with the given ray, fills in data about the intersection, and returns `true` if the ray hit anything. Because a Boolean value is returned, this method can be put in a conditional check, just as you used `Input.GetMouseButton-Down()` earlier.

For now, the code emits a console message to indicate when an intersection occurred. This console message displays the 3D coordinates of the point where the ray hit (the x, y, z values we discussed in chapter 2). But it can be hard to visualize where exactly the ray hit; similarly, it can be hard to tell where the center of the screen is (the location where the ray shoots through). Let's add visual indicators to address both problems.

3.1.3   Adding visual indicators for aiming and hits

Our next step is to add two kinds of visual indicators: an aiming spot at the center of the screen and a mark in the scene where the ray hit. For a first-person shooter, the latter is usually bullet holes, but for now, you're going to put a blank sphere on the spot (and use a coroutine to remove the sphere after 1 second). Figure 3.3 shows what you'll see.

> **DEFINITION**   *Coroutines* are a way of handling tasks that execute incrementally over time. In contrast, most functions make the program wait until they finish.

First, let's add indicators to mark where the ray hits. Listing 3.2 shows the script after making this addition. Run around the scene, shooting; it's pretty fun seeing the sphere indicators!

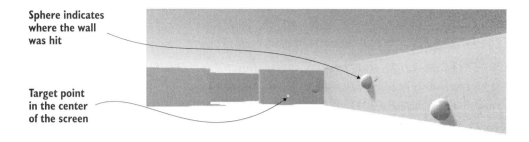

Sphere indicates where the wall was hit

Target point in the center of the screen

Figure 3.3   Shooting repeatedly after adding visual indicators for aiming and hits

Listing 3.2   `RayShooter` script with sphere indicators added

```
using System.Collections;
using System.Collections.Generic;
using UnityEngine;

public class RayShooter : MonoBehaviour {
  private Camera cam;

  void Start() {
    cam = GetComponent<Camera>();
  }

  void Update() {
    if (Input.GetMouseButtonDown(0)) {
      Vector3 point = new Vector3(cam.pixelWidth/2, cam.pixelHeight/2, 0);
      Ray ray = cam.ScreenPointToRay(point);
      RaycastHit hit;
      if (Physics.Raycast(ray, out hit)) {
        StartCoroutine(SphereIndicator(hit.point));
      }
    }
  }

  private IEnumerator SphereIndicator(Vector3 pos) {
    GameObject sphere = GameObject.CreatePrimitive(PrimitiveType.Sphere);
    sphere.transform.position = pos;

    yield return new WaitForSeconds(1);

    Destroy(sphere);
  }
}
```

This function is mostly the same raycasting code from listing 3.1.

Launch a coroutine in response to a hit.

Coroutines use IEnumerator functions.

The yield keyword tells coroutines where to pause.

Remove this GameObject and clear its memory.

The new method is `SphereIndicator()`, plus a one-line modification in the existing `Update()` method. This method creates a sphere at a point in the scene and then removes that sphere a second later. Calling `SphereIndicator()` from the raycasting code ensures that there will be visual indicators showing exactly where the ray hit.

This function is defined with IEnumerator, and that type is tied in with the concept of coroutines.

Technically, coroutines aren't asynchronous (asynchronous operations don't stop the rest of the code from running; think of downloading an image in the script of a website), but through clever use of enumerators, Unity makes coroutines behave similarly to asynchronous functions. The secret sauce in coroutines is the yield keyword; that keyword causes the coroutine to temporarily pause, handing back the program flow and picking up again from that point in the next frame. In this way, coroutines seemingly run in the background of a program, through a repeated cycle of running partway and then returning to the rest of the program.

As the name indicates, StartCoroutine() sets a coroutine in motion. Once a coroutine is started, it keeps running until the function is finished; it pauses along the way. Note the subtle but significant point that the method passed to StartCoroutine() has a set of parentheses following the name: this syntax means you're calling that function, as opposed to passing its name. The called function runs until it hits a yield command, at which point the function pauses.

SphereIndicator() creates a sphere at a specific point, pauses for the yield statement, and then destroys the sphere after the coroutine resumes. The length of the pause is controlled by the value returned at yield. A few types of return values work in coroutines, but the most straightforward is to return a specific length of time to wait. Returning WaitForSeconds(1) causes the coroutine to pause for 1 second. Create a sphere, pause for 1 second, and then destroy the sphere: that sequence sets up a temporary visual indicator.

Listing 3.2 gave you indicators to mark where the ray hits. But you also want an aiming spot in the center of the screen.

Listing 3.3 Visual indicator for aiming

```
...
void Start() {
  cam = GetComponent<Camera>();

  Cursor.lockState = CursorLockMode.Locked;    Hide the mouse cursor at
  Cursor.visible = false;                       the center of the screen.
}

void OnGUI() {                    This is just the rough
  int size = 12;         ←       size of this font.
  float posX = cam.pixelWidth/2 - size/4;
  float posY = cam.pixelHeight/2 - size/2;                 The GUI.Label() command
  GUI.Label(new Rect(posX, posY, size, size), "*");   ←   displays text onscreen.
}
...
```

Another new method has been added to the RayShooter class, called OnGUI(). Unity comes with both a basic and more advanced UI system. Because the basic system has a lot of limitations, we'll build a more flexible advanced UI in future chapters, but for now, it's much easier to display a point in the center of the screen by using the basic UI. Much like `Start()` and `Update()`, every `MonoBehaviour` automatically responds to an `OnGUI()` method. That function runs every frame right after the 3D scene is rendered, resulting in everything drawn during `OnGUI()` appearing on top of the 3D scene (imagine stickers applied to a painting of a landscape).

> **DEFINITION** *Render* is the action of the computer drawing the pixels of the 3D scene. Although the scene is defined using x-, y-, and z-coordinates, the actual display on your monitor is a 2D grid of colored pixels. To display the 3D scene, the computer needs to calculate the color of all the pixels in the 2D grid; running that algorithm is referred to as *rendering*.

Inside `OnGUI()`, the code defines 2D coordinates for the display (shifted slightly to account for the size of the label) and then calls `GUI.Label()`. That method displays a text label. Because the string passed to the label is an asterisk (*), you end up with that character displayed in the center of the screen. Now it's much easier to aim in our nascent FPS game!

Listing 3.3 also adds cursor settings to the `Start()` method. All that's happening is that the values are being set for cursor visibility and locking. The script will work perfectly fine if you omit the cursor values, but these settings make first-person controls work a bit more smoothly. The mouse cursor will stay in the center of the screen, and to avoid cluttering the view, will turn invisible and will reappear only when you press Esc.

> **WARNING** Always remember that you can press Esc to unlock the mouse cursor in order to move it away from the middle of the Game view. While the mouse cursor is locked, it's impossible to click the Play button and stop the game.

That wraps up the first-person shooting code . . . well, that wraps up the player's end of the interaction, anyway, but we still need to take care of targets.

3.2 Scripting reactive targets

Being able to shoot is all well and good, but at the moment, players don't have anything to shoot at. We're going to create a target object and give it a script that will respond to being hit. Or rather, we'll slightly modify the shooting code to notify the target when hit, and then the script on the target will react when notified.

3.2.1 Determining what was hit

First, you need to create a new object to shoot at. Create a new cube object (GameObject > 3D Object > Cube) and then scale it up vertically by setting the Y scale to 2 and leaving X and Z at 1. Position the new object at 0, 1, 0 to put it on the floor in the middle of the room, and name the object `Enemy`.

Create a new script called `ReactiveTarget` and attach that to the newly created box. Soon, you'll write code for this script, but leave it as the default for now; you're creating this script file ahead of time because the next code listing requires it to exist in order to compile.

Go back to RayShooter and modify the raycasting code according to the following listing. Run the new code and shoot the new target; debug messages appear in the console instead of sphere indicators in the scene.

Listing 3.4 Detecting whether the target object was hit

```
...
if (Physics.Raycast(ray, out hit)) {                              Retrieve the object
  GameObject hitObject = hit.transform.gameObject;     ◁─────    the ray hit.
  ReactiveTarget target = hitObject.GetComponent<ReactiveTarget>();
  if (target != null) {                          ◁─
    Debug.Log("Target hit");                               Check for the ReactiveTarget
  } else {                                                 component on the object.
    StartCoroutine(SphereIndicator(hit.point));
  }
}
...
```

Notice that you retrieve the object from RaycastHit, just as the coordinates were retrieved for the sphere indicators. Technically, the hit information doesn't return the game object hit; it indicates the Transform component hit. You can then access game-Object as a property of transform.

Then, you use the GetComponent() method on the object to check whether it's a reactive target (that is, whether it has the ReactiveTarget script attached). As you saw previously, that method returns components of a specific type that are attached to the GameObject. If no component of that type is attached to the object, GetComponent() won't return anything. You check whether null was returned and run different code in each case.

If the hit object is a reactive target, the code emits a debug message instead of starting the coroutine for sphere indicators. Now let's inform the target object about the hit so it can react.

3.2.2 Alerting the target that it was hit

All that's needed in the code is a one-line change, as shown next.

Listing 3.5 Sending a message to the target object

```
...
if (target != null) {              Call a method of the target instead
  target.ReactToHit();     ◁────   of just emitting the debug message.
} else {
  StartCoroutine(SphereIndicator(hit.point));
}
...
```

Now the shooting code calls a method of the target, so let's write that target method. In the `ReactiveTarget` script, write in the code from the next listing. The target object will fall over and disappear when you shoot it; refer to figure 3.4.

Listing 3.6   `ReactiveTarget` script that dies when hit

```
using System.Collections;
using System.Collections.Generic;
using UnityEngine;

public class ReactiveTarget : MonoBehaviour {

  public void ReactToHit() {          Method called by
    StartCoroutine(Die());            the shooting script
  }

  private IEnumerator Die() {          Topple the enemy, wait 1.5 seconds,
    this.transform.Rotate(-75, 0, 0);  and then destroy the enemy.

    yield return new WaitForSeconds(1.5f);

    Destroy(this.gameObject);          A script can destroy itself (just
  }                                    as it could a separate object).
}
```

Most of this code should be familiar to you from previous scripts, so we'll go over it only briefly. First, you define the `ReactToHit()` method, because that's the method name called in the shooting script. This method starts a coroutine that's similar to the sphere indicator code from earlier; the main difference is that it operates on the object of this script rather than creating a separate object. Expressions like `this.gameObject` refer to the GameObject that this script is attached to (and the `this` keyword is optional, so code could refer to `gameObject` without anything in front of it).

The first line of the coroutine function makes the object tip over. As discussed in chapter 2, rotations can be defined as an angle around each of the three coordinate axes, x, y, and z. Because we don't want the object to rotate side to side, leave Y and Z as 0 and assign an angle to the X rotation.

Figure 3.4   The target object falling over when hit

> **NOTE** The transform is applied instantly, but you may prefer seeing the movement when objects topple over. Once you start looking beyond this book for more advanced topics, you might want to look up *tweens*, systems used to make objects move smoothly over time.

The second line of the method uses the `yield` keyword that's so significant to coroutines, pausing the function there and returning the number of seconds to wait before resuming. Finally, the game object destroys itself in the last line of the function. `Destroy(this.gameObject)` is called after the wait time, just as the code called `Destroy(sphere)` before.

> **WARNING** Be sure to call `Destroy()` on `this.gameObject` and not simply `this`! Don't get confused between the two; `this` refers only to this script component, whereas `this.gameObject` refers to the object the script is attached to.

The target now reacts to being shot—great! But it doesn't do anything else on its own, so let's add more behavior to make this target a proper enemy character.

3.3   Basic wandering AI

A static target isn't terribly interesting, so let's write code that'll make the enemy wander around. Code for wandering around is pretty much the simplest example of artificial intelligence (AI), or computer-controlled entities. In this case, the entity is an enemy in a game, but it could also be a robot in the real world or a voice that plays chess, for example.

3.3.1   Diagramming how basic AI works

Multiple approaches to AI exist (seriously, AI is a major area of research for computer scientists). For our purposes, we'll stick with a simple one. As you become more experienced and your games get more sophisticated, you'll probably want to explore the various approaches to AI.

Figure 3.5 depicts the basic process. In every frame, the AI code will scan around its environment to determine whether it needs to react. If an obstacle appears in its way, the enemy turns to face a different direction. Regardless of whether the enemy needs to turn, it will always move forward steadily. As such, the enemy will ping-pong around the room, always moving forward and turning to avoid walls.

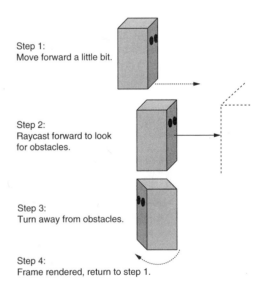

Step 1:
Move forward a little bit.

Step 2:
Raycast forward to look for obstacles.

Step 3:
Turn away from obstacles.

Step 4:
Frame rendered, return to step 1.

Figure 3.5   Basic AI: cyclical process of moving forward and avoiding obstacles

The code will look pretty familiar, because it moves enemies forward by using the same commands as moving the player forward. The AI code will also use raycasting, similar to, but in a different context from, shooting.

3.3.2 "Seeing" obstacles with a raycast

As you saw in the introduction to this chapter, raycasting is a technique that's useful for multiple tasks within 3D simulations. One easily grasped task is shooting, but another task raycasting can be useful for is scanning around the scene. Given that scanning around the scene is a step in AI code, that means raycasting is used in AI code.

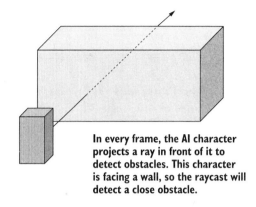

In every frame, the AI character projects a ray in front of it to detect obstacles. This character is facing a wall, so the raycast will detect a close obstacle.

Figure 3.6 Using raycasting to "see" obstacles

Earlier, you created a ray that originated from the camera, because that's where the player was looking from. This time, you'll create a ray that originates from the enemy. The first ray shot out through the center of the screen, but this time the ray will shoot forward in front of the character; figure 3.6 illustrates this. Then, just as the shooting code used `RaycastHit` information to determine whether anything was hit and where, the AI code will use `RaycastHit` information to determine whether anything is in front of the enemy and, if so, how far away.

One difference between raycasting for shooting and raycasting for AI is the radius of the ray. For shooting, the ray was treated as infinitely thin, but for AI, the ray will be treated as having a large cross section. In terms of the code, this means using the `SphereCast()` method instead of `Raycast()`. The reason for this difference is that bullets are tiny, whereas checking for obstacles in front of the character requires us to account for the width of the character.

Create a new script called `WanderingAI`, attach that to the target object (alongside the `ReactiveTarget` script), and write the code from the next listing. Play the scene now and you should see the enemy wandering around the room; you can still shoot the target, and it will react the same way as before.

Listing 3.7 Basic `WanderingAI` script

```
using System.Collections;
using System.Collections.Generic;
using UnityEngine;

public class WanderingAI : MonoBehaviour {
  public float speed = 3.0f;
  public float obstacleRange = 5.0f;

  void Update() {
    transform.Translate(0, 0, speed * Time.deltaTime);
```

Values for the speed of movement and the distance at which to react to obstacles

Move forward continuously every frame, regardless of turning.

```
        Ray ray = new Ray(transform.position, transform.forward);
        RaycastHit hit;
        if (Physics.SphereCast(ray, 0.75f, out hit)) {
          if (hit.distance < obstacleRange) {
            float angle = Random.Range(-110, 110);
            transform.Rotate(0, angle, 0);
          }
        }
      }
    }
```

A ray at the same position and pointing in the same direction as the character

Turn toward a semi-random new direction.

Perform raycasting with a circular volume around the ray.

This listing adds a couple of variables to represent the speed of movement and the distance at which the AI reacts to obstacles. Then, `transform.Translate()` is added in the `Update()` method to move forward continuously (including the use of `deltaTime` for frame rate–independent movement). In `Update()`, you'll also see raycasting code that looks a lot like the shooting script from earlier; again, the same technique of raycasting is being used here to see instead of shoot. The ray is created using the enemy's position and direction, instead of using the camera.

As explained earlier, the raycasting calculation is done using the `Physics.Sphere-Cast()` method. This method takes a radius parameter to determine how far around the ray to detect intersections, but in every other respect, it's exactly the same as `Physics.Raycast()`. This similarity includes how the command fills in hit information, checks for intersections just as before, and uses the `distance` property to be sure to react only when the enemy gets near an obstacle (as opposed to a wall across the room).

When the enemy has a nearby obstacle right in front of it, the code rotates the character a semi-random amount toward a new direction. I say *semi-random* because the values are constrained to the minimum and maximum values that make sense for this situation. Specifically, we use the `Random.Range()` method, which Unity provides for obtaining a random value between constraints. In this case, the constraints were just slightly beyond an exact left or right turn, allowing the character to turn sufficiently to avoid obstacles.

3.3.3   *Tracking the character's state*

One oddity of the current behavior is that the enemy keeps moving forward after falling over from being hit. That's because, right now, the `Translate()` method runs every frame no matter what. Let's make small adjustments to the code to keep track of whether the character is alive—or to put it in another (more technical) way, we want to track the alive state of the character.

Having the code keep track of and respond differently to the current state of the object is a common code pattern in many areas of programming, not just AI. More sophisticated implementations of this approach are referred to as *state machines*, or possibly even *finite-state machines*.

DEFINITION A *finite-state machine* (*FSM*) is a code structure in which the current state of the object is tracked, well-defined transitions exist between states, and the code behaves differently based on the state.

We're not going to implement a full FSM, but it's no coincidence that a common place to see the initials *FSM* is in discussions of AI. A full FSM would have many states for the many behaviors of a sophisticated AI application, but in this basic AI, we need to track only whether the character is alive. The next listing adds a Boolean value, isAlive, toward the top of the script, and the code needs occasional conditional checks of that value. With those checks in place, the movement code runs only while the enemy is alive.

Listing 3.8 WanderingAI script with alive state added

```
...
private bool isAlive;    ⟵——  Boolean value to track
                               whether the enemy is alive

void Start() {
  isAlive = true;    ⟵—— Initialize that value.
}

void Update() {                    Move only if the
  if (isAlive) {     ⟵——          character is alive.
    transform.Translate(0, 0, speed * Time.deltaTime);
    ...
  }
}
                                        Public method allowing outside
public void SetAlive(bool alive) {   ⟵—— code to affect the "alive" state
  isAlive = alive;
}
...
```

The ReactiveTarget script can now tell the WanderingAI script whether the enemy is alive.

Listing 3.9 ReactiveTarget tells WanderingAI when it dies

```
...
public void ReactToHit() {
  WanderingAI behavior = GetComponent<WanderingAI>();
  if (behavior != null) {       ⟵
    behavior.SetAlive(false);         Check if this character has a
  }                                   WanderingAI script; it might not.
  StartCoroutine(Die());
}
...
```

AI code structure

The AI code in this chapter is contained within a single class so that learning and understanding it is straightforward. This code structure is perfectly fine for simple AI needs, so don't be afraid that you've done something wrong and that a more complex code structure is an absolute requirement. For more complex AI needs (such as a game with a wide variety of highly intelligent characters), a more robust code structure can help facilitate developing the AI.

As alluded to in chapter 1's example for composition versus inheritance, sometimes you'll want to split chunks of the AI into separate scripts. Doing so will enable you to mix and match components, generating unique behavior for each character. Think about the similarities and differences among your characters, and those differences will guide you as you design your code architecture. For example, if your game has some enemies that move by charging headlong at the player and some that slink around in the shadows, you may want to make `Locomotion` a separate component. Then you can create scripts for both `LocomotionCharge` and `LocomotionSlink`, and use different `Locomotion` components on different enemies.

The exact AI code structure you want depends on the design of your specific game; there's no one right way to do it. Unity makes it easy to design flexible code architectures like this.

3.4   *Spawning enemy prefabs*

At the moment, only one enemy is in the scene, and when it dies, the scene is empty. Let's make the game spawn enemies so that whenever the enemy dies, a new one appears. This is easily done in Unity by using prefabs.

3.4.1   *What is a prefab?*

Prefabs are a flexible approach to visually defining interactive objects. In a nutshell, a *prefab* is a fully fleshed-out game object (with components already attached and set up) that doesn't exist in any specific scene but rather exists as an asset that can be copied into any scene.

This copying can be done manually, to ensure that the enemy object (or other prefab) is the same in every scene. More importantly, though, prefabs can also be spawned from code; you can place copies of the object into the scene by using commands in scripts and not only by doing so manually in the visual editor.

> **DEFINITION**   An *asset* is any file that shows up in the Project view; these could be 2D images, 3D models, code files, scenes, and so on. I mentioned this term briefly in chapter 1 but didn't emphasize it until now.

A copy of a prefab is called an *instance*, analogous to *instance* referring to a specific code object created from a class. Try to keep the terminology straight: *prefab* refers to the game object existing outside of any scene; *instance* refers to a copy of the object that's placed in a scene.

DEFINITION Also analogous to object-oriented terminology, *instantiate* is the action of creating an instance.

3.4.2 Creating the enemy prefab

To create a prefab, first create an object in the scene that will become the prefab. Because our enemy object will become a prefab, we've already done this first step. Now all we do is drag the object down from the Hierarchy view and drop it in the Project view; this will automatically save the object as a prefab (see figure 3.7).

Back in the Hierarchy view, the original object's name will turn blue to signify that it's now linked to a prefab. We don't actually want the object in the scene anymore (we're going to spawn the prefab, not use the instance already in the scene), so delete the enemy object now. If you want to edit the prefab further, just double-click the prefab in the Project view to open it and then click the back arrow at the top left of the Hierarchy view to close it again.

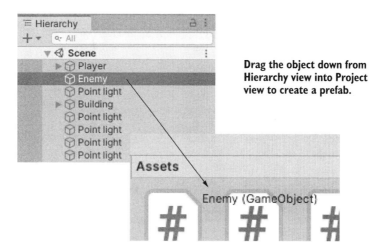

Drag the object down from Hierarchy view into Project view to create a prefab.

Figure 3.7 Drag objects from Hierarchy to Project to create prefabs.

WARNING The interface for working with prefabs has improved a lot since earlier versions of Unity, but editing prefabs can still cause confusion. For example, you are not technically in any scene after you double-click a prefab, so remember to click the back arrow in the Hierarchy view when you are done editing the prefab. In addition, if you nest prefabs (so that one prefab contains other prefabs), working with them can get confusing.

Now we have the actual prefab object to spawn in the scene, so let's write code to create instances of the prefab.

3.4.3 Instantiating from an invisible SceneController

Although the prefab itself doesn't exist in the scene, an object must be in the scene for the enemy spawning code to attach to. We'll create an empty game object and can attach the script to that, but the object won't be visible in the scene.

TIP   The use of empty GameObjects for attaching script components is a common pattern in Unity development. This trick is used for abstract tasks that don't apply to any specific object in the scene. Unity scripts are intended to be attached to visible objects, but not every task makes sense that way.

Choose GameObject > Create Empty, rename the new object `Controller`, and ensure that its position is 0, 0, 0. (Technically, the position doesn't matter because the object isn't visible, but putting it at the origin will make life simpler if you ever parent anything to it.) Create a script called `SceneController`.

Listing 3.10   `SceneController` that spawns the enemy prefab

```
using System.Collections;
using System.Collections.Generic;
using UnityEngine;

public class SceneController : MonoBehaviour {              Serialized variable for
    [SerializeField] GameObject enemyPrefab;  ◁────────     linking to the prefab object
    private GameObject enemy;  ◁───────────
                                              Private variable to keep track of
    void Update() {                           the enemy instance in the scene

        if (enemy == null) {                          ◁────────
            enemy = Instantiate(enemyPrefab) as GameObject;        Spawn a new enemy
            enemy.transform.position = new Vector3(0, 1, 0);       only if one isn't already
            float angle = Random.Range(0, 360);                    in the scene.
            enemy.transform.Rotate(0, angle, 0);
        }
    }
}
```

Method that copies the prefab object (label pointing to `enemy = Instantiate...` block)

Attach this script to the controller object, and in the Inspector you'll see a variable slot for the enemy prefab. This works similarly to public variables, but there's an important difference.

TIP   To reference objects in Unity's editor, I recommend decorating variables with `SerializeField` instead of declaring them to be public. As explained in chapter 2, public variables show up in the Inspector (in other words, they're serialized by Unity), so most tutorials and sample code you'll see use public variables for all serialized values. But these variables can also be modified by other scripts (these are public variables, after all), whereas the `Serialize-Field` attribute allows you to keep the variables private. C# defaults to `private` if a variable isn't explicitly made public, and that's better in most cases because you want to expose that variable in the Inspector but don't want the value to be changed by other scripts.

WARNING   Prior to version 2019.4, Unity had a bug in which `SerializeField` would cause the compiler to emit a warning about that field not being initialized. If you ever encounter this bug, the script still functions fine, so technically you can just ignore those warnings or get rid of them by adding `= null` to those fields.

Drag the prefab asset up from Project to the empty variable slot. When the mouse gets near, you should see the slot highlight to indicate that the object can be linked there (see figure 3.8). Once the enemy prefab is linked to the `SceneController` script, play the scene to see the code in action. An enemy will appear in the middle of the room just as before, but now if you shoot the enemy, it will be replaced by a new enemy. That's much better than just one enemy that's gone forever!

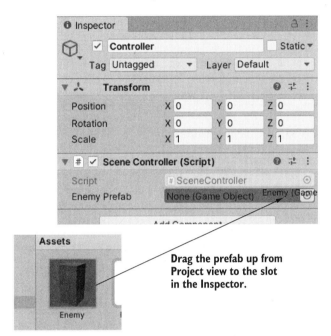

Figure 3.8   Link the enemy prefab to the script's prefab slot.

TIP This approach of dragging objects onto the Inspector's variable slots is a handy technique that comes up in a lot of scripts. Here we linked a prefab to the script, but you can also link to objects in the scene and can even link to specific components (rather than the overall GameObject). In future chapters, we'll use this technique often.

The core of this script is the `Instantiate()` method, so take note of that line. When we instantiate the prefab, that creates a copy in the scene. By default, `Instantiate()` returns the new object as a generic `Object` type, but `Object` is pretty useless directly, and we need to handle it as a `GameObject`. In C#, use the `as` keyword for typecasting to convert from one type of code object into another type (written with the syntax `original-object as new-type`).

The instantiated object is stored in `enemy`, a private variable of the `GameObject` type. (Keep the distinction between a prefab and an instance of the prefab straight: `enemyPrefab` stores the prefab; `enemy` stores the instance.) The `if` statement that checks the stored object ensures that `Instantiate()` is called only when `enemy` is empty (or `null`, in coder-speak). The variable starts out empty, so the instantiating code runs once right from the beginning of the session. The object returned by `Instantiate()` is then stored in enemy so that the instantiating code won't run again.

Because the enemy destroys itself when shot, that empties the enemy variable and causes `Instantiate()` to be run again. In this way, an enemy is always in the scene.

Destroying GameObjects and memory management

It's somewhat unexpected for existing references to become `null` when an object destroys itself. In a memory-managed programming language like C#, normally you aren't able to directly destroy objects; you can only dereference them so that they can be destroyed automatically. This is still true within Unity, but the way GameObjects are handled behind the scenes makes it look like they were destroyed directly.

To display objects in the scene, Unity has to have a reference to all objects in its scene graph. As such, even if you removed all references to the GameObject in your code, this scene graph reference would still prevent the object from being destroyed automatically. Because of this, Unity provides the `Destroy()` method to tell the game engine, "Remove this object from the scene graph." As part of that behind-the-scenes functionality, Unity also overloads the `==` operator to return `true` when checking for `null`. Technically, that object still exists in memory, but it may as well not exist any longer, so Unity has it appearing as `null`. You could confirm this by calling `Get-InstanceID()` on the destroyed object.

Note that the developers of Unity have considered changing this behavior to more standard memory management. If they do, this spawning code will need to change as well, probably by swapping the `(enemy==null)` check with a new parameter like `(enemy.isDestroyed)`.

(If most of this discussion was Greek to you, just don't worry about it; this was a tangential technical discussion for people interested in these obscure details.)

3.5   Shooting by instantiating objects

All right, let's add another bit of functionality to the enemies. Much as we did with the player, first we made them move—now let's make them shoot! As I mentioned back when introducing raycasting, that was just one of the approaches to implementing shooting. Another approach involves instantiating prefabs, so let's take that approach to making the enemies shoot back. The goal of this section is to see figure 3.9 when playing.

3.5.1   Creating the projectile prefab

This time, shooting will involve a projectile in the scene. Shooting with raycasting was basically instantaneous, registering a hit the moment the mouse was clicked, but this time enemies are going to emit fireballs that fly through the air. Admittedly, they'll be moving pretty fast, but not instantaneously, giving the player a chance to dodge out of the way. Instead of using raycasting to detect hits, we'll use collision detection (the same collision system that keeps the moving player from passing through walls).

**Figure 3.9   Enemy shooting
a fireball at the player.**

The code will spawn fireballs in the same way that enemies spawn: by instantiating a prefab. As explained in the previous section, the first step when creating a prefab is to create an object in the scene that will become the prefab, so let's create a fireball.

To start, choose GameObject > 3D Object > Sphere. Rename the new object `Fireball`. Now create a new script, also called `Fireball`, and attach that script to this object. Eventually, we'll write code in this script, but leave it as the default for now while we work on a few other parts of the `Fireball` object. So that it appears like a fireball and not just a gray sphere, we're going to give the object a bright orange color. Surface properties such as color are controlled using materials.

> **DEFINITION**   A *material* is a packet of information that defines the surface properties of any 3D object that the material is attached to. These surface properties can include color, shininess, and even subtle roughness.

Choose Assets > Create > Material. Name the new material something like `Flame` and drag it onto the object in the scene. Select the material in the Project view in order to see the material's properties in the Inspector. As figure 3.10 shows, click the color swatch labeled Albedo (that's a technical term that refers to the main color of a surface). Clicking that will bring up a color picker in its own window; slide both the rainbow-colored ring and the main picking area to set the color to orange.

We're also going to brighten the material to make it look more like fire. Adjust the Emission value (one of the other attributes in the Inspector). The check box is off by default, so turn it on to brighten up the material.

Now you can turn the fireball object into a prefab by dragging the object down from Hierarchy into Project, just as you did with the enemy prefab. As with the enemy, we need only the prefab now, so delete the instance in the Hierarchy. Great—we have a new prefab to use as a projectile! Next up is writing code to shoot using that projectile.

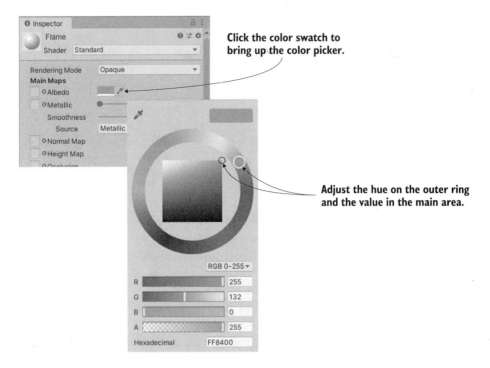

Click the color swatch to bring up the color picker.

Adjust the hue on the outer ring and the value in the main area.

Figure 3.10 Setting the color of a material

3.5.2 *Shooting the projectile and colliding with a target*

Let's make adjustments to the enemy in order to emit fireballs. Because code to recognize the player will require a new script (just like ReactiveTarget was required by the code to recognize the target), first create a new script and name it PlayerCharacter. Attach this script to the player object in the scene. Now open up WanderingAI and add to the code from this listing.

Listing 3.11 WanderingAI additions for emitting fireballs

Add these two fields before any methods, just as in SceneController.

```
...
[SerializeField] GameObject fireballPrefab;
private GameObject fireball;
...
if (Physics.SphereCast(ray, 0.75f, out hit)) {
   GameObject hitObject = hit.transform.gameObject;
   if (hitObject.GetComponent<PlayerCharacter>()) {
      if (fireball == null) {
         fireball = Instantiate(fireballPrefab) as GameObject;
         fireball.transform.position =
            transform.TransformPoint(Vector3.forward * 1.5f);
         fireball.transform.rotation = transform.rotation;
```

Player is detected in the same way as the target object in RayShooter.

Instantiate() method here is just as it was in SceneController.

Same null GameObject logic as SceneController

Place the fireball in front of the enemy and point in the same direction.

```
    }
  }
  else if (hit.distance < obstacleRange) {
    float angle = Random.Range(-110, 110);
    transform.Rotate(0, angle, 0);
  }
}
...
```

You'll notice that all the annotations in this listing refer to similar (or the same) bits in previous scripts. Previous code listings showed everything needed for emitting fireballs; now we're mashing together and remixing bits of code to fit in the new context.

Just as in `SceneController`, you need to add two `GameObject` fields toward the top of the script: a serialized variable for linking the prefab to, and a private variable for keeping track of the instance created by the code. After doing a raycast, the code checks for the `PlayerCharacter` on the object hit; this works just as the shooting code checking for `ReactiveTarget` on the object hit. The code that instantiates a fireball when there isn't already one in the scene works like the code that instantiates an enemy. The positioning and rotation are different, though; this time, you place the instance just in front of the enemy and point it in the same direction.

Once all the new code is in place, a new Fireball Prefab slot will appear in the Inspector when you select the Enemy prefab, like the Enemy Prefab slot in the `Scene-Controller` component. Click the Enemy prefab in the Project view (double-click to actually open the prefab, but just a single click selects it), and the Inspector will show that object's components, as if you'd selected an object in the scene. Although the earlier warning about interface awkwardness often applies when editing prefabs, the interface makes it easy to adjust the components on a prefab without opening it, and that's all we're doing. As shown in figure 3.11, drag the Fireball prefab from Project onto the Fireball Prefab slot in the Inspector (again, just as you did with `SceneController`).

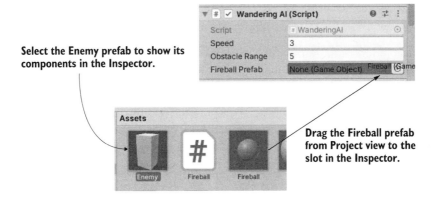

Select the Enemy prefab to show its components in the Inspector.

Drag the Fireball prefab from Project view to the slot in the Inspector.

Figure 3.11 Link the fireball prefab to the script's prefab slot.

Now the enemy will fire at the player when the player is directly ahead of it . . . well, try to fire. The bright orange sphere appears in front of the enemy but just sits there because we haven't written its script yet. Let's do that now.

Listing 3.12 Fireball script that reacts to collisions

```
using System.Collections;
using System.Collections.Generic;
using UnityEngine;

public class Fireball : MonoBehaviour {
  public float speed = 10.0f;
  public int damage = 1;

  void Update() {
    transform.Translate(0, 0, speed * Time.deltaTime);    ⟵ Move forward in the direction it faces.
  }

  void OnTriggerEnter(Collider other) {      ⟵ Called when another object collides with this trigger
    PlayerCharacter player = other.GetComponent<PlayerCharacter>();
    if (player != null) {       ⟵
      Debug.Log("Player hit");       Check if the other object is a PlayerCharacter.
    }
    Destroy(this.gameObject);
  }
}
```

The crucial new bit to this code is the `OnTriggerEnter()` method, called automatically when the object has a collision, such as with the walls or with the player. At the moment, this code won't work entirely; if you run it, the fireball will fly forward thanks to the `Translate()` line, but the trigger won't run, queuing up a new fireball by destroying the current one. A couple of other adjustments need to be made to components on the `Fireball` object. The first change is making the collider a trigger. To adjust that, go to the Inspector and click the Is Trigger check box in the Sphere Collider component.

> **TIP** A collider component set as a trigger will still react to touching/overlapping other objects but will no longer stop other objects from physically passing through.

The fireball also needs a Rigidbody, a component used by the physics system in Unity. By giving the fireball a Rigidbody component, you ensure that the physics system is able to register collision triggers for that object. Click Add Component at the bottom of the Inspector and choose Physics > Rigidbody. In the component that's added, deselect Use Gravity (see figure 3.12) so that the fireball won't be pulled down by gravity.

Play now, and fireballs are destroyed when they hit something. Because the fireball-emitting code runs whenever a fireball isn't already in the scene, the enemy will shoot more fireballs at the player. Now just one more thing remains for shooting at the player: making the player react to being hit.

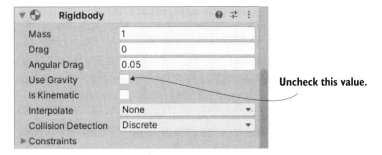

Figure 3.12 Turn off gravity in the Rigidbody component.

3.5.3 Damaging the player

Earlier, you created a `PlayerCharacter` script but left it empty. Now you'll write code to have the player react to being hit.

Listing 3.13 Player that can take damage

```
using System.Collections;
using System.Collections.Generic;
using UnityEngine;

public class PlayerCharacter : MonoBehaviour {
  private int health;

  void Start() {
    health = 5;        ⟵——— Initialize the health value.
  }

  public void Hurt(int damage) {      | Decrement the player's health.
    health -= damage;          ⟵
    Debug.Log($"Health: {health}");   ⟵   Construct the message by
  }                                        using string interpolation.
}
```

The listing defines a field for the player's health and reduces the health on command. In later chapters, we'll go over text displays to show information on the screen, but for now, we can display information about the player's health only by using debug messages.

> **DEFINITION** *String interpolation* is a mechanism to insert the evaluation of code (for example, the value of a variable) into a string. Several programming languages support string interpolation, including C#. For example, look at the health message in listing 3.13.

Now you need to go back to the `Fireball` script to call the player's `Hurt()` method. Replace the debug line in the `Fireball` script with `player.Hurt(damage)` to tell the player they've been hit. And that's the final bit of code we need!

Whew! That was a pretty intense chapter, with lots of code introduced. Combining the previous chapter with this one, you now have most of the functionality in place for a first-person shooter.

Summary

- A ray is an imaginary line projected into the scene.
- Raycasting operations are useful for both shooting and sensing obstacles.
- Making a character wander around involves basic AI.
- New objects are spawned by instantiating prefabs.
- Coroutines are used to spread out functions over time.

Developing
graphics for your game

This chapter covers

- Understanding art assets used in game development
- Building prototype levels through whiteboxing
- Using 2D images in Unity
- Importing custom 3D models
- Crafting particle effects

We've been focusing mostly on how the game functions and not as much on how the game looks. That was no accident—this book is mostly about programming games in Unity. Still, it's important to understand how to work on and improve the visuals. Before we get back to the book's main focus on coding various parts of the game, let's spend a chapter learning about game art so that your projects won't always end up with just blank boxes sliding around.

All of the visual content in a game is made up of art assets. But what exactly does that mean?

4.1   Understanding art assets

An *art asset* is an individual unit of visual information (usually a file) used by the game. This overarching umbrella term applies to all visual content: image files are art assets, 3D models are art assets, and so on. Indeed, an art asset is simply a specific type of asset, which you've learned is any file used by the game (such as a script)—hence the main Assets folder in Unity. Table 4.1 describes the five main kinds of art assets used in building a game.

Table 4.1   Types of art assets

Type of art asset	Definition
2D image	Flat pictures. To make a real-world analogy, 2D images are like paintings and photographs.
3D model	3D virtual objects (almost a synonym for *mesh objects*). To make a real-world analogy, 3D models are like sculptures.
Material	A packet of information that defines the surface properties of any object that the material is attached to. These surface properties can include color, shininess, and even subtle roughness.
Animation	Packets of information that define the movement of the associated object. These are detailed movement sequences created ahead of time, as opposed to code that calculates positions on the fly.
Particle system	An orderly mechanism for creating and controlling large numbers of small moving objects. Many visual effects, like fire, smoke, or spraying water, are created this way.

Creating art for a new game generally starts with either 2D images or 3D models because those assets form a base on which everything else relies. As the names imply, *2D images* are the foundation of 2D graphics, whereas *3D models* are the foundation of 3D graphics. Specifically, 2D images are flat pictures. Even if you have no previous familiarity with game art, you're probably already familiar with 2D images from the graphics used on websites; 3D models, on the other hand, may need to be defined for a newcomer.

> **DEFINITION** A *model* is a 3D virtual object. Chapter 1 introduced the term *mesh object*, and *3D model* is practically a synonym. The terms are frequently used interchangeably, but *mesh object* strictly refers to the geometry of the 3D object (the connected lines and shapes), whereas *model* is a bit more ambiguous and often includes other attributes of the object.

The next two types of assets on the list are *materials* and *animations*. Unlike 2D images and 3D models, materials and animations don't do anything in isolation and are much harder for newcomers to understand. 2D images and 3D models are easily understood through real-world analogs: paintings for the former, sculptures for the latter. Materials and animations aren't as directly relatable to the real world. Instead, both are abstract packets of information that layer onto 3D models. In fact, materials were already introduced in a basic sense in chapter 3.

> **DEFINITION** A *material* is a packet of information that defines the surface properties (color, shininess, and so forth) of any object that it's attached to. Defining surface properties separately enables multiple objects to share a material (all the castle walls, for example).

Continuing the art analogy, you can think of a material as the medium (clay, brass, marble, and so on) that the sculpture is made of. Similarly, an animation is also an abstract layer of information that's attached to a visible object.

> **DEFINITION** An *animation* is a packet of information that defines the movement of the associated object. Because these movements can be defined independently from the object itself, they can be used in a mix-and-match way with multiple objects.

For a concrete example, think about a character walking around. The overall position of the character is handled by the game's code (for example, the movement scripts you wrote in chapter 2). But the detailed movements of feet hitting the ground, arms swinging, and hips rotating are an animation sequence that's being played back; that animation sequence is an art asset.

To help you understand how animations and 3D models relate, let's make an analogy with puppeteering: the 3D model is the puppet, the animator is the puppeteer who makes the puppet move, and the animation is a recording of the puppet's movements. The movements defined this way are created ahead of time and are usually small-scale movements that don't change the overall positioning of the object. This is in contrast to the sort of large-scale movements that were done in code in previous chapters.

The final kind of art asset from table 4.1 is a particle system. *Particle systems* are useful for creating visual effects, like fire, smoke, or spraying water.

> **DEFINITION** A *particle system* is an orderly mechanism for creating and controlling large numbers of moving objects. These moving objects are usually small—hence the name *particle*—but they don't have to be.

The particles (the individual objects under the control of a particle system) can be any mesh object that you choose. But for most effects, the particles will be a square displaying a picture (a flame spark or a smoke puff, for example).

Much of the work of creating game art is done in external software, not within Unity itself. Materials and particle systems are created within Unity, but the other art assets are created using external software. Refer to appendix B to learn more about external tools; a variety of art applications are used for creating 3D models and animation. 3D models created in an external tool are then saved as an art asset that's imported by Unity. I use Blender when explaining how to model in appendix C (download it from www.blender.org), but that's just because Blender is open source and thus available to all readers.

> **NOTE** The project download for this chapter includes a folder named *scratch*. Although that folder is in the same place as the Unity project, it's not part of the Unity project; that's where I put extra external files.

As you work through the project for this chapter, you'll see examples of most of these types of art assets (animations are a bit too complex for now and are addressed later in the book). You're going to build a scene that uses 2D images, 3D models, materials, and a particle system. In some cases, you'll bring in already existing art assets and learn how to import them into Unity, but at other times (especially with the particle system), you'll create the art asset from scratch within Unity.

This chapter only scratches the surface of game art creation. Because this book focuses on how to program in Unity, extensive coverage of art disciplines would reduce how much the book could cover. Creating game art is a giant topic in and of itself, easily able to fill several books. In most cases, a game programmer would need to partner with a game artist who specializes in that discipline. That said, it's extremely useful for game programmers to understand how Unity works with art assets and possibly even create their own rough stand-ins to be replaced later (commonly known as *programmer art*).

> **NOTE** Nothing in this chapter directly requires projects from the previous chapters. But you'll want to have movement scripts like the ones from chapter 2 so that you can walk around the scene you'll build. If necessary, you can grab the player object and scripts from the project download. Similarly, this chapter ends with moving objects that are similar to the ones created in previous chapters.

4.2   *Building basic 3D scenery: Whiteboxing*

The first content creation topic we'll go over is *whiteboxing*. This process is usually the first step in building a level on the computer (after designing the level on paper). As the name suggests, you block out the walls of the scene with blank geometry (white boxes). Looking at the list of art assets in table 4.1, this blank scenery is the most basic sort of 3D model, and it provides a base on which to display 2D images.

If you think back to the primitive scene you created in chapter 2, that was basically whiteboxing (you just hadn't learned the term yet). Some of this section will be a rehash of work done in the beginning of chapter 2, but we'll cover the process a lot faster this time, as well as discuss more new terminology.

> **NOTE** Another term that is frequently used is *grayboxing*. It means the same thing. I tend to use *whiteboxing* because that was the term I first learned, but others use grayboxing, which is just as accepted. The actual color used varies anyway, similar to the way blueprints aren't necessarily blue.

4.2.1 Whiteboxing explained

Blocking out the scene with blank geometry serves a couple of purposes. First, this process enables you to quickly build a sketch that will be progressively refined over time. This activity is closely associated with level design and/or level designers.

> **DEFINITION** *Level design* is the discipline of planning and creating scenes (or levels) in the game. A *level designer* is a practitioner of level design.

As game development teams have grown in size and team members have become more specialized, a common level-building workflow is for the level designer to create a first version of the level through whiteboxing. This rough level is then handed over to the art team for visual polish. But even on a tiny team, where the same person is both designing levels and creating art for the game, this workflow of first doing whiteboxing and then polishing the visuals generally works best. You have to start somewhere, after all, and whiteboxing gives a clear foundation on which to build up the visuals.

A second purpose served by whiteboxing is that the level quickly reaches a playable state. The level may not be finished (indeed, a level right after whiteboxing is *far* from finished), but this rough version is functional and can support gameplay. At a minimum, the player can walk around the scene (think of the demo in chapter 2). In this way, you can test to make sure the level is coming together well (for example, are the rooms the right size for this game?) before investing a lot of time and energy in detailed work. If something is off (say you realize the spaces need to be bigger), changing and retesting is much easier in the whiteboxing stage.

Moreover, being able to play the under-construction level is a huge morale boost. Don't discount this benefit: building all the visuals for a scene can take a great deal of time, and having to wait a long time before you can experience any of that work in the game can start to feel like a slog. Whiteboxing builds a complete (if primitive) level right away, and it's exciting to then play the game as it continually improves.

All right, so you understand why levels start with whiteboxing. Now let's build a level!

4.2.2 Drawing a floor plan for the level

Building a level on the computer follows designing the level on paper. We're not going to get into a huge discussion about level design; just as chapter 2 noted about game design, level design (which is a subset of game design) is a large discipline that could fill an entire book by itself. For our purposes, we're going to draw a basic level, with little design going into the plan, in order to give us a target to work toward.

Figure 4.1 is a top-down drawing of a simple layout with four rooms connected by a central hallway. That's all we need for a plan right now: a bunch of separated areas and interior walls to place. In a real game, your plan would be more extensive and include things like enemies and items.

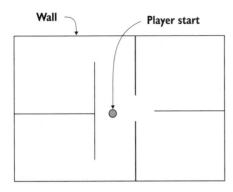

**Figure 4.1   Floor plan for the level:
four rooms and a central corridor**

You could practice whiteboxing by building this floor plan, or you could draw your own simple level to practice that step too. The specifics of the room layout matter little for this exercise. The important thing for our purposes is to have a floor plan drawn so that we can move forward with the next step.

4.2.3   *Laying out primitives according to the plan*

Building the whitebox level in accordance with the drawn floor plan involves positioning and scaling a bunch of blank boxes to be the walls in the diagram. As described in section 2.2.1, choose GameObject > 3D Object > Cube to create a blank box that you can position and scale as needed.

> **More advanced level editing within Unity**
>
> In the workflow featured in this chapter, the level is first blocked out with primitives, and then the final-level geometry is built in an external 3D art tool. However, Unity also offers ProBuilder, a more robust tool for level editing. You could still choose to use that for blocking out a level that gets detailed in an external 3D art tool, but ProBuilder could even be your sole level-design tool.
>
> Open the Package Manager window (choose Window > Package Manager) and search the Unity Registry for ProBuilder. Once that package is installed, it operates as described on the Unity website (https://unity.com/features/probuilder).
>
> Meanwhile, a different approach to editing the level is called *constructive solid geometry* (CSG). In that approach, you use shapes referred to as *brushes*, and everything from the initial prototype to final-level geometry is built within Unity. Go to Realtime CSG (https://realtimecsg.com) for more information.

The first object will be the floor of the scene. In the Inspector, rename the object and lower it to -0.5 Y to account for the height of the box itself (figure 4.2 depicts this). Then stretch the object along the x- and z-axes.

Name of the object

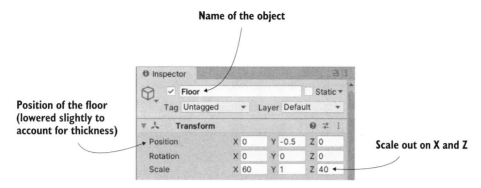

Position of the floor (lowered slightly to account for thickness)

Scale out on X and Z

Figure 4.2 Inspector view of the box positioned and scaled for the floor

Repeat these steps to create the walls of the scene. You probably want to clean up the Hierarchy view by making the walls children of a common base object (remember, position the root object at 0, 0, 0, and then drag objects onto it in Hierarchy), but that's not required. Also put a few simple lights around the scene so that you can see it; referring to chapter 2, create lights by selecting them in the Light submenu of the GameObject menu. The level should look something like figure 4.3 once you're done with whiteboxing.

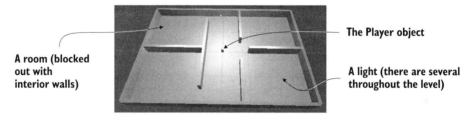

The Player object

A room (blocked out with interior walls)

A light (there are several throughout the level)

Figure 4.3 Whitebox level of the floor plan in figure 4.1

Set up your player object or camera to move around (create the player with a character controller and movement scripts; refer to chapter 2 if you need a full explanation). Now you can walk around the primitive scene to experience your work and test it out. And that's how you do whiteboxing! Pretty simple—but all you have right now is blank geometry, so let's dress up the geometry with pictures on the walls.

Exporting whitebox geometry to external art tools

Much of the work when adding visual polish to the level is done in external 3D art applications like Blender. Because of this, you may want to have the whitebox geometry in your art tool to refer to. By default, there's no export option for primitives laid out within Unity, but Unity offers an optional package (called FBX Exporter) that adds this functionality to the editor.

(continued)
Open the Package Manager and search for FBX Exporter. This is a preview package, so you'll need to select Show Preview Packages in the Package Manager window's Advanced menu. Once that package is installed, it operates as described in the Unity documentation (http://mng.bz/AOYW).

Incidentally, you don't need this package for levels made with ProBuilder, the advanced level-editing tool mentioned earlier, since that tool already has a model exporter.

4.3   *Texturing the scene with 2D images*

The level at this point is a rough sketch. It's playable, but clearly a lot more work needs to be done on the visual appearance of the scene. The next step in improving the look of the level is applying textures.

> **DEFINITION**   A *texture* is a 2D image being used to enhance 3D graphics. That's the totality of what the term means; don't confuse yourself by thinking that any of the uses of textures are part of how the term is defined. No matter how the image is being used, it's still referred to as a texture.

> **NOTE**   *Texture* is routinely used as both a verb and a noun. In addition to the noun definition, the word describes the action of using 2D images in 3D graphics.

Textures have multiple uses in 3D graphics, but the most straightforward use is to be displayed on the surface of 3D models. Later in this chapter, we'll discuss how this works for more complex models, but for our whiteboxed level, the 2D images will act as wallpaper covering the walls (see figure 4.4).

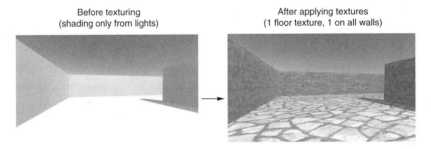

Before texturing
(shading only from lights)

After applying textures
(1 floor texture, 1 on all walls)

Figure 4.4   Comparing the level before and after textures

As you can see from the comparison in figure 4.4, textures turn what was an obviously unreal digital construct into a brick wall. Other uses for textures include masks to cut out shapes and normal maps to make surfaces bumpy. Later, you may want to look up more information about textures in the resources mentioned in appendix D.

4.3.1 Choosing a file format

A variety of file formats is available for saving 2D images, so which should you use? Unity supports the use of many file formats, so you could choose any of the ones shown in table 4.2.

Table 4.2 2D image file formats supported by Unity

File type	Pros and cons
PNG	Commonly used on the web. Lossless compression; has an alpha channel.
JPG	Commonly used on the web. Lossy compression; no alpha channel.
GIF	Commonly used on the web. Lossy compression; no alpha channel. (Technically, the loss isn't from compression; rather, data is lost when the image is converted to 8-bit. Ultimately, it amounts to the same thing.)
BMP	Default image format on Windows. No compression; no alpha channel.
TGA	Commonly used for 3D graphics; obscure everywhere else. No or lossless compression; has an alpha channel.
TIFF	Commonly used for digital photography and publishing. No or lossless compression; no alpha channel.
PICT	Default image format on old Macs. Lossy compression; no alpha channel.
PSD	Native file format for Adobe Photoshop. No compression; has an alpha channel. The main reason to use this file format would be the advantage of using Photoshop files directly.

> **DEFINITION** The *alpha channel* is used to store transparency information in an image. The visible colors come in three *channels* of information: Red, Green, and Blue. Alpha is an additional channel of information that isn't visible but controls the transparency of the image.

Although Unity will accept any of the image types shown in table 4.2 to import and use as a texture, the file formats vary considerably in the features they support. Two factors are particularly important for 2D images imported as textures: how is the image compressed, and does it have an alpha channel?

The alpha channel is a straightforward consideration. Because the alpha channel is used often in 3D graphics, an image that has an alpha channel is preferred.

Image compression is a slightly more complicated consideration, but it boils down to "lossy compression is bad." Both no compression and lossless compression preserve the image quality, whereas lossy compression reduces the image quality (hence the term *lossy*) as part of reducing the file size.

Between these two considerations, the two file formats I recommend for Unity textures are PNG and TGA. Targas (TGA) used to be the favorite file format for texturing 3D graphics, before PNG became widely used on the internet. These days, PNG is almost equivalent technologically but is much more widespread, because it's useful both on the web and as a texture.

PSD is also commonly recommended for Unity textures, because it's an advanced file format and because it's convenient that the same file you work on in Photoshop also works in Unity. But I tend to prefer keeping work files separate from "finished" files that are exported over to Unity (this same mindset comes up again later with 3D models).

The upshot is that all the images I provide in the example projects are PNG, and I recommend that you work with that file format as well. With this decision made, it's time to bring some images into Unity and apply them to the blank scene.

4.3.2   Importing an image file

Let's start creating and preparing the textures we'll use. The images used to texture levels are usually tileable so that they can be repeated across large surfaces like the floor.

> **DEFINITION**   A *tileable* image (sometimes referred to as a *seamless tile*) is an image in which opposite edges match up when placed side by side. This way, the image can be repeated without any visible seams between the repeats. The concept for 3D texturing is just like wallpaper on web pages.

You can obtain tileable images in several ways, including by manipulating photographs or even painting them by hand. Tutorials and explanations of these techniques can be found in numerous books and websites, but we don't want to get bogged down with that right now. Instead, let's grab a couple of tileable images from one of the many websites that offer a catalog of such images for 3D artists to use.

I obtained a couple of images from www.textures.com (see figure 4.5) to apply to the walls and floor of the level. Find a couple of images you think look good for the floor and walls; I chose BrickRound0067 and BrickLargeBare0032.

Figure 4.5   Seamlessly tiling stone and brick images obtained from Textures.com

Download the images you want and prepare them for use as textures. Technically, you could use the images directly as they were downloaded, but they aren't ideal for use as textures. Although they're certainly tileable (the important reason you're using these images), they aren't the right size and are the wrong file format.

The size (in pixels) of a texture should be in powers of 2. For reasons of technical efficiency, graphics chips like to handle textures in sizes that are 2^N: 4, 8, 16, 32, 64, 128, 256, 512, 1024, 2048 (the next number is 4096, but at that point the image is too big to use as a texture). In your image editor (Photoshop, GIMP, or whatever; refer to appendix B), scale the downloaded image to 256 × 256 pixels, and save it as a PNG.

Now drag the files from their location in the computer into the Project view in Unity. This will copy the files into your Unity project (see figure 4.6), at which point they're imported as textures and can be used in the 3D scene. If dragging the file over would be awkward, you could instead right-click in Project and select Import New Asset to access a file picker.

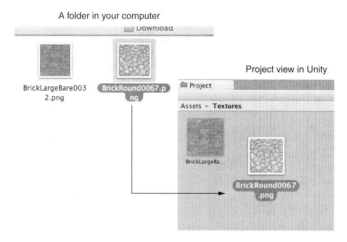

Figure 4.6   Drag images from outside Unity to import them into the Project view.

> **TIP** Organizing your assets into separate folders is probably a good idea as your projects start to get more complex. In the Project view, create folders for Scripts and Textures and then move assets into the appropriate folders. Simply drag files to their new folder.

> **WARNING** Unity has several keywords that it responds to in folder names, with special ways of handling the contents of these special folders. Those keywords are Resources, Plugins, Editor, and Gizmos. Later in the book, we'll go over what some of these special folders do, but for now, avoid naming any folders with those words.

Now the images are imported into Unity as textures, ready to use. But how do we apply the textures to objects in the scene?

4.3.3   *Applying the image*

Technically, textures aren't applied to geometry directly. Instead, textures can be part of materials, and materials are applied to geometry. As explained in the introduction, a material is a set of information defining the properties of a surface; that information can include a texture to display on that surface. This indirection is significant because the same texture can be used with multiple materials. That said, typically each texture goes with a different material, so for convenience Unity allows you to drop a texture onto an object and then it creates a new material automatically.

If you drag a texture from Project view onto an object in the scene, Unity will create a new material and apply it to the object. Figure 4.7 illustrates the maneuver. Try that now with the texture for the floor.

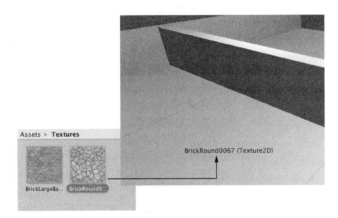

Assets ▶ Textures

BrickRound0067 (Texture2D)

BrickLargeBa...   BrickRound0...

Figure 4.7   One way to apply textures is to drag them from Project onto Scene objects.

Besides this convenient method of automatically creating materials, the "proper" way to create a material is to choose Assets > Create > Material; the new asset will appear in the Project view. Now select the material to show its properties in the Inspector (you'll see something like figure 4.8) and drag a texture to the main texture slot; the setting is called Albedo (that's a technical term for the base color), and the texture slot is the square to the left side of the label. Meanwhile, drag the material up from Project onto an object in the scene to apply the material to that object. Try these steps now with the texture for the wall: create a new material, drag the wall texture into this material, and drag the material onto a wall in the scene.

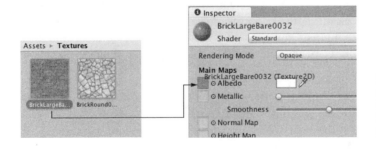

Assets ▶ Textures

BrickLargeBa...   BrickRound0...

ⓘ Inspector

BrickLargeBare0032

Shader Standard

Rendering Mode   Opaque

Main Maps
BrickLargeBare0032 (Texture2D)
○ Albedo
○ Metallic
   Smoothness
○ Normal Map
○ Height Map

Figure 4.8   Select a material to see it in the Inspector and then drag textures to the material properties.

You should now see the stone and brick images appear on the surface of the floor and wall objects, but the images look rather stretched out and blurry. The single image is being stretched out to cover the entire floor. Instead, you want the image to repeat a few times over the floor surface.

You can set this appearance by using the tiling property of the material. Select the material in Project and then change the tiling number in the Inspector (with separate X and Y values for tiling in each direction). Make sure you're setting the tiling of the main map and not the secondary map (this material optionally uses a secondary texture map for advanced effects). The default tiling is 1 (that's no tiling, with the image being stretched over the entire surface); change the numbers to something like 8 and see what happens in the scene. Change the numbers in both materials to tiling that looks good.

> **NOTE** Adjusting the tiling property like this is useful only for texturing white-box geometry. In a polished game, the floor and walls will be built with more intricate art tools, and that includes setting up their textures.

Great—now the scene has textures applied to the floor and walls! You can also apply textures to the sky of the scene. Let's look at that process.

4.4 Generating sky visuals by using texture images

The brick and stone textures provide a much more natural look to the walls and floor. Yet the sky is currently blank and unnatural; we also want a realistic look for the sky. The most common approach to this task is a special kind of texturing using pictures of the sky.

4.4.1 What is a skybox?

By default, the camera's background color is dark blue. Ordinarily, that color fills in any empty area of the view (for example, above the walls of this scene), but it's possible to render pictures of the sky as background. This is where a skybox comes in.

> **DEFINITION** A *skybox* is a cube surrounding the camera with pictures of the sky on each side. No matter what direction the camera is facing, it's looking at a picture of the sky.

Properly implementing a skybox can be tricky; figure 4.9 shows a diagram of how a skybox works. Rendering tricks are needed for the skybox to appear as a distant background. Fortunately, Unity already takes care of all that for you.

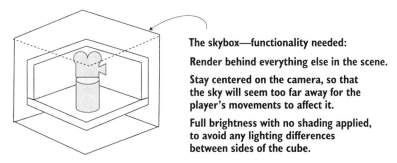

The skybox—functionality needed:

Render behind everything else in the scene.

Stay centered on the camera, so that the sky will seem too far away for the player's movements to affect it.

Full brightness with no shading applied, to avoid any lighting differences between sides of the cube.

Figure 4.9   Diagram of a skybox

New scenes come with a simple default skybox already assigned to them. This is why the sky has a gradient from light to dark blue, rather than being a flat dark blue. Open the lighting window (Window > Rendering > Lighting), switch to the Environment tab, and then note that the first setting is Skybox Material. This window has a multiple settings panels related to the advanced lighting system in Unity, but for now, we care about only the first setting.

Just like the brick textures earlier, skybox images can be obtained from a variety of websites. Search for *skybox textures* or simply get them from the book's sample project. For example, I obtained the TropicalSunnyDay set of skybox images from Heiko Irrgang at https://93i.de/. Once this skybox is applied to the scene, you will see something like figure 4.10.

Figure 4.10   Scene with background pictures of the sky

As with other textures, skybox images are first assigned to a material, and that gets used in the scene. Let's examine how to create a new skybox material.

4.4.2   Creating a new skybox material

First, create a new material (as usual, either right-click and choose Create, or choose Create from the Assets menu) and then select that material to see its settings in the Inspector. Next, you need to change the shader used by this material. The top of the material settings has a Shader menu (see figure 4.11). In section 4.3, we pretty much ignored this menu because the default works fine for most standard texturing, but a skybox requires a special shader.

> **DEFINITION**   A *shader* is a short program that outlines instructions for drawing a surface, including whether to use any textures. The computer uses these instructions to calculate the pixels when rendering the image. The most common shader takes the color of the material and darkens it according to the light, but shaders can also be used for all sorts of visual effects.

Every material has a shader that controls it (you could think of a material as an instance of a shader). New materials are set to the Standard shader by default. This shader displays the color of the material (including the texture) while applying light and shadows across the surface.

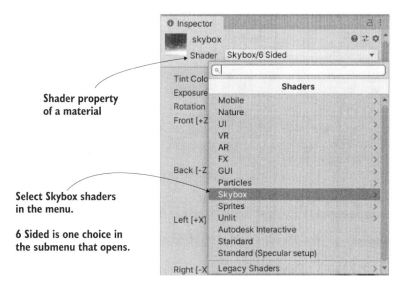

Shader property
of a material

Select Skybox shaders
in the menu.

6 Sided is one choice in
the submenu that opens.

Figure 4.11   The drop-down menu of available shaders

For skyboxes, Unity has a different shader. Click the menu to see the drop-down list (see figure 4.11) of all the available shaders. Select the Skybox section and choose 6 Sided in the submenu. With this shader active, the material now has six large texture slots (instead of only the small Albedo texture slot that the standard shader has). These six texture slots correspond to the six sides of a cube, so these images should match up at the edges to appear seamless. For example, figure 4.12 shows the images for the sunny skybox.

Figure 4.12   Six images for the sides of a skybox

Import the skybox images into Unity the same way you brought in the brick textures: drag the files into the Project view or right-click in Project and select Import New Asset. We need to change one subtle import setting; click the imported texture to see its properties in the Inspector and change the Wrap Mode setting (shown in figure 4.13) from Repeat to Clamp. Don't forget to click Apply when you're done. Ordinarily, textures can be tiled repeatedly over a surface, and for this to appear seamless, opposite edges of the image bleed together. But this blending of edges can create faint lines in the sky where images meet, so the Clamp setting (similar to the `Clamp()` function in chapter 2) will limit the boundaries of the texture and get rid of this blending.

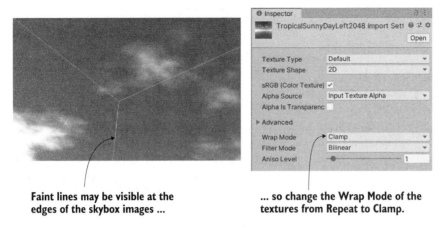

Faint lines may be visible at the
edges of the skybox images ...

... so change the Wrap Mode of the
textures from Repeat to Clamp.

Figure 4.13 Correct faint edge lines by adjusting the Wrap mode.

Now you can drag these images to the texture slots of the skybox material. The image names correspond to the texture slot to assign them to (such as left or front). Once all six textures are linked up, you can use this new material as the skybox for the scene. Open the lighting window again and set this new material to the Skybox slot; either drag the material to that slot, or click the tiny circle icon to bring up a file picker. Now click Play to see the new skybox.

> **TIP** By default, Unity will display the skybox (or at least its main color) in the editor's Scene view. You may find this color distracting while editing objects, so you can toggle the skybox on or off. Across the top of the Scene view's pane are buttons that control what's visible; look for the Effects button to toggle the skybox on or off.

Woo-hoo—you've learned how to create sky visuals for your scene! A skybox is an elegant way to create the illusion of a vast atmosphere surrounding the player. The next step in polishing the visuals in your level is to create more complex 3D models.

4.5 *Working with custom 3D models*

In the previous sections, we looked at applying textures to the large flat walls and floors of the level. But what about more detailed objects? What if you want, say, interesting furniture in the room? You can accomplish that by building 3D models in external 3D art apps. Recall the definition from the introduction to this chapter: 3D models are the mesh objects in the game (the three-dimensional shapes). Well, you're going to import a 3D mesh of a simple bench.

Applications widely used for modeling 3D objects include Autodesk Maya and Autodesk 3ds Max. Both are expensive commercial tools, so the sample for this chapter uses the open source app Blender. The sample download includes a .blend file that you can use; figure 4.14 depicts the bench model in Blender. If you're interested in learning how to model your own objects, you'll find an exercise in appendix C about modeling this bench in Blender.

Besides custom-made models created by yourself or an artist you're working with, many 3D models are available for download from game art websites. One great resource for 3D models is the Unity Asset Store, accessible within Unity or at https://assetstore.unity.com.

This includes both the 3D mesh geometry and a texture applied to the mesh.

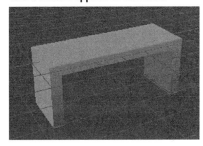

Figure 4.14   The bench model in Blender

4.5.1   *Which file format to choose?*

After you obtain a model made in an external art tool, you need to export the asset from that software. Just as with 2D images, multiple file formats are available for you to use when exporting the 3D model, and these file types have various pros and cons. Table 4.3 lists the 3D file formats that Unity supports.

Table 4.3   3D Model file formats supported by Unity

File type	Pros and cons
FBX	Mesh and animation; recommended option when available.
COLLADA (DAE)	Mesh and animation; another good option when FBX isn't available.
OBJ	Mesh only; this is a text format, so sometimes useful for streaming over the internet.
3DS	Mesh only; a pretty old and primitive model format.
DXF	Mesh only; a pretty old and primitive model format.
Maya	Works via FBX; requires this application to be installed.
3ds Max	Works via FBX; requires this application to be installed.
Blender	Works via FBX; requires this application to be installed.

Choosing an option boils down to whether the file supports animation. Because COLLADA and FBX are the only two options that include animation data, those are the two options to choose. Whenever it's available (not all 3D tools have it as an export option), FBX export tends to work best, but if you're using a tool without FBX export, then COLLLADA works well too. In our case, Blender supports FBX export, so we'll use that file format.

> ### gITF file format
>
> While FBX is the best 3D format with built-in support, you may instead want to use gITF files in Unity. This newer 3D file format sees increased use these days. The gITF specification is developed by the Khronos Group, the same people behind COLLADA, and they maintain a Unity add-on at https://github.com/KhronosGroup/UnityGLTF.
>
> Personally, I find their gITF plugin unwieldy and prefer the GLTFUtility package made by a user named Siccity, available at https://github.com/Siccity/GLTFUtility.

Note that the bottom of table 4.3 lists several 3D art applications. Unity allows you to directly drop those applications' files into your project. This functionality seems handy at first but has some caveats.

For starters, Unity doesn't load those application files directly; instead, it exports the model behind the scenes and loads that exported file. Because the model is being exported to FBX anyway, it's preferable to do that step explicitly. Furthermore, this export requires you to have the relevant application installed. This requirement is a big hassle if you plan to share files among multiple computers (for example, a team of developers working together). I don't recommend using 3D art application files directly in Unity.

4.5.2   *Exporting and importing the model*

All right, it's time to export the model from Blender and then import it into Unity. First, open the bench in Blender and then choose File > Export > FBX. Once the file is saved, import it into Unity the same way that you import images. Drag the FBX file from the computer into Unity's Project view or right-click in Project and choose Import New Asset. The 3D model will be copied into the Unity project and show up ready to be put in the scene.

> **NOTE**   The sample download includes the .blend file so that you can practice exporting the FBX file from Blender. Even if you don't end up modeling any-thing yourself, you may need to convert downloaded models into a format Unity accepts. If you want to skip all steps involving Blender, use the provided FBX file.

You should change a few import settings immediately. First, Unity defaults imported models to a very small scale (refer to figure 4.15, which shows what you see in the Inspector when you select the model); change the Scale Factor to 50 to partially coun-teract the 0.01 unit conversion. You may also want to click the Generate Colliders check box, but that's optional; without a collider, you can walk through the bench. Then, switch to the Animation tab in the import settings and deselect Import Anima-tion (this model doesn't have animation). Click Apply at the bottom after making these changes.

Default size is too small, so set the scale to 50.

Optional: Generate a collider or you can walk through the bench.

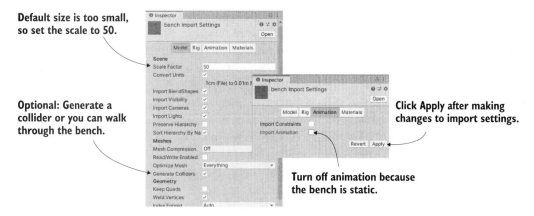

Click Apply after making changes to import settings.

Turn off animation because the bench is static.

Figure 4.15 Adjust import settings for the 3D model.

That takes care of the imported mesh. Now for the texture. Import the bench texture (the image in figure 4.16) in the same way as the bricks for walls earlier: drag the image file from this project's scratch folder into Unity's Project view, or right-click in Project and select Import New Asset. The image looks somewhat odd, with different parts of the image appearing on different parts of the bench; the model's texture coordinates were edited to define this mapping of image to mesh.

This image relates to the model by using texture coordinates.

To understand the concept of texture coordinates, refer to appendix C.

Figure 4.16 The 2D image for the bench texture

DEFINITION *Texture coordinates* are an extra set of values for each vertex that assign polygons to areas of the texture image. Think about it like wrapping paper; the 3D model is the box being wrapped, the texture is the wrapping paper, and the texture coordinates represent the points on the box where the wrapping paper will go.

NOTE Even if you don't want to model the bench, you may want to read the detailed explanation of texture coordinates in appendix C. Texture coordinates (as well as other related terms like *UVs* and *mapping*) can be useful to understand when programming games.

When Unity imported the FBX file, it also generated a material with the same settings as the material in Blender. If the image file used in Blender has been imported into Unity, the generated material will automatically link to that texture. If the automatic linkage doesn't work right, or if you need to use a different texture image, then you can extract the model's material for further editing. Refer back to figure 4.15; under the Materials tab, you should find a button labeled Extract Materials. Now you can select the material asset and then drag images to Albedo just as you did for brick walls.

New materials are often too shiny, so you may want to reduce the Smoothness setting to 0 (smoother surfaces are shinier). Finally, having adjusted everything as needed, you can put the bench in the scene. Drag the model up from the Project view and place it in one room of the level; as you drag the mouse, you should see it in the scene. Once you drop the bench in place, you should see something like figure 4.17. Congratulations—you've created a textured model for the level!

> **NOTE** We're not going to do it in this chapter, but typically, you'd also replace the whitebox geometry with models created in an external tool. The new geometry might look essentially identical, but you'll have much more flexibility in controlling the texture.

Figure 4.17   The imported bench in the level

Animating characters with Mecanim

The model you created is static, sitting still where placed. You can also animate in Blender and then play the animation in Unity. The process of creating 3D animation is long and involved, and this isn't a book about animation, so we're not going to discuss that here. As has already been mentioned for modeling, a lot of existing resources can help you learn more about 3D animation. But be warned: it is a *huge* topic. There's a reason *animator* is a specialized role within game development.

Unity has a sophisticated system called *Mecanim* for managing animations on models. The special name Mecanim identifies the newer, more advanced animation system that was added to Unity as a replacement for the older animation system. The older system is still around, identified as legacy animation. But it may be phased out in a future version of Unity, at which point Mecanim will be *the* animation system.

Although we don't work with any animations in this chapter, we'll play animations on characters in future chapters.

4.6 Creating effects by using particle systems

Besides 2D images and 3D models, the remaining type of visual content that game artists create is a particle system. The definition in this chapter's introduction explained that particle systems are orderly mechanisms for creating and controlling large numbers of moving objects. Particle systems are useful for creating visual effects like fire, smoke, or spraying water. The fire effect in figure 4.18 was created using a particle system.

Whereas most other art assets are created in external tools and imported into the project, particle systems are created within Unity itself. Unity provides flexible and powerful tools for creating particle effects.

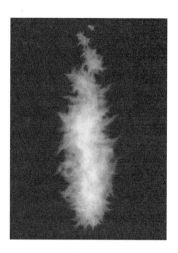

Figure 4.18   Fire effect created using a particle system

NOTE Much like the situation with the Mecanim animation system, Unity used to have an older legacy particle system and gave its newer system a special name, Shuriken. At this point, the legacy particle system has been phased out, so the separate name is no longer necessary.

To begin, create a new particle system and watch the default effect play. From the GameObject menu, choose Effects > Particle System, and you'll see basic white puffballs spraying upward from the new object. Or rather, you'll see particles spraying upward while you have the object selected. When you select a particle system, the particle playback panel is displayed in the corner of the screen and indicates the amount of time that has elapsed (see figure 4.19).

The default effect looks pretty neat already, but let's go through parameters you can use to customize the effect.

**Pause or reset the particle
effect playing in the scene.**

**Click and drag the label
Playback Time to play
back and forth.**

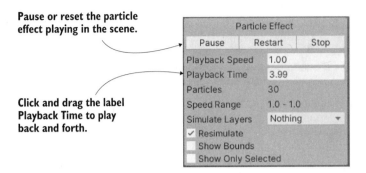

Figure 4.19   Playback panel for a particle system

4.6.1   *Adjusting parameters on the default effect*

Figure 4.20 shows the entire list of settings for a particle system. We're not going to go through every single setting in that list; instead, we'll look at those relevant to making the fire effect. Once you understand how a few of the settings work, the rest should be fairly self-explanatory. Each setting's label is, in fact, a whole information panel. Initially, only the first information panel is expanded; the rest of the panels are collapsed. Click the setting's label to expand that information panel.

> **TIP**   Many of the settings are controlled by a curve displayed at the bottom of the Inspector. That curve represents how the value changes over time: the left side of the graph indicates when the particle first appears, the right side indicates when the particle is gone, the bottom is a value of 0, and the top is the maximum value. Drag points around the graph and double-click or right-click the curve to insert new points.

Adjust parameters of the particle system as indicated in figure 4.20, and it'll look more like a jet of flame.

Looping: The particle system keeps playing forever; leave the default.

Lifetime: How long the particle exists; reduce to 3.

Speed: How fast the particle is moving; reduce to 1.

Size: How big the particle is; leave the default.

Rotation: The orientation of the particle; click the arrow menu to change to Between Two Constants, and set to 0 and 180.

Color: Tint the particles. We want a dim orange, like RGB values 182, 101, 58.

Local simulation space is fine for a still particle system, but World may be better for a system that's moving.

Emission: How quickly particles are emitted; leave the default.

Shape: The shape of the area emitted from. The default is a wide cone, but we want a small box to make a tight jet of flame (set to Box, and all numbers to 0.2)

Size over Lifetime: The particle grows and shrinks. The default is off; turn this on and click the arrow to set a curve. The bottom of this image shows a curve that quickly grows and then slowly shrinks back to 0.

Rotation over Lifetime: The particle rotates while it moves. The default is off; turn this on and set Random Between to -80 and 80 to make different particles rotate in different directions.

Renderer: Set what each particle looks like. You could even set this to a mesh, but leave it as Billboard and drag a new material (explained shortly).

Select settings' curves (e.g., Size over Lifetime) to edit them here. Add points to the curve by double-clicking or by right-clicking and choosing Add Key.

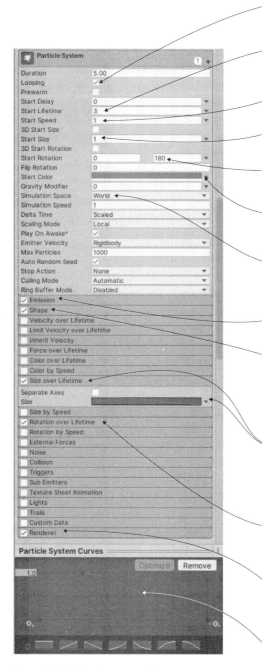

Figure 4.20 The Inspector displays settings for a particle system (pointing out settings for the fire effect).

4.6.2   *Applying a new texture for fire*

Now the particle system looks more like a jet of flame, but the effect still needs the particles to look like flame, not white blobs. That requires importing a new image into Unity. Figure 4.21 depicts the image I painted; I made an orange dot and used the Smudge tool to draw out the tendrils of the flame (and then I drew the same thing in yellow).

Figure 4.21   The image used for fire particles

Whether you use this image from the sample project, draw your own, or download a similar one, you need to import the image file into Unity. As explained previously, drag image files into the Project view, or choose Assets > Import New Asset.

Just as with 3D models, textures aren't applied to particle systems directly. You add the texture to a material and apply that material to the particle system. Create a new material and then select it to see its properties in the Inspector. Drag the fire image from Project up to the texture slot. That links the fire texture to the fire material, so now you want to apply the material to the particle system. Figure 4.22 shows how to do this: select the particle system, expand Renderer at the bottom of the settings, and drag the material onto the Material slot.

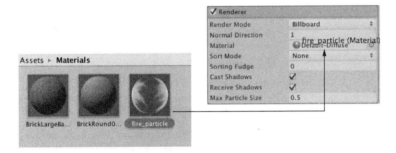

Figure 4.22   Assign a material to the particle system.

As you did for the skybox material, you need to change the shader for a particle material. Click the Shader menu near the top of the material settings to see the list of available shaders. Instead of the standard default, a material for particles needs one of the shaders under the Particles submenu. As shown in figure 4.23, in this case, we want Standard Unlit. Now switch the material's Rendering Mode to Additive. This will make the particles appear to be hazy and brighten the scene, just like a fire.

> **DEFINITION**   *Additive* is a shader effect that adds the color of the particle to the color behind it, as opposed to replacing the pixels. This makes the pixels brighter and makes black on the particle turn invisible. These shaders have the same visual effect as the Additive layer effect in Photoshop.

After choosing the particle shader, change Rendering Mode to Additive.

From the material's Shader menu, choose Particles > Standard Unlit.

Figure 4.23   Setting the shader for the fire particle material

WARNING Changing this shader may cause Unity to emit a warning about needing to `apply to systems`. Click the Apply to Systems button at the bottom of the Inspector.

With the fire material assigned to the fire particle effect, it'll now look like figure 4.18. This looks like a pretty convincing jet of flame, but the effect doesn't work only when sitting still. Next, let's attach it to an object that moves around.

4.6.3   Attaching particle effects to 3D objects

Create a sphere (remember, GameObject > 3D Object > Sphere). Create a new script called `BackAndForth` and attach it to the new sphere.

Listing 4.1   Moving an object back and forth along a straight path

```
using System.Collections;
using System.Collections.Generic;
using UnityEngine;

public class BackAndForth : MonoBehaviour {
    public float speed = 3.0f;
    public float maxZ = 16.0f;          ⊲  These are the positions the
    public float minZ = -16.0f;             object moves between.

    private int direction = 1;          ⊲  Which direction is the
                                            object currently moving in?
    void Update() {
        transform.Translate(0, 0, direction * speed * Time.deltaTime);

        bool bounced = false;
        if (transform.position.z > maxZ || transform.position.z < minZ) {
            direction = -direction;
            bounced = true;                 Apply a second movement in the
        }                                   new direction if the object switched
        if (bounced) {              ⊲       directions.
            transform.Translate(0, 0, direction * speed * Time.deltaTime);
        }
    }
}
```

Toggle the direction back and forth.

Run this script, and the sphere glides back and forth in the central corridor of the level. Now you can make the particle system a child of the sphere, and the fire will move with the sphere. Just as with the walls of the level, in the Hierarchy view, drag the particle object onto the sphere object.

> **WARNING**   You usually have to reset the position of an object after making it the child of another object. For example, we want the particle system at 0, 0, 0 (this is relative to the parent). Unity will preserve the placement of an object from before it was linked as a child.

Now the particle system moves along with the sphere. However, the fire isn't deflecting from the movement, which looks unnatural. That's because, by default, particles move correctly only in the local space of the particle system. To complete the flaming sphere, find Simulation Space in the particle system settings (it's in the top panel of figure 4.20) and switch from Local to World.

> **NOTE**   In this script, the object moves back and forth in a straight line, but video games commonly have objects moving around complex paths. Unity comes with support for complex navigation and paths; see https://docs.unity3d .com/Manual/Navigation.html to read about it.

I'm sure that, at this point, you're itching to apply your own ideas and add more content to this sample game. You should do that—you could create more art assets, or even test your skills by bringing in the shooting mechanics developed in chapter 3. In the next chapter, we'll switch gears to a different game genre and start over with a new game. Even though future chapters will switch to other game genres, everything from these first four chapters will still apply and be useful.

Summary

- *Art asset* is the term for all individual graphics.
- Whiteboxing is a useful first step for level designers to block out spaces.
- Textures are 2D images displayed on the surface of 3D models.
- 3D models are created outside Unity and imported as FBX files.
- Particle systems are used to create many visual effects (fire, smoke, water, and so on).

Part 2

Getting comfortable

You've built your first game prototypes in Unity, so now you're ready to stretch yourself by tackling other game genres. At this point, the rhythms of working in Unity should feel familiar: create a script with such and such function, drag this object to that slot in the Inspector, and so forth. You're not tripping over details of the interface so much anymore, which means the remaining chapters don't need to rehash the basics. Let's run through a succession of additional projects that will progressively teach you more and more about developing games in Unity.

5

Building a Memory game using Unity's 2D functionality

This chapter covers

- Displaying 2D graphics in Unity
- Making objects clickable
- Loading new images programmatically
- Maintaining and displaying state by using UI text
- Loading levels and restarting the game

Up to now, we've been working with 3D graphics, but you can also work with 2D graphics in Unity. So in this chapter, you'll build a 2D game. You're going to develop the classic children's game Memory: you'll display a grid of card backs, reveal the card front when it's clicked, and score matches. These mechanics cover the basics you need to know to develop 2D games in Unity.

Although Unity originated as a tool for 3D games, it's used often for 2D games as well. Unity has had built-in 2D graphics support since version 4.3 in 2013, but even before then 2D games were already being developed in Unity (especially mobile games that took advantage of Unity's cross-platform nature). In prior versions of Unity, game developers required a third-party framework to emulate 2D graphics within Unity's 3D scenes. Eventually, the core editor and game engine were modified to incorporate 2D graphics, and this chapter will teach you about that functionality.

The 2D workflow in Unity is more or less the same as the workflow to develop a 3D game: import art assets, drag them into a scene, and write scripts to attach to the objects. The primary kind of art asset in 2D graphics is called a *sprite*.

> **DEFINITION**   *Sprites* are 2D images displayed directly on the screen, as opposed to images displayed on the surface of 3D models (that is, *textures*).

You can import 2D images into Unity as sprites in much the same way you can import images as textures (see chapter 4). Technically, these sprites will be objects in 3D space, but they'll be flat surfaces all oriented perpendicular to the z-axis. Because they'll all face the same direction, you can point the camera straight at the sprites, and players will be able to discern their movements only along the x- and y-axes (in two dimensions).

In chapter 2, we discussed the coordinate axes: having three dimensions adds a z-axis perpendicular to the x- and y-axes you were already familiar with. Two dimensions are just those x- and y-axes (that's what your teacher was talking about in math class!).

5.1 Setting up everything for 2D graphics

You're going to create the classic game of Memory. For those unfamiliar with this game, a series of cards are dealt out facedown. Every card has a matching card located somewhere else, but the player sees only the reverse side of the card. The player can turn over two cards at a time, attempting to find matching cards; if the two cards chosen aren't a match, they'll flip back, and then the player can guess again.

Figure 5.1 shows a mock-up of the game we're going to build; compare this to the road map diagram from chapter 2. The mock-up this time depicts exactly what the player will see (whereas the mock-up for our 3D scene depicted the space around the player and then where the camera went for the player to see through). Now that you know what you'll be building, it's time to get to work!

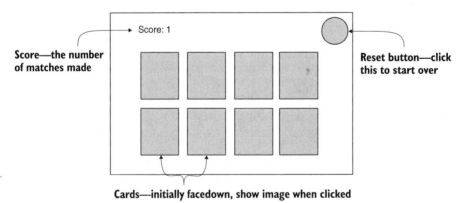

Figure 5.1   Mock-up of what the Memory game will look like

5.1.1 Preparing the project

The first step is to gather up and display graphics for our game. In much the same way as building the 3D demo previously, you want to start the new game by putting together the minimum set of graphics for the game to operate, and after that's in place, you can start programming the functionality.

That means you'll need to create everything depicted in figure 5.1: card backs for hidden cards, a series of card fronts for when they turn over, a score display in one corner, and a reset button in the opposite corner. We also need a background for the screen, so all together, our art requirements sum up to figure 5.2.

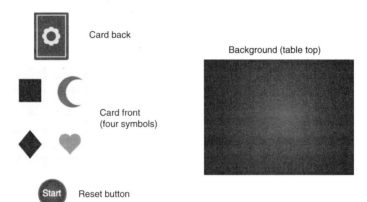

Card back

Card front
(four symbols)

Reset button

Background (table top)

Figure 5.2 Art assets required for the Memory game

TIP As always, a finished version of the project, including all necessary art assets, can be downloaded from http://mng.bz/VBY5, this book's website. You can copy the images from there to use in your own project.

Gather the required images and then create a new project in Unity. In the New Project window that comes up, you'll notice project templates (shown in figure 5.3) that let you switch between 2D and 3D mode. In previous chapters, we've worked with 3D graphics, and because that's the default value, we haven't been concerned with this setting. In this chapter, though, you'll want to select the 2D template when creating a new project.

With the new project for this chapter created and set for 2D, we can start putting our images into the scene.

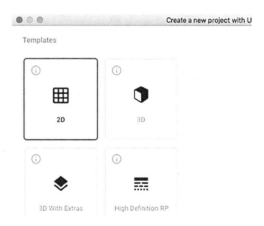

Figure 5.3 Create new projects in either 2D or 3D mode with these buttons.

2D Editor mode and 2D Scene view

The 2D/3D setting for new projects adjusts two settings within Unity's editor, both of which you can adjust manually later if you wish. Those two settings are the 2D Editor mode and the 2D Scene view. The 2D Scene view controls how the scene is displayed within Unity; toggle the 2D button along the top of the Scene view.

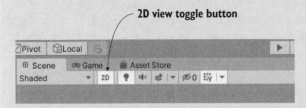

You set 2D Editor mode by opening the Edit menu and selecting Editor from the Project Settings drop-down list. Within those settings, you'll see the Default Behavior Mode setting with selections for either 3D or 2D.

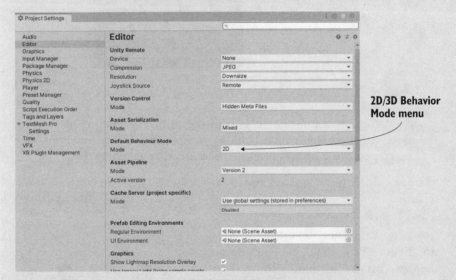

Default Behavior Mode setting within Edit > Project Settings > Editor

Setting the editor to 2D mode causes imported images to be set to Sprite. As you saw in chapter 4, images normally import as textures, but that's easy to switch in the Inspector. Just select the asset to see its settings, and remember to click Apply after making any changes.

2D Editor mode also causes new scenes to lack the default 3D lighting setup; this lighting doesn't harm 2D scenes, but it's unnecessary. If you ever need to remove it manually, delete the directional light that comes with new scenes and turn off the skybox in the lighting window (click the tiny circle icon for a file picker and choose None from the list).

5.1.2 Displaying 2D images (aka sprites)

Drag all the image files into the Project view to import them, ensuring that the images are imported as sprites and not textures. (This is automatic if the editor is set to 2D. Select an asset to see its import settings in the Inspector.) Now drag the `table_top` sprite (our background image) up from the Project view into the empty scene. As with mesh objects, in the Inspector there's a Transform component for the sprite; type 0, 0, 5 to position the background image.

> **TIP** Another import setting to take note of is Pixels Per Unit. Because Unity was previously a 3D engine that had 2D graphics grafted in, one unit in Unity isn't necessarily one pixel in the image. You could set the Pixels Per Unit setting to 1:1, but I recommend leaving it at the default of 100:1 (because the physics engine doesn't work properly at 1:1, and the default is better for compatibility with others' code).

Creating packed sprite atlases

Although we're going to use separate images in this project, you can have multiple sprites laid out in a single image. The image is usually called a *sprite sheet* when numerous frames of an animation are combined into one image, but the more general term for multiple images combined into one is an *atlas*.

Animated sprites are common in 2D games, and we'll implement those in the next chapter. Multiple frames can be imported as multiple images, but games usually have all the frames of animation laid out in a sprite sheet. Basically, all the separate frames appear as a grid on one large image.

In addition to keeping frames of animation together, sprite atlases are also often used for still images. That's because atlases can optimize the performance of sprites in two ways: by reducing the amount of wasted space in images by packing them tightly, and by reducing the draw calls of the video card (every new image that's loaded causes a bit more work for the video card).

Sprite atlases can be created using external tools like TexturePacker (see appendix B), and that approach will certainly work. But Unity includes sprite-packing functionality, which packs together multiple sprites automatically. To use this feature, enable Sprite Packer in Editor settings (choose Edit > Project Settings and switch the Mode to Always Enabled). Now you can create Sprite Atlas assets that contain individual sprites. For more information, look at Unity's documentation at http://mng.bz/ZxOZ.

The 0s for the X and Y positions are straightforward (this sprite will fill the entire screen, so you want it at the center), but that 5 for the Z position might seem odd. For 2D graphics, shouldn't only X and Y matter? Well, X and Y are the only values that matter for positioning the object on the 2D screen, but the Z value still matters for stacking objects.

Lower Z values are closer to the camera, so sprites with lower Z values are displayed on top of other sprites (refer to figure 5.4). Accordingly, the background sprite

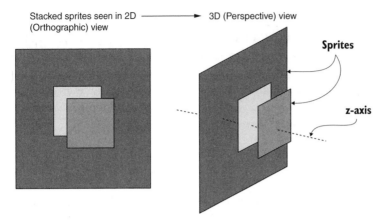

Figure 5.4   How sprites stack along the z-axis

should have the highest Z value. You'll set your background to a positive Z position, and then give everything else a 0 or negative Z position.

Other sprites will be positioned with values with up to two decimal places because of the Pixels Per Unit setting mentioned earlier. A ratio of 100:1 means that 100 pixels in the image are 1 unit in Unity; put another way, 1 pixel is 0.01 units. But before you put any more sprites into the scene, let's set up the camera for this game.

5.1.3   *Switching the camera to 2D mode*

Now let's adjust settings on the main camera in the scene. You might think that because the Scene view is set to 2D, what you see in Unity is what you'll see in the game. Somewhat unintuitively, though, that isn't the case.

> **WARNING**   Whether or not the Scene view is set to 2D has nothing to do with the camera view in the running game.

It turns out that, regardless of whether the Scene view is set to 2D mode, the camera in the game is set independently. This can be handy in many situations so that you can toggle the Scene view back to 3D to work on certain effects within the scene. This disconnect does mean that what you see in Unity isn't necessarily what you see in the game, and it can be easy for beginners to forget this.

The most important camera setting to adjust is Projection. The camera projection is probably already correct because you created the new project in 2D mode, but this is still important to know about and worth double-checking. Select the camera in Hierarchy to show its settings in the Inspector, and then look for the Projection setting (see figure 5.5). For 3D graphics, the setting should be Perspective, but for 2D graphics, the camera projection should be Orthographic.

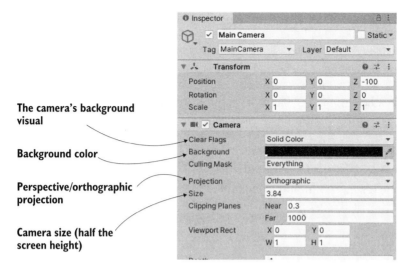

The camera's background visual

Background color

Perspective/orthographic projection

Camera size (half the screen height)

Figure 5.5   Camera settings to adjust for 2D graphics

DEFINITION   *Orthographic* is the term for a flat camera view that has no apparent perspective. This is the opposite of a Perspective camera view, in which closer objects appear larger and lines recede into the distance.

Although the Projection mode is the most important camera setting for 2D graphics, we have a few other settings to adjust as well. Next, we'll look at Size, which is under Projection. The camera's orthographic size determines the size of the camera view from the center of the screen up to the top of the screen. In other words, set Size to half the pixel dimensions of the screen you want. If you later set the resolution of the deployed game to the same pixel dimensions, you'll get pixel-perfect graphics.

DEFINITION   *Pixel-perfect* means one pixel on the screen corresponds to one pixel in the image (otherwise, the video card will make the images subtly blurry while scaling up to fit the screen).

Let's say you want a pixel-perfect 1024 × 768 screen. That means the camera height should be 384 pixels. Divide that by 100 (because of the pixels-to-units scale) and you get 3.84 for the camera size. Again, that math is SCREEN_SIZE / 2 / 100f (f as in float, rather than an int value). Given that the background image is 1024 × 768 (select the asset to check its dimensions), then clearly this value of 3.84 is what we want for our camera.

The remaining adjustments to make in the Inspector are the camera's background color and Z position. As mentioned previously for sprites, higher Z positions are further away into the scene. As such, the camera should have a pretty low Z position; set the position of the camera to 0, 0, –100. Next make sure the camera's Clear Flag is set to Solid Color instead of Skybox; this setting determines the camera background. The camera's background color should probably be black; the default color is blue, and that'll look odd displayed along the sides if the screen is wider than the background image (which is likely). Click the color swatch next to Background and set the color picker to black.

Now save the scene as Scene and click Play. You'll see the Game view filled with our tabletop sprite. As you saw, getting to this point wasn't completely straightforward (again, that's because Unity was a 3D game engine that has recently had 2D graphics grafted in). But the tabletop is completely bare, so our next step is to put a card on the table.

5.2   Building a card object and making it react to clicks

Now that the images are all imported and ready to use, let's build the card objects that form the core of this game. In Memory, all the cards are initially face down, and they're face up only temporarily, when you choose a pair of cards to turn over. To implement this functionality, you're going to create objects that consist of multiple sprites stacked on top of one another. Then, you'll write code that makes the cards reveal themselves when clicked with the mouse.

5.2.1   Building the object out of sprites

Drag one of the card images into the scene. Use one of the card fronts, because you'll add a card back on top to hide the image. Technically, the position right now doesn't matter, but eventually it will, so you may as well position the card at -3, 1, 0. Now drag the card_back sprite into the scene. Make this new sprite a child of the previous card sprite (remember, in the Hierarchy, drag the child object onto the parent object) and then set its position to 0, 0, -0.1 (Keep in mind that this position is relative to the parent, so this means, "Put it at the same X and Y but move it closer on Z.")

> **NOTE**   In this setup, the back of the card and the front of the card are separate objects. That makes the graphics simpler to set up, and revealing the "front" is as simple as turning off the "back." However, since Unity is always 3D even when the scene looks 2D, you could make a 3D card that flips over. That would be more complex to set up but may have advantages for certain graphical effects. There's no one right way to implement things, just different pros and cons to balance.

> **TIP**   Instead of the Move, Rotate, and Scale tools that we used in 3D, in 2D mode we use a single manipulation tool called the *Rect tool*. In 2D mode, this tool is selected automatically, or you can click the fifth control button in the top-left corner of Unity. With this tool active, click and drag objects to do all three operations (move/rotate/scale) in two dimensions.

With the card back in place, as depicted in figure 5.6, the graphics are ready for a reactive card that can be revealed.

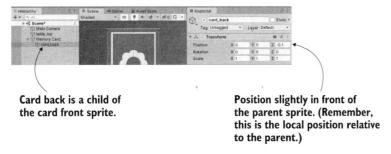

Card back is a child of the card front sprite.

Position slightly in front of the parent sprite. (Remember, this is the local position relative to the parent.)

Figure 5.6 Hierarchy linking and position for the card back sprite

5.2.2 Mouse input code

In order to respond when the player clicks them, the card sprites need to have a collider component. New sprites don't have a collider by default, so they can't be clicked. You're going to attach a collider to the root card object, but not to the card back, so that only the card front and not the card back will receive mouse clicks.

To do this, select the root card object in Hierarchy (don't click the card in the scene, because the card back is on top and you'll select that part instead). Then click the Add Component button in the Inspector. Select Physics 2D (not Physics, because that system is for 3D physics and this is a 2D game) and then choose a box collider.

Besides a collider, the card needs a script in order to be reactive to the player clicking it, so let's write some code. Create a new script called `MemoryCard` and attach it to the root card object (again, not the card back). This listing shows the code that makes the card emit debug messages when clicked.

Listing 5.1 Emitting debug messages when clicked

```
dusing System.Collections;
using System.Collections.Generic;
using UnityEngine;

public class MemoryCard : MonoBehaviour {          The function is called when
    public void OnMouseDown() {          ←        the object is clicked.
        Debug.Log("testing 1 2 3");      ←        Just emit a test message
    }                                               to the console for now.
}
```

TIP If you're not in this habit yet, organizing your assets into separate folders is probably a good idea. Create folders for scripts and drag files within the Project view. Be careful to avoid the special folder names Unity responds to: Resources, Plugins, Editor, and Gizmos. Later in the book, we'll go over what some of these special folders do, but for now avoid naming any folders with those words.

Nice—we can click the card now! Just like Update(), OnMouseDown() is another function provided by MonoBehaviour, this time responding when the object is clicked. Play the game and watch messages appear in the console. But this only prints to the console for testing; we want the card to be *revealed*.

5.2.3 Revealing the card on a click

Rewrite the code to match this listing (the code won't run quite yet, but don't worry).

Listing 5.2 Script that hides the back when the card is clicked

```
using System.Collections;
using System.Collections.Generic;
using UnityEngine;

public class MemoryCard : MonoBehaviour {
    [SerializeField] GameObject cardBack;          ⟵  Variable that appears
                                                       in the Inspector
    public void OnMouseDown() {
        if (cardBack.activeSelf) {                 ⟵  Run deactivate code only if the
            cardBack.SetActive(false);                 object is currently active/visible.
        }                                          ⟵  Set the object to
    }                                                  inactive/invisible.
}
```

We've made two key additions to the script: a reference to an object in the scene, and the SetActive() method that deactivates that object. The first part, the reference to an object in the scene, is similar to what we've done in previous chapters: mark the variable as serialized and then drag the object from Hierarchy over to the variable in the Inspector. With the object reference set, the code will now affect the object in the scene.

The second key addition to the code is the SetActive command. This command will deactivate any GameObject, making that object invisible. If we now drag card_back in the scene to this script's variable in the Inspector, the card back disappears when you click the card during a game. Hiding the card back will reveal the card front; we've accomplished yet another important task for the Memory game! But this is still only one card, so now let's create a bunch of cards.

> **TIP** Forgetting to drag over the object when a script has a serialized variable is a fairly common mistake, so it's useful to recognize that error message in the Console tab. Code that uses a serialized variable that hasn't been set will throw a null reference error. Actually, a null reference error gets thrown *any* time the code attempts to use a variable not set yet, whether or not it's a serialized variable.

5.3   *Displaying the various card images*

We've programmed a card object that initially shows the card back but reveals itself when clicked. That was a single card, but the game needs a whole grid of cards, with different images on most cards. We'll implement the grid of cards by using a couple of concepts seen in previous chapters, along with some concepts you haven't seen before. Chapter 3 introduced the concepts of using an invisible `SceneController` component and instantiating clones of an object. The `SceneController` will apply different images to different cards this time.

5.3.1   *Loading images programmatically*

The game we're creating has four card images. All eight cards on the table (two for each symbol) will be created by cloning the same original, so all cards will initially have the same symbol. We'll have to change the image on the card in the script, loading different images programmatically.

To examine how images can be assigned programmatically, let's write simple test code (which will be replaced later) to demonstrate the technique. First, add this code to the `MemoryCard` script.

Listing 5.3   Test code to demonstrate changing the sprite image

```
...
[SerializeField] Sprite image;   ⟵——— Reference to the Sprite
void Start() {                          asset that will be loaded
    GetComponent<SpriteRenderer>().sprite = image;   ⟵——— Set the sprite for
}                                                          this SpriteRenderer
...                                                        component.
```

After you save this script, the new `image` variable will appear in the Inspector because it has been set as serialized. Drag a sprite up from the Project view (pick one of the card images, and not the same as the image already in the scene) and drop it on the Image slot. Now run the scene and you'll see the new image on the card.

The key to understanding this code is to know about the `SpriteRenderer` component. You'll notice in figure 5.7 that the card back object has just two components: the standard `Transform` component on all objects in the scene, and a new component called `SpriteRenderer`. This component makes the GameObject into a sprite object and determines which sprite asset will be displayed. Note that the first property in the component is called `sprite` and links to one of the sprites in the Project view; the property can be manipulated in code, and that's precisely what this script does.

As it did with `CharacterController` and custom scripts in previous chapters, the `GetComponent()` method returns other components on the same object, so we use it to reference the `SpriteRenderer` object. The `sprite` property of `SpriteRenderer` can be set to any sprite asset, so this code sets that property to the `Sprite` variable declared at the top (which we filled with a sprite asset in the editor).

**Sprite asset displayed
on this Sprite object**

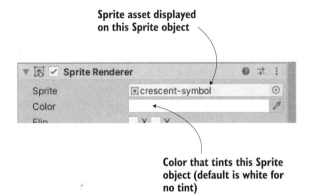

**Color that tints this Sprite
object (default is white for
no tint)**

**Figure 5.7   A sprite object in the
scene has the `SpriteRenderer`
component attached to it.**

Well, that wasn't too hard! But it's only a single image. We have four images to use, so now delete the new code from listing 5.3 (it was only a demonstration of how the technique works) to prepare for the next section.

5.3.2   Setting the image from an invisible SceneController

Recall that, in chapter 3, we created an invisible object in the scene to control spawning objects. We're going to take that approach here as well, using an invisible object to control more abstract features that aren't tied to any specific object in the scene.

First, create an empty GameObject (remember, choose GameObject > Create Empty). Then create a new script, `SceneController`, in the Project view, and drag this script asset onto the controller GameObject. Before writing code in the new script, add the contents of the next listing to the `MemoryCard` script instead of what you saw in listing 5.3.

Listing 5.4   New public methods in `MemoryCard`

```
...
[SerializeField] SceneController controller;

private int _id;
public int Id {
    get {return _id;}        ◁── Added getter function (an idiom
}                                 common in languages like C# and Java)

public void SetCard(int id, Sprite image) {   ◁────── Public method that
    _id = id;                                          other scripts can use
    GetComponent<SpriteRenderer>().sprite = image;  ◁── to pass new sprites
}                                                        to this object
...
```

**SpriteRenderer code line
just as in the deleted code
demonstration**

The primary change from previous listings is that we're now setting the sprite image in `SetCard()` instead of `Start()`. Because that's a public method that takes a sprite as a parameter, you can call this function from other scripts and set the image on this object. Note that SetCard() also takes an ID number as a parameter, and the code stores that number. Although we don't need the ID quite yet, soon we'll write code that compares cards for matches, and that comparison will rely on the IDs of the cards.

> **NOTE** Depending on what programming languages you've used in the past, you may not be familiar with the concept of *getters* and *setters.* Long story short, they are functions that run when you attempt to access the property associated with them (for example, retrieving the value of card.Id). There are multiple reasons to use getters and setters, but in this case the Id property is read-only because we have a function to only get the value and not set it.

Finally, note that the code has a variable for the controller. Even as SceneController starts cloning card objects to fill the scene, the card objects also need a reference to the controller to call its public methods. As usual, when the code references objects in the scene, drag the controller object in Unity's editor to the serialized variable slot in the Inspector. Do this once for this single card, and all of the copies to come later will have the reference as well. With that additional code now in MemoryCard, write this code in SceneController.

Listing 5.5 First pass at `SceneController` for the Memory game

```
using System.Collections;
using System.Collections.Generic;
using UnityEngine;

public class SceneController : MonoBehaviour {
    [SerializeField] MemoryCard originalCard;        Reference for the
                                                     card in the scene
    [SerializeField] Sprite[] images;
                                                     An array for references
    void Start() {                                   to the sprite assets
        int id = Random.Range(0, images.Length);
        originalCard.SetCard(id, images[id]);        Call the public method we
    }                                                added to MemoryCard.
}
```

For now, this is a short snippet to demonstrate the concept of manipulating cards from SceneController. Most of this should already be familiar to you (for example, in Unity's editor, drag the card object to the serialized variable slot in the Inspector), but the array of images is new. As shown in figure 5.8, in the Inspector you can set the number of elements. Type in 4 for the array length and then drag the sprites for card images onto the array slots. Now these sprites can be accessed in the array, like any other object reference.

Incidentally, we used the Random.Range() method in chapter 3, so hopefully you recall that. The exact boundary values didn't matter there, but this time it's important to note that the minimum value is inclusive and may be returned, whereas the return value is always below the maximum.

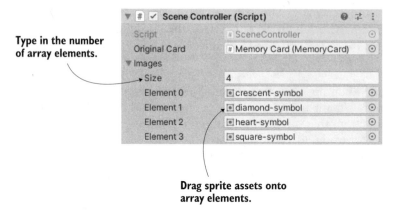

Type in the number of array elements.

Drag sprite assets onto array elements.

Figure 5.8   The filled-in array of sprites

Click Play to run this new code. You'll see different images being applied to the revealed card each time you run the scene. The next step is to create a whole grid of cards instead of only one.

5.3.3   *Instantiating a grid of cards*

SceneController already has a reference to the card object, so now you'll use the Instantiate() method (see the next listing) to clone the object numerous times, as we did when spawning objects in chapter 3.

Listing 5.6   Cloning the card eight times and positioning in a grid

```
using System.Collections;
using System.Collections.Generic;
using UnityEngine;

public class SceneController : MonoBehaviour {
  public const int gridRows = 2;
  public const int gridCols = 4;                    Values for how many grid
  public const float offsetX = 2f;                  spaces to make and how
  public const float offsetY = 2.5f;                far apart to place them

  [SerializeField] MemoryCard originalCard;
  [SerializeField] Sprite[] images;                 Position of the first
                                                    card; all other cards
  void Start() {                                    will be offset from
    Vector3 startPos = originalCard.transform.position;   here.

    for (int i = 0; i < gridCols; i++) {           Nested loops to define both
      for (int j = 0; j < gridRows; j++) {          columns and rows of the grid
        MemoryCard card;
        if (i == 0 && j == 0) {                     Container reference for either
          card = originalCard;                      the original card or the copies
        } else {
          card = Instantiate(originalCard) as MemoryCard;
```

```
        }

        int id = Random.Range(0, images.Length);
        card.SetCard(id, images[id]);

        float posX = (offsetX * i) + startPos.x;
        float posY = -(offsetY * j) + startPos.y;
        card.transform.position = new Vector3(posX, posY, startPos.z);
      }                                          ◁─────────
    }
  }
}
```

> **For 2D graphics, you need to offset only X and Y; keep Z the same.**

Although this script is much longer than the previous listing, there's not a lot to explain because most of the additions are straightforward variable declarations and math. The oddest bit of this code is probably the if/else statement that begins if (i == 0 && j == 0). That conditional either uses the original card object for the first grid slot or clones the card object for all other grid slots. Because the original card already exists in the scene, if you copied the card at every iteration of the loop, you'd end up with one too many cards in the scene. The cards are then positioned by offsetting them according to the number of iterations through the loop.

> **TIP** Just as when moving 3D objects, 2D objects could have transform.position incremented repeatedly in Update() to achieve smooth movement over time. But as you saw when moving the first-person player, collision detection isn't applied when adjusting transform.position directly. For that reason, the next chapter's code will move sprites by adjusting rigidbody2D.velocity.

Run the code now, and a grid of eight cards will be created (as depicted in figure 5.9). The last step in preparing the grid of cards is to organize them into pairs instead of keeping them random.

Figure 5.9 The grid of eight cards, which are revealed when you click them

5.3.4 Shuffling the cards

Instead of making every card random, we'll define an array of all the card IDs (numbers 0 through 3 twice, for a pair of each card) and then shuffle that array. We'll then use this array of card IDs when setting cards, rather than making each one random.

Listing 5.7   Placing cards from a shuffled list

```
...
void Start() {           ◁──── Much of this listing is context to
    Vector3 startPos = originalCard.transform.position;     show where the additions go.

    int[] numbers = {0, 0, 1, 1, 2, 2, 3, 3};    ◁──── Declare an integer array
    numbers = ShuffleArray(numbers);    ◁───              with a pair of IDs for all
                                                          four card sprites.
    for (int i = 0; i < gridCols; i++) {    Call a function that will shuffle
        for (int j = 0; j < gridRows; j++) {    the elements of the array.
            MemoryCard card;
            if (i == 0 && j == 0) {
                card = originalCard;
            } else {
                card = Instantiate(originalCard) as MemoryCard;
            }

            int index = j * gridCols + i;       Retrieve IDs from the shuffled list
            int id = numbers[index];    ◁────   instead of random numbers.
            card.SetCard(id, images[id]);

            float posX = (offsetX * i) + startPos.x;
            float posY = -(offsetY * j) + startPos.y;
            card.transform.position = new Vector3(posX, posY, startPos.z);
        }
    }
}
                                                          An implementation of the
private int[] ShuffleArray(int[] numbers) {    ◁──── Knuth shuffle algorithm
    int[] newArray = numbers.Clone() as int[];
    for (int i = 0; i < newArray.Length; i++ ) {
        int tmp = newArray[i];
        int r = Random.Range(i, newArray.Length);
        newArray[i] = newArray[r];
        newArray[r] = tmp;
    }
    return newArray;
}
...
```

Now, when you click Play, the grid of cards will be a shuffled assortment that reveals exactly two of each card image. The array of cards was run through the *Knuth* (also known as *Fisher-Yates*) shuffle algorithm, a simple yet effective way of shuffling the elements of an array. This algorithm loops through the array and swaps every element of the array with another randomly chosen array position.

You can click all the cards to reveal them, but the game of Memory is supposed to proceed in pairs. We need a bit more code.

5.4 *Making and scoring matches*

The last step in making a fully functional Memory game is checking for matches. Although we now have a grid of cards that are revealed when clicked, the various cards don't affect each other in any way. In the game of Memory, every time a pair of cards is revealed, we should check to see if the revealed cards match.

This abstract logic—checking for matches and responding appropriately—requires that cards notify `SceneController` when they've been clicked. That requires the additions to `SceneController` shown in the next listing.

Listing 5.8   `SceneController`, which must keep track of revealed cards

```
...
private MemoryCard firstRevealed;
private MemoryCard secondRevealed;

public bool canReveal {
    get {return secondRevealed == null;}          Getter function that returns false if
}                                                  a second card is already revealed
...
public void CardRevealed(MemoryCard card) {
    // initially empty
}
...
```

The `CardRevealed()` method will be filled in momentarily; we need the empty scaffolding for now to refer to in `MemoryCard` without any compiler errors. Note that we have a read-only getter again, this time used to determine whether another card can be revealed. The player can reveal another card only when two cards aren't already revealed.

We also need to modify `MemoryCard` to call the (currently empty) method in order to inform `SceneController` when a card is clicked. Modify the code in `MemoryCard` according to this listing.

Listing 5.9   `MemoryCard` modifications for revealing cards

```
...
public void OnMouseDown() {                              Check the controller's
    if (cardBack.activeSelf && controller.canReveal) {   canReveal property to
        cardBack.SetActive(false);                       make sure only two cards
        controller.CardRevealed(this);                   are revealed at a time.
    }
}                                                Notify the controller when
                                                 this card is revealed.

public void Unreveal() {
    cardBack.SetActive(true);          A public method so that SceneController
}                                      can hide the card again (by turning
...                                    card_back back on)
```

If you were to put a debug statement inside CardRevealed() to test the communication between objects, you'd see the test message appear whenever you click a card. Let's first handle one revealed pair.

5.4.1 Storing and comparing revealed cards

The card object was passed into CardRevealed(), so let's start keeping track of the revealed cards.

Listing 5.10 Keeping track of revealed cards in `SceneController`

```
...
public void CardRevealed(MemoryCard card) {
  if (firstRevealed == null) {          ⊲————  Store card objects in one of the
    firstRevealed = card;                       two card variables, depending
  } else {                                       on whether the first variable is
    secondRevealed = card;                       already occupied.
    Debug.Log("Match? " + (firstRevealed.Id == secondRevealed.Id));   ⊲———
  }
}                                               Compare the IDs of the two revealed cards.
...
```

The listing stores the revealed cards in one of the two card variables, depending on whether the first variable is already occupied. If the first variable is empty, fill it; if it's already occupied, fill the second variable and check the card IDs for a match. The Debug statement prints either true or false in the console.

At the moment, the code doesn't respond to matches—it only checks for them. Now let's program the response.

5.4.2 Hiding mismatched cards

We'll use coroutines again because the reaction to mismatched cards should pause to allow the player to see the cards. Refer to chapter 3 for a full explanation of coroutines; long story short, using a coroutine will allow us to pause before checking for a match. This listing shows more code for you to add to SceneController.

Listing 5.11 `SceneController` scores a match or hides missed matches

```
...
private int score = 0;     ⊲———  Add to the list near the
...                               top of SceneController
public void CardRevealed(MemoryCard card) {
   if (firstRevealed == null) {
     firstRevealed = card;
   } else {                            The only changed line in this function,
     secondRevealed = card;            which calls the coroutine when both
     StartCoroutine(CheckMatch());  ⊲— cards are revealed
   }
}
```

```
private IEnumerator CheckMatch() {
  if (firstRevealed.Id == secondRevealed.Id) {          Increment the score if the revealed
    score++;                                             cards have matching IDs.
    Debug.Log($"Score: {score}");
  }                                                      Construct the message by
  else {                                                 using string interpolation.
    yield return new WaitForSeconds(.5f);

    firstRevealed.Unreveal();                            Unreveal the cards if
    secondRevealed.Unreveal();                           they do not match.
  }

  firstRevealed = null;                                  Clear out the variables whether
  secondRevealed = null;                                 or not a match was made.
}
...
```

First, add a score value to track. Then, launch a coroutine to CheckMatch() when a second card is revealed. That coroutine has two code paths, depending on whether the cards match. If they match, the coroutine doesn't pause; the yield command gets skipped over. If the cards don't match, the coroutine pauses for half a second before calling Unreveal() on both cards, hiding them again. Finally, whether or not a match was made, the variables for storing cards are both nulled out, paving the way for revealing more cards.

When you play the game, mismatched cards will display briefly before hiding again. Debug messages appear when you score matches, but we want the score displayed as a label on the screen.

5.4.3 Text display for the score

Displaying information to the player is half of the reason for a UI in a game (the other half is receiving input from the player. UI buttons are discussed in the next section).

> **DEFINITION** *UI* stands for *user interface*. Another closely related term is *GUI*, or *graphical user interface*, which refers to the visual part of the interface, such as text and buttons, and which is what a lot of people mean when they say UI.

Unity has multiple ways to create text displays, but using the TextMeshPro package is the best approach. This advanced text system was developed externally and later acquired by Unity.

TextMeshPro may already be installed (when creating a new project, Unity installs several commonly used packages), but if not, then you must install it in Package Manager. From the menu, choose Window > Package Manager to open that window and scroll down to TextMeshPro in the list on the left, as shown in figure 5.10. Select that package and then click the Install button.

With that package installed, you can create a TextMeshPro object in the scene by going to the GameObject menu and choosing 3D Object > Text – TextMeshPro. Since

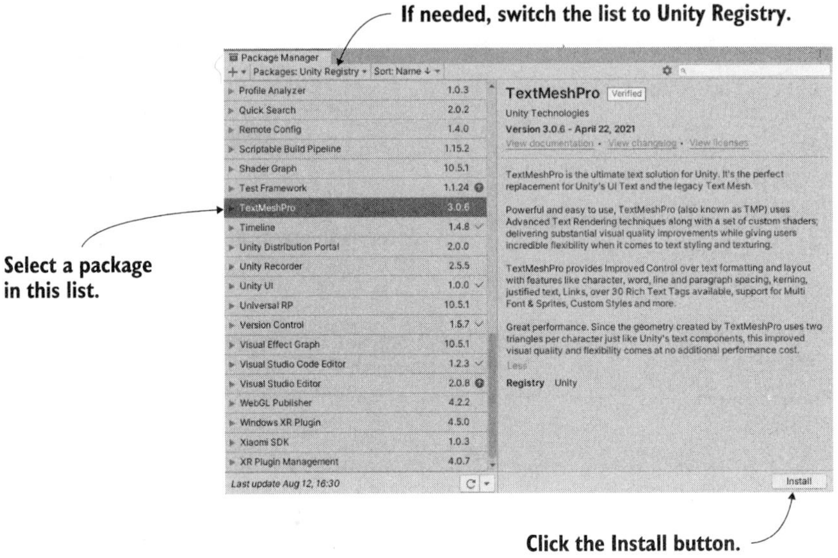

If needed, switch the list to Unity Registry.

Select a package in this list.

Click the Install button.

Figure 5.10 Installing TextMeshPro via Package Manager

this will be the first time TextMeshPro is used in this project, the TMP Importer window will automatically appear. Click the Import TMP Essentials button, and after the required resources finish downloading, the text object will appear in the scene.

> **NOTE** 3D text might sound incompatible with a 2D game, but don't forget that this is technically a 3D scene that looks flat because it's being seen through an orthographic camera. That means we can put 3D objects into the 2D game if we want—they're displayed in a flat perspective.

> **WARNING** TextMeshPro is also listed under GameObject > UI. Later chapters cover Unity's UI system, and you'll use that other GameObject instead in those chapters. Don't get the two versions confused; while both are Text-MeshPro objects, we are not using Unity's advanced UI system in this chapter.

Select the new text object to see its settings in the Inspector. Position this object at -2.3, 3.1, -10; that's 230 pixels to the left and 310 pixels up, putting it in the top-left corner and nearer to the camera so that it'll appear on top of other game objects. Also decrease Width to 5 and Height to 1 since the new text starts out huge.

Scroll down to the TextMeshPro settings. We could customize the text in tons of ways but are going to leave most of the defaults for now. Figure 5.11 shows the settings we'll change, and you can learn about them all in the Unity documentation (http://mng.bz/RqQP).

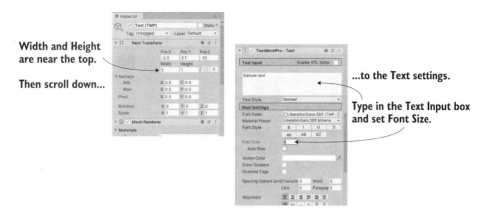

Figure 5.11 Inspector settings for this text object

Enter `Score:` in the big Text Input box and decrease Font Size to 8. Manipulating this text object during the game requires just a few adjustments in the scoring code.

Listing 5.12 Displaying the score on a text object

```
...
using TMPro;       ⟵—— Include TextMeshPro code.
...
[SerializeField] TMP_Text scoreLabel;
...
private IEnumerator CheckMatch() {
  if (firstRevealed.Id == secondRevealed.Id) {
     score++;
     scoreLabel.text = $"Score: {score}";
  }
...
```

As you can see, `text` is a property of the object that you can set to a new string. Put the `score` variable into the string to display that value.

Drag the text object in the scene to the `scoreLabel` variable you added to `Scene-Controller` and then click Play. Now you should see the score displayed while you play the game and make matches. Huzzah—the game works!

5.5   *Restart button*

At this point, the Memory game is fully functional. You can play the game, and all the essential features are in place. But this playable core is still lacking the overarching functionality that players expect or need in a finished game. For example, right now you can play the game only once; you need to quit and restart to play again. Let's add a control to the screen so that players can start the game over without having to quit.

This functionality divides into two tasks: create a UI button and reset the game when that button is clicked. Figure 5.12 shows what the game will look like with the Start button.

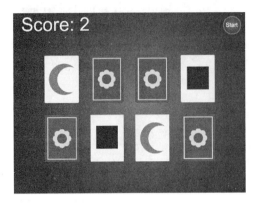

Figure 5.12   Complete Memory game screen, including the Start button

Neither task is specific to 2D games, by the way. All games need UI buttons, and all games need the ability to reset. We'll go over both topics to round out this chapter.

5.5.1   *Programming a UIButton component by using SendMessage*

First, place the button sprite in the scene by dragging it up from the Project view. Give it a position like 4.5, 3.25, -10; that will place the button in the top-right corner (that's 450 pixels to the right and 325 pixels up) and move it nearer to the camera so that it'll appear on top of other game objects. Because we want to be able to click this object, give it a collider (just as with the card object, choose Add Component > Physics 2D > Box Collider 2D).

> **NOTE**   As alluded to in the previous section, Unity provides multiple ways to create UI displays, including an advanced UI system introduced in later versions of Unity. For now, we'll build the single button out of standard display objects. A future chapter will teach you about the advanced UI functionality; the UI for both 2D and 3D games is ideally built with that system.

Now create a new script called UIButton and assign it to the button object.

Listing 5.13   Code to make a generic and reusable UI button

```
using System.Collections;
using System.Collections.Generic;
using UnityEngine;

public class UIButton : MonoBehaviour {                       Reference a target object
    [SerializeField] GameObject targetObject;          ◁─────  to inform about clicks.
    [SerializeField] string targetMessage;
    public Color highlightColor = Color.cyan;
```

```
public void OnMouseEnter() {
  SpriteRenderer sprite = GetComponent<SpriteRenderer>();
  if (sprite != null) {
    sprite.color = highlightColor;          ⟵  Tint the button when the
  }                                              mouse hovers over it.
}
public void OnMouseExit() {
  SpriteRenderer sprite = GetComponent<SpriteRenderer>();
  if (sprite != null) {
    sprite.color = Color.white;
  }
}

public void OnMouseDown() {                         The button's size
  transform.localScale = new Vector3(1.1f, 1.1f, 1.1f);  ⟵  pops a bit when
}                                                        it's clicked.
public void OnMouseUp() {
  transform.localScale = Vector3.one;
  if (targetObject != null) {                    Send a message to the target
    targetObject.SendMessage(targetMessage);  ⟵  object when the button is clicked.
  }
}
}
```

The majority of this code happens inside a series of OnMouseSomething functions. Like Start() and Update(), these are a series of functions automatically available to all script components in Unity. MouseDown was already mentioned in section 5.2.2, but these other functions also respond to mouse interactions if the object has a collider. MouseEnter and MouseExit are a pair of events used for hovering the mouse cursor over an object: MouseEnter triggers when the mouse cursor first moves over an object, and MouseExit triggers when the mouse cursor moves away. Similarly, MouseDown and MouseUp are a pair of events for clicking the mouse. MouseDown triggers when the mouse button is physically pressed, and MouseUp triggers when the mouse button is released.

You can see that this code tints the sprite when the mouse hovers over it and scales the sprite when it's clicked. In both cases, you can see that the change (in color or scale) happens when the mouse interaction begins, and then the property returns to the default (either white or scale 1) when the mouse interaction ends. For scaling, the code uses the standard transform component that all GameObjects have. For tint, though, the code uses the SpriteRenderer component that sprite objects have; the sprite is set to a color that's defined in Unity's editor through a public variable.

In addition to returning the scale to 1, SendMessage() is called when the mouse is released. SendMessage() calls the function of the given name in all components of that GameObject. Here, the target object for the message, as well as the message to send, are both defined by serialized variables. This way, the same UIButton component can be used for all sorts of buttons, with the target of different buttons set to different objects in the Inspector.

Normally, when doing OOP in a strongly typed language like C#, you need to know the type of a target object in order to communicate with that object (for example, to call a public method of the object, like calling `targetObject.SendMessage()` itself). But scripts for UI elements may have lots of types of targets, so Unity provides the `SendMessage()` method to communicate specific messages with a target object even if you don't know exactly what type of object it is.

> **WARNING**   Using `SendMessage()` is less efficient for the CPU than calling public methods on known types (that is, using `object.SendMessage("Method")` versus `component.Method()`), so use `SendMessage()` only when it's a big win in terms of making the code simpler to understand and work with. As a general rule, that will be the case only if lots of different types of objects could be receiving the message. In situations like that, the inflexibility of inheritance or even interfaces will hinder the game development process and discourage experimentation.

With this code written, wire up the public variables in the button's Inspector. The highlight color can be set to whatever you'd like (although the default cyan looks pretty good on a blue button). Meanwhile, put the `SceneController` object in the target object slot, and then type `Restart` as the message.

If you play the game now, the Reset button in the top-right corner changes color in response to the mouse and makes a slight visual pop when clicked. But an error message will be emitted when you click the button; in the console, you'll see an error about there not being a receiver for the Restart message. That's because we haven't written a `Restart()` method in `SceneController`, so let's add that.

5.5.2   *Calling LoadScene from SceneController*

The `SendMessage()` method from the button attempts to call `Restart()` in the `SceneController`, so let's add that now.

Listing 5.14   `SceneController` code that reloads the level

```
...
using UnityEngine.SceneManagement;     ⟵─── Include SceneManagement code.
...
public void Restart() {
    SceneManager.LoadScene("Scene");   ⟵─┐ If your scene has a different name,
}                                        └ change the name in this string.
...
```

You can see the one thing `Restart()` does is call `LoadScene()`. That method loads a saved scene asset (the file created when you click Save Scene in Unity). Pass the name of the scene you want to load into the method. In my case, the scene was saved with the name `Scene`, but if you used a different name, pass that to the method instead.

Click Play to see what happens. Reveal a few cards and make a few matches. If you then click the Reset button, the game starts over, with all cards hidden and a score of 0. Great, just what we wanted!

As the name `LoadScene()` indicates, this method can load different scenes. But what exactly happens when a scene loads, and why does this reset the game? What happens is that everything from the current level (all objects in the scene, and thus all scripts attached to those objects) is flushed from memory, and then everything from the new scene is loaded. Because the new scene is the saved asset of the current scene (in this case), everything is flushed from memory and then reloaded from scratch.

> **TIP** You can mark specific objects to exclude from the default memory flush when a level is loaded. Unity provides the `DontDestroyOnLoad()` method to keep an object around in multiple scenes. You'll use this method on parts of the code architecture in later chapters.

Another game successfully completed! Well, *completed* is a relative term; you could always implement more features, but everything from the initial plan is done. Many of the concepts from this 2D game apply to 3D games as well, especially the checking of game state and loading levels. It's time to switch gears yet again and move away from this Memory game and on to new projects.

Summary

- Displaying 2D graphics in Unity uses an orthographic camera.
- For pixel-perfect graphics, the camera size should be half the screen height.
- Clicking sprites requires that you first assign 2D colliders to them.
- New images for sprites can be loaded programmatically.
- UI text can be made using 3D text objects.
- Loading levels resets the scene.

Creating
a basic 2D platformer

6

This chapter covers

- Moving sprites around continuously
- Playing sprite-sheet animation
- Working with 2D physics (collision, gravity)
- Implementing camera control for side-scrolling games

Let's create a new game and continue learning about Unity's 2D functionality. Chapter 5 covered the fundamental concepts, so this chapter builds on those to create a more elaborate game. Specifically, you are going to build the core functionality of a 2D platform game. Also called a *platformer*, this common type of 2D action game is best known for classics like *Super Mario Brothers*: a character viewed from the side runs and jumps on platforms, and the view scrolls around to follow. Figure 6.1 shows what the end result will be.

This project will teach concepts like moving the player left and right, playing the sprite's animation, and adding the ability to jump. We'll also go over several special features common in platform games, like one-way floors and moving platforms.

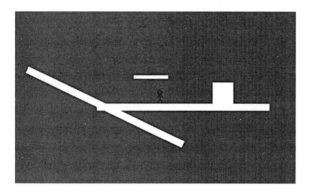

Figure 6.1 The final product of this chapter

Going from this shell to a full game mostly means repeating those concepts over and over.

To get started, create a new project in 2D mode as in the last chapter: from Unity Hub, choose New, or from the File menu choose New Project; then select 2D in the window that appears. In the new project, create two folders, called `Sprites` and `Scripts`, to contain the various assets. You could adjust the camera as in chapter 5, but for now just reduce Size to 4. This project doesn't require a perfect camera setup, although you would need to adjust the size for a polished game that's ready for release.

> **TIP** The camera icon in the center of the screen can get in the way, so you can hide it by using the Gizmos menu. Along the top of the Scene view is a label for Gizmos. That term refers to the abstract shapes and icons in the editor. Click Gizmos for an alphabetical list and then click the icon next to Camera.

Now save the empty scene (and of course click Save periodically while you work) to create the Scene asset in this project. Everything is empty at the moment, so the first step will be bringing in art assets.

6.1 Setting up the graphics

Before you can program the functionality of a 2D platform game, you need to import images into the project (remember, images in a 2D game are referred to as *sprites* instead of *textures*) and then place those sprites into the scene. This game will be the shell of a 2D platform game, with a player-controlled character running around a basic and mostly empty scene, so all you need are a couple of sprites for the platforms and for the player. Let's go over each separately, because although the images in this example are simple, some nonobvious considerations are involved.

6.1.1 Placing the scenery

Simply put, you need a single blank white image to use here. An image called blank.png is included in the sample project for this chapter; download the sample project and copy blank.png from there. Then drag the PNG into the Sprites folder of your new project, and make sure in the Inspector that Import Settings indicate it's a Sprite rather than a Texture (that should be automatic for a 2D project, but it's worth double-checking).

What you're doing now is essentially the same as the whiteboxing from chapter 4, but in 2D instead of 3D. Whiteboxing in 2D is done with sprites rather than meshes but maintains the same activity of blocking out blank floors and walls for the player to move around.

To place the floor object, drag the blank sprite into the scene as shown in figure 6.2 (around Position 0.15, -1.27, 0), set Scale to 50, 2, 1, and change its name to Floor. Then drag in another blank sprite, set its Scale to 6, 6, 1, place it on the floor off to the right (around Position 2, -0.63, 0), and name it Block.

Simple enough; now the floor and block are done. The other object you need is a character for the player.

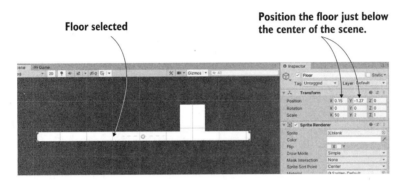

Figure 6.2   Floor platform placement

6.1.2   *Importing sprite sheets*

The only other art asset you need is the player's sprite, so also copy stickman.png from the sample project. But unlike the blank image, this PNG is a series of separate sprites assembled into one image. As shown in figure 6.3, the stickman image is the frames of two animations: standing idle and a walk cycle.

We're not going into detail on how to animate, but suffice to say that *idle* and *cycle* are both common terms used by game developers. Idle refers to subtle movement while doing nothing, and cycle is an animation that loops continuously.

As explained in chapter 5, an image file may be a bunch of sprite images packed together, rather than just a single sprite. Images like this are called *sprite sheets* when the multiple sprite images are frames of an animation. In Unity, an image imported as multiple sprites will still appear in the Project view as a single asset, but if you click the arrow on the asset, it'll expand and show all the individual sprite images. Figure 6.4 shows how that looks.

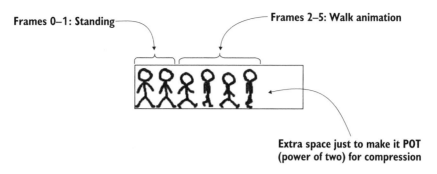

Frames 0–1: Standing

Frames 2–5: Walk animation

Extra space just to make it POT (power of two) for compression

Figure 6.3 Stickman sprite sheet—six frames in a row

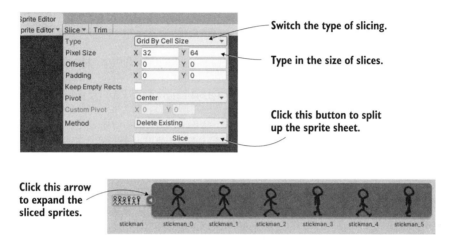

Switch the type of slicing.

Type in the size of slices.

Click this button to split up the sprite sheet.

Click this arrow to expand the sliced sprites.

Figure 6.4 Slicing a sprite sheet into separate frames

Drag stickman.png into the Sprites folder to import the image, but this time change a lot of Import Settings in the Inspector. Select the sprite asset, set Sprite Mode to Multiple, and then click Sprite Editor to open that window. Click Slice at the top left of the window, set Type to Grid By Cell Size (shown in figure 6.4), use Size 32, 64 (this is the size of each frame in the sprite sheet), and click Slice to see the frames split up. Now close the Sprite Editor window and click Apply to keep the changes.

NOTE The Sprite Editor window requires the 2D Sprite package. Creating a new 2D project should have automatically installed that package, but if not, then open Window > Package Manager and look for 2D Sprite in the list on the left side of the window. Select that package and then click the Install button.

WARNING The buttons on top of the Sprite Editor window get hidden if the window is too small. If you don't see the Slice button, try dragging the corner of the window to resize it.

The sprite asset is now split up, so click the arrow to expand the frames. Drag one (probably the first) stickman sprite into the scene, place it standing on the middle of the floor, and name it `Player`. There, the player object is in the scene!

6.2 *Moving the player left and right*

Now that the graphics are set up, let's start programming the player's movement. First off, the player entity in the scene needs a couple of additional components for us to control. As mentioned briefly in previous chapters, the physics simulation in Unity acts on objects with the special Rigidbody component, and you want physics (collisions and gravity in particular) to act on the character.

Meanwhile, the character also needs a Collider component to define its boundaries for collision detection. The difference between these components is subtle but important: the Collider defines the shape for physics to act on, and the Rigidbody tells the physics simulation what objects to act on.

> **NOTE** These components are kept separate (even though they are closely related) because many objects that don't need the physics simulation themselves *do* need to collide with other objects that *are* acted on by physics.

One other subtlety to be aware of is that Unity has a separate physics system for 2D games instead of 3D physics. Thus, in this chapter you'll be using components from the Physics 2D section instead of the regular Physics section of the list.

Select Player in the scene. In the Inspector, click Add Component and then choose Physics 2D > Rigidbody 2D, as shown in figure 6.5. Then click Add Component again to add Physics 2D > Box Collider 2D. The Rigidbody needs a small amount of fine-tuning, so in the Inspector set Collision Detection as Continuous, turn on Constraints > Freeze Rotation Z (normally, the physics simulation will attempt to rotate objects while moving them, but characters in games don't behave like normal objects), and reduce Gravity Scale to 0 (you'll reset this later, but for now you don't want gravity). The player entity is now ready for the script that controls movement.

Click Add Component, then Physics 2D, and then scroll down to Rigidbody.

After the component is added, look at the settings in the Inspector...

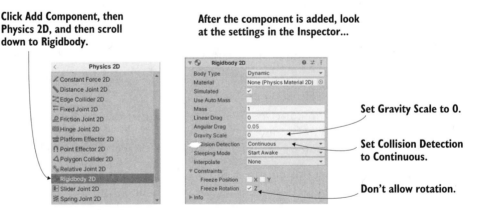

Set Gravity Scale to 0.

Set Collision Detection to Continuous.

Don't allow rotation.

Figure 6.5   Add and adjust the Rigidbody 2D component

6.2.1 *Writing keyboard controls*

To begin, you'll make the player move left and right; vertical movement is important also in a platformer, but you'll deal with that later. Create a C# script called `Platformer-Player` in the Scripts folder, and then drag that onto the Player object in the scene. Open the script and write the code from this listing.

> **Listing 6.1 `PlatformerPlayer` script to move with arrow keys**

```csharp
using System.Collections;
using System.Collections.Generic;
using UnityEngine;

public class PlatformerPlayer : MonoBehaviour {
  public float speed = 4.5f;

  private Rigidbody2D body;

  void Start() {
    body = GetComponent<Rigidbody2D>();          // Need this other component
                                                 // attached to this GameObject
  }

  void Update() {
    float deltaX = Input.GetAxis("Horizontal") * speed;
    Vector2 movement = new Vector2(deltaX, body.velocity.y);   // Set only horizontal
    body.velocity = movement;                                  // movement; preserve
  }                                                            // preexisting vertical
}                                                              // movement.
```

After writing the code, click Play and you can move the player by using the arrow keys. The code is fairly similar to movement code in previous chapters, with the main difference being that it acts on `Rigidbody2D` instead of `CharacterController`. `Character-Controller` is for 3D, so for a 2D game you use a `Rigidbody` component. Note that the movement is applied to `Rigidbody`'s `velocity`, rather than something like `position`.

> **NOTE** This code doesn't need to use delta time. In previous chapters, we needed to factor in the time between frames to achieve frame rate–independent movement, but we don't need to do that in this chapter. Here, we are adjusting velocity, which is inherently frame-rate independent, rather than position. In previous chapters, we were adjusting position directly.

> **TIP** By default, Unity applies a bit of acceleration to arrow key input. That can feel sluggish for a platformer, though. For snappier control, increase Sensitivity and Gravity of Horizontal input to 6. To find those settings, choose Edit > Project Settings > Input Manager; you'll see a long list, but Horizontal is the first section.

Great—this project is most of the way there for horizontal movement! You need to address only collision detection.

6.2.2 Colliding with the block

As you've probably noticed, the player walks through the block right now. There are no colliders on the floor or block, so the player can move through them. To fix this, add Box Collider 2D to Floor and Block: select each object in the scene, click Add Component in the Inspector, and choose Physics 2D > Box Collider 2D.

And that's all you need to do! Click Play now, and the player won't be able to move through the block. As with moving the player in chapter 2, if you had adjusted the player's position directly, collision detection wouldn't work. But Unity's built-in collision detection can work if you apply the movement to the player's physics components. In other words, moving `Transform` `.position` would have ignored collision detection, so instead you manipulated `Rigidbody2D` `.velocity` in the `movement` script.

Adding colliders to more complex art could be slightly trickier, but frankly not much harder in that case. Even if the art is not exactly a rectangle, you may still want to use box colliders and roughly surround the shape of obstacles in the scene. Alternatively, you could try other collider shapes, including arbitrary custom polygon shapes. Figure 6.6 illustrates how to work with polygon colliders for oddly shaped objects.

Anyway, collision detection is now working, so the next step is making the player animate along with its movement.

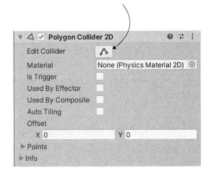

Click this button to drag around points in the scene.

Figure 6.6 Edit the shape of the polygon collider with the Edit Collider button.

6.3 Playing the sprite's animation

When stickman.png was imported, it was split into multiple frames for animating. Now let's *play* that animation, so that the player isn't sliding around but appears to be walking.

6.3.1 Explaining the Mecanim animation system

As mentioned briefly in chapter 4, the animation system in Unity is called *Mecanim*. It's designed so that you can visually set up a complex network of animations for a character and then control those animations with a minimum of code. The system is most useful for 3D characters (thus, we cover it in more detail in future chapters) but is still useful for 2D characters too.

The heart of the animation system is composed of two kinds of assets: *animation* clips and *animator* controllers. Notice *animation* versus *animator*: clips are the individual animation loops to play, whereas the controller is the network controlling when to play animations. This network is a *state machine* diagram, and the states in the diagram are different animations that could be playing. The controller shifts between states in reaction to conditions it is watching, and plays a different animation in each state.

Unity will create both kinds of assets automatically when you drag a 2D animation into the scene. That is, when you drag the frames of an animation into the scene, Unity will automatically create an animation clip and an animator controller using those frames. As depicted in figure 6.7, expand all the frames of the sprite asset, select frames 0–1, drag them into the scene, and type the name `stickman_idle` in the confirmation window.

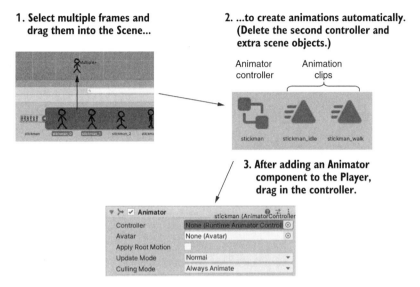

1. Select multiple frames and drag them into the Scene...

2. ...to create animations automatically. (Delete the second controller and extra scene objects.)

Animator controller   Animation clips

3. After adding an Animator component to the Player, drag in the controller.

Figure 6.7   Steps to use sprite-sheet frames in an Animator component

The action of dragging frames into the Scene view creates two things in the Asset view: a clip named `stickman_idle` and a controller named `stickman_0`. This action also creates an object called `stickman_0` in the scene, but you don't need that, so delete it. Rename the controller `stickman` with no suffix. Great—you created the character's idle animation!

Now repeat the process for the walk animation. Select frames 2–5, drag them into the scene, and name the animation `stickman_walk`. This time, delete both `stickman_2` in the scene and the new controller in Assets; only one animator controller is needed to control both animation clips, so keep the old one and delete `stickman_2`, the newly created one.

To apply the controller to your player character, select Player in the scene and click Add Component to choose Miscellaneous > Animator. As shown in figure 6.7, drag the stickman controller into the controller slot in the Inspector. With the Player still selected, open Window > Animation > Animator (shown in figure 6.8). Animations in the Animator window are displayed as blocks, referred to as *states*, and the controller switches between states when running. This particular controller already has the idle state in it, but you need to add a walking state; drag the `stickman_walk` animation clip from Assets into the Animator window.

By default, the idle animation will play too fast. To decrease the idle speed, select the idle animation state, and in the right-hand panel set the Speed setting to 0.2. With that change, the animations are all set up for the next step.

Click the Parameters tab.

Then click the + button to add a float parameter called speed.

Each of these blocks is an animation state. The Animator switches between states while running, playing the animation for that state.

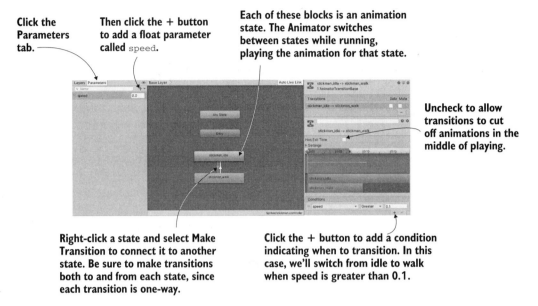

Uncheck to allow transitions to cut off animations in the middle of playing.

Right-click a state and select Make Transition to connect it to another state. Be sure to make transitions both to and from each state, since each transition is one-way.

Click the + button to add a condition indicating when to transition. In this case, we'll switch from idle to walk when speed is greater than 0.1.

Figure 6.8   Animator window, showing animation states and transitions

6.3.2   *Triggering animations from code*

Now that you've set up animation states in the animator controller, you can switch between those states to play the different animations. As mentioned in the preceding section, a state machine switches states in reaction to conditions it is watching. In Unity's animation controllers, those conditions are referred to as *parameters,* so let's add one. Figure 6.8 pointed out the relevant controls: select the Parameters tab and click the + button for a menu of parameter types. Add a float parameter called speed.

Next, you need to switch between animation states based on that parameter. Right-click stickman_idle and select Make Transition; that'll start dragging out an arrow from the idle state. Click stickman_walk to connect to that state, and because transitions are unidirectional, also right-click stickman_walk to transition back.

Now select the transition from idle (you can click the arrows themselves), uncheck Has Exit Time, and click the + at the bottom to add a condition (again, shown in figure 6.8). Make the condition speed Greater (than) 0.1 so the states will transition in that condition. Now do it again for the walk-to-idle transition: select the transition from walk, uncheck Has Exit Time, add a condition, and make the condition speed Less (than) 0.1.

Finally, the PlatformerPlayer script can manipulate the animator controller, as shown in this listing.

Listing 6.2 Triggering animations along with moving

```
...
private Animator anim;
...
void Start() {
  body = GetComponent<Rigidbody2D>();          ⟵── Existing code to help show
  anim = GetComponent<Animator>();                  where to position new code
}

                                                 Speed is greater than zero
                                                 even if velocity is negative.
void Update() {
  ...
  anim.SetFloat("speed", Mathf.Abs(deltaX));   ⟵── Floats aren't always exact, so
  if (!Mathf.Approximately(deltaX, 0)) {       ⟵── compare using Approximately().
    transform.localScale = new Vector3(Mathf.Sign(deltaX), 1, 1);   ⟵┐
  }                                                When moving, scale positive or
}                                                  negative 1 to face right or left.
...
```

Wow, that was barely any code for controlling the animations! Most of the work is handled by Mecanim, and only a small amount of code is needed to operate the animations. Play the game and move around to watch the player sprite animate. This game is really coming along, so on to the next step!

6.4 Adding the ability to jump

The player can move back and forth but isn't yet moving vertically. Vertical movement (both falling off ledges and jumping to higher platforms) is an important part of platform games, so let's implement that next.

6.4.1 Falling from gravity

Somewhat counterintuitively, before you can make the player jump, it needs gravity to jump against. As you may recall, earlier you set Gravity Scale to 0 on the player's Rigidbody. That was so the player wouldn't fall because of gravity. Well, turn that back to 1 now: select the Player object in the scene, find Rigidbody in the Inspector, and then type 1 in Gravity Scale.

Gravity is now affecting the player, but (assuming you had added a Box Collider to the Floor object) the floor is holding them up. Walk off the sides of the floor to fall into oblivion. By default, gravity affects the player somewhat weakly, so you'll want to increase the magnitude of its effect. The physics simulation includes a global gravity setting, which you can adjust in the Edit menu. Specifically, choose Edit > Project Settings > Physics 2D. As shown in figure 6.9, at the top of the various controls and settings, you should see Gravity Y; change that to -40.

You may have noticed one subtle issue: the falling player sticks to the side of the floor. To see this problem, walk off the edge of the platform and immediately reverse direction to move back toward the platform. Ugh, not good! Fortunately, Unity makes that easy to fix. Just add the Physics 2D > Platform Effector 2D components to Block

In this long list of settings, you
need to change only the intensity
of Gravity here at the top.

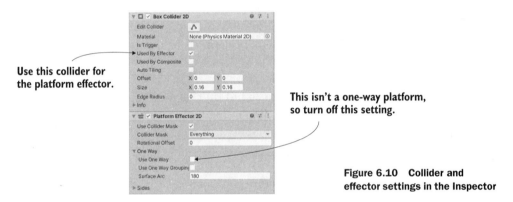

Figure 6.9   Gravity intensity
in Physics settings

and Floor. This effector makes objects in the scene behave more like platforms in a
platform game. Figure 6.10 points out two settings to adjust: Set Used By Effector on
the collider, and turn off Use One Way on the effector (we'll use this latter setting for
other platforms, but not now).

Use this collider for
the platform effector.

This isn't a one-way platform,
so turn off this setting.

Figure 6.10   Collider and
effector settings in the Inspector

That takes care of the downward part of vertical movement, but you still need to take
care of the upward part.

6.4.2   Applying an upward impulse

The next action you need is jumping. That is an upward jolt applied when the player
clicks the Jump button (we'll use the spacebar). Although your code directly changed
the velocity for horizontal movement, you're going to leave vertical velocity alone so
gravity can do its work. Instead, objects can be influenced by other forces besides gravity, so you'll add an upward force. Add this code to the `PlatformerPlayer` script.

Listing 6.3   Jumping when pressing the spacebar

```
...
public float jumpForce = 12.0f;
...
```

```
body.velocity = movement;
if (Input.GetKeyDown(KeyCode.Space)) {
    body.AddForce(Vector2.up * jumpForce, ForceMode2D.Impulse);
}
...
```
Existing code to help show
where to position new code

Add force only when the spacebar is pressed.

The important line is the `AddForce()` command. The code adds an upward force to the Rigidbody and does so in impulse mode. An *impulse* is a sudden jolt, as opposed to a continuously applied force. This code, then, applies a sudden upward jolt when the spacebar is pressed.

Meanwhile, gravity continues to affect the jumping player, resulting in a nice arc when the player jumps. You may have noticed another issue, however, so let's address that.

6.4.3 *Detecting the ground*

The jump control has one subtle problem: the player can jump in midair! If the player is already in midair (either because they jumped or because they are falling), pressing the spacebar applies an upward force, but it shouldn't. Instead, the jump control should work only when the player is on the ground. You therefore need to detect when the player is on the ground.

Listing 6.4   Checking if the player is on the ground

```
...
private BoxCollider2D box;
...
box = GetComponent<BoxCollider2D>();            Get this component to use the
...                                              player's collider as an area to check.
body.velocity = movement;

Vector3 max = box.bounds.max;
Vector3 min = box.bounds.min;
Vector2 corner1 = new Vector2(max.x, min.y - .1f);    Check below the
Vector2 corner2 = new Vector2(min.x, min.y - .2f);    collider's min Y values.
Collider2D hit = Physics2D.OverlapArea(corner1, corner2);

bool grounded = false;
if (hit != null) {           If a collider was detected
    grounded = true;         under the player . . .
}
                                                      . . . add grounded to
if (grounded && Input.GetKeyDown(KeyCode.Space)) {    the jump condition.
...
```

With this code in place, the player can no longer jump in midair. This addition to the script checks for colliders below the player and takes them into account in the conditional statement for jumping. Specifically, the code first gets the bounds of the player's collision box and then looks for overlapping colliders in an area of the same width just below the player. The result of that check is stored in the grounded variable and used in the conditional.

6.5   *Additional features for a platform game*

At this point, the most crucial aspects of the player's movement, walking and jumping, are implemented. Let's round out this platformer demo by adding new functionality to the environment around the player.

Designing levels by using tilemaps

For our project, the floors and platforms are blank, white rectangles. A finished game should have nicer graphics, but an image the size of a level would be way too big for the computer to handle. The most common solution to this problem is to use *tilemaps*. In a nutshell, that's a technique for constructing a larger, combined image out of lots of small tiling images. This image shows an example of a tilemap.

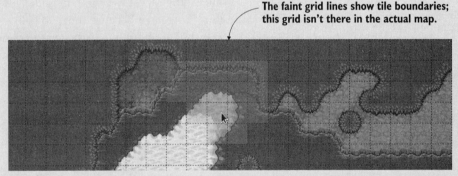

The faint grid lines show tile boundaries; this grid isn't there in the actual map.

Image courtesy of Tiled (www.mapeditor.org), using tiles by OpenGameArt.org (https://lpc.opengameart.org/).

Tilemap

Note that the map is constructed of small blocks that are repeated throughout the map. In that way, no single image is very large, but the entire screen can be covered with custom artwork. An official tilemap system for Unity is available by looking for 2D Tilemap Editor in Window > Package Manager.

You can find details in the Unity documentation (https://docs.unity3d.com/Manual/class-Tilemap.html). Alternatively, you could use an external library like SuperTiled2-Unity (www.seanba.com/supertiled2unity), which imports tilemaps created in Tiled, a popular (and free) tilemap editor.

6.5.1   *Unusual floors: Slopes and one-way platforms*

Right now, this demo has normal, level floors to stand on. Many interesting kinds of platforms are used in platform games, though, so let's implement a few other options. The first unusual floor you'll create is a slope. Duplicate the Floor object, set the duplicate's rotation to 0, 0, -25, move it off to the left side (around -3.47, -1.27, 0), and name it Slope. Refer all the way back to figure 6.1 to see what this looks like.

If you play now, the player already slides up and down correctly when moving but slowly slides down because of gravity when idle. To address this, let's turn off gravity for the player when the player is both standing on the ground and idle. Fortunately, you already detect the ground, so that can be reused in the new code. Indeed, only a single new line is needed.

Listing 6.5   Turning off gravity when standing on the ground

```
. . .
body.gravityScale = (grounded && Mathf.Approximately(deltaX, 0)) ? 0 : 1;   ⟵
if (grounded && Input.GetKeyDown(KeyCode.Space)) {   ⟵
. . .
```
Existing code to help show where to position new code

Check both on ground and not moving.

With that adjustment to the movement code, your player character correctly navigates slopes. Next, one-way platforms are another sort of unusual floor common in platformers. I'm talking about platforms that you can jump through but still stand on; the player bonks their head against the bottom of normal, fully solid platforms.

Because they're fairly common in platform games, Unity provides functionality for one-way platforms. As you may recall, when you added the Platform Effector component earlier, a one-way setting was turned off. Now turn that on! To create a new platform, duplicate the Floor object, scale the duplicate 10, 1, 1, place it above the floor around position -1.68, 0.11, 0, and name the object Platform. Oh, and don't forget to turn on Use One Way in the Platform Effector component.

The player jumps through the platform from below, but stands on it when coming down from above. We have one possible issue to fix, shown in figure 6.11. Unity may display the platform sprite on top of the player (to see this more easily, test with Jump Force set to 7), but you probably want the player on top. You could adjust the player's Z position as you did in chapter 5, but this time you'll adjust something else to show another option. Sprite renderers have a sorting order that can be used to control which sprites appear on top. Set Order in Layer to 1 in the Player's Sprite Renderer component.

That takes care of both sloped floors and one-way platforms. I'm going to cover one more sort of unusual floor, but it is significantly more complex to implement.

The platform may overlap the player, but we want it the other way around.

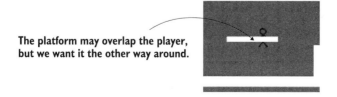

Figure 6.11   Platform sprite overlapping the player sprite

6.5.2   *Implementing moving platforms*

A third sort of unusual floor common in platform games is the moving platform. Implementing one requires both a new script to control the platform itself and changes in the player's movement script to handle moving platforms. You're going to write a script that takes two positions, start and finish, and makes the platform bounce between them. First, create a new C# script called MovingPlatform and write this code in it.

Listing 6.6   MovingPlatform script for floors that move back and forth

```csharp
using System.Collections;
using System.Collections.Generic;
using UnityEngine;

public class MovingPlatform : MonoBehaviour {
  public Vector3 finishPos = Vector3.zero;       ◁─── Position to move to
  public float speed = 0.5f;

  private Vector3 startPos;                       ┐ How far along the "track"
  private float trackPercent = 0;        ◁────────┘ between start and finish
  private int direction = 1;             ◁───┐
                                             │ Current movement direction
  void Start() {
    startPos = transform.position;       ◁───┐ Placement in the scene is
  }                                           │ the position to move from

  void Update() {
    trackPercent += direction * speed * Time.deltaTime;
    float x = (finishPos.x - startPos.x) * trackPercent + startPos.x;
    float y = (finishPos.y - startPos.y) * trackPercent + startPos.y;
    transform.position = new Vector3(x, y, startPos.z);

    if ((direction == 1 && trackPercent > .9f) ||
      (direction == -1 && trackPercent < .1f)) {   ◁───┐ Change direction at
      direction *= -1;                                  │ both start and end.
    }
  }
}
```

Drawing custom gizmos

The majority of the code you'll write is for the running game, but Unity scripts can also affect Unity's *editor*. An often-overlooked feature of Unity is the ability to add new menus and windows. Your scripts can also draw custom helper images in the Scene view; such helper images are called *gizmos*.

You're already familiar with gizmos like the green boxes to display colliders. Those are built into Unity, but you can also draw your own gizmos in scripts. For example, drawing a line that shows the movement path of the platform could be useful, as shown here.

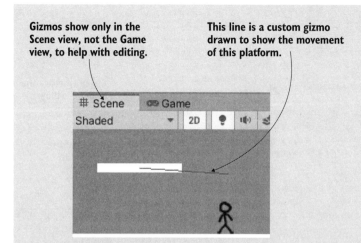

Gizmos show only in the Scene view, not the Game view, to help with editing.

This line is a custom gizmo drawn to show the movement of this platform.

A custom gizmo

The code for drawing that line is simple. Usually, when writing code that affects Unity's editing interface, you need to add `using UnityEditor;` at the top (because most editor functions reside in that namespace), but in this case, you don't even need that. Add this method to the `MovingPlatform` script:

```
...
void OnDrawGizmos() {
  Gizmos.color = Color.red;
  Gizmos.DrawLine(transform.position, finishPos);
}
...
```

You need to know a few things about this code. One, it all happens in a method called `OnDrawGizmos()`. Like `Start()` or `Update()`, `OnDrawGizmos()` is another method name Unity recognizes. Within the method are two lines of code: one sets the drawing color, and the other tells Unity to draw a line from the platform's position to the finish position.

Similar commands are used for other gizmo shapes. `DrawLine()` is used to define a line by using start and end points, but the similar command `DrawRay()` is used to draw a line in a given direction. That's handy for visualizing raycasts coming from AI characters.

Gizmos are visible only in the Scene view by default, but note that the Game view has a Gizmos button along the top. Oh, and although this project is a 2D game, drawing custom gizmos works just as well in 3D games.

Drag this script onto the platform object. Great—the platform moves left and right when you play the scene! Now you need to adjust the player's movement script to attach the player to the moving platform. Here are the changes to make.

Listing 6.7   Handling moving platforms in `PlatformerPlayer`

```
...
  body.AddForce(Vector2.up * jumpForce, ForceMode2D.Impulse);
}

MovingPlatform platform = null;
if (hit != null) {
  platform = hit.GetComponent<MovingPlatform>();
}
if (platform != null) {
  transform.parent = platform.transform;
} else {
  transform.parent = null;
}
anim.SetFloat("speed", Mathf.Abs(deltaX));
...
```

Check whether the platform under the player is a moving platform.

Either attach to the platform or clear transform.parent.

Existing code to help show where to position new code

Now the player moves with the platform after jumping on it. This change mostly comes down to attaching the player as a child of the platform; remember, when you set a parent object, the child object moves with the parent. Listing 6.7 uses `GetComponent()` to check whether the ground detected is a moving platform. If so, it sets that platform as the player's parent; otherwise, the player is detached from any parent.

There's a big problem, though: the player inherits the platform's scale, resulting in weird scaling. That can be fixed by counter-scaling (scaling the player down to counteract the platform's scale up).

Listing 6.8   Correcting scaling of the player

```
...
  anim.SetFloat("speed", Mathf.Abs(deltaX));

  Vector3 pScale = Vector3.one;
  if (platform != null) {
    pScale = platform.transform.localScale;
  }
  if (!Mathf.Approximately(deltaX, 0)) {
    transform.localScale = new Vector3(
    Mathf.Sign(deltaX) / pScale.x, 1/pScale.y, 1);
  }
}
...
```

Default scale 1 if not on moving platform

Replace existing scaling with new code.

The math for counter-scaling is straightforward: set the player to 1 divided by the platform's scale. When the player's scale is then multiplied by the platform's scale, that leaves a scale of 1. The only tricky bit of this code is multiplying by the sign of the movement value; as you may recall from earlier, the player is flipped based on the movement direction.

And that's moving platforms fully implemented. This platformer demo needs only one final touch.

6.5.3　Camera control

Moving the camera is the final feature you'll add to this 2D platformer. Create a script called `FollowCam`, drag it onto the camera, and then write the following in it.

Listing 6.9　`FollowCam` script to move with the player

```
using System.Collections;
using System.Collections.Generic;
using UnityEngine;

public class FollowCam : MonoBehaviour {
  public Transform target;

  void LateUpdate() {
    transform.position = new Vector3(
    target.position.x, target.position.y, transform.position.z);
  }
}
```

Preserve the Z position while changing X and Y.

With that code written, drag the Player object to the script's `target` slot in the Inspector. Play the scene, and the camera moves around, keeping the player at the center of the screen. You can see that the code applies the target object's position to the camera, and you set the player as the target object. Note that the method name is `LateUpdate()` instead of `Update()`; that's yet another name Unity recognizes. `LateUpdate()` also executes every frame, but it happens after `Update()` every frame.

It's slightly jarring that the camera moves *exactly* with the player at all times. The camera in most platformers has all kinds of subtle but complicated behavior, highlighting different parts of the level as the player moves around. In fact, camera control for platform games is a surprisingly deep topic; try searching for "platform game camera" and see all the results. In this case, though, you're just going to make the camera's movement smoother and less jarring; this listing makes that adjustment.

Listing 6.10　Smoothing the camera movement

```
...
public float smoothTime = 0.2f;

private Vector3 velocity = Vector3.zero;
...
void LateUpdate() {
  Vector3 targetPosition = new Vector3(
  target.position.x, target.position.y, transform.position.z);

  transform.position = Vector3.SmoothDamp(transform.position,
  targetPosition, ref velocity, smoothTime);
}
...
```

Preserve Z position while changing X and Y.

Smooth transition from current to target position

The main change is calling a function called SmoothDamp(); the other changes (like adding time and velocity variables) are all to support that function. That's a function Unity provides for making values smoothly transition to a new value. In this case, the values are the positions of the camera and target.

The camera moves smoothly with the player now. You implemented the player's movement, several kinds of platforms, and now camera control. Looks like this chapter's project is finished!

Summary

- Sprite sheets are a common way to handle 2D animation.
- Characters in games don't behave like objects in the real world, so you must adjust their physics accordingly.
- Rigidbody objects can be controlled either by applying forces or by setting their velocity directly.
- Levels in 2D games are often constructed with tilemaps.
- A simple script can make the camera smoothly follow the player.

7

Putting
a GUI onto a game

This chapter covers

- Comparing old and newer GUI systems
- Creating a canvas for the interface
- Positioning UI elements by using anchor points
- Adding interactivity to the UI (buttons, sliders, and so on)
- Broadcasting and listening for events from the UI

In this chapter, you'll build a 2D interface display for a 3D game. So far, we've focused on the virtual scene itself while building a first-person demo. But every game needs abstract interaction and information displays in addition to the virtual scene the gameplay takes place in. This is true for all games, whether they're 2D or 3D, first-person shooters or puzzle games. So, while the techniques in this chapter will be used on a 3D game, they apply to 2D games as well.

These abstract interaction displays are referred to as the *UI*, or more specifically, the *GUI*. GUI (short for Graphical User Interface) refers to the visual part of the interface, such as text and buttons (see figure 7.1). Technically, the UI includes

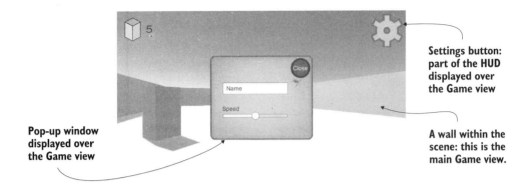

Settings button: part of the HUD displayed over the Game view

Pop-up window displayed over the Game view

A wall within the scene: this is the main Game view.

Figure 7.1   The GUI you'll create for a game

nongraphical controls, such as the keyboard or game pad, but people tend to be referring to the graphical parts when they say "user interface."

Although any software requires some sort of UI in order for the user of that software to control it, games often use their GUI in a slightly different way from other software. In a website, for example, the GUI basically *is* the website (in terms of visual representation). In a game, though, text and buttons are often an additional overlay on top of the Game view, a kind of display called a *heads-up display* (*HUD*).

> **DEFINITION** A *heads-up display* (*HUD*) superimposes graphics on top of the view of the world. The concept of a HUD originated with military jets— its purpose was to enable pilots to see crucial information without having to look down. Similarly, a GUI superimposed on the Game view is referred to as the HUD.

This chapter shows how to build the game's HUD by using the UI tools in Unity. As you saw in chapter 5, Unity provides multiple ways to create UI displays. This chapter demonstrates the advanced UI system that replaced Unity's first UI system. I also discuss the previous UI system and the advantages of the newer system.

To learn about the UI tools in Unity, you'll build on top of the FPS project from chapter 3. The project in this chapter involves these steps:

1. Planning the interface
2. Placing UI elements on the display
3. Programming interactions with the UI elements
4. Making the GUI respond to events in the scene
5. Making the scene respond to actions on the GUI

Copy the project from chapter 3 and open the copy to start working in this chapter. As usual, the art assets you need are in the sample download. With those files set up, you're ready to start building the game's UI.

NOTE All the examples in this chapter are built on top of the FPS game created in chapter 3. But the content of this chapter is largely independent of that base project; we'll just add a graphical interface on top of the existing game demo. Although I've suggested that you download the chapter 3 project, you're free to use whatever game demo you'd like.

7.1 Before you start writing code . . .

To start building the HUD, you first need to understand how the UI system works. Unity provides multiple approaches to building a game's HUD, so we need to go over how those systems work. Then we can briefly plan the UI and prepare the art assets that we'll need.

7.1.1 Immediate mode GUI or advanced 2D interface?

From its first version, Unity has come with an immediate mode GUI system. The immediate mode system makes it easy to put a clickable button on the screen. Listing 7.1 shows the code to do that: simply attach this script to any object in the scene.

DEFINITION *Immediate mode* refers to explicitly issuing draw commands every frame—instead of defining all the visuals once, and then for every frame the system knows what to draw without you having to tell it again. The latter approach is called *retained mode*.

For another example of immediate mode UI, recall the target cursor displayed in chapter 3. This GUI system is entirely based on code, with no work done in Unity's editor.

Listing 7.1 Example of a button using the immediate mode GUI

```
using System.Collections;
using System.Collections.Generic;
using UnityEngine;

public class BasicUI : MonoBehaviour {          Function called every frame
    void OnGUI() {                              after everything else renders
        if (GUI.Button(new Rect(10, 10, 40, 20), "Test")) {     Parameters: position
            Debug.Log("Test button");                           X, pos Y, width,
        }                                                       height, text label
    }
}
```

The core of the code in this listing is the `OnGUI()` method. Much like `Start()` and `Update()`, every `MonoBehaviour` automatically responds to `OnGUI()`. That function runs every frame after the 3D scene is rendered, providing a place to put GUI drawing commands. This code draws a button; note that the command for a button is executed every frame (that is, in immediate mode style). The button command is used in a conditional that responds when the button is clicked.

Because the immediate mode GUI makes it easy to get a few buttons onscreen with minimal effort, we'll sometimes use it for examples in future chapters. But default buttons are about the only thing easy to create with that system, so more recent versions of Unity now have a new interface system based on 2D graphics laid out in the editor. This newer interface system takes a bit more effort to set up, but you'll probably want to use it in finished games because it produces more polished results.

The newer UI system works in retained mode, so the graphics are laid out once and then drawn every frame without needing to be continually redefined. In this system, graphics for the UI are placed in Unity's editor. This provides two advantages over the immediate mode UI: (1) you can see what the UI looks like while placing UI elements, and (2) this system makes it straightforward to customize the UI with your own images.

NOTE   Chapter 1 mentioned that Unity has three UI systems (which are compared at http://mng.bz/205X) because successively developed systems improved on their predecessor. This book covers the second UI system (Unity UI, or uGUI) because it is still preferred over the incomplete third UI system (UI Toolkit).

To use this system, you're going to import images and then drag objects into the scene. Next, let's plan how this UI will look.

7.1.2   Planning the layout

The HUD for most games comprises a few UI controls repeated over and over. Therefore, this project doesn't need to be terribly complex in order for you to learn how to build a game's UI. You're going to put a score display and a Settings button in the corners of the screen over the main Game view (see figure 7.2). The Settings button will bring up a pop-up window, which will have both a text field and a slider.

For this example, those input controls will be used for setting the player's name and movement speed, but ultimately those UI elements could control any settings relevant to your game. Well, that plan is pretty simple! The next step is bringing in the images that are needed.

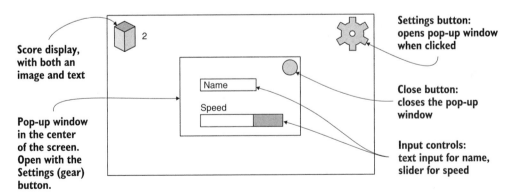

Figure 7.2   Planned GUI

7.1.3 Importing UI images

This UI requires some images to display for things like buttons. The UI is built from 2D images like the graphics in chapter 5, so you'll follow the same two steps:

1. Import images (if needed, set them to Sprite).
2. Drag the sprites into the scene.

To accomplish these steps, first drag the images into Project view to import them. Then, in the Inspector, change their Texture Type setting to Sprite (2D and UI).

> **WARNING** The Texture Type setting defaults to Texture in 3D projects and to Sprite in 2D projects. If you want sprites in a 3D project, you need to manually adjust this setting.

Get all the necessary images from the sample download (see figure 7.3) and then import them into your project. Make sure all the imported assets are set to Sprite; you'll probably need to adjust Texture Type in the settings displayed after importing.

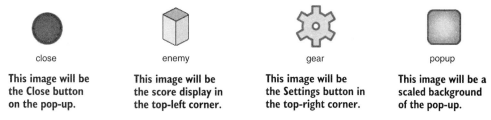

close	enemy	gear	popup
This image will be the Close button on the pop-up.	This image will be the score display in the top-left corner.	This image will be the Settings button in the top-right corner.	This image will be a scaled background of the pop-up.

Figure 7.3 Images that are needed for this chapter's project

These sprites comprise the buttons, score display, and pop-up that you'll create. Now that the images are imported, let's put these graphics onto the screen.

7.2 Setting up the GUI display

The art assets are the same kind of 2D sprites we used in chapter 5, but we'll use those assets in the scene a bit differently. Unity provides special tools to make the images a HUD that's displayed over the 3D scene, rather than displaying the images as part of the scene. Some special tricks are used when positioning UI elements, because of the needs of a display that may change on different screens.

7.2.1 Creating a canvas for the interface

One of the most fundamental and nonobvious aspects of how the UI system works is that all images must be attached to a canvas object.

> **TIP** Canvas is a special kind of object that Unity renders as the UI for a game.

Open the GameObject menu to see the objects you can create; in the UI category, choose Canvas. A canvas object will appear in the scene (it may be clearer to rename the object HUD Canvas). This object represents the entire extent of the screen, and it's huge compared to the 3D scene because it scales one pixel of the screen to one unit in the scene.

> **WARNING**   When you create a canvas object, an EventSystem object is automatically created too. That object is required for UI interaction, but you can otherwise ignore it.

Switch to 2D view mode (refer to figure 7.4) and double-click the canvas in the Hierarchy to zoom out and view it fully. The 2D view mode is automatic when the entire project is 2D, but in a 3D project, this toggle must be clicked to switch between the UI and the main scene. To return to viewing the 3D scene, toggle off the 2D view mode and then double-click the building to zoom in to that object.

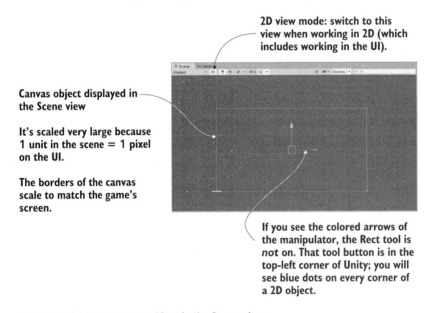

2D view mode: switch to this view when working in 2D (which includes working in the UI).

Canvas object displayed in the Scene view

It's scaled very large because 1 unit in the scene = 1 pixel on the UI.

The borders of the canvas scale to match the game's screen.

If you see the colored arrows of the manipulator, the Rect tool is *not* on. That tool button is in the top-left corner of Unity; you will see blue dots on every corner of a 2D object.

Figure 7.4   A blank canvas object in the Scene view

> **TIP**   Don't forget this tip from chapter 4: across the top of the Scene view's pane are buttons that control what's visible, so look there for the Effects button to turn off the skybox.

The canvas has settings that you can adjust. The first is the Render Mode option. Leave this at the default setting (Screen Space—Overlay), but you should know what the three possible settings mean:

- *Screen Space—Overlay*—Renders the UI as 2D graphics on top of the camera view. (This is the default setting.)
- *Screen Space—Camera*—Also renders the UI on top of the camera view, but UI elements can rotate for perspective effects.
- *World Space*—Places the canvas object within the scene, as if the UI were part of the 3D scene.

The two modes besides the initial default can sometimes be useful for specific effects but are slightly more complicated.

The other important setting is Pixel Perfect. This setting causes the rendering to subtly adjust the position of images so that they're always perfectly crisp and sharp (as opposed to blurring them when positioned between pixels). Go ahead and select that check box. Now the HUD canvas is set up, but it's still blank and needs sprites.

7.2.2 Buttons, images, and text labels

The canvas object defines an area to display as the UI, but it still requires sprites to display. Referring to the UI mock-up in figure 7.2, you'll see an image of the block/enemy in the top-left corner, text displaying the score next to that, and a gear-shaped button in the top-right corner. Accordingly, the UI section of the GameObject menu contains options to create an image, text, or button. Create one of each, but using the TextMeshPro version when applicable. That is, choose GameObject > UI > Image, then Text - TextMeshPro, then Button - TextMeshPro.

> **NOTE** Just as in chapter 5, you need to have the TextMeshPro package installed, so go to Window > Package Manager if no TextMeshPro versions are displayed in the menu of UI objects. The TMP Importer window will automatically appear when you create a TextMeshPro object for the first time. Click the Import TMP Essentials button.

To display correctly, UI elements need to be a child of the canvas object. Unity does this automatically, but remember that, as usual, you can drag objects around the Hierarchy view to make parent-child linkages (see figure 7.5).

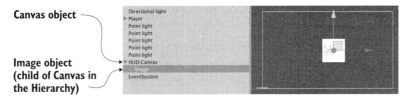

Figure 7.5   Canvas with an image linked in the Hierarchy view

Objects within the canvas can be parented together for positioning purposes, just like any other objects in the scene. For example, you should drag the text object onto the image so that the text will move with the image. The default button object also has a text object as its child, but this project's button doesn't need a text label, so delete the default text object.

Roughly position the UI elements into their corners. In the next section, we'll make the positions exact; for now, just drag the objects until they're pretty much in position. Click and drag the image object to the top left of the canvas; the button goes in the top right.

TIP   As noted in chapter 5, you use the Rect tool in 2D mode. I described it as a single manipulation tool that encompasses all three transforms: Move, Rotate, and Scale. These operations have to be separate tools in 3D but are combined in 2D because that's one less dimension to worry about. In 2D mode, this tool is selected automatically, or you can click the button near the top-left corner of Unity.

At the moment, the images are blank. If you select a UI object and look at the Inspector, you should see a Source Image slot near the top of the image component. As shown in figure 7.6, drag over sprites (remember, not textures!) from the Project view to assign images to the objects. Assign the enemy sprite to the image object, and the gear sprite to the button object (click Set Native Size after assigning sprites to properly size the image object).

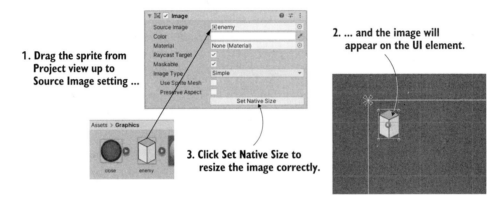

Figure 7.6   Assigning 2D sprites to the Image property of UI elements.

That took care of the appearance of both the enemy image and the gear button. As for the text object, the Inspector has a bunch of settings (see figure 7.7). First, type a single number in the large Text Input box; this text will be overwritten later, but it's useful because it looks like a score display within the editor. The text is the wrong size, so change the Font Size to 24. Also click the first Font Style button for Bold, and then change Vertex Color to black. You also want to set this label to left horizontal alignment and middle vertical alignment. For now, the remaining settings can be left at their default values.

NOTE   The most commonly adjusted property that we didn't just touch on is the font. To use a TrueType font with TextMeshPro, first import the font into Unity and then choose Window > TextMeshPro > Font Asset Creator.

Now that sprites have been assigned to the UI images and the score text is set up, you can click Play to see the HUD on top of the 3D game. The canvas displayed in Unity's editor shows the bounds of the screen, and UI elements are drawn onto the screen in the positions shown in figure 7.8.

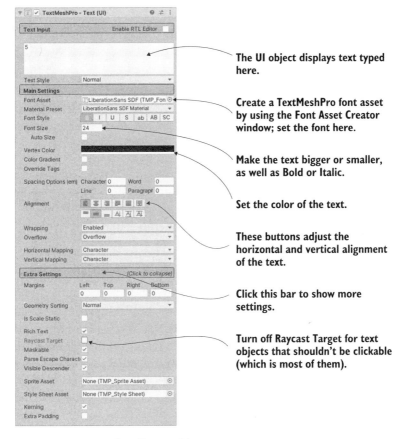

The UI object displays text typed here.

Create a TextMeshPro font asset by using the Font Asset Creator window; set the font here.

Make the text bigger or smaller, as well as Bold or Italic.

Set the color of the text.

These buttons adjust the horizontal and vertical alignment of the text.

Click this bar to show more settings.

Turn off Raycast Target for text objects that shouldn't be clickable (which is most of them).

Figure 7.7   Settings for a UI text object

The canvas displayed in Scene view

HUD overlays the 3D level in Game view.

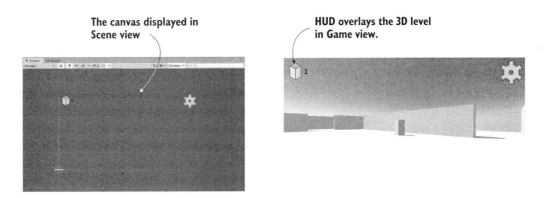

Figure 7.8   The GUI as seen in the editor (left) and when playing the game (right)

Great, you made a HUD with 2D images displayed over the 3D game! One more complex visual setting remains: positioning UI elements relative to the canvas.

7.2.3 *Controlling the position of UI elements*

All UI objects have an anchor, displayed in the editor as an X shape (see figure 7.9). An *anchor* is a flexible way of positioning objects on the UI.

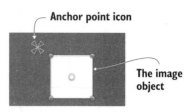

Anchor point icon

The image object

> **DEFINITION** The *anchor* of an object is the point where an object attaches to the canvas or screen. That object's position is measured relative to the anchor.

Figure 7.9   The anchor point of an image object

Positions are values like "50 pixels on the x-axis." But that leaves the question: 50 pixels from what? This is where anchors come in. The purpose of an anchor is to keep the object in place relative to the anchor point, whereas the anchor moves around relative to the canvas. The anchor is defined as something like "center of the screen," and then the anchor will stay centered while the screen changes size. Similarly, setting the anchor to the right-hand side of the screen will keep the object rooted to the right-hand side even if the screen changes size (for example, if the game is played on different monitors).

The easiest way to understand what I'm talking about is to see it in action. Select the image object and look over at the Inspector. Anchor settings will appear right below the transform component (see figure 7.10). By default, UI elements have their anchor set to Center, but you want to set the anchor to Top Left for this image; figure 7.10 shows how to adjust that by using the Anchor Presets.

Click the Anchor button (it looks like a target) to open the entire Anchor Presets menu.

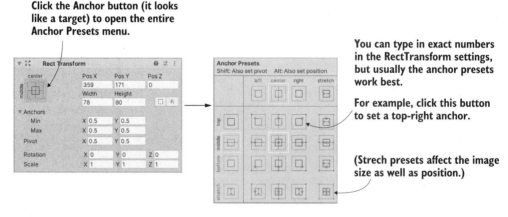

You can type in exact numbers in the RectTransform settings, but usually the anchor presets work best.

For example, click this button to set a top-right anchor.

(Strech presets affect the image size as well as position.)

Figure 7.10   How to adjust anchor settings

Change the gear button's anchor as well. Set it to Top Right for this object; click the top-right Anchor Preset. Now try scaling the window left and right: click and drag on the side of the game's view. Thanks to the anchors, the UI objects will stay in their corners while the canvas changes size. As figure 7.11 shows, these UI elements are now rooted in place while the screen moves.

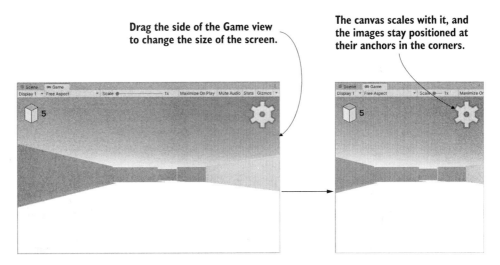

Drag the side of the Game view to change the size of the screen.

The canvas scales with it, and the images stay positioned at their anchors in the corners.

Figure 7.11   Anchors stay in place while the screen changes size.

TIP Anchor points can adjust scale as well as position. We're not going to explore that functionality in this chapter, but each corner of the image can be rooted to a different corner of the screen. In figure 7.11, the images didn't change size, but we could adjust the anchors so that when the screen changes size, the image stretches with it.

All of the visual setup is done, so it's time to program interactivity.

7.3   Programming interactivity in the UI

Before you can interact with the UI, you need to have a mouse cursor. As you may recall, we adjusted Cursor settings in the Start() method of the RayShooter code. Those settings lock and hide the mouse cursor, a behavior that works for the controls in an FPS game but that interferes with using the UI. Remove those lines from Ray-Shooter so that you can click the HUD.

While you have RayShooter open, you could also make sure not to shoot while interacting with the GUI. Here is the code for that.

Listing 7.2   Adding a GUI check to the code in `RayShooter`

```
using UnityEngine.EventSystems;     ⟵── Include UI system code frameworks.
...
void Update() {
  if (Input.GetMouseButtonDown(0) &&          ⟵┐ Italicized code was already in
!EventSystem.current.IsPointerOverGameObject()) {  ⟵┘ script; shown for reference.
    Vector3 point = new Vector3(            Check that GUI isn't being used.
      camera.pixelWidth/2, camera.pixelHeight/2, 0);
    ...
```

Now you can play the game and click the button, although it doesn't do anything yet. You can watch the tinting of the button change as you mouse over it and click. This mouseover and click behavior is a default tint that can be changed for each button, but the default looks fine for now. You could speed up the default fading behavior; Fade Duration is a setting in the button component, so try decreasing that to 0.01 to see how the button changes.

> **TIP** Sometimes the default interaction controls of the UI also interfere with the game. Remember the EventSystem object that was created automatically along with the canvas? That object controls the UI interaction controls, and by default it uses the arrow keys to interact with the GUI. You may need to turn off the arrow keys to avoid interacting with the GUI by accident: to do this, deselect the Send Navigation Event check box in the settings for EventSystem.

But nothing else happens when you click the button because you haven't yet linked it up to any code. Let's take care of that next.

7.3.1 *Programming an invisible UIController*

In general, UI interaction is programmed with a standard series of steps that's the same for all UI elements:

1. Create a UI object in the scene (the button created in the previous section).
2. Write a script to call when the UI is operated.
3. Attach that script to an object in the scene.
4. Link UI elements (such as buttons) to the object with that script.

To follow these steps, first we need to create a controller object to link to the button. Create a script called UIController and drag that script onto the controller object in the scene.

Listing 7.3 `UIController` script used to program buttons

```
using System.Collections;
using System.Collections.Generic;
using UnityEngine;                          ⟵─── Import the TextMeshPro
using TMPro;                                          code framework.

public class UIController : MonoBehaviour {
    [SerializeField] TMP_Text scoreLabel;   ⟵─── Reference the Text object in the
                                                  scene to set the text property.
    void Update() {
        scoreLabel.text = Time.realtimeSinceStartup.ToString();
    }

    public void OnOpenSettings() {          ⟵─── Method called by
        Debug.Log("open settings");               Settings button
    }
}
```

TIP You might be wondering why we need separate objects for Scene-Controller and UIController. Indeed, this scene is so simple that you could have one controller handling both the 3D scene and the UI. As the game gets more complex, though, it'll become increasingly useful for the 3D scene and the UI to be separate modules, communicating indirectly. This notion extends well beyond games to software in general: software engineers refer to this principle as *separation of concerns*.

Now drag objects to component slots to wire them up. Drag the Score label (the text object we created before) to the UIController text slot. The code in UIController sets the text displayed on that label. Currently, the code displays a timer to test the text display; that will later be changed to the score.

Next, add an OnClick entry to the button to drag the controller object onto. Select the button to see its settings in the Inspector. Toward the bottom, you should see an On Click panel; initially that panel is empty, but you can click the + button to add an entry (as you can see in figure 7.12). Each entry defines a single function that gets called when that button is clicked; the listing has both a slot for an object and a menu for the function to call. Drag the controller object to the object slot, and then look for UIController in the menu; select OnOpenSettings() in that section.

On Click event panel near the bottom of the settings

Drag an object in the scene to the object slot; then choose a function in the menu.

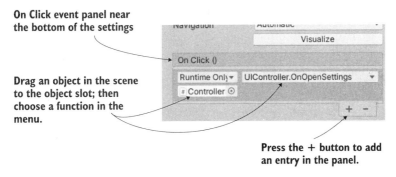

Press the + button to add an entry in the panel.

Figure 7.12   The On Click panel toward the bottom of the button settings

Responding to other mouse events

OnClick is the only event that the button component exposes, but UI elements can respond to multiple interactions. To go beyond the default interactions, use an Event-Trigger component.

Add a new component to the button object and look for the Event section of the component's menu. Select EventTrigger from that menu. Although the button's OnClick responded to only a full click (the mouse button being pressed down and then released), let's try responding to the mouse button being pressed but not released. Perform the same steps as for OnClick, only responding to a different event. First add another method to UIController:

(continued)
```
...
public void OnPointerDown() {
    Debug.Log("pointer down");
}
...
```

Now click Add New Event Type to add a new type to the EventTrigger component. Choose Pointer Down for the event. This will create an empty panel for that event, just like `OnClick` had. Click the + button to add an event listing, drag the controller object to this entry, and select `OnPointerDown()` in the menu. There you go!

Play the game and click the button to output debug messages in the console. Again, the code is currently random output to test the button's functionality. We want to open a settings pop-up, so let's create that pop-up window next.

7.3.2   *Creating a pop-up window*

The UI has a button to open a pop-up window, but there's no pop-up yet. That will be a new image object, along with several controls (such as buttons and sliders) attached to that object. The first step is to create a new image, so choose GameObject > UI > Image. Just as before, the new image has a slot in the Inspector called Source Image. Drag a sprite to that slot to set this image. This time, use the sprite called popup.

Ordinarily, the sprite is stretched over the entire image object; this was how the score and gear images worked, and you clicked the Set Native Size button to resize the object to the size of the image. This behavior is the default for image objects, but the pop-up will use a sliced image instead.

> **DEFINITION**   A *sliced image* is split into nine sections that scale differently from one another. By scaling the edges of the image separately from the middle, you ensure that the image can scale to any size you want, and it maintains its sharp, crisp edges. In other development tools, these kinds of images often have "9" somewhere in the name (such as 9-slice, 9-patch, scale-9) to indicate the nine sections of the image.

As you can see in figure 7.13, the image component has an Image Type setting. This setting defaults to Simple, which was the correct image type earlier. For the pop-up, though, set Image Type to Sliced. Unity will probably display an error, complaining that the image doesn't have a border, so we'll correct that next.

The error happens because the popup sprite doesn't have the nine border sections defined yet. To set that up, first select the popup sprite in the Project view. In the Inspector, you should see the Sprite Editor button (see figure 7.14); click that button, and the Sprite Editor window will appear.

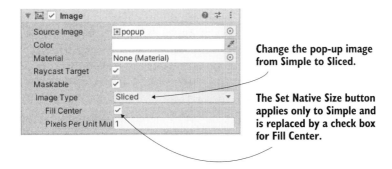

Change the pop-up image from Simple to Sliced.

The Set Native Size button applies only to Simple and is replaced by a check box for Fill Center.

Figure 7.13   Settings for the image component, including Image Type

> **WARNING**   As mentioned in chapter 6, the Sprite Editor window requires the 2D Sprite package. Creating a 2D project may automatically install that package, but for this project, you need to open Window > Package Manager and look for 2D Sprite in the list on the left side of the window. Select that package and then click the Install button.

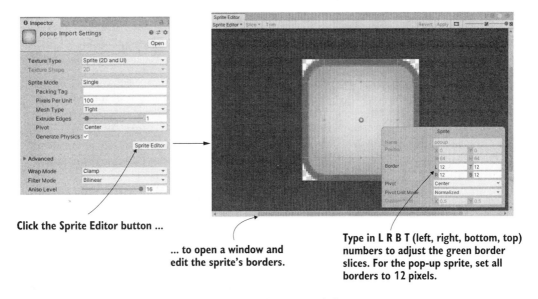

Click the Sprite Editor button ...

... to open a window and edit the sprite's borders.

Type in L R B T (left, right, bottom, top) numbers to adjust the green border slices. For the pop-up sprite, set all borders to 12 pixels.

Figure 7.14   Sprite Editor button in the Inspector and a pop-up window

In the Sprite Editor, you can see green lines that indicate how the image will be sliced. Initially, the image won't have any border (all of the Border settings are 0). Increase the border width to 12 for all four sides, which will result in the border shown in figure 7.14. Because all four sides (Left, Right, Bottom, and Top) have the border set to 12 pixels wide, the border lines will intersect into nine sections. Close the editor window and apply the changes.

Now that the sprite has the nine sections defined, the sliced image will work correctly (and the Image component settings will show Fill Center; make sure that setting is on). Click and drag the blue indicators in the corner of the image to scale it (switch to the Rect tool described in chapter 5 if you don't see any scale indicators). The border sections will maintain their size while the center portion scales.

Because the border sections maintain their size, a sliced image can be scaled to any size and still have crisp edges. This is perfect for UI elements—different windows may be different sizes but should still look the same. For this pop-up, enter a width of 250 and a height of 200 to make it look like figure 7.15 (also, center it on position 0, 0, 0).

Figure 7.15   Sliced image scaled to dimensions of the pop-up

TIP   The way that UI images stack on top of each other is determined by their order in the Hierarchy view. In the Hierarchy list, drag the pop-up object above other UI objects (always staying attached to the canvas, of course). Now move the pop-up around within the Scene view; you can see how images overlap the pop-up window. Finally, drag the pop-up to the bottom of the canvas hierarchy so that it will display on top of everything else.

The pop-up object is set up now, so write some code for it. Create a script called Set-tingsPopup and drag that script onto the pop-up object.

Listing 7.4   SettingsPopup script for the pop-up object

```
using System.Collections;
using System.Collections.Generic;
using UnityEngine;

public class SettingsPopup : MonoBehaviour {
    public void Open() {
        gameObject.SetActive(true);        // Turn the object on to
    }                                      // open the window.
    public void Close() {
        gameObject.SetActive(false);       // Deactivate this object
    }                                      // to close the window.
}
```

Next, open UIController to make a few adjustments.

Listing 7.5 Adjusting UIController to handle the pop-up

```
...
[SerializeField] SettingsPopup settingsPopup;
void Start() {
    settingsPopup.Close();          ◁         Close the pop-up when
}                                              the game starts.
...
public void OnOpenSettings() {
    settingsPopup.Open();           ◁         Replace the debug text with
}                                              the pop-up's method.
...
```

This code adds a slot for the pop-up object, so drag the pop-up to UIController. The pop-up will be closed initially when you play the game, and it'll open when you click the Settings button.

At the moment, there's no way to close it again, so add a button to the pop-up. The steps are pretty much the same as for the button created earlier: choose GameObject > UI> Button - TextMeshPro, position the new button in the top-right corner of the pop-up, drag the close sprite to this UI element's Source Image property, and then click Set Native Size to correctly resize the image. Unlike with the previous button, we want this text label, so select the text object and type Close in the text field, reduce Font Size to 14, and set Vertex Color to white. In the Hierarchy view, drag this button onto the pop-up object so that it will be a child of the pop-up window. And as a final touch of polish, adjust the button transition to a Fade Duration value of 0.01 and a darker Normal Color setting of 210, 210, 210, 255.

To make the button close the pop-up, it needs an OnClick entry; click the + button on the button's On Click panel, drag the pop-up window into the object slot, and choose SettingsPopup > Close() from the function list. Now play the game, and this button will close the pop-up window.

The pop-up window has been added to the HUD. The window is currently blank, though, so let's add controls to it.

7.3.3 Setting values using sliders and input fields

As with the buttons we made earlier, adding controls to the settings pop-up involves two main steps. You create UI elements attached to the canvas and link those objects to a script. The input controls we need are a text field and a slider, as well as a static text label to identify the slider. Choose GameObject > UI > InputField - TextMeshPro to create the text field, GameObject > UI > Slider to create the slider object, and Game-Object > UI > Text - TextMeshPro to create the text label object (see figure 7.16).

Make all three objects children of the pop-up by dragging them in the Hierarchy view and then position them as indicated in the figure, lined up in the middle of the pop-up. To make a label for the slider, set the text object to Speed and color it black.

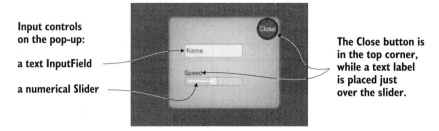

Input controls on the pop-up:

a text InputField

a numerical Slider

The Close button is in the top corner, while a text label is placed just over the slider.

Figure 7.16   Input controls added to the pop-up window

The input field is for typing in text, and the content of the big text box is shown before the player types something else; set this value to Name. You can leave the options Content Type and Line Type at their defaults; if desired, you can use Content Type to restrict typing to things like only letters or only numbers, whereas you can use Line Type to switch from a single line to multiline text.

> **WARNING**   You won't be able to click the slider if the text label covers it. Move the text object above the slider in the Hierarchy, or better yet turn off the Raycast Target setting (expand Extra Settings as shown in figure 7.7) so that mouse clicks will ignore this object.

> **WARNING**   You should probably leave the Input Field at the default size for this example, but if you do decide to shrink it, reduce only the Width, not the Height. If you set the Height to less than 30, that's too small for the text to appear.

As for the slider itself, several settings appear toward the bottom of the component inspector. Min Value is set to 0 by default; leave that. Max Value defaults to 1, but make it 2 for this example. Similarly, both Value and Whole Numbers can be left at their defaults; Value controls the starting value of the slider, and Whole Numbers constrains it to 0, 1, 2 rather than decimal values (a constraint we don't want).

And that wraps up all the objects. Now you need to write the code that the objects are linked to; add the methods shown in the following listing to SettingsPopup.

Listing 7.6   SettingsPopup methods for the pop-up's input controls

```
...
public void OnSubmitName(string name) {          Triggers when the user
    Debug.Log(name);                             types in the input field
}
public void OnSpeedValue(float speed) {          Triggers when the user
    Debug.Log($"Speed: {speed}");                adjusts the slider
}
...                                              Constructs the message using
                                                 string interpolation
```

Great! We have methods for the controls to use. Now select the input object, and at the bottom of the settings you'll see an On End Edit panel; events listed here are triggered when the user finishes typing. Add an entry to this panel, drag the pop-up to the object slot, and choose `SettingsPopup.OnSubmitName()` in the function list.

> **WARNING** Be sure to select the function in the End Edit panel's top section, Dynamic String, and not the bottom section, Static Parameters. The `OnSubmit-Name()` function appears in both sections, but selecting it under Static Parameters will send only a single string defined ahead of time; *dynamic string* refers to whatever value is typed in the input field.

Follow these same steps for the slider: look for the event panel toward the end of the component settings (in this case, the panel is OnValueChanged), click + to add an entry, drag in the settings pop-up, and choose `SettingsPopup.OnSpeedValue()` in the list of dynamic value functions.

Now both of the input controls are connected to code in the pop-up's script. Play the game, and watch the console while you move the slider or press Enter after typing input.

Saving settings between plays by using PlayerPrefs

A few methods are available for saving persistent data in Unity, and one of the simplest is called `PlayerPrefs`. Unity provides an abstracted way (that is, you don't worry about the details) to save small amounts of information that work on all platforms (with their differing filesystems). `PlayerPrefs` isn't too useful for large amounts of data (in future chapters, we'll use other methods to save the game's progress), but it's perfect for saving settings.

`PlayerPrefs` provides simple commands to get and set named values (it works a lot like a hash table or dictionary). For example, you can save the speed setting by adding the line `PlayerPrefs.SetFloat("speed", speed);` inside the `OnSpeed-Value()` method of the `SettingsPopup` script. That method will save the float in a value called `speed`.

Similarly, you'll want to initialize the slider to the saved value. Add the following code to `SettingsPopup`:

```
using UnityEngine.UI;     ◁——— Import the UI code framework.
...
[SerializeField] Slider speedSlider;
void Start() {
    speedSlider.value = PlayerPrefs.GetFloat("speed", 1);
}
...
```

Note that the `get` command has both the value to get as well as a default value in case `speed` wasn't previously saved.

Although the controls generate debug output, they still don't affect the game. Making the HUD affect the game (and vice versa) is the topic of the final section of this chapter.

7.4   *Updating the game by responding to events*

Up to now, the HUD and main game have been ignoring each other, but they ought to be communicating back and forth. That could be accomplished via script references, as you've done for other sorts of inter-object communication, but that approach would have major downsides. In particular, doing so would tightly couple the scene and the HUD; you want to keep them fairly independent of each other so that you can freely edit the game without worrying that you've broken the HUD.

To alert the UI of actions in the scene, we're going to use a broadcast messenger system. Figure 7.17 illustrates how this event messaging system works: scripts can register to listen for an event, other code can broadcast an event, and listeners will be alerted about broadcast messages. Let's go over a messaging system to accomplish that.

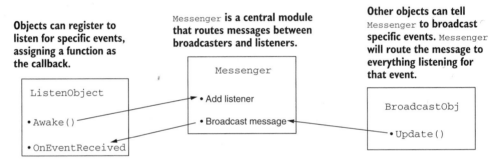

Figure 7.17   Diagram of the broadcast event system we'll implement

> **TIP**   C# does have a built-in system for handling events, so you might wonder why we don't use that. Well, the built-in event system enforces targeted messages, whereas we want a broadcast messenger system. A targeted system requires the code to know exactly where messages originate from; broadcasts can originate from anywhere.

7.4.1   *Integrating an event system*

To alert the UI of actions in the scene, we're going to use a broadcast messenger system. Although Unity doesn't have this feature built in, you can download a good code library for this purpose. This messenger system is great for providing a decoupled way of communicating events to the rest of the program. When some code broadcasts a message, that code doesn't need to know anything about the listeners, allowing for a great deal of flexibility in switching around or adding objects.

Create a script called `Messenger` and paste in the code from https://github.com/jhocking/from-unity-wiki/blob/main/Messenger.cs. Then, you also need to create a script called `GameEvent` and fill it with the code from listing 7.7.

Listing 7.7 `GameEvent` script to use with `Messenger`

```
public static class GameEvent {
   public const string ENEMY_HIT = "ENEMY_HIT";
   public const string SPEED_CHANGED = "SPEED_CHANGED";
}
```

This script defines constants for a couple of event messages; the messages are more organized this way, and you don't have to remember and type the message string all over the place.

Now the event messenger system is ready to use, so let's start using it. First, we'll communicate from the scene to the HUD, and then we'll go in the other direction.

7.4.2 Broadcasting and listening for events from the scene

Up to now, the score display has displayed a timer as a test of the text display functionality. But we want to display a count of enemies hit, so let's modify the code in `UIController`. First, delete the entire `Update()` method, because that was the test code. When an enemy dies, it will emit an event, so the following listing makes `UIController` listen for that event.

Listing 7.8 Adding event listeners to `UIController`

```
...
private int score;

void OnEnable() {
   Messenger.AddListener(GameEvent.ENEMY_HIT, OnEnemyHit);      ⟵ Declare which method responds to the ENEMY_HIT event.
}
void OnDisable() {
   Messenger.RemoveListener(GameEvent.ENEMY_HIT, OnEnemyHit);   ⟵ When an object is deactivated, remove the listener to avoid errors.
}

void Start() {
   score = 0;
   scoreLabel.text = score.ToString();    ⟵ Initialize the score to 0.

   settingsPopup.Close();
}

private void OnEnemyHit() {
   score += 1;                            ⟵ Increment the score in response to the event.
   scoreLabel.text = score.ToString();
}
...
```

First notice the `OnEnable()` and `OnDisable()` methods. Much like `Start()` and `Update()`, every `MonoBehaviour` automatically responds when the object is activated or deactivated. A listener gets added and removed in `OnEnable()`/`OnDisable()`. This listener is part of the broadcast messaging system, and it calls `OnEnemyHit()` when that message is received. `OnEnemyHit()` increments the score and then puts that value in the score display.

The event listeners are set up in the UI code, so now we need to broadcast that message whenever an enemy is hit. The code to respond to hits is in `RayShooter`, so emit the message as shown here.

Listing 7.9   Broadcast event message from `RayShooter`

```
...
if (target != null) {
   target.ReactToHit();
   Messenger.Broadcast(GameEvent.ENEMY_HIT);      ⟵┐  Message broadcast
} else {                                            │  added to hit response
   ...
```

Play the game after adding that message and watch the score display when you shoot an enemy. You should see the count going up every time you make a hit. That covers sending messages from the 3D game to the 2D interface, but we also want an example going in the other direction.

7.4.3   *Broadcasting and listening for events from the HUD*

In the previous section, an event was broadcast from the scene and received by the HUD. In a similar way, UI controls can broadcast a message that both players and enemies listen for. In this way, the settings pop-up can affect the settings of the game. Open `WanderingAI` and add this code.

Listing 7.10   Event listener added to `WanderingAI`

```
...
public const float baseSpeed = 3.0f;   ⟵┐  Base speed that is adjusted
...                                      │  by the speed setting
void OnEnable() {
   Messenger<float>.AddListener(GameEvent.SPEED_CHANGED, OnSpeedChanged);
}
void OnDisable() {
   Messenger<float>.RemoveListener(GameEvent.SPEED_CHANGED, OnSpeedChanged);
}
...
private void OnSpeedChanged(float value) {   ⟵┐  Method that was declared in
   speed = baseSpeed * value;                 │  listener for event SPEED_CHANGED
}
...
```

OnEnable() and OnDisable() add and remove, respectively, an event listener here, too, but the methods have a value this time. That value is used to set the speed of the wandering AI.

> **TIP** The code in the previous section used a generic event, but this messaging system can also pass a value along with the message. Supporting a value in the listener is as simple as adding a type definition; note the <float> added to the listener command.

Now make the same changes in FPSInput to affect the speed of the player. The code in the next listing is almost the same as that in listing 7.10, except that the player has a different number for baseSpeed.

Listing 7.11 Event listener added to `FPSInput`

```
...
public const float baseSpeed = 6.0f;        ◁──┐  This value is changed
...                                             │  from listing 7.10.
void OnEnable() {
    Messenger<float>.AddListener(GameEvent.SPEED_CHANGED, OnSpeedChanged);
}
void OnDisable() {
    Messenger<float>.RemoveListener(GameEvent.SPEED_CHANGED, OnSpeedChanged);
}
...
private void OnSpeedChanged(float value) {
    speed = baseSpeed * value;
}
...
```

Finally, broadcast the speed values from SettingsPopup in response to the slider.

Listing 7.12 Broadcast message from `SettingsPopup`

```
public void OnSpeedValue(float speed) {
    Messenger<float>.Broadcast(GameEvent.SPEED_CHANGED, speed);   ◁──┐
    ...                                                              │
                         Send slider value as <float> event. ───────┘
}
```

Now the enemy and player have their speed changed when you adjust the slider. Click Play and try it out!

Exercise: Changing the speed of spawned enemies

Currently, the speed value is updated only for enemies already in the scene and not for newly spawned enemies; new enemies aren't created at the correct speed setting. I'll leave it as an exercise for you to figure out how to set the speed on spawned enemies. Here's a hint: add a SPEED_CHANGED listener to SceneController, because that script is where enemies are spawned from.

You now know how to build a graphical interface by using the new UI tools offered by Unity. This knowledge will come in handy in all future projects, even as we explore different game genres.

Summary

- Unity has both an immediate mode GUI system as well as a newer system based on 2D sprites.
- Using 2D sprites for a GUI requires that the scene have a canvas object.
- UI elements can be anchored to relative positions on the adjustable canvas.
- Set the Active property to turn UI elements on and off.
- A decoupled messaging system is a great way to broadcast events between the interface and the scene.

Creating a third-person 3D game: Player movement and animation

In this chapter, you'll create another 3D game, but this time you'll be working in a new game genre. In chapter 2, you built a movement demo for a first-person game. Now you're going to write another movement demo, but this time it'll involve third-person movement. The most important difference is the placement of the camera relative to the player: a player sees through their character's eyes in first-person view, and the camera is placed *outside* the character in third-person view. This view is probably familiar to you from adventure games, like the long-lived *Legend of Zelda* series or the more recent *Uncharted* series. (Skip ahead to figure 8.3 if you want to see a comparison of first-person and third-person views.)

The project in this chapter is one of the more visually exciting prototypes we'll build in this book. Figure 8.1 shows how the scene will be constructed. Compare this with the diagram of the first-person scene we created in chapter 2 (figure 2.2).

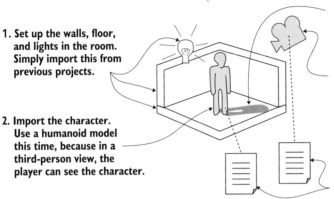

1. Set up the walls, floor, and lights in the room. Simply import this from previous projects.

2. Import the character. Use a humanoid model this time, because in a third-person view, the player can see the character.

3. Turn on shadows for this scene. We can see the player now, so shadows are important.

4. Position the camera for this demo. The camera should be outside the character, looking down at it.

5. Write movement scripts for the camera and player. First write code to orbit the camera around the character; then write code to move the character around (including jumping!).

Figure 8.1   Road map for the third-person movement demo

You can see that the room construction is the same, and the use of scripts is much the same. But the look of the player, as well as the placement of the camera, are different in each case. Again, what defines this as a third-person view is that the camera is outside the player's character and looking inward at that character. You'll use a model that looks like a humanoid character (rather than a primitive capsule) because now players can actually see themselves.

Recall that two of the types of art assets discussed in chapter 4 were 3D models and animations. As mentioned in earlier chapters, the term *3D model* is almost a synonym for *mesh object*; the 3D model is the static shape defined by vertices and polygons (that is, mesh geometry). For a humanoid character, this mesh geometry is shaped into a head, arms, legs, and so forth (see figure 8.2).

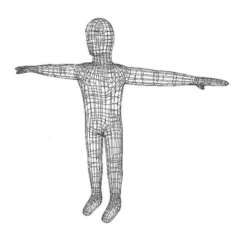

Figure 8.2   Wireframe view of the model we'll use in this chapter

As usual, we'll focus on the last step in the road map: programming objects in the scene. Here's a recap of our plan of action:

1. Import a character model into the scene.
2. Implement camera controls to look at the character.
3. Write a script that enables the player to run around on the ground.
4. Add the ability to jump to the movement script.
5. Play animations on the model based on its movements.

Copy the project from chapter 2 to modify it, or create a new Unity project (be sure it's set to 3D, not the 2D project from chapter 5) and copy over the scene file from chapter 2's project. Either way, also grab the scratch folder from this chapter's download to get the character model we'll use.

> **NOTE** You're going to build this chapter's project in the walled area from chapter 2. You'll keep the walls and lights but replace the player and all the scripts. If you need the sample files, download them from that chapter.

Assuming you're starting with the completed project from chapter 2 (the movement demo, not later projects), let's delete everything we don't need for this chapter. First, disconnect the camera from the player in the Hierarchy list (drag the camera object off the player object). Now delete the player object; if you hadn't disconnected the camera first, that would be deleted too, but what you want is to delete only the player capsule and leave the camera. Alternatively, if you already deleted the camera by accident, create a new camera object by choosing GameObject > Camera.

Delete all the scripts as well (which involves removing the script component from the camera and deleting the files in the Project view), leaving only the walls, floor, and lights.

8.1 Adjusting the camera view for third-person

Before you can write code to make the player move around, you need to put a character in the scene and set up the camera to look at that character. You'll import a faceless humanoid model to use as the player character, and then place the camera above at an angle to look down at the player obliquely. Figure 8.3 compares what the scene looks like in first-person view with what the scene will look like in third-person view (shown with a few large blocks, which you'll add in this chapter). You've prepared the scene already, so now you'll put a character model into the scene.

First-person demo   Third-person demo

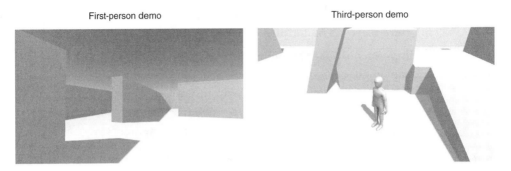

Figure 8.3   Side-by-side comparison of first-person and third-person views

8.1.1   *Importing a character to look at*

The scratch folder for this chapter's download includes both the model and the texture. As you'll recall from chapter 4, FBX is the model, and TGA is the texture. Import the FBX file into the project: either drag the file into the Project view, or right-click in the Project view and select Import New Asset.

Then look in the Inspector to adjust import settings for the model. Later in the chapter, you'll adjust imported animations, but for now, you need to make only a couple of adjustments in the Model and Materials tabs. First, go to the Model tab and change the Scale Factor value to 10 (to partially counteract the Convert Units value of 0.01) so that the model will be the correct size.

A bit farther down, you'll find the Normals option (see figure 8.4). This setting controls how lighting and shading appear on the model, using a 3D math concept known as, well, *normals*.

Set the Scale Factor to partially counteract the Convert Units value. This determines how big the model is in Unity, compared to how big it was in the 3D art tool.

Select how to handle Normals on the model.

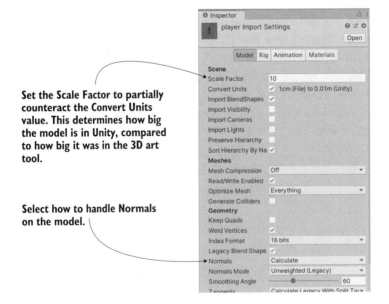

Figure 8.4   Import settings for the character model

DEFINITION   *Normals* are direction vectors sticking out of polygons that tell the computer which direction the polygon is facing. This facing direction is used for lighting calculations.

The default setting for Normals is Import, which will use the normals defined in the imported mesh geometry. But this particular model doesn't have correctly defined normals and will react in odd ways to lights. Instead, change the setting to Calculate so that Unity will calculate a vector for the facing direction of every polygon. Once you've adjusted these settings, click the Apply button in the Inspector.

Next, import the TGA file into the project (in order to assign this image as the texture on the player's material). Go to the Materials tab and click the Extract Materials button. Extract to whatever location you feel like; then select the material that appeared and drag the texture image onto the Albedo texture slot in the Inspector. Once the texture is applied, you won't see a dramatic change in the model's color (this texture image is mostly white), but shadows that are painted into the texture will improve the look of the model.

With the texture applied, drag the player model from the Project view up into the scene. Position the character at 0, 1.1, 0 so that it'll be in the center of the room and raised up to stand on the floor. We have a third-person character in the scene!

NOTE   The imported character has arms stuck straight out to each side, rather than the more natural arms-down pose. That's because animations haven't been applied yet; that arms-out position is referred to as the *T-pose*, and the standard is for animated characters to default to a T-pose before they're animated.

8.1.2   *Adding shadows to the scene*

Before we move on, I want to explain a bit about the shadow being cast by the character. We take shadows for granted in the real world, but shadows aren't guaranteed in the game's virtual world. Fortunately, Unity can handle this detail, and shadows are turned on for the default light that comes with new scenes.

Select the directional light in your scene and then look in the Inspector for the Shadow Type option. That setting (figure 8.5) is already on Soft Shadows for the default light, but notice that the menu also has a No Shadows option.

That's all you need to do to set up shadows in this project, but there's a lot more you should know about shadows in games. Calculating the shadows in a scene is a particularly time-consuming part of computer graphics, so games often cut corners and fake things in various ways to achieve the visual look desired.

The kind of shadow cast from the character is referred to as *real-time* shadow because the shadow is calculated while the game is running and moves around with moving objects. A perfectly realistic lighting setup would have all objects casting and receiving shadows in real time, but in order for the shadow calculations to run fast enough, the appearance of real-time shadows can be primitive, plus the game may even limit which lights cast shadows. Note that only the directional light is casting shadows in this scene.

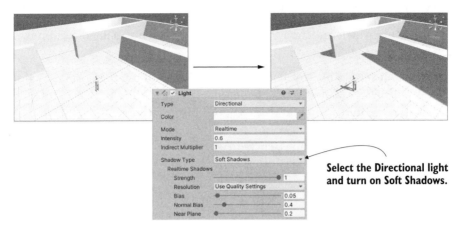

Figure 8.5   Before and after casting shadows from the directional light

Another common way of handling shadows in games is with a technique called *light-mapping*.

> **DEFINITION**   *Lightmaps* are textures applied to the level geometry, with pictures of the shadows baked into the texture image.

> **DEFINITION**   Drawing shadows onto a model's texture is referred to as *baking* the shadows.

Because these images are generated ahead of time (rather than while the game is running), they can be very elaborate and realistic. On the downside, because the shadows are generated ahead of time, they won't move. As such, lightmaps are great to use for static-level geometry, but not for dynamic objects like characters. Lightmaps are generated automatically rather than being painted by hand. The computer calculates how the lights in the scene will illuminate the level while subtle darkness builds up in corners.

Whether or not to use real-time shadows or lightmaps isn't an all-or-nothing choice. You can set the Culling Mask property on a light so that real-time shadows are used only for certain objects, allowing you to use the higher-quality lightmaps for other objects in the scene. Similarly, though you almost always want the main character to cast shadows, sometimes you don't want the character to receive shadows; all mesh objects (in either Mesh Renderer or Skinned Mesh Renderer components) have settings to cast and receive shadows. Figure 8.6 shows how those settings appear when you select the floor.

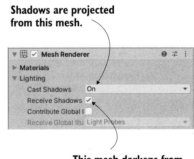

Figure 8.6   The Cast Shadows and Receive Shadows settings in the Inspector

DEFINITION *Culling* is a general term for removing unwanted things. The word comes up a lot in computer graphics in many contexts, but in this case *culling mask* is the set of objects you want to remove from shadow casting.

All right, now you understand the basics of how to apply shadows to your scenes. Lighting and shading a level can be a big topic in itself (books about level editing will often spend multiple chapters on lightmapping), but here we'll restrict ourselves to turning on real-time shadows on one light. And with that, let's turn our attention to the camera.

8.1.3 Orbiting the camera around the player character

In the first-person demo, the camera was linked to the player object in Hierarchy view so that they'd rotate together. In third-person movement, though, the player character will be facing different directions independently of the camera. Therefore, you don't want to drag the camera onto the player character in the Hierarchy view this time. Instead, the camera's code will move its position along with the character but will rotate independently of the character.

First, place the camera where you want it to be relative to the player; I went with position 0, 3.5, -3.75 to put the camera above and behind the character (reset rotation to 0, 0, 0 if needed). Then create a script called OrbitCamera and write the code from listing 8.1. Attach the script component to the camera and then drag the player character into the target slot of the script. Now you can play the scene to see the camera code in action.

Listing 8.1   Camera script for rotating around a target while looking at it

```
using System.Collections;
using System.Collections.Generic;
using UnityEngine;

public class OrbitCamera : MonoBehaviour {          Serialized reference to the
    [SerializeField] Transform target;          ◁─── object to orbit around

    public float rotSpeed = 1.5f;

    private float rotY;
    private Vector3 offset;

    void Start() {                                              Store the starting position
        rotY = transform.eulerAngles.y;                        offset between the camera
        offset = target.position - transform.position;    ◁──  and the target.
    }

    void LateUpdate() {
        float horInput = Input.GetAxis("Horizontal");          Either rotate the camera
        if (!Mathf.Approximately(horInput, 0)) {          ◁──  slowly using arrow keys . . .
            rotY += horInput * rotSpeed;
        } else {
```

Maintain the starting offset, shifted according to the camera's rotation.

```
            rotY += Input.GetAxis("Mouse X") * rotSpeed * 3;      ⊲——┐  . . . or rotate
      }                                                              │  quickly with
                                                                     │  the mouse.
      Quaternion rotation = Quaternion.Euler(0, rotY, 0);
      transform.position = target.position - (rotation * offset);
      transform.LookAt(target);    ⊲——┐
                                       │  No matter where the camera is relative
   }                                   │  to the target, always face the target.
}
```

As you're reading through the listing, note the serialized variable for `target`. The code needs to know which object to orbit the camera around, so this variable is serialized to appear within Unity's editor and have the player character linked to it. The next couple of variables are rotation values that are used in the same way as in the camera control code from chapter 2.

And an `offset` value is declared; `offset` is set within `Start()` to store the position difference between the camera and target. This way, the relative position of the camera can be maintained while the script runs. In other words, the camera will stay at the initial distance from the character regardless of which way it rotates. The remainder of the code is inside the `LateUpdate()` function.

> **TIP** Remember, `LateUpdate()` is another method provided by Mono-Behaviour and it's similar to `Update()`; it's a method run every frame. The difference, as the name implies, is that `LateUpdate()` is called on all objects after `Update()` has run on all objects. This way, you can ensure that the camera updates after the target has moved.

First, the code increments the rotation value based on input controls. This code looks at two input controls—horizontal arrow keys and horizontal mouse movement—so a conditional is used to switch between them. The code checks whether horizontal arrow keys are being pressed; if they are, then it uses that input, but if not, it checks the mouse. By checking the two inputs separately, the code can rotate at different speeds for each type of input.

Next, the code positions the camera based on the position of the target and the rotation value. The `transform.position` line is probably the biggest "aha!" in this code, because it provides crucial math that you haven't seen before. Multiplying a position vector by a quaternion results in a position that's shifted over according to that rotation (note that the rotation angle was converted to a quaternion by using `Quaternion.Euler`). This rotated position vector is then added as the offset from the character's position to calculate the position for the camera. Figure 8.7 illustrates the steps of the calculation and provides a detailed breakdown of this rather conceptually dense line of code.

> **NOTE** The more mathematically astute among you may be thinking, "Hmm, that transforming-between-coordinate-systems thing in chapter 2 . . . can't I do that here, too?" Yes, you could transform the offset position by using a rotated coordinate system to get the rotated offset, but that would require setting up the rotated coordinate system first, and it's more straightforward not to need that step.

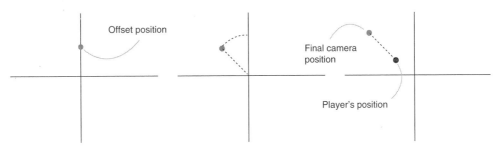

Figure 8.7   The steps for calculating the camera's position

Finally, the code uses the LookAt() method to point the camera at the target; this function points one object (not just cameras) at another object. The rotation value calculated previously was used to position the camera at the correct angle around the target, but in that step the camera was only positioned and not rotated. Thus, without the final LookAt() line, the camera position would orbit around the character but wouldn't necessarily be looking at it. Go ahead and comment out that line to see what happens.

Cinemachine

We just wrote a custom script for controlling the camera. However Unity also offers Cinemachine, a suite of tools for advanced camera control. That package would be overkill for the straightforward camera behavior in this chapter, but for many projects, Cinemachine is well worth experimenting with.

Open the Package Manager window (Window > Package Manager) and search the Unity Registry for Cinemachine. Read more about it at http://mng.bz/PXvP.

The camera has its script for orbiting around the player character; next up is code that moves the character around.

8.2 *Programming camera-relative movement controls*

Now that the character model is imported into Unity and you've written code to control the camera view, it's time to program controls for moving around the scene. Let's program camera-relative controls that'll move the character in various directions when arrow keys are pressed, as well as rotate the character to face those different directions.

What does "camera-relative" mean?

The whole notion of *camera-relative* is a bit nonobvious but crucial to understand. This is similar to the local versus global distinction mentioned in previous chapters: "left" points in different directions when you mean "left of the local object" or "left of the entire world." In a similar way, when you "move the character to the left," do you mean toward the character's left, or the left side of the screen?

The camera in a first-person game is placed inside the character and moves with it, so no distinction exists between the character's left and the camera's left. A third-person view places the camera outside the character, though, and thus the camera's left may be pointed in a different direction from the character's left. For example, the directions are literally opposite if the camera is looking at the front of the character. As such, you have to decide what you want to have happen in your specific game and controls setup.

Although games occasionally do it the other way, most third-person games make their controls camera-relative. When the player presses the left button, the character moves to the left of the screen, not the character's left. Over time and through experiments with trying out different control schemes, game designers have figured out that players find the controls more intuitive and easier to understand when "left" means "left-hand side of the screen" (which, not coincidentally, is also the player's left).

Implementing camera-relative controls involves two primary steps: first rotate the player character to face the direction of the controls and then move the character forward. Let's write the code for these two steps next.

8.2.1 *Rotating the character to face movement direction*

First you'll write code to make the character face in the direction of the arrow keys. Create a C# script called `RelativeMovement` that uses the code from listing 8.2. Drag that script onto the player character and then link the camera to the `target` property of the script component (just as you linked the character to the target of the camera script). Now the character will face different directions when you press the controls, facing directions relative to the camera, or stand still when you're not pressing any arrow keys (that is, when rotating using the mouse).

Listing 8.2 Rotating the character relative to the camera

```
using System.Collections;
using System.Collections.Generic;
using UnityEngine;

public class RelativeMovement : MonoBehaviour {
    [SerializeField] Transform target;

    void Update() {
        Vector3 movement = Vector3.zero;

        float horInput = Input.GetAxis("Horizontal");
        float vertInput = Input.GetAxis("Vertical");
        if (horInput != 0 || vertInput != 0) {

            Vector3 right = target.right;
            Vector3 forward = Vector3.Cross(right, Vector3.up);
            movement = (right * horInput) + (forward * vertInput);

            transform.rotation = Quaternion.LookRotation(movement);
        }
    }
}
```

This script needs a reference to the object to move relative to.

Start with vector (0, 0, 0) and add movement components progressively.

Handle movement only while arrow keys are pressed.

Calculate the player's forward direction by using the cross product of the target's right direction.

LookRotation() calculates a quaternion facing in that direction.

Add together the input in each direction to get the combined movement vector.

This listing starts the same way listing 8.1 did, with a serialized variable for `target`. Just as the previous script needed a reference to the object it would orbit around, this script needs a reference to the object it'll move relative to. Then we get to the `Update()` function. The first line of the function declares a `Vector3` value of 0, 0, 0. The remaining code will replace this vector if the player is pressing any buttons, but it's important to have a default value in case there isn't any input.

Next, check the input controls, just as you have in previous scripts. Here's where X and Z values are set in the movement vector, for horizontal movement around the scene. Remember that `Input.GetAxis()` returns 0 if no button is pressed, and it varies between 1 and –1 when those keys are being pressed; putting that value in the movement vector sets the movement to the positive or negative direction of that axis (the x-axis is left/right, and the z-axis is forward/backward).

The next several lines calculate the camera-relative movement vector. Specifically, we need to determine the sideways and forward directions to move in. The sideways direction is easy; the target transform has a property called `right`, and that will point to the camera's right because the camera was set as the target object. The forward direction is trickier, because the camera is angled forward and down into the ground, but we want the character to move around perpendicular to the ground. This forward direction can be determined using the cross product.

DEFINITION   The *cross product* is one kind of mathematical operation that can be done on two vectors. Long story short, the cross product of two vectors is a new vector pointed perpendicular to both input vectors. Think about the 3D coordinate axes: the z–axis is perpendicular to both the x- and y-axes. Don't confuse cross product with dot product; the dot product (explained later in the chapter) is a different but also commonly seen vector math operation.

In this case, the two input vectors are the right and up directions. Remember that we already determined the camera's right. Meanwhile, `Vector3` has several shortcut properties for common directions, including the direction pointed straight up from the ground. The vector perpendicular to both of those points in the direction the camera faces, but aligned perpendicular to the ground.

Add the inputs in each direction to get the combined movement vector. The final line of code applies that movement direction to the character by converting `Vector3` into a quaternion by using `Quaternion.LookRotation()` and assigning that value. Try running the game now to see what happens!

Smoothly rotating (interpolating) by using lerp

Currently, the character's rotation snaps instantly to different directions, but it'd look better if the character smoothly rotated. You can do so using a mathematical operation called *lerp*. First add this variable to the script:

```
public float rotSpeed = 15.0f;
```

Then replace the existing `transform.rotation` line at the end of listing 8.2 with the following code:

```
    ...
    Quaternion direction = Quaternion.LookRotation(movement);
    transform.rotation = Quaternion.Lerp(transform.rotation,
        direction, rotSpeed * Time.deltaTime);
  }
 }
}
```

Now, instead of snapping directly to the `LookRotation()` value, that value is used indirectly as the target direction to rotate toward. The `Quaternion.Lerp()` method smoothly changes between the current and target rotations.

The term for smoothly changing from one value to another is *interpolate*; you can interpolate between two of any kind of value, not just rotation values. *Lerp* is a quasi-acronym for *linear interpolation*, and Unity provides lerp methods for vectors and float values too (to interpolate positions, colors, or anything else). Quaternions also have a closely related alternative method for interpolation called *slerp* (for *spherical linear interpolation*). For slower turns, slerp rotations may look better than lerp.

Incidentally, this code uses Lerp() in a somewhat nontraditional way. Normally, the third value changes over time, but we are instead keeping the third value constant and changing the *first* value. In traditional usage, the start and end points are constant, but here we keep moving the start closer to the end, resulting in smooth interpolation toward that endpoint. This nontraditional use is explained at the Unity Answers website (http://answers.unity.com/answers/730798/view.html).

Currently, the character is rotating in place without moving; in the next section, you'll add code for moving the character around.

> **NOTE** Because moving sideways uses the same keyboard controls as orbiting the camera, the character will slowly rotate while the movement direction points sideways. This doubling up of the controls is desired behavior in this project.

8.2.2 Moving forward in that direction

As you'll recall from chapter 2, in order to move the player around the scene, you need to add a character controller component to the player object. Select the player and then choose Component > Physics > Character Controller. In the Inspector, you should slightly reduce the controller's radius to 0.4, but otherwise the default settings are all fine for this character model. Here's what you need to add in the Relative-Movement script.

Listing 8.3 Adding code to change the player's position

```
using System.Collections;
using System.Collections.Generic;
using UnityEngine;

[RequireComponent(typeof(CharacterController))]          The surrounding lines are
public class RelativeMovement : MonoBehaviour {          context for placing the
...                                                      RequireComponent() method.
public float moveSpeed = 6.0f;

private CharacterController charController;

void Start() {
    charController = GetComponent<CharacterController>();
}
    void Update() {
        ...
        movement = (right * horInput) + (forward * vertInput);
        movement *= moveSpeed;
        movement = Vector3.ClampMagnitude(movement, moveSpeed);
        ...
    }
```

A pattern you've seen in previous chapters, used for getting access to other components.

The facing directions are magnitude 1, so multiply with the desired speed value.

Limit diagonal movement to the same speed as movement along an axis.

```
movement *= Time.deltaTime;
charController.Move(movement);
    }
}
```

Always multiply movements by deltaTime to make them frame-rate independent.

If you play the game now, you will see the character (stuck in a T-pose) moving around in the scene. Pretty much the entirety of this listing is code you've already seen, so I'll review everything briefly.

First, a `RequireComponent` attribute is at the top of the code. As explained in chapter 2, `RequireComponent` will force Unity to make sure the GameObject has a component of the type passed into the command. This line is optional; you don't have to require it, but without this component, the script will have errors.

Next, a movement value is declared, followed by getting this script a reference to the character controller. As you'll recall from previous chapters, `GetComponent()` returns other components attached to the given object, and if the object to search on isn't explicitly defined, then it's assumed to be `this.gameObject.GetComponent()` (the same object as this script).

Movement values are still assigned based on the input controls, but now you also account for the movement speed. Multiply all movement axes by the movement speed, and then use `Vector3.ClampMagnitude()` to limit the vector's magnitude to the movement speed. The clamp is needed because, otherwise, diagonal movement would have a greater magnitude than movement directly along an axis (picture the sides and hypotenuse of a right triangle).

Finally, at the end, you multiply the movement values by `deltaTime` to get frame rate–independent movement (recall that *frame rate–independent* means the character moves at the same speed on different computers with different frame rates). Pass the movement values to `CharacterController.Move()` to make the movement.

This handles all the horizontal movement. Next, let's take care of vertical movement.

8.3   *Implementing the jump action*

In the previous section, you wrote code to make the character run around on the ground. In the chapter introduction, I also mentioned making the character jump, so let's do that now. Most third-person games do have a control for jumping. And even if they don't, they almost always have vertical movement from the character falling off ledges. Our code will handle both jumping and falling. Specifically, this code will have gravity pulling the player down at all times, but occasionally an upward jolt will be applied when the player jumps.

Before you write this code, let's add a few raised platforms to the scene. The game currently has nothing to jump on or fall from! Create a couple more cube objects, and then modify their positions and scale to give the player platforms to jump on. In the sample project, I added two cubes and used these settings: Position 5, 0.75, 5 and Scale 4, 1.5, 4; Position 1, 1.5, 5.5, and Scale 4, 3, 4. Figure 8.8 shows the raised platforms.

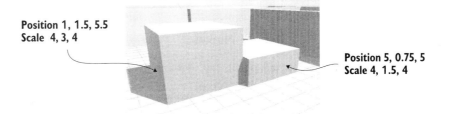

Position 1, 1.5, 5.5
Scale 4, 3, 4

Position 5, 0.75, 5
Scale 4, 1.5, 4

Figure 8.8   A couple of raised platforms added to the sparse scene

8.3.1 *Applying vertical speed and acceleration*

As mentioned when you first started writing the `RelativeMovement` script in listing 8.2, the movement values are calculated in separate steps and added to the movement vector progressively. This listing adds vertical movement to the existing vector.

Listing 8.4   Adding vertical movement to the `RelativeMovement` script

```
...
public float jumpSpeed = 15.0f;
public float gravity = -9.8f;
public float terminalVelocity = -10.0f;
public float minFall = -1.5f;

private float vertSpeed;
...
void Start() {
    vertSpeed = minFall;          ←── Initialize the vertical speed to the
    ...                                minimum falling speed at the
}                                      start of the existing function.

void Update() {
    ...
    if (charController.isGrounded) {     ←── CharacterController has an
        if (Input.GetButtonDown("Jump")) {   isGrounded property to check if
            vertSpeed = jumpSpeed;           the controller is on the ground.
        } else {
            vertSpeed = minFall;
        }                            If not on the ground, apply gravity
    } else {              ←──        until terminal velocity is reached.
        vertSpeed += gravity * 5 * Time.deltaTime;
        if (vertSpeed < terminalVelocity) {
            vertSpeed = terminalVelocity;
        }
    }
    movement.y = vertSpeed;          This is existing code, simply
                                     for reference on where the
    movement *= Time.deltaTime;   ←── new code goes.
    charController.Move(movement);
}
}
```

React to the Jump button while on the ground.

As usual, you start by adding a few new variables to the top of the script for various movement values, and initialize the values correctly. Then, you skip down to just after the big if statement for horizontal movement, where you'll add another big if statement for vertical movement. Specifically, the code will check whether the character is on the ground, because the vertical speed will be adjusted differently in each case. CharacterController includes isGrounded for checking whether the character is on the ground; this value is true if the bottom of the character controller collided with anything in the last frame.

If the character is on the ground, the vertical speed value (the private vertSpeed variable) should be reset to nothing. The character isn't falling while on the ground, so its vertical speed is 0; if the character then steps off a ledge, you're going to get a nice, natural-looking motion because the falling speed will accelerate from nothing.

> **NOTE**   Well, the vertical speed is not *exactly* 0; you're setting the value to min-Fall, a slight downward movement, so that the character will always be pressing down against the ground while running around horizontally. Some downward force is required for running up and down on uneven terrain.

The exception to this grounded speed value occurs if the jump button is clicked. In that case, the vertical speed should be set to a high number. The if statement checks Get-ButtonDown(), a new input function that works much like GetAxis() does, returning the state of the indicated input control. And much like Horizontal and Vertical input axes, the exact key assigned to Jump is defined by going to Input Manager settings under Edit > Project Settings (the default key assignment is Space—that is, the spacebar).

Getting back to the larger if condition, if the character is not on the ground, then the vertical speed should be constantly reduced by gravity. Note that this code doesn't simply set the speed value but rather decrements it; this way, it's not a constant speed but rather a downward acceleration, resulting in a realistic falling movement. Jumping will happen in a natural arc, as the character's upward speed gradually reduces to 0 and it starts falling instead.

Finally, the code makes sure the downward speed doesn't exceed terminal velocity. Note that the operator is less than and not greater than, because downward is a negative speed value. Then, after the big if statement, assign the calculated vertical speed to the y-axis of the movement vector.

And that's all you need for realistic vertical movement! By applying a constant downward acceleration when the character isn't on the ground, and adjusting the speed appropriately when the character is on the ground, the code creates nice falling behavior. But this all depends on detecting the ground correctly, and a subtle glitch remains that you need to fix.

8.3.2   *Modifying the ground detection to handle edges and slopes*

As explained in the previous section, the isGrounded property of CharacterController indicates whether the bottom of the character controller collided with anything in the last frame. Although this approach to detecting the ground works the majority of the time, you'll probably notice that the character seems to float in the air while stepping off edges.

That's because the collision area of the character is a surrounding capsule (you can see it when you select the character object), and the bottom of this capsule will still be in contact with the ground when the player steps off the edge of the platform. Figure 8.9 illustrates the problem. This won't do at all!

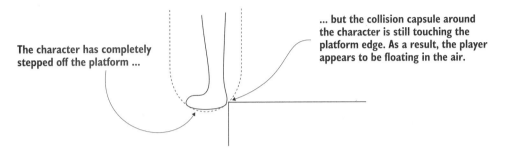

The character has completely stepped off the platform ...

... but the collision capsule around the character is still touching the platform edge. As a result, the player appears to be floating in the air.

Figure 8.9   **Diagram showing the character controller capsule touching the platform edge**

Similarly, if the character stands on a slope, the current ground detection will cause problematic behavior. Try it now by creating a sloped block against the raised platforms. Create a new cube object and set its transform values to Position -1.5, 1.5, 5, Rotation 0, 0, -25, and Scale 1, 4, 4.

If you jump onto the slope from the ground, you'll find that you can jump again from midway up the slope and thereby ascend to the top. That's because the slope touches the bottom of the capsule obliquely, and the code currently considers any collision on the bottom to be solid footing. Again, this won't do; the character should slide back down, not have a solid footing to jump from.

> **NOTE**   Sliding back down is desired only on steep slopes. On shallow slopes, such as uneven ground, you want the player to run around unaffected. If you want one to test on, make a shallow ramp by creating a cube and set it to Position 5.25, 0.25, 0.25, Rotation 0, 90, 75, Scale 1, 6, 3.

All these problems have the same root cause: checking for collisions on the bottom of the character isn't a great way to determine whether the character is on the ground. Instead, let's use raycasting to detect the ground. In chapter 3, the AI used raycasting to detect obstacles in front of it; let's use the same approach to detect surfaces below the character. Cast a ray straight down from the player's position. If it registers a hit just below the character's feet, the player is standing on the ground.

This introduces a new situation to handle: when the raycast doesn't detect ground below the character, but the character controller is colliding with the ground. As in figure 8.9, the capsule still collides with the platform while the character is walking off the edge. Figure 8.10 adds raycasting to the diagram to show what will happen now:

the ray doesn't hit the platform, but the capsule does touch the edge. The code needs to handle this special situation.

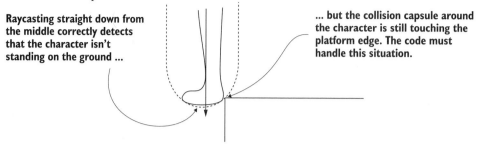

Raycasting straight down from the middle correctly detects that the character isn't standing on the ground ...

... but the collision capsule around the character is still touching the platform edge. The code must handle this situation.

Figure 8.10   Diagram of raycasting downward while stepping off a ledge

In this case, the code should make the character slide off the ledge. The character will still fall (because it's not standing on the ground), but it'll also push away from the point of collision (because it needs to move the capsule away from the platform it's hitting). Thus, the code will detect collisions with the character controller and respond to those collisions by nudging away. This listing adjusts the vertical movement with everything we just discussed.

Listing 8.5   Using raycasting to detect the ground

```
...
private ControllerColliderHit contact;          Needed to store collision
...                                             data between functions

        bool hitGround = false;
        RaycastHit hit;                         Check if the player is falling.
        if (vertSpeed < 0 &&
            Physics.Raycast(transform.position, Vector3.down, out hit)) {
            float check =
                (charController.height + charController.radius) / 1.9f;
            hitGround = hit.distance <= check;          Distance to check against
        }                                               (extend slightly beyond the
                                                        bottom of the capsule)
        if (hitGround) {
            if (Input.GetButtonDown("Jump")) {
                vertSpeed = jumpSpeed;
            } else {
                vertSpeed = minFall;
            }
        } else {
            vertSpeed += gravity * 5 * Time.deltaTime;
            if (vertSpeed < terminalVelocity) {
                vertSpeed = terminalVelocity;       Respond slightly differently
            }                                       depending on whether the character
                                                    is facing the contact point.
            if (charController.isGrounded) {
                if (Vector3.Dot(movement, contact.normal) < 0) {
                    movement = contact.normal * moveSpeed;
```

Instead of using isGrounded, check the raycasting result.

Raycasting didn't detect ground, but the capsule is touching the ground.

```
                    } else {
                        movement += contact.normal * moveSpeed;
                    }
                }
            }
        movement.y = vertSpeed;

        movement *= Time.deltaTime;                    Store the collision data
        charController.Move(movement);                  in the callback when a
    }                                                   collision is detected.

    void OnControllerColliderHit(ControllerColliderHit hit) {    ◁————————
        contact = hit;
    }
}
```

This listing contains much of the same code as the previous listing; the new code is interspersed throughout the existing movement script, and this listing needs the existing code for context. The first line adds a new variable to the top of the Relative-Movement script. This variable is used to store data about collisions between functions.

The next several lines do raycasting. This code also goes below horizontal movement but before the if statement for vertical movement. The actual Physics.Raycast() call should be familiar from previous chapters, but the specific parameters are different this time. Although the position to cast a ray from is the same (the character's position), the direction will be down this time instead of forward. Then, you check how far away the raycast was when it hit something; if the distance of the hit is at the distance of the character's feet, the character is standing on the ground, so set hitGround to true.

> **WARNING** The way the check distance is calculated is not obvious, so let's go over that in detail. First, take the height of the character controller (which is the height without the rounded ends) and then add the rounded ends. Divide this value in half because the ray was cast from the middle of the character (that is, already halfway down) to get the distance to the bottom of the character. But you really want to check a little beyond the bottom of the character to account for tiny inaccuracies in the raycasting, so divide by 1.9 instead of 2 to get a distance that's slightly too far.

Having done this raycasting, use hitGround instead of isGrounded in the if statement for vertical movement. Most of the vertical movement code will remain the same, but add code to handle when the character controller collides with the ground even though the player isn't over the ground (that is, when the player walks off the edge of the platform). We've added a new isGrounded conditional, but note that it's nested inside the hitGround conditional so that isGrounded is checked only when hitGround doesn't detect the ground.

The collision data includes a normal property (again, a normal vector says which way something is facing) that tells us the direction to move away from the point of collision. But one tricky thing is that you want the nudge away from the contact point to be handled differently depending on in which direction the player is already moving. When the previous horizontal movement is toward the platform, you want to replace that movement so that the character won't keep moving in the wrong direction; but when facing away from the edge, you want to add to the previous horizontal movement in order to keep the forward momentum away from the edge. The movement vector's facing relative to the point of collision can be determined using the dot product.

> **DEFINITION**   The *dot product* is another mathematical operation that can be done on two vectors. The dot product of two vectors ranges between N and $-N$ (with N determined by multiplying the magnitude of the input vectors). Positive N means they point in exactly the same direction, and $-N$ means they point in exactly opposite directions. Don't confuse dot product and cross product; the cross product is a different but also commonly seen vector math operation.

Vector3 includes a Dot() function to calculate the dot product of two given vectors. If you calculate the dot product between the movement vector and the collision normal, that will return a negative number when the two directions face away from each other, and a positive number when the movement and the collision face the same direction.

The very end of listing 8.5 adds a new method to the script. In the previous code, you were checking the collision normal, but where did that information come from? It turns out that collisions with the character controller are reported through a call-back function called OnControllerColliderHit() that MonoBehaviour provides; in order to respond to the collision data anywhere else in the script, that data must be stored in an external variable. That's all the method is doing here: storing the collision data in contact so that this data can be used within the Update() method.

Now the errors are corrected around platform edges and on slopes. Go ahead and play to test it out by stepping over edges and jumping onto the steep slope. This movement demo is almost complete. The character is moving around the scene correctly, so only one thing remains: animating the character out of the T-pose.

8.4   Setting up animations on the player character

Besides the more complex shape defined by mesh geometry, a humanoid character needs animations. In chapter 4, you learned that an animation is a packet of information that defines movement of the associated 3D object. The concrete example I gave was of a character walking around, and that situation is exactly what you're going to be doing now!

The character is going to run around the scene, so you'll assign animations that make the arms and legs swing back and forth. Figure 8.11 shows what the game will look like when the character has an animation playing while it moves around the scene.

A good analogy for understanding 3D animation is puppeteering: 3D models are the puppets, the animator is the puppeteer, and an animation is a recording of the puppet's movements. Animations can be created with a few approaches; most character

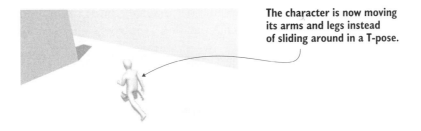

The character is now moving its arms and legs instead of sliding around in a T-pose.

Figure 8.11   Character moving around with a run animation playing

animation in modern games (certainly all the animations on this chapter's character) uses a technique called *skeletal animation*.

> **DEFINITION**   In *skeletal animation*, a series of bones is set up inside the model, and then the bones are moved around during the animation. When a bone moves, the model's surface linked to that bone moves along with it.

As the name implies, skeletal animation makes the most intuitive sense when simulating the skeleton inside a character (figure 8.12 illustrates this), but the skeleton is an abstraction that's useful anytime you want a model to bend and flex while still having a definite structure to its movement (for example, a tentacle that waves around). Although the bones move rigidly, the model surface around the bones can bend and flex.

Achieving the result illustrated in figure 8.11 involves several steps: first, define animation clips in the imported file, then set up the controller to play those animation clips, and finally, incorporate that animation controller in your code. The animations on the character model will be played back according to the movement scripts you'll write.

Of course, the very first thing you need to do, before any of those steps, is turn on the animation system. Select the player model in the Project view to see its Import

Bone (invisible in Unity)   Visible mesh

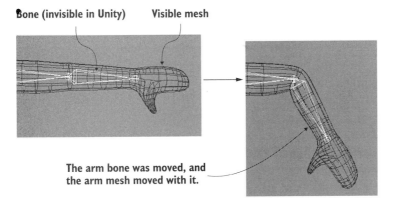

The arm bone was moved, and the arm mesh moved with it.

Figure 8.12   Skeletal animation of a humanoid character

settings in the Inspector. Select the Animation tab and make sure Import Animation is checked. Then go to the Rig tab and switch Animation Type from Generic to Humanoid (this is a humanoid character, naturally). Note that this last menu also has a Legacy setting; Generic and Humanoid are both settings within the umbrella term Mecanim.

Explaining Unity's Mecanim animation system

Unity has a sophisticated system for managing animations on models, called Mecanim. You were introduced to this animation system in chapter 6 with the caveat that we'd go into more detail later, so some of this chapter will be a review of previous explanations, now focusing on 3D animations instead of 2D.

The name *Mecanim* identifies the newer, more advanced animation system that was added to Unity as a replacement for the older animation system. The older system is still around, identified as Legacy animation, but it may be phased out in a future version of Unity, at which point Mecanim will simply be *the* animation system.

Although the animations you're going to use are all included in the same FBX file as our character model, one of the major advantages of Mecanim's approach is that you can apply animations from other FBX files to a character. For example, all of the human enemies can share a single set of animations. This has multiple advantages, including keeping all your data organized (models can go in one folder, whereas animations go in another folder) as well as saving time spent animating each separate character.

Click the Apply button at the bottom of the Inspector to lock these settings onto the imported model and then continue defining animation clips.

> **WARNING** You may notice a warning (not an error) in the console that says, `conversion warning: spine3 is between humanoid transforms`. That specific warning isn't a cause for worry; it indicates that the skeleton in the imported model has extra bones beyond the skeleton that Mecanim expects.

8.4.1   *Defining animation clips in the imported model*

The first step in setting up animations for our character is defining the various animation clips that'll be played. If you think about a lifelike character, different movements can happen at different times: sometimes the player is running around, sometimes the player is jumping on platforms, and sometimes the character is just standing there with its arms down. Each movement is a separate clip that can play individually.

Often, imported animations come as a single long timeline that can be cut up into shorter individual animations. To split up the animation clips, first select the Animations tab in the Inspector. You'll see a Clips panel, shown in figure 8.13; this lists all the defined animation clips, which initially are one imported clip. You'll notice + and − buttons at the bottom of the list; you use these buttons to add and remove clips on the list. Ultimately, you need four clips for this character, so add and remove clips as necessary while you work.

Animation clips listed by name, along with the start and end frames

+/– buttons to add more clips to the list

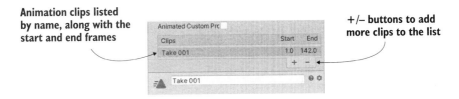

Figure 8.13   The Clips list in Animation settings

When you select a clip, information about that clip (shown in figure 8.14) will appear in the area below the list. The top of this information area shows the name of this clip, and you can type in a new name. Name the first clip idle. Define Start and End frames for this animation clip; this allows you to slice a chunk out of the longer imported animation. The idle animation goes from frames 3 to 141 of the total time-line, so enter those numbers for Start and End. Next up are the Loop settings.

> **DEFINITION**   *Loop* refers to a recording that plays over and over repeatedly. A looping animation clip is one that plays again from the start as soon as play-back reaches the end.

The idle animation loops, so select both Loop Time and Loop Pose. Incidentally, the green indicator dot tells you when the pose at the beginning of the clip matches the pose at the end for correct looping; this indicator turns yellow when the poses are somewhat off, and it turns red when the start and end poses are completely different.

Below the Loop settings is a series of settings related to the root transform. The word *root* means the same thing for skeletal animation as it does for a hierarchy connected within Unity: the root object is the base object that everything else is connected to. Thus, the *animation root* can be thought of as the base of the character, and everything else moves relative to that base.

The name of the animation clip; type a new one here.

Set Start and End frames for this clip.

Turn on looping playback (including an option to blend together the start and end poses).

This color indicates how well the start and end poses match (for looping): Green signifies very matched. Yellow signifies somewhat similar poses. Red signifies completely different poses.

Select how each component of the root will be transformed (rotation, vertical position, horizontal position).

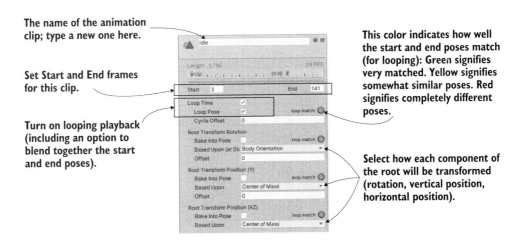

Figure 8.14   Information about the selected animation clip

A few settings can be used for setting up that base, and you may want to experiment here when working with your own animations. For our purposes, though, the three Based Upon menus should be set to Body Orientation, Center Of Mass, and Center Of Mass, in that order.

Now click Apply and you've added an idle animation clip to your character. Do the same for two more clips: walk starts at frame 144 and ends at 169, and run starts at 171 and ends at 190. All the other settings should be the same as for idle because they're also animation loops.

The fourth animation clip is jump, and the settings for that clip differ a bit. First, this isn't a loop but rather a still pose, so don't select Loop Time. Set the Start and End to 190.5 and 191; this is a single-frame pose, but Unity requires that Start and End be different. The animation preview below won't look quite right because of these tricky numbers, but this pose will look fine in the game. Click Apply to confirm the new animation clips, and then move on to the next step: creating the animator controller.

8.4.2 Creating the animator controller for these animations

The next step is to create the animator controller for this character. This step allows us to set up animation states and create transitions between those states. Various animation clips are played during different animation states, and then our scripts will cause the controller to shift between animation states.

This might seem like an odd bit of indirection—putting the abstraction of a controller between our code and the actual playing of animations. You may be familiar with systems that enable you to play animations directly from your code; indeed, the old Legacy animation system worked in exactly that way, with calls like `Play("idle")`. But this indirection enables us to share animations between models, rather than being able to play only animations that are internal to this model. In this chapter, we won't take advantage of this ability, but keep in mind that it can be helpful when you're working on a larger project. You can obtain your animations from several sources, including multiple animators, or you can buy individual animations from stores online (such as the Unity Asset Store).

Begin by creating a new animator controller asset (Assets > Create > Animator Controller—not Animation, a different sort of asset). In the Project view, you'll see an icon with a funny-looking network of lines on it (see figure 8.15); rename this asset `player`. Select the character in the scene and you'll notice this object has a component called Animator; any model that can be animated has this component, in addition to the Transform component and whatever else you've added. The Animator component has a Controller slot for you to link a specific animator controller, so drag and drop your new controller asset (and be sure to uncheck Apply Root Motion).

The animator controller is a tree of connected nodes (hence the icon on that asset) that you can see and manipulate by opening the Animator view. This is another view, just like Scene or Project (shown in figure 8.16), except this view isn't open by default. Choose Window > Animation and select Animator from this menu (be careful

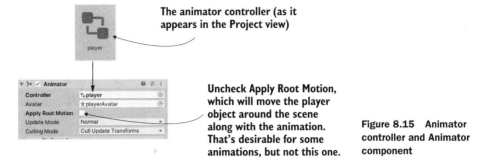

The animator controller (as it appears in the Project view)

Uncheck Apply Root Motion, which will move the player object around the scene along with the animation. That's desirable for some animations, but not this one.

Figure 8.15 Animator controller and Animator component

not to get confused with the Animation window; that's a separate selection from Animator). The node network displayed here is whichever animator controller is currently selected (or the animator controller on the selected character).

A series of number or Boolean values can be created here to control the animations. The currently active state transitions between states on the graph when these values change.

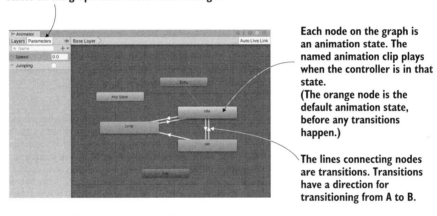

Each node on the graph is an animation state. The named animation clip plays when the controller is in that state.
(The orange node is the default animation state, before any transitions happen.)

The lines connecting nodes are transitions. Transitions have a direction for transitioning from A to B.

Figure 8.16 The Animator view with our completed animator controller

TIP Remember that you can move tabs around in Unity and dock them wherever you like to organize the interface. I like to dock the Animator right next to the Scene and Game tabs.

Initially, we have only two default nodes, for Entry and Any State. You're not going to use the Any State node. Instead, you'll drag in animation clips to create new nodes. In the Project view, click the arrow on the side of the model asset to expand that asset and see what it contains. Among the contents of this asset are the animation clips you defined (see figure 8.17), so drag those clips into the Animator view. Don't bother with the walking animation (that could be useful for other projects) and drag in idle, run, and jump.

Click the arrow to expand an asset and see its contents.

The imported model contains the various animation clips.

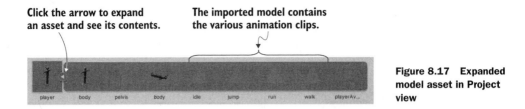

player   body   pelvis   body   idle   jump   run   walk   playerAv...

Figure 8.17   Expanded model asset in Project view

Right-click the Idle node and select Set As Layer Default State. That node will turn orange while the other nodes stay gray; the default animation state is where the network of nodes starts before the game has made any changes. You'll need to link the nodes together with lines indicating transitions between animation states; right-click a node and select Make Transition to start dragging out an arrow that you can click on another node to connect. Connect nodes in the pattern shown in figure 8.16 (be sure to make transitions in both directions for most nodes, but not from jump to run). These transition lines determine how the animation states connect to each other and control the changes from one state to another during the game.

The transitions rely on a set of controlling values, so let's create those parameters. At the top left is the Parameters tab (shown previously in figure 8.16); click that to see a panel with a + button for adding parameters. Add a float called `Speed` and a Boolean called `Jumping`. Those values will be adjusted by our code, and they'll trigger transitions between animation states. Click the transition lines to see their settings in the Inspector (see figure 8.18).

Click a transition to select it and see its settings.

Uncheck this value for most transitions, so that the animation can be interrupted.

Change this setting if the transition itself can also be interrupted.

These arrows control how long the transition takes (hold Alt while dragging the mouse to navigate this graph).

Define conditions for transitioning between animation states when the parameters change.

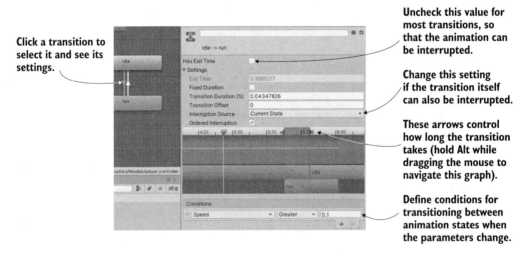

Figure 8.18   Transition settings in the Inspector

Here's where you'll adjust how the animation states change when the parameters change. For example, click the Idle-to-Run transition to adjust the conditions of that transition. Under Conditions, add one and set it to Speed, Greater, and `0.1`. Turn off

Has Exit Time (that would force playing the animation all the way through, as opposed to cutting short immediately when the transition happens). Then, click the arrow next to the Settings label to see that entire menu; other transitions should be able to interrupt this one, so change the Interruption Source menu from None to Current State. Repeat this for all the transitions in table 8.1.

Table 8.1   Conditions for all transitions in this animator controller

Transition	Condition	Interruption
Idle-to-Run	Speed greater than 0.1	Current state
Run-to-Idle	Speed less than 0.1	None
Idle-to-Jump	Jumping is true	None
Run-to-Jump	Jumping is true	None
Jump-to-Idle	Jumping is false	None

In addition to these menu-based settings is a complex visual interface, shown in figure 8.18, just above the Condition setting. This graph allows you to visually adjust the length in time of a transition. The default transition time looks fine for both transitions between Idle and Run, but all of the transitions to and from Jump should be shorter so that the character will snap faster to the jump animation. The shaded area of the graph indicates how long the transition takes; to see more detail, Alt+left-click (or Option+left-click on a Mac) the graph to pan across it and Alt+right-click to scale it (these are the same controls as navigating in the Scene view). Use the arrows on top of the shaded area to shrink it to under 4 milliseconds for all three Jump transitions.

Finally, you can perfect the animation network by selecting the animation nodes one at a time and adjusting the ordering of transitions. The Inspector will show a list of all transitions to and from that node; you can drag items in the list (their drag handles are the icon on the left side) to reorder them. Make sure the Jump transition is on top for both the Idle and Run nodes so that the Jump transition has priority over the other transitions.

While you're looking at these settings, you can also change the playback speed if the animation looks too slow (Run looks better at 1.5 speed). The animator controller is set up, so now you can operate the animations from the movement script.

8.4.3   *Writing code that operates the animator*

Finally, you'll add methods to the `RelativeMovement` script. As explained earlier, most of the work of setting up animation states is done in the animator controller; only a small amount of code is needed to operate a rich and fluid animation system, shown here.

Listing 8.6   Setting values in the Animator component

```
...
private Animator animator;
...
animator = GetComponent<Animator>();          Added inside the
...                                            Start() function

        animator.SetFloat("Speed", movement.sqrMagnitude);

        if (hitGround) {
            if (Input.GetButtonDown("Jump")) {
                vertSpeed = jumpSpeed;
            } else {
                vertSpeed = minFall;
                animator.SetBool("Jumping", false);
            }
        } else {
            vertSpeed += gravity * 5 * Time.deltaTime;
            if (vertSpeed < terminalVelocity) {
                vertSpeed = terminalVelocity;
            }
            if (contact != null ) {
                animator.SetBool("Jumping", true);
            }

            if (charController.isGrounded) {
                if (Vector3.Dot(movement, contact.normal) < 0) {
                    movement = contact.normal * moveSpeed;
                } else {
                    movement += contact.normal * moveSpeed;
                }
            }
        }
...
```

Just below the entire if statement for horizontal movement

Don't trigger this value right at the beginning of the level.

Again, much of this listing is repeated from previous listings; the animation code is a handful of lines interspersed throughout the existing movement script. Pick out the `animator` lines to find additions to make in your code.

The script needs a reference to the Animator component, and then the code sets values (either floats or Booleans) on the animator. The only somewhat nonobvious bit of code is the condition (`contact != null`) before setting the `Jumping` Boolean. That condition prevents the animator from playing the jump animation when the game starts. Even though the character is technically falling for a split second, no collision data is generated until the character touches the ground for the first time.

And there you have it! Now we have a nice third-person movement demo, with camera-relative controls and character animation playing.

Summary

- Third-person view means the camera moves around the character instead of inside the character.
- Simulated shadows, like real-time shadows and lightmaps, improve the graphics.
- Controls can be relative to the camera instead of relative to the character.
- You can improve on Unity's ground detection by casting a ray downward.
- Sophisticated animation set up with Unity's animator controller results in life-like characters.

Adding interactive devices and items within the game

This chapter covers

- Programming doors that the player can open
- Enabling physics simulations that scatter a stack of boxes
- Building collectible items that players store in their inventory
- Using code to manage game state, such as inventory data
- Equipping and using inventory items

Implementing functional items is the next topic we're going to focus on. Previous chapters covered various elements of a complete game: movement, enemies, the UI, and so forth. But our projects have lacked anything to interact with other than enemies, nor have they had much in the way of game state. In this chapter, you'll learn how to create functional devices like doors.

We'll also discuss collecting items, which involves both interacting with objects in the level and tracking game state. Games often have to track state like the player's current stats, progress through objectives, and so on. The player's inventory is an example of this sort of state, so you'll build a code architecture that can keep track of items collected by the player. By the end of this chapter, you'll have built a dynamic space that really feels like a game!

We'll start by exploring devices (such as doors) that are operated with keypresses from the player. After that, you'll write code to detect when the player collides with objects in the level, enabling interactions like pushing objects around or collecting inventory items. Then you'll set up a robust Model-View-Controller (MVC) style of code architecture to manage data for the collected inventory. Finally, you'll program interfaces to make use of the inventory for gameplay, such as requiring a key to open a door.

> **WARNING** Previous chapters were relatively self-contained and didn't technically require projects from earlier chapters, but this time some of the code listings make edits to scripts from chapter 8. If you skipped directly to this chapter, download the sample project for chapter 8 to build on that.

The example project will have these devices and items randomly strewn about the level. A polished game would have a lot of careful design behind the placement of items, but we don't need to carefully plan out a level that only tests functionality. However, even though the placement of objects doesn't require a plan, the bullet points at the start of the chapter lay out the order in which we'll implement things. As usual, the explanations build up the code step by step, but if you want to see all the finished code in one place, you can download the sample project.

9.1 Creating doors and other devices

Although levels in games consist mostly of static walls and scenery, they also usually incorporate a lot of functional devices. I'm talking about objects that the player can interact with and operate—things like lights that turn on or a fan that starts turning. The specific devices can vary a lot and are mostly limited only by your imagination, but almost all of them use the same sort of code to have the player activate the device. You'll implement a couple of examples in this chapter, and then you should be able to adapt this same code to work with all sorts of other devices.

9.1.1 Doors that open and close on a keypress

The first kind of device you'll program is a door that opens and closes, and you're going to start with operating the door by pressing a key. You could have lots of devices in a game, and lots of ways to operate those devices. We're eventually going to look at a couple of variations, but doors are the most common interactive devices found in games, and using items with a keypress is the most straightforward approach to start with.

The scene has a few spots where a gap exists between walls, so place a new object that blocks the gap. I created a new cube object and then set its transform to Position 2.5, 1.5, 17 and Scale 5, 3, 0.5, creating the door shown in figure 9.1.

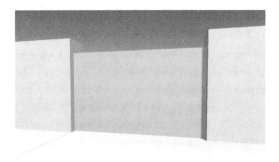

Figure 9.1   Door object fit into a gap in the wall

Create a C# script, call it DoorOpenDevice, and put that script on the door object. This code will cause the object to operate as a door.

Listing 9.1   Script that opens and closes the door on command

```csharp
using System.Collections;
using System.Collections.Generic;
using UnityEngine;

public class DoorOpenDevice : MonoBehaviour {
    [SerializeField] Vector3 dPos;              ← Amount to offset the position
                                                  by when the door opens

    private bool open;      ← Boolean to keep track of
                              the open state of the door
    public void Operate() {
        if (open) {                             ← Open or close the door
            Vector3 pos = transform.position - dPos;   depending on the open state.
            transform.position = pos;
        } else {
            Vector3 pos = transform.position + dPos;
            transform.position = pos;
        }
        open = !open;
    }
}
```

The first variable defines the offset that's applied when the door opens. The door will move this amount when it opens, and then it will subtract this amount when it closes. The second variable is a private Boolean for tracking whether the door is open or closed. In the Operate() method, the object's transform is set to a new position, adding or subtracting the offset depending on whether the door is already open; then open is toggled on or off.

As with other serialized variables, dPos appears in the Inspector. But this is a Vector3 value, so instead of one input box, we have three, all under the one variable name. Type in the relative position of the door when it opens; I decided to have the door slide down to open, so the offset is 0, -2.9, 0 (because the door object has a height of 3, moving down 2.9 leaves a tiny sliver of the door sticking up out of the floor).

> **NOTE** The transform is applied instantly, but you may prefer seeing the movement when the door opens. As mentioned in chapter 3, you can use tweens to make objects move smoothly over time. The word *tween* means different things in different contexts, but in game programming it refers to code commands that cause objects to move around; appendix D mentions tweening systems for Unity.

Other code needs to call Operate() to make the door open and close (the single function call handles both cases). You don't yet have that other script on the player, so writing that is the next step.

9.1.2 Checking distance and facing before opening the door

Create a new script and name it DeviceOperator. This listing implements a control key that operates nearby devices.

Listing 9.2 Device control key for the player

```
using System.Collections;
using System.Collections.Generic;
using UnityEngine;

public class DeviceOperator : MonoBehaviour {        How far away from the
  public float radius = 1.5f;                         player to activate devices

  void Update() {                                     Respond when the named
    if (Input.GetKeyDown(KeyCode.C)) {                key is pressed down.
      Collider[] hitColliders =
          Physics.OverlapSphere(transform.position, radius);
      foreach (Collider hitCollider in hitColliders) {
        hitCollider.SendMessage("Operate",
          SendMessageOptions.DontRequireReceiver);    SendMessage() tries to
      }                                               call the named function,
    }                                                 regardless of the target's
  }                                                   type.
}
```

OverlapSphere() returns a list of nearby objects.

The majority of this listing should look familiar, but a crucial new method is at the center. First, establish a value for how far away to operate devices from. Then, in the Update() function, look for keyboard input. Just as the RelativeMovement script uses GetButtonDown() and a button from the project's input settings, this time you'll use GetKeyDown() for input from a specific letter key.

Now we get to the crucial new method: `OverlapSphere()`. This method returns an array of all objects that are within a given distance of a given position. By passing in the position of the player and the `radius` variable, this method detects all objects near the player. What you do with this list can vary (perhaps you set off a bomb and want to apply an explosive force), but in this situation you want to attempt to call `Operate()` on all nearby objects.

That method is called via `SendMessage()` instead of the typical dot notation, an approach you also saw with UI buttons in previous chapters. As was the case there, you use `SendMessage()` because you don't know the exact type of the target object, and that command works on all GameObjects. But this time you're going to pass the `Dont-RequireReceiver` option to the method. This is because most of the objects returned by `OverlapSphere()` won't have an `Operate()` method; normally, `SendMessage()` prints an error message if nothing in the object received the message, but in this case the error messages would be distracting because you already know most objects will ignore the message.

Once the code is written, you can attach this script to the player object. Now you can open and close the door by standing near it and pressing the key.

You can fix one little detail. Currently, it doesn't matter which way the player is facing, as long as the player is close enough. But you could also adjust the script to operate only devices the player is facing, so let's do that. Recall from chapter 8 that you can calculate the dot product for checking facing. That's a mathematical operation done on a pair of vectors that returns a range between $-N$ and N, with N meaning they point in exactly the same direction and $-N$ when they point in exactly opposite directions. Well, N is 1 when the vectors are normalized, resulting in an easy-to-work-with range from -1 to 1.

> **DEFINITION** When a vector is *normalized*, the result continues to point in the same direction, but its length (also referred to as its *magnitude*) is adjusted to 1. Many mathematical operations work best with normalized vectors, so Unity provides properties that return normalized vectors.

Here is the new code in the `DeviceOperator` script.

Listing 9.3   Adjusting `DeviceOperator` to operate only devices that the player faces

```
...
foreach (Collider hitCollider in hitColliders) {
    Vector3 hitPosition = hitCollider.transform.position;
    hitPosition.y = transform.position.y;          ⟵──── Vertical correction so
                                                          the direction won't
                                                          point up or down
    Vector3 direction = hitPosition - transform.position;
    if (Vector3.Dot(transform.forward, direction.normalized) > .5f) {  ⟵──┐
        hitCollider.SendMessage("Operate",
            SendMessageOptions.DontRequireReceiver);      Send the message only
    }                                                     when facing the right
}                                                                direction.
}
...
```

To use the dot product, you first determine the direction to check against. That would be the direction from the player to the object; make a direction vector by subtracting the position of the player from the position of the object (with the vertical position corrected, so that the direction will be horizontal instead of pointing down at the lowered door). Then call `Vector3.Dot()` with both that direction vector and the forward direction of the player. When the dot product is close to 1 (specifically, this code checks whether it is greater than 0.5), the two vectors are close to pointing in the same direction.

With this adjustment made, the door won't open and close when the player faces away from it, even if the player is close. And this same approach to operating devices can be used with any sort of device. To demonstrate that flexibility, let's create another example device.

9.1.3 *Operating a color-changing monitor*

We've created a door that opens and closes, but that same device-operating logic can be used with any sort of device. You're going to create another device that's operated in the same way; this time, you'll create a color-changing display on the wall.

Create a new cube and place it so that one side is barely sticking out of the wall. For example, I went with Position 10.9, 1.5, -5. Now create a new script called `ColorChangeDevice` and attach that script (listing 9.4) to the wall display. Run up to the wall monitor and press the same "operate" key as used with the door; you should see the display change color, as figure 9.2 illustrates.

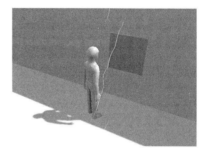

Figure 9.2 Color-changing display embedded in the wall

> **Listing 9.4 Script for a device that changes color**

```
using System.Collections;
using System.Collections.Generic;
using UnityEngine;

public class ColorChangeDevice : MonoBehaviour {
    public void Operate() {
        Color random = new Color(Random.Range(0f,1f),
            Random.Range(0f,1f), Random.Range(0f,1f));
        GetComponent<Renderer>().material.color = random;
    }
}
```

Declare a method with the same name as the door script.

The numbers are RGB values that range from 0 to 1.

The color is set in the material attached to the object.

To start with, declare the same function name as the door script used. `Operate` is the function name that the device operator script uses, so you need to use that name for it to be triggered. Inside this function, the code assigns a random color to the object's material (remember, color isn't an attribute of the object itself, but rather the object has a material, and that material can have a color).

> **NOTE** Although the color is defined with Red, Blue, and Green components, as is standard in most computer graphics, the values in Unity's `Color` object vary between `0` and `1`, instead of `0` and `255`, as is common in most places (including Unity's color picker UI).

All right, so we've gone over one approach to interacting with devices in the game and have even implemented a couple of devices to demonstrate. Another way of interacting with items is by bumping into them, so let's go over that next.

9.2   Interacting with objects by bumping into them

In the previous section, devices were operated by keyboard input from the player, but that's not the only way players can interact with items in the level. Another straightforward approach is to respond to collisions with the player. Unity handles most of that for you, by having collision detection and physics built into the game engine. Unity will detect collisions for you, but you still need to program the object to respond.

We'll go over three collision responses that are useful for games:

- Push away and fall over
- Trigger a device in the level
- Disappear on contact (for item pickups)

9.2.1   Colliding with physics-enabled obstacles

To start, you're going to create a pile of boxes and then cause the pile to collapse when the player runs into it. Although the physics calculations involved are complicated, Unity has all of that built in and will scatter the boxes in a realistic way.

By default, Unity doesn't use its physics simulation to move objects around. That can be enabled by adding a Rigidbody component to the object. This concept was first discussed in chapter 3, because the enemy's fireballs also needed a Rigidbody component. As I explained in that chapter, Unity's physics system will act only on objects that have a Rigidbody component. Look for Rigidbody by clicking Add Component and going to the Physics (not Physics 2D!) menu.

Create a new cube object and then add a Rigidbody component to it. Create several such cubes and position them in a neat stack. For example, in the sample download, I created five boxes and stacked them into two tiers (see figure 9.3).

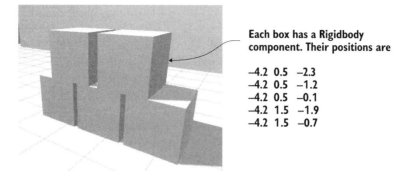

Each box has a Rigidbody
component. Their positions are

–4.2 0.5 –2.3
–4.2 0.5 –1.2
–4.2 0.5 –0.1
–4.2 1.5 –1.9
–4.2 1.5 –0.7

Figure 9.3   Stack of five boxes to collide with

The boxes are now ready to react to physics forces. To have the player apply a force to the boxes, make the small addition shown in the following listing to the `Relative-Movement` script (this is one of the scripts written in chapter 8) that's on the player.

Listing 9.5   Adding physics force to the `RelativeMovement` script

```
...
public float pushForce = 3.0f;        ⟵  Amount of force to apply
...
void OnControllerColliderHit(ControllerColliderHit hit) {        Check if the
   contact = hit;                                                 collided object has a
                                                                  Rigidbody to receive
   Rigidbody body = hit.collider.attachedRigidbody;    ⟵        physics forces.
   if (body != null && !body.isKinematic) {
      body.velocity = hit.moveDirection * pushForce;   ⟵   Apply velocity to
   }                                                         the physics body.
}
...
```

There's not much to explain about this code: whenever the player collides with something, check whether the collided object has a Rigidbody component. If so, apply a velocity to that Rigidbody.

Play the game and then run into the pile of boxes; you should see them scatter around realistically. And that's all you have to do to activate physics simulation on a stack of boxes in the scene! Unity has physics simulation built in, so you don't have to write much code. That simulation can cause objects to move around in response to collisions, but another possible response is firing trigger events, so let's use those trigger events to control the door.

9.2.2   Operating the door with a trigger object

Previously, the door was operated by a keypress. This time it will open and close in response to the character colliding with another object in the scene.

Create yet another door and place it in another wall gap (I duplicated the previous door and moved the new door to -2.5, 1.5, -17). Now create a new cube to use for the trigger object, and select the Is Trigger check box for the collider (this step was illustrated when making the fireball in chapter 3). In addition, set the trigger object to the Ignore Raycast layer; the top-right corner of the Inspector has a Layer menu. Finally, you should turn off Cast Shadows from this object (remember, this setting is under Mesh Renderer when you select the object).

> **WARNING** These tiny steps are easy to miss but important: To use an object as a trigger, be sure to turn on Is Trigger. In the Inspector, look for the check box in the Collider component. Also, change the layer to Ignore Raycast so that the trigger object won't show up in raycasting.

> **NOTE** When trigger objects were introduced in chapter 3, the object needed to have a Rigidbody component added. Rigidbody isn't required for the trigger this time because the trigger will be responding to the player (versus colliding with a wall, the earlier situation). For triggers to work, either the trigger or the object entering the trigger needs to have Unity's physics system enabled; a Rigidbody component fulfills this requirement, but so does the player's character controller.

Position and scale the trigger object so that it both encompasses the door and surrounds an area around the door; I used Position -2.5, 1.5, -17 (same as the door) and Scale 7.5, 3, 6. Additionally, you may want to assign a semitransparent material to the object so that you can visually distinguish trigger volumes from solid objects. Create a new material by using the Assets menu, and select the new material in the Project view. Looking at the Inspector, the top setting is Rendering Mode (currently set to the default value of Opaque); select Transparent in this menu.

Now click the Albedo color swatch to bring up the Color Picker window. Pick green in the main part of the window, and lower the alpha by using the bottom slider. Drag this material from Project onto the object; figure 9.4 shows the trigger with this material.

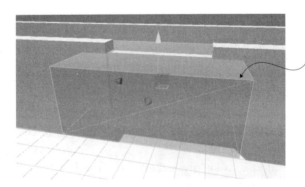

Box with a semitransparent material surrounding the door it triggers

Figure 9.4 Trigger volume surrounding the door it will trigger

DEFINITION *Triggers* are often referred to as *volumes* rather than objects to conceptually differentiate solid objects from objects you can move through.

Play the game now and you can freely move through the trigger volume. Unity still registers collisions with the object, but those collisions don't affect the player's movement anymore. To react to the collisions, you need to write code. Specifically, you want this trigger to control the door. Create a new script called `DeviceTrigger`.

Listing 9.6 Code for a trigger that controls a device

```
using System.Collections;
using System.Collections.Generic;
using UnityEngine;

public class DeviceTrigger : MonoBehaviour {          List of target objects that
    [SerializeField] GameObject[] targets;            this trigger will activate

    void OnTriggerEnter(Collider other) {             OnTriggerEnter() is called
        foreach (GameObject target in targets) {      when another object enters
            target.SendMessage("Activate");           the trigger volume . . .
        }
    }

    void OnTriggerExit(Collider other) {              . . . whereas OnTriggerExit()
        foreach (GameObject target in targets) {      is called when an object
            target.SendMessage("Deactivate");         leaves the trigger volume.
        }
    }
}
```

This listing defines an array of target objects for the trigger; even though it'll be a list of only one most of the time, it's possible to have multiple devices controlled by a single trigger. Loop through the array of targets to send a message to all the targets. This loop happens inside the `OnTriggerEnter()` and `OnTriggerExit()` methods. These functions are called once when another object first enters and exits the trigger (as opposed to being called over and over while the object is inside the trigger volume).

Notice that the messages being sent are different from before; now you need to define the `Activate()` and `Deactivate()` functions on the door. Add the code in the next listing to the `DoorOpenDevice` script.

Listing 9.7 Adding activate and deactivate functions to the `DoorOpenDevice` script

```
. . .
public void Activate() {              Open the door only if it isn't already open.
    if (!open) {
        Vector3 pos = transform.position + dPos;
        transform.position = pos;
        open = true;
    }
}
```

```
public void Deactivate() {                    Close the door only if it isn't already closed.
  if (open) {                      ◄─────
    Vector3 pos = transform.position - dPos;
    transform.position = pos;
    open = false;
  }
}
...
```

The new `Activate()` and `Deactivate()` methods are much the same code as the `Operate()` method from earlier, except now separate functions open and close the door instead of only one function that handles both cases.

With all the necessary code in place, you can now use the trigger volume to open and close the door. Put the `DeviceTrigger` script on the trigger volume and then link the door to the `targets` property of that script; in the Inspector, first set the size of the array and then drag objects from the Hierarchy view over to slots in the targets array. Because you have only one door that you want to control with this trigger, type 1 in the array's Size field and then drag that door into the target slot.

With all of this done, play the game and watch what happens to the door when the player walks toward and away from it. It'll open and close automatically as the player enters and leaves the trigger volume.

That's another great way to put interactivity into levels! But this trigger volume approach doesn't work only with devices like doors; you can also use this approach to make collectible items.

Exercise: Trigger devices in 2D platformer

In this chapter, you've implemented triggers in a 3D game, but the logic is almost exactly the same to do this in a 2D game; you'd just be reacting to 2D colliders instead, using OnTrigger2D. As an exercise, go back to the 2D platform game from chapter 6 and implement trigger volumes and devices in that platformer.

9.2.3 Collecting items scattered around the level

Many games include items that can be picked up by the player. These items include equipment, health packs, and power-ups. The basic mechanism of colliding with items to pick them up is simple; most of the complicated stuff happens after items are picked up, but we'll get to that a bit later.

Create a sphere object and place it hovering at about waist height in an open area of the scene. Make the object small (like Scale 0.5, 0.5, 0.5), but otherwise prepare it as you did with the large trigger volume. Select the Is Trigger setting in the collider, set the object to the Ignore Raycast layer, and then create a new material to give the object a distinct color. Because the object doesn't cover much, you don't need to make it semitransparent, so don't turn down the alpha slider this time. Also, as mentioned in chapter 8, settings are available for removing the shadows cast from this object; whether to use the shadows is a judgment call, but for small pickup items like this, I prefer to turn them off.

Now that the object in the scene is ready, create a new script to attach to that object. Call the script `CollectibleItem`.

```
using System.Collections;
using System.Collections.Generic;
using UnityEngine;

public class CollectibleItem : MonoBehaviour {        Type the name of this
    [SerializeField] string itemName;            ◁──── item in the Inspector.

    void OnTriggerEnter(Collider other) {
        Debug.Log($"Item collected: {itemName}");
        Destroy(this.gameObject);
    }
}
```

This script is extremely short and simple. Give the item a `name` value so that different items can be in the scene. `OnTriggerEnter()` destroys itself. A debug message is also being printed to the console; eventually it will be replaced with useful code.

> **WARNING** Be sure to call `Destroy()` on `this.gameObject` and not `this`! Don't get confused between the two; `this` refers only to this script component, whereas `this.gameObject` refers to the object the script is attached to.

Back in Unity, the variable you added to the code should become visible in the Inspector. Type in a name to identify this item; I went with `energy` for my first item. Then duplicate the item a few times and change the name of the copies; I also created `ore`, `health`, and `key` (these names must be exact because they'll be used in code later). Also create separate materials for each item to give them distinct colors: I used light blue energy, dark gray ore, pink health, and yellow key.

> **TIP** Rather than a name, as we've done here, items in more complex games often have an identifier used to look up further data. For example, one item might be assigned ID 301, and ID 301 correlates to a certain display name, image, description, and so forth.

Now make prefabs of the items so you can clone them throughout the level. In chapter 3, I explained that dragging an object from the Hierarchy view down to the Project view will turn that object into a prefab; do that for all four items.

> **NOTE** The object's name will turn blue in the Hierarchy list; blue names indicate objects that are instances of a prefab. Right-click a prefab instance to pick Select Prefab and select the prefab that the object is an instance of.

Drag out instances of the prefabs and place the items in open areas of the level; even drag out multiple copies of the same item to test with. Play the game and run into items to collect them. That's pretty neat, but at the moment nothing happens when you collect an item. You're going to start keeping track of the items collected; to do that, you need to set up the inventory code structure.

9.3   Managing inventory data and game state

Now that you've programmed the features of collecting items, you need background data managers (similar to web coding patterns) for the game's inventory. The code you'll write will be similar to the MVC architectures behind many web applications. The advantage of these data managers is in decoupling data storage from the objects that are displayed onscreen, allowing for easier experimentation and iterative development. Even when the data and/or displays are complex, changes in one part of the application don't affect other parts of the application.

That said, such structures vary a lot among games, because not every game has the same data-management needs. For example, a role-playing game will have high data-management needs, so you probably want to implement something like an MVC architecture. A puzzle game, though, has little data to manage, so building a complex decoupled structure of data managers would be overkill. Instead, the game state can be tracked in the scene-specific controller objects (indeed, that's how we handled game state in previous chapters).

In this project, you need to manage the player's inventory. Let's set up the code structure needed for that.

9.3.1   Setting up player and inventory managers

The general idea here is to split up all the data management into separate, well-defined modules, with each managing its own area of responsibility. You're going to create separate modules to maintain player state in `PlayerManager` (things like the player's health) and maintain the inventory list in `InventoryManager`. These data managers will behave like the *model* in MVC; the *controller* is an invisible object in most scenes (it wasn't needed here, but recall `SceneController` in previous chapters), and the rest of the scene is analogous to the *view*.

A higher-level *manager of managers* will keep track of all the separate modules. Besides keeping a list of all the managers, this higher-level manager will control the life cycles of the various managers—in particular, initializing them at the start. All the other scripts in the game will be able to access these centralized modules by going through the main manager. Specifically, other code can use static properties in the main manager to connect with the specific module desired.

For the main manager to reference other modules in a consistent way, these modules must all inherit properties from a common base. You're going to do that with an interface; many programming languages (including C#) allow you to define a sort of blueprint that other classes need to follow. Both `PlayerManager` and `InventoryManager` will

Design patterns for accessing centralized shared modules

Over the years, a variety of design patterns have emerged to solve the problem of connecting parts of a program to centralized modules that are shared throughout the program. For example, the Singleton pattern was enshrined in the original "Gang of Four" book about design patterns.

But that pattern has fallen out of favor with many software engineers, so they use alternative patterns like service locator and dependency injection. In my code, I use a compromise between the simplicity of static variables and the flexibility of a service locator.

This design leaves the code simple to use while also allowing for swapping in different modules. For example, requesting `InventoryManager` by using a singleton will always refer to the exact same class, and thus will tightly couple your code to that class; conversely, requesting `Inventory` from a service locator leaves the option to return either `InventoryManager` or `DifferentInventoryManager`. Sometimes it's handy to be able to switch between slightly different versions of the same module (deploying the game on different platforms, for example).

implement a common interface (called `IGameManager` in this case), and then the main `Managers` object can treat both `PlayerManager` and `InventoryManager` as type `IGameManager`. Figure 9.5 illustrates the setup I'm describing.

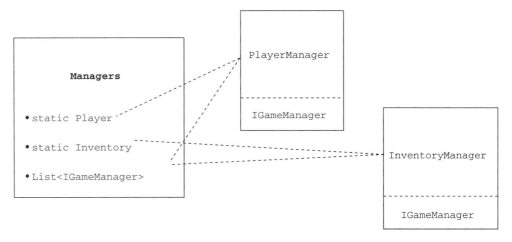

Figure 9.5 Diagram of the various modules and how they're related

Incidentally, whereas all of the code architecture I've been talking about consists of invisible modules that exist in the background, Unity still requires scripts to be linked to objects in the scene in order to run that code. As you've done with the scene-specific controllers in previous projects, you're going to create an empty GameObject to link these data managers to.

9.3.2 *Programming the game managers*

All right, so that explains all the concepts behind what you'll do; it's time to write the code. To start, create a new script called `IGameManager`.

Listing 9.9   Base interface that the data managers will implement

```
public interface IGameManager {
    ManagerStatus status {get;}          ◁──┐  This is an enum you
                                             │  need to define.
    void Startup();
}
```

Hmm, there's barely any code in this file. Note that it doesn't even inherit from `MonoBehaviour`; an interface doesn't do anything on its own and exists only to impose structure on other classes. This interface declares one property (a variable that has a getter function) and one method; both need to be implemented in any class that implements this interface. The `status` property tells the rest of the code whether this module has completed its initialization. The purpose of `Startup()` is to handle the initialization of the manager, so initialization tasks happen there and the function sets the manager's status.

Notice that the property is of type `ManagerStatus`. That's an enum you haven't written yet, so create the `ManagerStatus` script.

Listing 9.10   `ManagerStatus`: possible states for `IGameManager` status

```
public enum ManagerStatus {
    Shutdown,
    Initializing,
    Started
}
```

This is another file with barely any code in it. This time, you're listing the possible states that managers can be in, thereby enforcing that the `status` property will always be one of these listed values.

Now that `IGameManager` is written, you can implement it in other scripts. Listings 9.11 and 9.12 contain code for `InventoryManager` and `PlayerManager`, respectively.

Listing 9.11   `InventoryManager`

```
using System.Collections;
using System.Collections.Generic;
using UnityEngine;

public class InventoryManager : MonoBehaviour, IGameManager {
    public ManagerStatus status {get; private set;}          ◁──┐

    public void Startup() {
        Debug.Log("Inventory manager starting...");          ◁──┐
```

Property can be read from anywhere but set only within this script.

Any long-running startup tasks go here.

```
        status = ManagerStatus.Started;
    }
}
```
> For long-running tasks, use status Initializing instead.

Listing 9.12 PlayerManager

```
using System.Collections;
using System.Collections.Generic;
using UnityEngine;

public class PlayerManager : MonoBehaviour, IGameManager {
    public ManagerStatus status {get; private set;}

    public int health {get; private set;}
    public int maxHealth {get; private set;}

    public void Startup() {
        Debug.Log("Player manager starting...");

        health = 50;
        maxHealth = 100;

        status = ManagerStatus.Started;
    }

    public void ChangeHealth(int value) {
        health += value;
        if (health > maxHealth) {
            health = maxHealth;
        } else if (health < 0) {
            health = 0;
        }

        Debug.Log($"Health: {health}/{maxHealth}");
    }
}
```
> Both inherit a class and implement an interface.

> These values could be initialized with saved data.

> Other scripts can't set health directly but can call this function.

For now, `InventoryManager` is a shell that will be filled in later, whereas `Player-Manager` has all the functionality needed for this project. These managers both inherit from the `MonoBehaviour` class and implement the `IGameManager` interface. That means the managers gain all the functionality of `MonoBehaviour` while also needing to implement the structure imposed by `IGameManager`. The structure in `IGameManager` was one property and one method, so the managers define those two things.

The `status` property was defined so that the status could be read from anywhere (the getter is public) but set only within this script (the setter is private). The method in the interface is `Startup()`, so both managers define that function. In both managers, initialization completes right away (`InventoryManager` doesn't do anything yet, whereas `PlayerManager` sets a couple of values), so the status is set to `Started`. But data modules may have long-running tasks as part of their initialization (such as loading saved data), in which case `Startup()` will launch those tasks and set the manager's status to `Initializing`. Change `status` to `Started` after those tasks complete.

Great! We're finally ready to tie everything together with a main manager of managers. Create one more script and call it `Managers`.

Listing 9.13   The manager of managers!

```
using System.Collections;
using System.Collections.Generic;
using UnityEngine;                                    Ensure that the various
                                                      managers exist.
[RequireComponent(typeof(PlayerManager))]     ⊲────┘
[RequireComponent(typeof(InventoryManager))]          Static properties
                                                      that other code
public class Managers : MonoBehaviour {               uses to access
    public static PlayerManager Player {get; private set;}   ⊲──┘ managers
    public static InventoryManager Inventory {get; private set;}

    private List<IGameManager> startSequence;   ⊲──┐ The list of managers to loop through
                                                   │ during the startup sequence
    void Awake() {
        Player = GetComponent<PlayerManager>();
        Inventory = GetComponent<InventoryManager>();

        startSequence = new List<IGameManager>();
        startSequence.Add(Player);
        startSequence.Add(Inventory);

        StartCoroutine(StartupManagers());   ⊲──┐ Launch the startup
    }                                           │ sequence asynchronously.

    private IEnumerator StartupManagers() {
        foreach (IGameManager manager in startSequence) {
            manager.Startup();
        }

        yield return null;

        int numModules = startSequence.Count;
        int numReady = 0;                          Keep looping until all
                                                   managers are started.
        while (numReady < numModules) {   ⊲──┘
            int lastReady = numReady;
            numReady = 0;

            foreach (IGameManager manager in startSequence) {
                if (manager.status == ManagerStatus.Started) {
                    numReady++;
                }
            }

            if (numReady > lastReady)
                Debug.Log($"Progress: {numReady}/{numModules}");
            yield return null;               ⊲──┐
        }                                       │ Pause for one frame
                                                │ before checking again.
        Debug.Log("All managers started up");
    }
}
```

The most important parts of this pattern are the static properties at the top. Those enable other scripts to use syntax like `Managers.Player` or `Managers.Inventory` to access the various modules. Those properties are initially empty, but they're filled immediately when the code runs in the `Awake()` method.

> **TIP** Like `Start()` and `Update()`, `Awake` is another method automatically provided by `MonoBehaviour`. It's similar to `Start()`, running once when the code first starts running. But in Unity's code-execution sequence, `Awake()` runs even sooner than `Start()`, allowing for initialization tasks that absolutely must run before any other code modules.

The `Awake()` method also lists the startup sequence, and then launches the coroutine to start all the managers. Specifically, the function creates a `List` and then uses `List.Add()` to add the managers.

> **DEFINITION** `List` is a collection data structure provided by C#. List objects are similar to arrays: they're declared with a specific type and store a series of entries in sequence. But a list can change size after being created, whereas arrays are created at a static size that can't change later.

Because all the managers implement `IGameManager`, this code can list them all as that type and can call the `Startup()` method defined in each. The startup sequence is run as a coroutine so that it will run asynchronously, with other parts of the game proceeding too (for example, a progress bar animated on a startup screen).

The startup function first loops through the entire list of managers and calls `Startup()` on each one. Then it enters a loop that keeps checking whether the managers have started up and won't proceed until they all have. Once all the managers are started, the startup function finally alerts us to this fact before finally completing.

> **TIP** The managers you wrote earlier have such simple initialization that no waiting is required, but in general this coroutine-based startup sequence can elegantly handle long-running asynchronous startup tasks like loading saved data.

Now all of the code structure has been written. Go back to Unity and create a new empty GameObject; as usual with these sorts of empty code objects, position it at 0, 0, 0 and give the object a descriptive name like `Game Managers`. Attach the `Managers`, `PlayerManager`, and `InventoryManager` script components to this new object.

When you play the game now, no visible change in the scene should occur, but in the console, you should see a series of messages logging the progress of the startup sequence. Assuming the managers are starting up correctly, it's time to start programming the inventory manager.

9.3.3 *Storing inventory in a collection object: List vs. Dictionary*

The list of items collected could also be stored as a `List` object. This listing adds a list of items to `InventoryManager`.

Listing 9.14 Adding items to `InventoryManager`

```
...
private List<string> items;

public void Startup() {
    Debug.Log("Inventory manager starting...");

    items = new List<string>();     ⟵—— Initialize the empty item list.

    status = ManagerStatus.Started;
}

private void DisplayItems() {        ⟵┐  Print console message of
    string itemDisplay = "Items: ";     │  the current inventory.
    foreach (string item in items) {
        itemDisplay += item + " ";
    }
    Debug.Log(itemDisplay);
}

public void AddItem(string name) {   ⟵┐  Other scripts can't manipulate the
    items.Add(name);                     │  item list directly but can call this.

    DisplayItems();
}
...
```

This listing makes two key additions to `InventoryManager`: a `List` object to store items in and a public method, `AddItem()`, that other code can call. This function adds the item to the list and then prints the list to the console. Now let's make a slight adjustment in the `CollectibleItem` script to call the new `AddItem()` method.

Listing 9.15 Using the new `InventoryManager` in `CollectibleItem`

```
...
void OnTriggerEnter(Collider other) {
    Managers.Inventory.AddItem(itemName);
    Destroy(this.gameObject);
}
...
```

Now when you run around collecting items, you should see your inventory growing in the console messages. This is pretty cool, but it does expose one limitation of `List` data structures: as you collect multiples of the same type of item (such as collecting a second Health item), you'll see both copies listed, instead of aggregating all items of the same type (refer to figure 9.6). Depending on your game, you may want the inventory to track each item separately, but in most games, the inventory should aggregate multiple copies of the same item. It's possible to accomplish this using `List`, but it's done more naturally and efficiently using `Dictionary` instead.

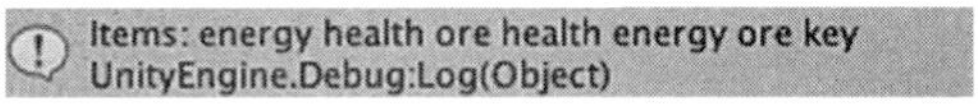

> Items: energy health ore health energy ore key
> UnityEngine.Debug:Log(Object)

Figure 9.6 Console message with multiples of the same item listed multiple times

> **DEFINITION** Dictionary is another collection data structure provided by C#. Entries in the dictionary are accessed by an identifier (or key) rather than by their position in the list. This is similar to a hash table but more flexible, because the keys can be literally any type (for example, "Return the entry for this GameObject").

Change the code in InventoryManager to use Dictionary instead of List. Replace everything from listing 9.14 with the code from this listing.

Listing 9.16 Dictionary of items in InventoryManager

```
...
private Dictionary<string, int> items;           ◁─────  Dictionary is declared with two
                                                          types: the key and the value.
public void Startup() {
   Debug.Log("Inventory manager starting...");

   items = new Dictionary<string, int>();

   status = ManagerStatus.Started;
}

private void DisplayItems() {
   string itemDisplay = "Items: ";
   foreach (KeyValuePair<string, int> item in items) {
      itemDisplay += item.Key + "(" + item.Value + ") ";
   }
   Debug.Log(itemDisplay);
}

public void AddItem(string name) {
   if (items.ContainsKey(name)) {   ◁─────  Check for existing entries
      items[name] += 1;                     before entering new data.
   } else {
      items[name] = 1;
   }

   DisplayItems();
}
...
```

Overall, this code looks the same as before, but a few tricky differences exist. If you aren't already familiar with Dictionary data structures, note that this one was declared with two types. Whereas List was declared with only one type (the type of values that'll be listed), a Dictionary declares both the type of key (that is, what the identifiers will be) and the type of value.

A bit more logic exists in the AddItem() method. Before, every item was appended to the List, but now you need to check whether the Dictionary already contains that item; that's what the `ContainsKey()` method is for. If it's a new entry, then you'll start the count at 1, but if the entry already exists, then increment the stored value. Play with the new code and you'll see that the inventory messages have an aggregated count of each item (refer to figure 9.7).

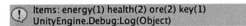
Items: energy(1) health(2) ore(2) key(1)
UnityEngine.Debug:Log(Object)

Figure 9.7   Console message with multiples of the same item aggregated

Whew, finally, collected items are managed in the player's inventory! This probably seems like a lot of code to handle a relatively simple problem, and if this were the entire purpose, then, yeah, it would be over-engineered. The point of this elaborate code architecture, though, is to keep all the data in separate flexible modules, a useful pattern when the game gets more complex. For example, now you can write UI displays, and the separate parts of the code will be much easier to handle.

9.4   *Inventory UI for using and equipping items*

The collection of items in your inventory can be used in multiple ways within the game, but all of those uses first rely on some sort of inventory UI so that players can see their collected items. Then, when the inventory is being shown to the player, you can program interactivity into the UI by enabling players to click their items. Again, you'll program a couple of specific examples (equipping a key and consuming health packs), and then you should be able to adapt this code to work with other types of items.

> **NOTE**   As mentioned in chapter 7, Unity has both an older immediate mode GUI and a newer sprite-based UI system. We'll use the immediate mode GUI in this chapter because that system is faster to implement and requires less setup; less setup is great for practice exercises. The sprite-based UI system is more polished, though, and for an actual game, you'd want a more polished interface.

9.4.1   *Displaying inventory items in the UI*

To show the items in a UI display, you first need to add a couple more methods to `InventoryManager`. Right now, the item list is private and accessible only within the manager. To display the list, that information must have public methods for accessing the data. Add two methods shown in the following listing to `InventoryManager`.

Listing 9.17   Adding data access methods to `InventoryManager`

```
...
public List<string> GetItemList() {                          Returns a List of all
    List<string> list = new List<string>(items.Keys);       the Dictionary keys
    return list;
}
                                          Returns how many of that
                                          item are in inventory
public int GetItemCount(string name) {
    if (items.ContainsKey(name)) {
```

```
        return items[name];
    }
    return 0;
}
...
```

The `GetItemList()` method returns a list of items in the inventory. You might be thinking, "Wait a minute, didn't we just spend lots of effort to convert the inventory away from a `List`?" The difference now is that each type of item will appear only once in the list. If the inventory contains two health packs, for example, the word `health` will still appear only once in the list. That's because the `List` was created from the keys in the `Dictionary`, not from every individual item.

The `GetItemCount()` method returns a count of how many of a given item are in the inventory. For example, call `GetItemCount("health")` to ask, "How many health packs are in the inventory?" This way, the UI can display a number of each item along with displaying each item.

With these methods added to `InventoryManager`, you can create the UI display. Let's display all the items in a horizontal row across the top of the screen. The items will be displayed using icons, so you need to import those images into the project. Unity handles assets in a special way if those assets are in a folder called Resources.

> **TIP** Assets placed into the Resources folder can be loaded in code by using the `Resources.Load()` method. Otherwise, assets can be placed in scenes only through Unity's editor.

Figure 9.8 shows the four icon images, along with the directory structure showing where to put those images. Create a folder called `Resources` and then create a folder called `Icons` inside it.

Figure 9.8 Image assets for equipment icons placed inside the Resources folder

The icons are all set up, so create a new empty GameObject named `Controller` and then assign it a new script called `BasicUI`.

Listing 9.18   `BasicUI` to display the inventory

```
using System.Collections;
using System.Collections.Generic;
using UnityEngine;

public class BasicUI : MonoBehaviour {
```

```
void OnGUI() {
    int posX = 10;
    int posY = 10;
    int width = 100;
    int height = 30;
    int buffer = 10;

    List<string> itemList = Managers.Inventory.GetItemList();
    if (itemList.Count == 0) {
        GUI.Box(new Rect(posX, posY, width, height), "No Items");
    }
    foreach (string item in itemList) {
        int count = Managers.Inventory.GetItemCount(item);
        Texture2D image = Resources.Load<Texture2D>($"Icons/{item}");
        GUI.Box(new Rect(posX, posY, width, height),
                new GUIContent($"({count})", image));
        posX += width+buffer;
    }
}
```

Display a message if the inventory is empty. ← (points to `if (itemList.Count == 0)` line)

Method loads assets from the Resources folder. → (points to `Texture2D image = Resources.Load` line)

Shift sideways each time through the loop. ← (points to `posX += width+buffer;` line)

This listing displays the collected items in a horizontal row (see figure 9.9) along with displaying the number collected. As mentioned in chapter 3, every MonoBehaviour automatically responds to an OnGUI() method. That function runs every frame right after the 3D scene is rendered.

Figure 9.9   UI display of the inventory

Inside OnGUI(), first define a bunch of values for positioning UI elements. These values are incremented when you loop through all the items in order to position UI elements in a row. The specific UI element drawn is GUI.Box; those are noninteractive displays that show text and images inside boxes.

The Resources.Load() method is used to load assets from the Resources folder. This method is a handy way to load assets by name; notice that the name of the item is passed as a parameter. You have to specify a type to load. Otherwise, the return value for that method is a generic object.

The UI shows us what items have been collected. Now you can use the items.

9.4.2 *Equipping a key to use on locked doors*

Let's go over a couple of examples of using inventory items so that you can extrapolate out to any type of item you want. The first example involves equipping a key required to open the door.

At the moment, the `DeviceTrigger` script doesn't pay attention to your items (because that script was written before the inventory code). This listing shows how to adjust that script.

Listing 9.19 Requiring a key in `DeviceTrigger`

```
...
public bool requireKey;

void OnTriggerEnter(Collider other) {
   if (requireKey && Managers.Inventory.equippedItem != "key") {
      return;
   }
...
```

As you can see, all that's needed is a new public variable in the script and a condition that looks for an equipped key. The `requireKey` Boolean appears as a check box in the Inspector so that you can require a key from some triggers but not others. The condition at the beginning of `OnTriggerEnter()` checks for an equipped key in `Inventory-Manager`; that requires you to add the code from the next listing to `InventoryManager`.

Listing 9.20 Equipping code for `InventoryManager`

```
...
public string equippedItem {get; private set;}
...
public bool EquipItem(string name) {
   if (items.ContainsKey(name) && equippedItem != name) {    ◁──┐  Check that inventory
      equippedItem = name;                                          has the item and that
      Debug.Log($"Equipped {name}");                                the item isn't already
      return true;                                                  equipped.
   }

   equippedItem = null;
   Debug.Log("Unequipped");
   return false;
}
...
```

At the top, add the `equippedItem` property that gets checked by other code. Then add the public `EquipItem()` method to allow other code to change which item is equipped. That method equips an item if it isn't already equipped, or *unequips* if that item is already equipped.

Finally, in order for the player to equip an item, add that functionality to the UI. This listing adds a row of buttons for that purpose.

Listing 9.21   Adding equip functionality to `BasicUI`

```
...
        foreach (string item in itemList) {        ◁──┐  Italicized code was already in the
            ...                                          script, shown here for reference.
            posX += width+buffer;
        }

        string equipped = Managers.Inventory.equippedItem;
        if (equipped != null) {
            posX = Screen.width - (width+buffer);
            Texture2D image = Resources.Load($"Icons/{equipped}") as Texture2D;
            GUI.Box(new Rect(posX, posY, width, height),
                    new GUIContent("Equipped", image));
        }

        posX = 10;
        posY += height+buffer;
                                          ┌── Loop through all items
        foreach (string item in itemList) {   ◁── to make buttons.
            if (GUI.Button(new Rect(posX, posY, width, height),
                    $"Equip {item}")) {       ◁──┐
                Managers.Inventory.EquipItem(item);   Run the contained code
            }                                         if the button is clicked.
            posX += width+buffer;
        }
    }
}
```

Arrows annotations in the listing: "Display the currently equipped item." points to the `if (equipped != null)` block.

`GUI.Box()` is used again to display the equipped item. But that element is noninteractive, so the row of Equip buttons is drawn using `GUI.Button()` instead. That method creates a button that executes the code inside the `if` statement when clicked.

With all the necessary code in place, select the `requireKey` option in `DeviceTrigger` and then play the game. Try running into the trigger volume before equipping a key; nothing happens. Now collect a key and click the button to equip it. Running into the trigger volume opens the door.

Just for fun, you could put a key at Position -11, 5, -14 to add a simple gameplay challenge to see if you can figure out how to reach the key. Whether or not you try that, let's move on to using health packs.

9.4.3 Restoring the player's health by consuming health packs

Using items to restore the player's health is another generally useful example. That requires two code changes: a new method in `InventoryManager` and a new button in the UI (see listings 9.22 and 9.23, respectively).

Listing 9.22 New method in `InventoryManager`

```
...
public bool ConsumeItem(string name) {
    if (items.ContainsKey(name)) {        ◄——— Check whether the item is in inventory.
        items[name]--;
        if (items[name] == 0) {           ◄——— Remove the entry if the count goes to 0.
            items.Remove(name);

        }
    } else {                              ◄———┐  Response if that item isn't in inventory
        Debug.Log($"Cannot consume {name}");
        return false;
    }

    DisplayItems();
    return true;
}
...
```

Listing 9.23 Adding a health item to `BasicUI`

```
...
    foreach (string item in itemList) {                    ◄———┐ Italicized code was
        if (GUI.Button(new Rect(posX, posY, width, height),    │ already in script,
                $"Equip {item}")) {                            │ shown here for
            Managers.Inventory.EquipItem(item);                │ reference.
        }

        if (item == "health") {           ◄——— Start of new code
            if (GUI.Button(new Rect(posX, posY + height+buffer, width,
                    height), "Use Health")) {      ◄———┐ Run the contained code
                Managers.Inventory.ConsumeItem("health");  │ if the button is clicked.
                Managers.Player.ChangeHealth(25);
            }
        }

        posX += width+buffer;
    }
}
```

The new ConsumeItem() method is pretty much the reverse of AddItem(). It checks for an item in the inventory and decrements if the item is found. It has responses to a couple of tricky cases, such as if the item count decrements to 0. The UI code calls this new inventory method, and it calls the ChangeHealth() method that PlayerManager has had from the beginning.

If you collect some health items and then use them, you'll see health messages appear in the console. And there you go—multiple examples of how to use inventory items!

Summary

- Both keypresses and collision triggers can be used to operate devices.
- Objects with physics enabled can respond to collision forces or trigger volumes.
- Complex game state is managed via special objects that can be accessed globally.
- Collections of objects can be organized in `List` or `Dictionary` data structures.
- Tracking the equip state of items can be used to affect other parts of the game.

Part 3

Strong finish

You know a fair amount about Unity by now. You know how to program the player's controls, create enemies that wander around, and add interactive devices to the game. You even know how to build a game using both 2D and 3D graphics! That's *almost* everything you need to know to develop a complete game, but not quite. You still need to learn about a few final tasks, like putting audio in the game, and you need to understand how to put together all the disparate pieces we've been working with. This is the home stretch, with just four chapters left!

Connecting your
game to the internet

This chapter covers

- Generating dynamic visuals for the sky
- Downloading data using web requests in coroutines
- Parsing common data formats like XML and JSON
- Displaying images downloaded from the internet
- Sending data to a web server

In this chapter, you'll learn how to send and receive data over a network. The projects built in previous chapters represented a variety of game genres, but all have been isolated to the player's machine. Connecting to the internet and exchanging data is increasingly important for games in all genres.

Many games exist almost entirely over the internet, with constant connection to a community of other players; games of this sort are referred to as massively multiplayer online (MMO) and are most widely known through MMO role-playing games (MMORPGs). Even when a game doesn't require such constant connectivity, modern video games usually incorporate features like reporting scores to a global list of high scores, or they record analytics to help improve the game. Unity provides support for such networking, so we'll be going over those features.

Unity supports multiple approaches to network communication, since different approaches are better suited to different needs. This chapter covers the most general sort of internet communication: issuing HTTP requests.

What are HTTP requests?

I assume most readers know what HTTP requests are, but here's a quick primer just in case: Hypertext Transfer Protocol (HTTP) is a communication protocol for sending requests to and receiving responses from web servers. When you click a link on a web page, your browser (the client) sends out a request to a specific address, and then that server responds with the new page. HTTP requests can be set to a variety of methods, in particular either GET or POST, to retrieve or to send data.

HTTP requests are reliable, and that's why the majority of the internet is built around them. The requests themselves, as well as the infrastructure for handling such requests, are designed to be robust and handle a wide range of failures in the network.

As a good comparison, imagine how a modern single-page web application works (as opposed to old-school web development based on web pages generated server-side). In an online game built around HTTP requests, the project developed in Unity is essentially a thick client that communicates with the server in an Ajax style. However, the familiarity of this approach can be misleading for experienced web developers. Video games often have much more stringent performance requirements than web applications, and these differences can affect design decisions.

> **WARNING** Time scales can be vastly different between web apps and video games. Half a second can seem like a short wait for updating a website, but pausing even just a fraction of that time can be excruciating in the middle of a high-intensity action game. The concept of *fast* is definitely relative to the situation.

Online games usually connect to a server specifically intended for that game. For learning purposes, however, we'll connect to some freely available internet data sources, including both weather data and images we can download. The last section of this chapter requires you to set up a custom web server; that section is optional because of that requirement, although I'll explain an easy way to do it with open source software.

The plan for this chapter is to go over multiple uses of HTTP requests so you can learn how they work within Unity:

- Setting up an outdoor scene (in particular, building a sky that can react to the weather data)
- Writing code to request weather data from the internet

- Parsing the response and then modifying the scene based on the data
- Downloading and displaying an image from the internet
- Posting data to your own server (in this case, a log of weather conditions)

The actual game that you'll use for this chapter's project matters little. Everything in this chapter will add new scripts to an existing project and won't modify any of the existing code. For the sample code, I used the movement demo from chapter 2, mostly so we can see the sky in first-person view when it gets modified.

The project for this chapter isn't directly tied into the gameplay, but obviously for most games you create, you would want the networking tied to the gameplay (for example, spawning enemies based on responses from the server). On to the first step!

10.1 Creating an outdoor scene

Because we're going to be downloading weather data, we'll first set up an outdoor area where the weather will be visible. The trickiest part of that will be the sky, but first let's take a moment to apply outdoors-looking textures on the level geometry.

Just as in chapter 4, I obtained a couple of images from www.textures.com to apply to the walls and floor of the level. Remember to change the size of the downloaded images to a power of 2, such as 256 × 256.

Then import the images into the Unity project, create materials, and assign the images to the materials (that is, drag an image into the texture slot of the material). Drag the materials onto the walls or floor in the scene, and increase tiling in the material (try numbers like 8 or 9 in one or both directions) so that the image won't be stretched in an ugly way. Once the ground and walls are taken care of, it's time to address the sky.

10.1.1 Generating sky visuals by using a skybox

Start by importing the skybox images as you did in chapter 4. Once again, I obtained skybox images from www.93i.de/, but this time I got the DarkStormy set in addition to TropicalSunnyDay (the sky will be more complex in this project). Simply get them from the book's sample project or download skybox images you find elsewhere. Import these textures into Unity and (as explained in chapter 4) set their Wrap Mode to Clamp.

Now create a new material to use for this skybox. At the top of the settings for this material, click the Shader menu to see the drop-down list with all the available shaders. Move down to the Skybox section and choose 6-Sided in that submenu. With this shader active, the material now has six texture slots (instead of only the small Albedo texture slot that the standard shader had).

Drag the SunnyDay skybox images to the texture slots of the new material. The names of the images correspond to the texture slot to assign them to (top, front, and so on). Once all six textures are linked, you can use this new material as the skybox for the scene.

Assign this skybox material by opening the Lighting window (Window > Rendering > Lighting). Switch to the Environment tab and assign the material for your skybox to the Skybox slot at the top of the window (either drag the material over or click the little circle button next to the slot). Click Play and you should see something like figure 10.1.

Figure 10.1   Scene with background pictures of the sky

Great, now you have an outdoors scene! A skybox is an elegant way to create the illusion of a vast atmosphere surrounding the player. But the skybox shader built into Unity does have one significant limitation: the images can never change, resulting in a sky that appears completely static. We'll address that limitation by creating a new custom shader.

10.1.2 *Setting up an atmosphere that's controlled by code*

The images in the TropicalSunnyDay set look great for a sunny day, but what if we want to transition between sunny and overcast weather? This will require a second set of sky images (some pictures of a cloudy sky), so we need a new shader for the skybox.

As explained in chapter 4, a shader is a short program with instructions for how to render the image. This implies that you can program new shaders, and that is, in fact, the case. We're going to create a new shader that takes two sets of skybox images and transitions between them. Get a shader for this purpose from https://github.com/jhocking/from-unity-wiki/blob/main/SkyboxBlended.shader.

In Unity, create a new shader script: Go to the Create menu just like when you create a new C# script, but select a Standard Surface Shader instead. Name the asset `Skybox-Blended` and then double-click the shader to open the script. Copy the code from that webpage and paste it into the shader script. The top line is `Shader "Skybox/Blended"`, which tells Unity to add the new shader into the shader list under the Skybox category (the same category as the regular skybox).

> **NOTE** We won't go over all the details of the shader program right now. Shader programming is a pretty advanced computer graphics topic, thus outside the scope of this book. You may want to look that up after you've finished this book; if so, start with the Unity Manual at http://mng.bz/wQzQ.

Now you can set your material to the Skybox Blended shader. Again, select the material and then look for the Shader menu at the top of the material's settings. There are now 12 texture slots, in two sets of six images. Assign TropicalSunnyDay images to the first six textures just as before; for the remaining textures, use the DarkStormy set of skybox images.

This new shader also added a Blend slider near the top of the settings. The Blend value controls how much of each set of skybox images you want to display; when you adjust the slider from one side to the other, the skybox transitions from sunny to overcast. You can test by adjusting the slider and playing the game, but manually adjusting the sky isn't terribly helpful while the game is running, so let's write code to transition the sky.

Create an empty object in the scene and name it `Controller`. Create a new script and name it `WeatherController`. Drag that script onto the empty object and then write this listing in that script.

Listing 10.1 `WeatherController` script transitioning from sunny to overcast

```
using System.Collections;
using System.Collections.Generic;
using UnityEngine;

public class WeatherController : MonoBehaviour {
    [SerializeField] Material sky;        ◁      Reference the material in Project
    [SerializeField] Light sun;                   view, not only objects in the scene.

    private float fullIntensity;

    private float cloudValue = 0f;

    void Start() {                    Initial intensity of the light is
        fullIntensity = sun.intensity;   ◁   considered "full" intensity.
    }

    void Update() {
        SetOvercast(cloudValue);      Increment the value every frame
        cloudValue += .005f;   ◁   for a continuous transition.
    }
                                      Adjust both the material's Blend
    private void SetOvercast(float value) {   ◁   value and the light's intensity.
        sky.SetFloat("_Blend", value);
        sun.intensity = fullIntensity - (fullIntensity * value);
    }
}
```

I'll point out several things in this code, but the key new method is `SetFloat()`, which appears almost at the bottom. Everything up to that point should be fairly familiar, but that one is new. The method sets a number value on the material. The first parameter to that method defines *which* value specifically. In this case, the material has a property called `_Blend` (note that material properties in code start with an underscore).

As for the rest of the code, we define a few variables, including both the material and a light. For the material, you want to reference the blended skybox material we just created, but what's with the light? That's so that the scene will also darken when transitioning from sunny to overcast; as the Blend value increases, we'll turn down the light. The directional light in the scene acts as the main light and provides illumination everywhere. Drag both the material and the light onto the variables in the Inspector.

> **NOTE**   The advanced lighting system in Unity takes the skybox into account to achieve realistic results. But this lighting approach won't work right with a changing skybox, so you may want to freeze the lighting setup. In the Lighting window, you can turn off the Auto Generate check box at the bottom; then the setup will update only when you click the button. Set the Blend of the skybox to the middle for an average look and then click the Generate button (next to the Auto check box) to manually bake lightmaps (lighting information was saved in a new folder that's named after the scene).

When the script starts, it initializes the intensity of the light. The script will store the starting value and consider that to be the full intensity. This full intensity will be used later in the script when dimming the light.

Then the code increments a value every frame and uses that value to adjust the sky. Specifically, it calls `SetOvercast()` every frame, and that function encapsulates the multiple adjustments made to the scene. I've already explained what `SetFloat()` is doing, so we won't go over that again, and the last line adjusts the intensity of the light.

Now play the scene to watch the code running. You'll see the depiction in figure 10.2: over a couple of seconds, you'll see the scene transition from a sunny day to dark and overcast.

Sunny before transition   Overcast after transition

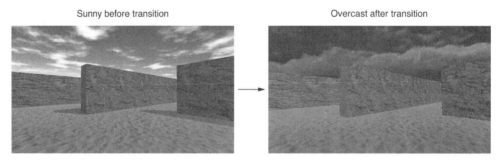

Figure 10.2   Before and after: scene transition from sunny to overcast

> **WARNING**   One unexpected quirk about Unity is that the `Blend` change on the material is permanent. Unity resets objects in the scene when the game stops running, but assets that were linked directly from the Project view (such as the skybox material) are changed permanently. This happens only within Unity's editor (changes don't carry over between plays after the game is deployed outside the editor), thus resulting in frustrating bugs if you forget about it.

Watching the scene transition from sunny to overcast is pretty cool. But this was all just a setup for the actual goal: having the weather in the game sync up to real-world weather conditions. For that, we need to start downloading weather data from the internet.

10.2 Downloading weather data from an internet service

Now that we've set up the outdoors scene, we can write code that will download weather data and modify the scene based on that data. This task will provide a good example of retrieving data by using HTTP requests. Many web services provide weather data; an extensive list is posted at ProgrammableWeb (www.programmableweb.com). I chose OpenWeather; the code examples use its API (application programming interface, a way to access their service using code commands instead of a graphical interface) located at http://openweathermap.org/api.

> **DEFINITION** A *web service,* or *web API,* is a server connected to the internet that returns data upon request. There's no technical difference between a web API and a website; a website is a web service that happens to return the data for a web page, and browsers interpret HTML data as a visible document.

> **NOTE** Web services often require you to register, even for free service. For example, if you go to the API page for OpenWeather, it has instructions for obtaining an API key, a value you will paste into requests.

The code you'll write will be structured around the same Managers architecture from chapter 9. This time, you'll have a WeatherManager class that gets initialized from the central manager of managers. WeatherManager will be in charge of retrieving and storing weather data, but to do so, it'll need the ability to communicate with the internet.

To accomplish that, you'll create a utility class called NetworkService to handle the details of connecting to the internet and making HTTP requests. WeatherManager can then tell NetworkService to make those requests and pass back the response. Figure 10.3 shows how this code structure will operate.

For this to work, obviously WeatherManager will need to have access to the Network-Service object. You're going to address this by creating the object in Managers and

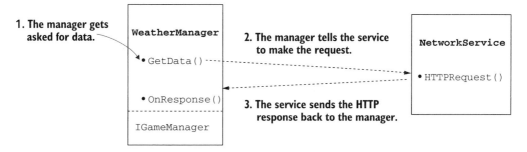

Figure 10.3 How the networking code will be structured

then injecting the NetworkService object into the various managers when they're initialized. In this way, not only will WeatherManager have a reference to the Network-Service, but so will any other managers you create later.

To start bringing over the Managers code architecture from chapter 9, first copy over ManagerStatus and IGameManager (remember that IGameManager is the interface that all managers must implement, whereas ManagerStatus is an enum that IGame-Manager uses). You'll need to modify IGameManager slightly to accommodate the new NetworkService class, so create a new script called NetworkService (delete :MonoBehaviour and otherwise leave it empty for now; you'll fill it in later) and then adjust IGameManager.

Listing 10.2   Adjusting `IGameManager` to include `NetworkService`

```
public interface IGameManager {
   ManagerStatus status {get;}              The startup function now
                                            takes one parameter: the
   void Startup(NetworkService service);  ⊲─── injected object.
}
```

Next let's create WeatherManager to implement this slightly adjusted interface. Create a new C# script.

Listing 10.3   Initial script for `WeatherManager`

```
using System.Collections;
using System.Collections.Generic;
using UnityEngine;

public class WeatherManager : MonoBehaviour, IGameManager {
   public ManagerStatus status {get; private set;}

   // Add cloud value here (listing 10.8)
   private NetworkService network;

   public void Startup(NetworkService service) {
      Debug.Log("Weather manager starting...");

      network = service;   ⊲──── Store the injected NetworkService object.

      status = ManagerStatus.Started;
   }
}
```

This initial pass at WeatherManager doesn't really do anything. For now, the class implements the minimum amount that IGameManager requires: declare the status property from the interface and implement the Startup() function. You'll fill in this empty framework over the next few sections. Finally, copy over Managers from chapter 9 and adjust it to start up WeatherManager.

Listing 10.4   Managers adjusted to initialize `WeatherManager`

```
using System.Collections;
using System.Collections.Generic;
using UnityEngine;

[RequireComponent(typeof(WeatherManager))]          Require the new manager instead
                                                    of player and inventory.
public class Managers : MonoBehaviour {
    public static WeatherManager Weather {get; private set;}

    private List<IGameManager> startSequence;

    void Awake() {
        Weather = GetComponent<WeatherManager>();

        startSequence = new List<IGameManager>();
        startSequence.Add(Weather);

        StartCoroutine(StartupManagers());
    }

    private IEnumerator StartupManagers() {              Instantiate NetworkService
        NetworkService network = new NetworkService();   to inject in all managers.

        foreach (IGameManager manager in startSequence) {
            manager.Startup(network);           
        }                                       Pass the network service to
        yield return null;                      managers during startup.

        int numModules = startSequence.Count;
        int numReady = 0;

        while (numReady < numModules) {
            int lastReady = numReady;
            numReady = 0;

            foreach (IGameManager manager in startSequence) {
                if (manager.status == ManagerStatus.Started) {
                    numReady++;
                }
            }

            if (numReady > lastReady)
                Debug.Log($"Progress: {numReady}/{numModules}");

            yield return null;
        }

        Debug.Log("All managers started up");
    }
}
```

And that's everything needed codewise for the `Managers` code architecture. As you have in previous chapters, create the game managers object in the scene and then attach both `Managers` and `WeatherManager` to the empty object. Even though the manager isn't doing anything yet, you can see startup messages in the console when it's set up correctly.

Whew, we had quite a few boilerplate things to get out of the way! Now we can get on with writing the networking code.

10.2.1 Requesting HTTP data using coroutines

NetworkService is currently an empty script, so you can write code in it to make HTTP requests. The primary class you need to know about is UnityWebRequest. Unity provides the UnityWebRequest class to communicate with the internet. Instantiating a request object using a URL will send a request to that URL.

Coroutines can work with the UnityWebRequest class to wait for the request to complete. Coroutines were introduced in chapter 3, where we used them to pause code for a set period of time. Recall the explanation given there: coroutines are special functions that seemingly run in the background of a program, in a repeated cycle of running partway and then returning to the rest of the program. When used along with the StartCoroutine() method, the yield keyword causes the coroutine to temporarily pause, handing back the program flow and picking up again from that point in the next frame.

In chapter 3, the coroutines yielded at WaitForSeconds(), an object that caused the function to pause for a specific number of seconds. Yielding a coroutine when sending a request will pause the function until that network request completes. The program flow here is similar to making asynchronous Ajax calls in a web application: first you send a request, then you continue with the rest of the program, and after some time you receive a response.

THAT WAS THE THEORY; NOW LET'S WRITE THE CODE

All right, let's implement this stuff in our code. First open the NetworkService script and replace the default template with the contents of this listing.

Listing 10.5 Making HTTP requests in NetworkService

```
using System;
using System.Collections;
using System.Collections.Generic;
using UnityEngine;
using UnityEngine.Networking;

public class NetworkService {                          URL to send request to
    private const string xmlApi =          ◄─┘
"http://api.openweathermap.org/data/2.5/weather?q=Chicago,
➡ us&mode=xml&appid=APIKEY";

    private IEnumerator CallAPI(string url, Action<string> callback) {
        using (UnityWebRequest request = UnityWebRequest.Get(url)) {   ◄──┐
                                                          Create UnityWebRequest
          yield return request.SendWebRequest();            object in GET mode.
```

Pause while downloading.

Check for errors in the response.

```
if (request.result == UnityWebRequest.Result.ConnectionError) {
    Debug.LogError($"network problem: {request.error}");
} else if (request.result == UnityWebRequest.Result.ProtocolError) {
    Debug.LogError($"response error: {request.responseCode}");
} else {
    callback(request.downloadHandler.text);     ⏴─┐
}
        }
    }

public IEnumerator GetWeatherXML(Action<string> callback) {
    return CallAPI(xmlApi, callback);     ⏴─┐
}
    }
```

Delegate can be called just like the original function.

Yield cascades through coroutine methods that call each other.

> **WARNING** The `Action` type (explained in "Understanding how the callback works") is contained in the `System` namespace; notice the additional `using` statements at the top of the script. Don't forget this detail in your scripts!

Remember the code design explained earlier: `WeatherManager` will tell `Network-Service` to go fetch data. All this code doesn't actually run yet; you're setting up code that will be called by `WeatherManager` a bit later. To explore this code listing, let's start at the bottom and work our way up.

WRITING COROUTINE METHODS THAT CASCADE THROUGH EACH OTHER

`GetWeatherXML()` is the coroutine method that outside code can use to tell `Network-Service` to make an HTTP request. Notice that this function has `IEnumerator` for its return type; methods used in coroutines must have `IEnumerator` declared as the return type.

It might look odd at first that `GetWeatherXML()` doesn't have a `yield` statement. Coroutines are paused by the `yield` statement, which implies that every coroutine must yield somewhere. It turns out that the yielding can cascade through multiple methods. If the initial coroutine method itself calls another method, and that other method yields part of the way through, then the coroutine will pause inside that second method and resume there. Thus, the `yield` statement in `CallAPI()` pauses the coroutine that was started in `GetWeatherXML()`; figure 10.4 shows this code flow.

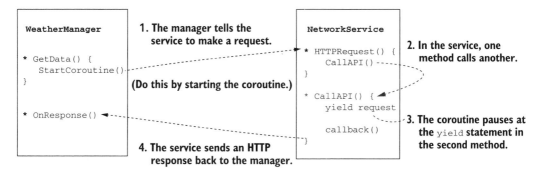

Figure 10.4   How the network coroutine works

The next potential head-scratcher is the `callback` parameter of type `Action`.

UNDERSTANDING HOW THE CALLBACK WORKS

When the coroutine is started, the method is called with a parameter called `callback`, and `callback` has the `Action` type. But what is an `Action`?

> **DEFINITION** The `Action` type is a delegate (C# has a few approaches to delegates, but this one is the simplest). Delegates are references to some other method/function. They allow you to store the function (or rather, a pointer to the function) in a variable and to pass that function as a parameter to another function.

If you're unfamiliar with the concept of delegates, realize that they enable you to pass around functions just as you do numbers and strings. Without delegates, you can't pass around functions to call later—you can only directly call the function immediately. With delegates, you can tell code about other methods to call later. This is useful for many purposes, especially for implementing callback functions.

> **DEFINITION** A *callback* is a function used to communicate back to the calling object. Object A could tell Object B about one of the methods in A. B could later call A's method to communicate back to A.

In this case, for example, the callback is used to communicate the response data back after waiting for the HTTP request to complete. In `CallAPI()`, the code first makes an HTTP request, then yields until that request completes, and finally uses `callback()` to send back the response.

Note the <> syntax used with the `Action` keyword; the type written in the angle brackets declares the parameters required to fit this `Action`. In other words, the function this `Action` points to must take parameters matching the declared type. In this case, the parameter is a single string, so the callback method must have a signature like this:

```
MethodName(string value)
```

The concept of a callback may make more sense after you've seen it in action, which you will in listing 10.6; this initial explanation is so that you'll recognize what's going on when you see that additional code.

The rest of listing 10.5 is pretty straightforward. The request object is created inside a `using` statement so that the object's memory will be cleaned up once we're done with that object. The conditional checks for errors in the HTTP response. There are two kinds of errors: the request could've failed because of a bad internet connection, or the response returned could have an error code. A `const` value is declared with the URL to make the request to. (Incidentally, you should replace `APIKEY` at the end with your OpenWeather API key.)

MAKING USE OF THE NETWORKING CODE

That wraps up the code in `NetworkService`. Now let's use `NetworkService` in `WeatherManager`.

> **Listing 10.6 Adjusting `WeatherManager` to use `NetworkService`**

```
...
public void Startup(NetworkService service) {
   Debug.Log("Weather manager starting...");

   network = service;
   StartCoroutine(network.GetWeatherXML(OnXMLDataLoaded));

   status = ManagerStatus.Initializing;
}
public void OnXMLDataLoaded(string data) {
   Debug.Log(data);

   status = ManagerStatus.Started;
}
...
```

Start loading data from the internet. → (points to `StartCoroutine(network.GetWeatherXML(OnXMLDataLoaded));`)

Instead of Started, make the status Initializing. → (points to `status = ManagerStatus.Initializing;`)

Callback method after the data is loaded → (points to `public void OnXMLDataLoaded(string data) {`)

Three primary changes are made to the code in this manager: starting a coroutine to download data from the internet, setting a different startup status, and defining a callback method to receive the response.

Starting the coroutine is simple. Most of the complexity behind coroutines was handled in `NetworkService`, so calling `StartCoroutine()` is all you need to do here. Then you set a different startup status, because the manager isn't finished initializing; it needs to receive data from the internet before startup is complete.

> **WARNING** Always start networking methods by using `StartCoroutine()`; don't just call the function normally. This can be easy to forget because creating request objects outside of a coroutine doesn't generate any sort of compiler error.

When you call the `StartCoroutine()` method, you need to invoke the method used as a parameter. That is, actually type the parentheses—`()`—and don't provide only the name of the function. In this case, the coroutine method needs a callback function as its one parameter, so let's define that function. We'll use `OnXMLDataLoaded()` for the callback; notice that this method has a string parameter, which fits the `Action<string>` declaration from `NetworkService`. The callback function doesn't do a lot right now; the debug line simply prints the received data to the console to verify that the data was received correctly. Then the last line of the function changes the startup status of the manager to say that it's completely started up.

Click Play to run the code. Assuming you have a solid internet connection, you should see a bunch of data appear in the console. This data is simply a long string, but the string is formatted in a specific way that we can make use of.

10.2.2 *Parsing XML*

Data that exists as a long string usually has individual bits of information embedded within the string. You extract those bits of information by parsing the string.

> **DEFINITION**   *Parsing* means analyzing a chunk of data and dividing it into separate pieces of information.

To parse the string, it needs to be formatted in a way that allows you (or rather, the parser code) to identify separate pieces. A couple of standard formats are commonly used to transfer data over the internet; one of the most common standard formats is *XML*.

> **DEFINITION**   XML stands for *Extensible Markup Language*. It's a set of rules for encoding documents in a structured way, similar to HTML web pages.

Fortunately, Unity (or rather Mono, the code framework built into Unity) provides functionality for parsing XML. The weather data we requested is formatted in XML, so we're going to add code to `WeatherManager` to parse the response and extract the cloudiness. Put the URL into a web browser to see the response data; there's a lot there, but we're interested only in the node that contains something like `<clouds value="40" name="scattered clouds"/>`.

In addition to adding code to parse XML, we're going to use the same messenger system as we did in chapter 7. That's because once the weather data is downloaded and parsed, we still need to inform the scene about that. Create a script called `Messenger` and paste in the code from https://github.com/jhocking/from-unity-wiki/blob/main/Messenger.cs.

Then you need to create a script called `GameEvent`. As explained in chapter 7, this messenger system is great for providing a decoupled way of communicating events to the rest of the program.

Listing 10.7 `GameEvent` code

```
public static class GameEvent {
    public const string WEATHER_UPDATED = "WEATHER_UPDATED";
}
```

Once the messenger system is in place, adjust `WeatherManager`.

Listing 10.8 Parsing XML in `WeatherManager`

```
using System;
using System.Xml;        ⟵── Be sure to add needed using statements.
...
public float cloudValue {get; private set;}      ⟵──
```
Cloudiness is modified internally but read-only elsewhere.

```
...
public void OnXMLDataLoaded(string data) {
    XmlDocument doc = new XmlDocument();
    doc.LoadXml(data);
    XmlNode root = doc.DocumentElement;

    XmlNode node = root.SelectSingleNode("clouds");
    string value = node.Attributes["value"].Value;
    cloudValue = Convert.ToInt32(value) / 100f;
    Debug.Log($"Value: {cloudValue}");

    Messenger.Broadcast(GameEvent.WEATHER_UPDATED);

    status = ManagerStatus.Started;
}
...
```

Parse XML into a searchable structure.

Pull out a single node from the data.

Convert the value to a 0–1 float.

Broadcast message to inform the other scripts.

You can see that the most important changes were made inside `OnXMLDataLoaded()`. Previously, this method simply logged the data to the console to verify that data was coming through correctly. This listing adds a lot of code to parse the XML.

First create a new empty XML document; this is an empty container that you can fill with a parsed XML structure. The next line parses the data string into a structure contained by the XML document. Then we start at the root of the XML tree so that everything can search up the tree in subsequent code.

At this point, you can search for nodes within the XML structure to pull out individual bits of information. In this case, `<clouds>` is the only node we're interested in. Find that node in the XML document and then extract the `value` attribute from that node. This data defines the cloud value as a 0–100 integer, but we're going to need it as a 0–1 float in order to adjust the scene later. Converting that is a simple bit of math added to the code.

Finally, after extracting out the cloudiness value from the full data, broadcast a message that the weather data has been updated. Currently, nothing is listening for that message, but the broadcaster doesn't need to know anything about listeners (indeed, that's the entire point of a decoupled messenger system). Later, we'll add a listener to the scene.

Great—we've written code to parse XML data! But before we move on to applying this value to the visible scene, I want to go over another option for data transfer.

10.2.3 Parsing JSON

Before continuing to the next step in the project, let's explore an alternative format for transferring data. XML is one common format for data transferred over the internet; another common one is *JSON*.

> **DEFINITION** *JSON* stands for *JavaScript Object Notation*. Similar in purpose to XML, JSON was designed to be a lightweight alternative. Although the syntax for JSON was originally derived from JavaScript, the format is not language-specific and is readily used with a variety of programming languages.

Unlike XML, Mono doesn't come with a parser for this format. Fortunately, numerous good JSON parsers are available. Unity itself provides a `JsonUtility` class, while externally developed options include Json.NET from Newtonsoft. I generally use Json.NET in my games, because Newtonsoft's library is widely used outside Unity in the whole .NET ecosystem. It can be installed using Unity's new Package Manager system, and that's how it's installed in the sample project.

> **WARNING** Json.NET has actually been packaged for Unity multiple times, and this book uses the package from jilleJr. However, recently Unity packaged Json.NET as com.unity.nuget.newtonsoft-json, and uses that as a dependency for other packages. Thus, if you have one of those other packages installed (such as Version Control), then you already have Json.NET in your project, and trying to install Json.NET a second time will cause errors. The easiest way to check is to expand the Packages folder (below Assets) in the Project view and look for Newtonsoft Json.

The GitHub page at http://mng.bz/7l4y has multiple sections about how to install, and "Installation via Pure UPM" explains the steps we need. As mentioned way back in chapter 1, the Unity Package Manager (UPM) is easiest to use with packages made by Unity itself. However, UPM is increasingly supported by external package authors as well; for example, the glTF package mentioned in chapter 4 is installed this way. While packages made by Unity are listed in the Package Manager window and can be selected there, externally created packages need to be installed by adjusting the manifest text file.

As explained by the GitHub page, navigate to the Unity project's folder on your computer, open the Packages folder in there, and then open manifest.json in any text editor. The installation documentation on GitHub lists all the text to paste into the package manifest, so do that. Installing a package always involves adding an entry in the `dependencies` block; in addition, some packages (for example, this JSON library) will also have `scopedRegistries` for you to add. Return to Unity, where it will take a moment for the new package to download.

Now you can use this library to parse JSON data. We've been getting XML from the OpenWeather API, but as it happens, OpenWeather can also send the same data formatted as JSON. To do that, modify `NetworkService` to request JSON.

Listing 10.9   Making `NetworkService` request JSON instead of XML

```
...
private const string jsonApi =                    ⟵——| The URL is slightly different this time.
"http://api.openweathermap.org/data/2.5/weather?q=Chicago,us&appid=APIKEY";
...
public IEnumerator GetWeatherJSON(Action<string> callback) {
    return CallAPI(jsonApi, callback);
}
...
```

This is pretty much the same as the code to download XML data, except that the URL is slightly different. The data returned from this request has the same values, but it's formatted differently. This time we're looking for a chunk like `"clouds":{"all":40}`.

There wasn't a ton of additional code required this time. That's because we set up the code for requests into nicely parceled separate functions, so every subsequent HTTP request will be easy to add. Nice! Now let's modify `WeatherManager` to request JSON data instead of XML.

Listing 10.10 Modifying `WeatherManager` to request JSON

```
...
using Newtonsoft.Json.Linq;        ◁─── Be sure to add the needed
...                                      using statement.
public void Startup(NetworkService service) {
   Debug.Log("Weather manager starting...");
                                                          Network
   network = service;                                     request
   StartCoroutine(network.GetWeatherJSON(OnJSONDataLoaded)); ◁── changed

   status = ManagerStatus.Initializing;
}
...
public void OnJSONDataLoaded(string data) {    Instead of an XML container,
   JObject root = JObject.Parse(data);  ◁──── parse into a JSON object.

   JToken clouds = root["clouds"];
   cloudValue = (float)clouds["all"] / 100f;        Syntax has changed, but
   Debug.Log($"Value: {cloudValue}");               this code is still doing
                                                     the same things.
   Messenger.Broadcast(GameEvent.WEATHER_UPDATED);

   status = ManagerStatus.Started;
}
...
```

As you can see, the code for working with JSON looks similar to the code for XML. The only real difference is that the data is parsed into a JSON object instead of an XML document container.

> **NOTE** Json.NET provides multiple approaches to parsing the data, and the alternative used here is referred to as *JSON Linq*. This alternative approach doesn't require as much setup, which is convenient for a small example like this. The main approach, however, requires first creating a new class with fields that mirror the structure of the JSON data. The data then populates this class by using the command `JsonConvert.DeserializeObject`.

> **DEFINITION** *Deserialize* means pretty much the same thing as *parse*, only with the implication that a code object is being created out of the data. This is the reverse of *serialize*, which means to encode a code object into a form that can be transferred and stored, such as a JSON string.

Aside from the different syntax, all the steps are the same. Extract the value from the data chunk (for some reason, the value is called `all` this time, but that's just a quirk of the API), do some simple math to convert the value to a 0–1 float, and broadcast an update message. With that done, it's time to apply the value to the visible scene.

10.2.4 Affecting the scene based on weather data

Regardless of exactly how the data is formatted, once the cloudiness value is extracted from the response data, we can use that value in the `SetOvercast()` method of `WeatherController`. Whether XML or JSON, the data string ultimately gets parsed into a series of words and numbers. The `SetOvercast()` method takes a number as a parameter. In section 9.1.2, we used a number incremented every frame, but we could just as easily use the number returned by the weather API. This shows the full `Weather-Controller` script again, after modifications.

> **Listing 10.11 `WeatherController` that reacts to downloaded weather data**

```
using System.Collections;
using System.Collections.Generic;
using UnityEngine;

public class WeatherController : MonoBehaviour {
    [SerializeField] Material sky;
    [SerializeField] Light sun;

    private float fullIntensity;

    void OnEnable() {                                      Add/remove event listeners.
        Messenger.AddListener(GameEvent.WEATHER_UPDATED, OnWeatherUpdated);
    }
    void OnDisable() {
        Messenger.RemoveListener(GameEvent.WEATHER_UPDATED, OnWeatherUpdated);
    }

    void Start() {
        fullIntensity = sun.intensity;
    }

    private void OnWeatherUpdated() {                      Use the cloudiness value
        SetOvercast(Managers.Weather.cloudValue);         from WeatherManager.
    }

    private void SetOvercast(float value) {
        sky.SetFloat("_Blend", value);
        sun.intensity = fullIntensity - (fullIntensity * value);
    }
}
```

Notice that the changes aren't only additions; several bits of test code got removed. Specifically, we removed the local cloudiness value that was incremented every frame; we don't need that anymore, because we'll use the value from `WeatherManager`.

A listener gets added and removed in `OnEnable()`/`OnDisable()` (these are the functions of `MonoBehaviour` called when the object is turned on or off). This listener is part of the broadcast messaging system and calls `OnWeatherUpdated()` when that message is received. `OnWeatherUpdated()` retrieves the cloudiness value from `Weather-Manager` and calls `SetOvercast()` using that value. In this way, the appearance of the scene is controlled by downloaded weather data.

Run the scene now and you'll see the sky update according to the cloudiness in the weather data. You may see it take time to request the weather; in a real game, you'd probably want to hide the scene behind a loading screen until the sky updates.

Game networking beyond HTTP

HTTP requests are robust and reliable, but the latency between making a request and receiving a response is too slow for many games. HTTP requests are therefore a good way of sending relatively slow-paced messages to a server (such as moves in a turn-based game, or submission of high scores for any game), but something like a multiplayer FPS would need a different approach to networking.

These approaches involve various communication technologies, as well as techniques to compensate for lag. Unity provides one API for multiplayer games, called MLAPI, but other options include Mirror or Photon.

The cutting edge for networked action games is a complex topic that goes beyond the scope of this book. You can look up more information on your own, starting with the Unity Multiplayer Networking site (https://docs-multiplayer.unity3d.com/).

Now that you know how to get numerical and string data from the internet, let's do the same thing with an image.

10.3 Adding a networked billboard

Although the responses from a web API are almost always text strings formatted in XML or JSON, many other sorts of data are transferred over the internet. Besides text data, the most common kind of data requested is images. The `UnityWebRequest` object can be used to download images too.

You're going to learn about this task by creating a billboard that displays an image downloaded from the internet. You need to code two steps: downloading an image to display and applying that image to the billboard object. As a third step, you'll improve the code so that the image will be stored to use on multiple billboards.

10.3.1 Loading images from the internet

First let's write the code to download an image. You're going to download some public domain landscape photography (see figure 10.5) to test with. The downloaded image won't be visible on the billboard yet; I'll show you a script to display the image in the next section, but before that, let's get the code in place that will retrieve the image.

Figure 10.5   Image of Moraine Lake in Banff National Park, Canada

The code architecture for downloading an image looks much the same as the architecture for downloading data. A new manager module (called ImagesManager) will be in charge of downloaded images to be displayed. Once again, the details of connecting to the internet and sending HTTP requests will be handled in NetworkService, and ImagesManager will call upon NetworkService to download images for it.

The first addition to the code is in NetworkService. This listing adds image downloading to that script.

Listing 10.12   Downloading an image in NetworkService

Put this const up near the top with the other URLs.

This callback takes a Texture2D instead of a string.

```
...
private const string webImage =
    "http://upload.wikimedia.org/wikipedia/commons/c/c5/Moraine_Lake_17092005.jpg";
...
public IEnumerator DownloadImage(Action<Texture2D> callback) {
    UnityWebRequest request = UnityWebRequestTexture.GetTexture(webImage);
    yield return request.SendWebRequest();
    callback(DownloadHandlerTexture.GetContent(request));
}
...
```

Retrieve the downloaded image by using the DownloadHandler utility.

The code that downloads an image looks almost identical to the code for downloading data. The primary difference is the type of callback method; note that the callback takes a Texture2D this time instead of a string. That's because you're sending back the relevant response: you downloaded a string of data previously—now you're downloading an image. This listing contains code for the new ImagesManager. Create a new script and enter this code.

Listing 10.13 Creating `ImagesManager` to retrieve and store images

```
using System;
using System.Collections;
using System.Collections.Generic;
using UnityEngine;

public class ImagesManager : MonoBehaviour, IGameManager {
   public ManagerStatus status {get; private set;}

   private NetworkService network;
                                           Variable to store the
   private Texture2D webImage;          ◄──┘ downloaded image

   public void Startup(NetworkService service) {
      Debug.Log("Images manager starting...");

      network = service;

      status = ManagerStatus.Started;
   }

   public void GetWebImage(Action<Texture2D> callback) {    Check whether the image
      if (webImage == null) {                            ◄──┘ is already stored.
         StartCoroutine(network.DownloadImage(callback));
      }
      else {
         callback(webImage);        ◄──┐ Invoke the callback right
      }                                  away (don't download) if
   }                                     there's a stored image.
}
```

The most interesting part of this code is `GetWebImage()`; everything else in this script consists of standard properties and methods that implement the manager interface. When `GetWebImage()` is called, it'll return (via a callback function) the web image. First, it'll check whether `webImage` already has a stored image. If not, it'll invoke the network call to download the image. If `webImage` already has a stored image, `GetWebImage()` will send back the stored image (rather than downloading the image anew).

> **NOTE** Currently, the downloaded image is never being stored, which means `webImage` will always be empty. Code that specifies what to do when `webImage` is *not* empty is already in place, so you'll adjust the code to store that image in the following sections. This adjustment is in a separate section because it involves some tricky code wizardry.

Of course, just like all manager modules, `ImagesManager` needs to be added to `Managers`, and this listing details the additions.

Listing 10.14 Adding the new manager to `Managers`

```
...
[RequireComponent(typeof(ImagesManager))]
...
```

```
public static ImagesManager Images {get; private set;}
...
void Awake() {
    Weather = GetComponent<WeatherManager>();
    Images = GetComponent<ImagesManager>();

    startSequence = new List<IGameManager>();
    startSequence.Add(Weather);
    startSequence.Add(Images);

    StartCoroutine(StartupManagers());
}
...
```

Unlike the way we set up `WeatherManager`, `GetWebImage()` in `ImagesManager` isn't called automatically on startup. Instead, the code waits until it's invoked; that'll happen in the next section.

10.3.2 Displaying images on the billboard

The `ImagesManager` you just wrote doesn't do anything until it's called upon, so now we'll create a billboard object that will call methods in `ImagesManager`. First create a new cube and then place it in the middle of the scene, at something like Position 0, 1.5, -5 and Scale 5, 3, 0.5 (see figure 10.6).

Billboard without image   Billboard with downloaded image

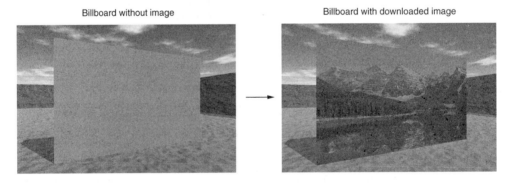

Figure 10.6   The billboard object, before and after displaying the downloaded image

You're going to create a device that operates just like the color-changing monitor in chapter 9. Copy the `DeviceOperator` script and put it on the player. As you may recall, that script will operate nearby devices when the C key is pressed. Also create a script for the billboard device called `WebLoadingBillboard`, put that script on the billboard object, and enter this code.

Listing 10.15   `WebLoadingBillboard` device script

```
using System.Collections;
using System.Collections.Generic;
```

```
using UnityEngine;

public class WebLoadingBillboard : MonoBehaviour {          Call the method in
    public void Operate() {                                 ImagesManager.
        Managers.Images.GetWebImage(OnWebImage);   ◁────┘
    }                                                       The downloaded image is
                                                            applied to the material in
    private void OnWebImage(Texture2D image) {              the callback.
        GetComponent<Renderer>().material.mainTexture = image;   ◁────┘
    }
}
```

This code does two primary things: it calls `ImagesManager.GetWebImage()` when the device is operated, and it applies the image from the callback function. Textures are applied to materials, so you can change the texture in the material that's on the billboard. Figure 10.6 shows what the billboard will look like after you play the game.

AssetBundles: How to download other kinds of assets

Downloading an image is fairly straightforward using `UnityWebRequest`, but what about other kinds of assets, like mesh objects and prefabs? `UnityWebRequest` has properties for text and images, but other assets are a bit more complicated.

Unity can download any kind of asset through a mechanism called AssetBundles. Long story short, you first package assets into a bundle, and then Unity can extract the assets after downloading the bundle. The details of both creating and downloading AssetBundles are beyond the scope of this book; if you want to learn more, start by reading the Unity Manual at http://mng.bz/m1X2 and http://mng.bz/5Zn1.

Great, the downloaded image is displayed on the billboard! But this code could be optimized further to work with multiple billboards. Let's tackle that optimization next.

10.3.3 *Caching the downloaded image for reuse*

As noted in section 10.3.1, `ImagesManager` doesn't yet store the downloaded image. That means the image will be downloaded over and over for multiple billboards. This is inefficient, because it'll be the same image each time. To address this, we're going to adjust `ImagesManager` to cache images that have been downloaded.

> **DEFINITION** *Cache* means to keep stored locally. The most common (but not only!) context involves files, such as images, downloaded from the internet.

The key is to provide a callback function in `ImagesManager` that first saves the image, and then calls the callback from `WebLoadingBillboard`. This is tricky to do (as opposed to the current code that directly uses the callback from `WebLoadingBillboard`) because the code doesn't know ahead of time what the callback from `WebLoadingBillboard` will be. Put another way, there's no way to write a method in `ImagesManager` that calls a specific method in `WebLoadingBillboard` because we don't yet know what that specific method will be. The way around this conundrum is to use lambda functions.

> **DEFINITION**   A *lambda function* (also called an *anonymous function*) is a function that doesn't have a name. These functions are usually created on the fly inside other functions.

Lambda functions are a tricky code feature supported in multiple programming languages, including C#. By using a lambda function for the callback in `ImagesManager`, the code can create the callback function on the fly by using the method passed in from `WebLoadingBillboard`. You don't need to know the method to call ahead of time, because this lambda function doesn't exist ahead of time! This listing shows how to do this voodoo in `ImagesManager`.

Listing 10.16   Lambda function for callback in `ImagesManager`

```
using System;
...
public void GetWebImage(Action<Texture2D> callback) {
    if (webImage == null) {
        StartCoroutine(network.DownloadImage((Texture2D image) => {
            webImage = image;
            callback(webImage);
        }));
    }
    else {
        callback(webImage);
    }
}
...
```

Store the downloaded image. → `webImage = image;`

The callback is used in the lambda function instead of being sent directly to NetworkService.

The main change is in the function passed to `NetworkService.DownloadImage()`. Previously, the code was passing through the same callback method from `WebLoading-Billboard`. After the change, though, the callback sent to `NetworkService` is a separate lambda function declared on the spot that called the method from `WebLoading-Billboard`. Take note of the syntax to declare a lambda function: `() => {}`.

Making the callback a separate function makes it possible to do more than call the method in `WebLoadingBillboard`; specifically, the lambda function also stores a local copy of the downloaded image. Thus, `GetWebImage()` has to download the image only the first time; all subsequent calls will use the locally stored image.

Because this optimization applies to subsequent calls, the effect will be noticeable only on multiple billboards. Let's duplicate the billboard object so that a second billboard will be in the scene. Select the billboard object, click Duplicate (look under the Edit menu or right-click), and move the duplicate over (for example, change the X position to 18).

Now play the game and watch what happens. When you operate the first billboard, a noticeable pause occurs while the image downloads from the internet. But when you then walk over to the second billboard, the image will appear immediately because it has already been downloaded.

This is an important optimization for downloading images (there's a reason web browsers cache images by default). One more major networking task remains to go over: sending data back to the server.

10.4 Posting data to a web server

We've gone over multiple examples of downloading data, but we still need to see an example of *sending* data. This last section does require you to have a server to send requests to, so this section is *optional*. But it's easy to download open source software to set up a server to test on.

I recommend XAMPP for a test server. Go to www.apachefriends.org to download XAMPP (on macOS you need to rename the .bz2 to .dmg) and follow the installation instructions. Once that's installed and the server is running, you can access XAMPP's htdocs folder with the address http://localhost/ just as you would a server on the internet. Once you have XAMPP up and running, create a folder called uia in htdocs; that's where you'll put the server-side script.

Whether you use XAMPP or your own existing web server, the actual task will be to post weather data to the server when the player reaches a checkpoint in the scene. This checkpoint will be a trigger volume, just like the door trigger in chapter 9. You need to create a new cube object, position it off to one side of the scene, set the collider to Trigger, and apply a semitransparent material as you did in chapter 9 (remember, set the material's Rendering Mode). Figure 10.7 shows the checkpoint object with a green semitransparent material applied.

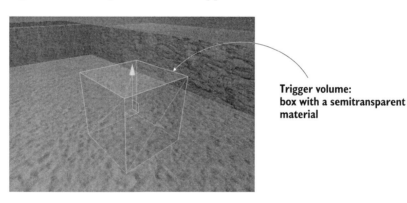

Trigger volume:
box with a semitransparent
material

Figure 10.7   The checkpoint object that triggers data sending

Now that the trigger object is in the scene, let's write the code that it invokes.

10.4.1 *Tracking current weather: Sending post requests*

The code that's invoked by the checkpoint object will cascade through several scripts. As with the code for downloading data, the code for sending data will involve `Weather-Manager` telling `NetworkService` to make the request, and `NetworkService` handles the details of HTTP communication. This shows the adjustments you need to make to `NetworkService`.

Listing 10.17   Adjusting `NetworkService` to post data

Address of the server-side script; change this if needed.

Added arguments to CallAPI() parameters

```
...
private const string localApi = "http://localhost/uia/api.php";
...
private IEnumerator CallAPI(string url, WWWForm form, Action<string>
        callback) {
    using (UnityWebRequest request = (form == null) ?
        UnityWebRequest.Get(url) : UnityWebRequest.Post(url, form)) {

        yield return request.SendWebRequest();

        if (request.result == UnityWebRequest.Result.ConnectionError) {
            Debug.LogError($"network problem: {request.error}");
        } else if (request.result == UnityWebRequest.Result.ProtocolError) {
            Debug.LogError($"response error: {request.responseCode}");
        } else {
            callback(request.downloadHandler.text);
        }
    }
}

public IEnumerator GetWeatherXML(Action<string> callback) {
    return CallAPI(xmlApi, null, callback);
}
public IEnumerator GetWeatherJSON(Action<string> callback) {
    return CallAPI(jsonApi, null, callback);
}

public IEnumerator LogWeather(string name, float cloudValue, Action<string>
        callback) {
    WWWForm form = new WWWForm();
    form.AddField("message", name);
    form.AddField("cloud_value", cloudValue.ToString());
    form.AddField("timestamp", DateTime.UtcNow.Ticks.ToString());

    return CallAPI(localApi, form, callback);
}
...
```

Either POST using WWWForm or GET without

Calls modified because of changed parameters

Define a form with values to send.

Send a timestamp along with the cloudiness.

First, notice that `CallAPI()` has a new parameter. This is a `WWWForm` object, a series of values to send along with the HTTP request. A condition in the code uses the presence of a WWWForm object to alter the request created. Normally we want to send a GET request, but WWWForm will change it to a POST request to send data. All the other changes in the code react to that central change (for example, modifying the GetWeather() code because of the CallAPI() parameters). The following code is what you need to add in WeatherManager.

Listing 10.18   Adding code to `WeatherManager` that sends data

```
...
public void LogWeather(string name) {
    StartCoroutine(network.LogWeather(name, cloudValue, OnLogged));
}
private void OnLogged(string response) {
    Debug.Log(response);
}
...
```

Finally, make use of this code by adding a checkpoint script to the trigger volume in the scene. Create a script called CheckpointTrigger, put that script on the trigger volume, and enter the contents of the next listing.

Listing 10.19   `CheckpointTrigger` script for the trigger volume

```
using System.Collections;
using System.Collections.Generic;
using UnityEngine;

public class CheckpointTrigger : MonoBehaviour {
    public string identifier;
                                          Track if the checkpoint has
    private bool triggered;        ⟵──┘   already been triggered.

    void OnTriggerEnter(Collider other) {
        if (triggered) {return;}

        Managers.Weather.LogWeather(identifier);   ⟵───  Call to send data.
        triggered = true;
    }
}
```

An Identifier slot will appear in the Inspector; name it something like checkpoint1. Run the code, and data will be sent when you enter the checkpoint. The response will indicate an error, though, because no script is on the server to receive the request. That's the last step in this section.

10.4.2 Server-side code in PHP

The server needs to have a script to receive data sent from the game. Coding server scripts is beyond the scope of this book, so we won't go into detail here. We'll just whip up a PHP script, because that's the easiest approach. Create a text file in htdocs (or wherever your web server is located) and name it api.php (listing 10.20).

Listing 10.20 Server script written in PHP that receives our data

```php
<?php

$message = $_POST['message'];              Extract post data into variables.
$cloudiness = $_POST['cloud_value'];
$timestamp = $_POST['timestamp'];
$combined = $message." cloudiness=".$cloudiness." time=".$timestamp."\n";

                                           Define the filename to write to.
$filename = "data.txt";
file_put_contents($filename, $combined, FILE_APPEND | LOCK_EX);      Write
                                                                     the file.
echo "Logged";

?>
```

Note that this script writes received data into data.txt, so you also need to put a text file with that name on the server. Once api.php is in place, you'll see weather logs appear in data.txt when triggering checkpoints in the game. Great!

Summary

- Skybox is designed for sky visuals that render behind everything else.
- Unity provides UnityWebRequest to download data.
- Common data formats like XML and JSON can be parsed easily.
- Materials can display images downloaded from the internet.
- UnityWebRequest can also post data to a web server.

Playing audio: Sound effects and music

This chapter covers

- Importing and playing audio clips for various sound effects
- Using 2D sounds for the UI and 3D sounds in the scene
- Modulating the volume of all sounds when they play
- Playing background music while the game is being played
- Fading in and out between different background tunes

Although graphics get most of the attention when it comes to content in video games, audio is crucial too. Most games play background music and have sound effects. Accordingly, Unity has audio functionality so that you can put sound effects and music into your games. Unity can import and play a variety of audio file formats, adjust the volume of sounds, and even handle sounds playing from a specific position within the scene.

> **NOTE** Audio is handled the same way for both 2D and 3D games. Although the sample project in this chapter is a 3D game, everything we'll do applies to 2D games as well.

This chapter starts off looking at sound effects rather than music. *Sound effects* are short clips that play along with actions in the game (such as a gunshot that plays when the player fires), whereas the sound clips for music are longer (often running into minutes) and playback isn't directly tied to events in the game. Ultimately, both boil down to the same kind of audio files and playback code, but the simple fact that the sound files for music are usually much larger than the short clips used for sound effects (indeed, files for music are often the largest files in the game!) merits covering them in a separate section.

The complete road map for this chapter will be to take a game without sound and do the following:

1. Import audio files for sound effects.
2. Play sound effects for the enemy and for shooting.
3. Program an audio manager to control volume.
4. Optimize the loading of music.
5. Control music volume separately from sound effects, including cross-fading tracks.

> **NOTE** In this chapter, we'll simply add audio capabilities on top of an existing game demo. All of the examples in this chapter are built on top of the FPS created in chapter 3, and you could download that sample project, but you're free to use whatever game demo you'd like.

Once you have an existing game demo copied to use for this chapter, you can tackle the first step: importing sound effects.

11.1 Importing sound effects

Before you can play any sounds, you obviously need to import the sound files into your Unity project. First, you'll collect sound clips in the desired file format, and then you'll bring the files into Unity and adjust them for your purposes.

11.1.1 Supported file formats

Much as you saw with art assets in chapter 4, Unity supports a variety of audio formats with different pros and cons. Table 11.1 lists the audio file formats that Unity supports.

The primary consideration differentiating audio files is the compression applied. Compression reduces a file's size but accomplishes that by throwing out a bit of information from the file. Audio compression is clever about throwing out only the least important information so that the compressed sound still sounds good.

Nevertheless, compression results in a small amount of loss of quality, so you should choose uncompressed audio when the sound clip is short and thus wouldn't be a large file. Longer sound clips (especially music) should use compressed audio,

Table 11.1   Audio file formats supported by Unity

File type	Pros and cons
WAV	Default audio format on Windows. Uncompressed sound file.
AIF	Default audio format on Mac. Uncompressed sound file.
MP3	Compressed sound file; sacrifices a bit of quality for much smaller files.
OGG	Compressed sound file; sacrifices a bit of quality for much smaller files.
MOD	Music tracker file format. A specialized kind of efficient digital music.
XM	Music tracker file format. A specialized kind of efficient digital music.

because the audio clip would be prohibitively large otherwise. Unity adds a small wrinkle to this decision, though.

> **TIP**   Although music should be compressed in the final game, Unity can compress the audio after you've imported the file. When developing a game in Unity, you usually want to use uncompressed file formats even for lengthy music, as opposed to importing compressed audio.

Because Unity will compress the audio after it's been imported, you should always choose either WAV or AIF file format. You'll probably need to adjust the import settings differently for short sound effects and longer music (in particular, to tell Unity when to apply compression), but the original files should always be uncompressed.

How digital audio works

In general, audio files store the waveform that'll be created in the speakers when the sound plays. Sound is a series of waves that travel through the air, and different sounds are made with different sizes and frequencies of sound waves. Audio files record these waves by sampling them repeatedly at short time intervals and saving the state of the wave at each sample.

Recordings that sample waves more frequently get a more accurate recording of them changing over time—the gaps between changes are smaller. But more frequent samples mean more data to save, resulting in a larger file. Compressed sound files reduce the file size through a number of tricks, including tossing out data at sound frequencies that aren't noticeable to listeners.

Music trackers are a special type of sequencer software used to create music. Whereas traditional audio files store the raw waveform for the sound, sequencers store something more akin to sheet music: the tracker file is a sequence of notes, with information like intensity and pitch stored with each note. These "notes" consist of little waveforms, but the total amount of data stored is reduced because the same note is used repeatedly throughout the sequence. Music composed this way can be efficient, but this is a fairly specialized sort of audio.

There are various ways to create sound files (appendix B mentions tools like Audacity, which can record sounds from a microphone), but for our purposes we'll download sounds from one of the many free sound websites. We're going to use clips downloaded from www.freesound.org in WAV file format.

> **WARNING**   "Free" sounds are offered under a variety of licensing schemes, so always make sure that you're allowed to use the sound clip in the way you intend. For example, many free sounds are for noncommercial use only.

The sample project uses the following public domain sound effects (of course, you can choose to download your own sounds; look for a 0 license listed on the side):

- "thump" by hy96
- "ding" by Daphne_in_Wonderland
- "swish bamboo pole" by ra_gun
- "fireplace" by leosalom

Once you have the sound files to use in your game, the next step is to import the sounds into Unity.

11.1.2   *Importing audio files*

After gathering some audio files, you need to bring them into Unity. Just as you did with art assets in chapter 4, you have to import audio assets into the project before they can be used in the game.

The mechanics of importing files are simple and are the same as with other assets: drag the files from their location on the computer to the Project view within Unity (create a folder called Sound FX to drag the files into). Well, that was easy! But just like other assets, these audio files have import settings (shown in figure 11.1) to adjust in the Inspector.

Leave the Force To Mono option unchecked. This refers to mono versus stereo sound. Often, sounds are recorded in stereo, resulting in two waveforms in the file, one for the left ear/speaker, and one for the right. To save on file size, you might want

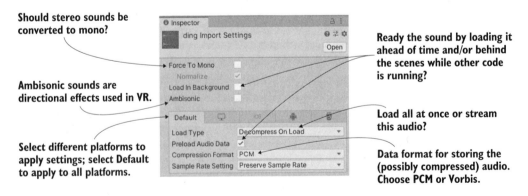

Figure 11.1   Import settings for audio files

to halve the audio information so that the same waveform is sent to both speakers rather than separate waves sent to the left and right speakers. (A Normalize setting, which applies only when mono is on, is grayed out when mono is off.)

Below Force To Mono, you'll see check boxes for Load In Background and Preload Audio Data. The preload setting relates to balancing playback performance and memory usage; preloading audio will consume memory while the sound waits to be used but will avoid having to wait to load. Thus, you don't want to preload long audio clips, but turn it on for short sound effects like this.

Meanwhile, loading audio in the background will allow the program to keep running while the audio is loading; this is generally a good idea for long music clips so that the program doesn't freeze. But this means the audio won't start playing right away. Usually you want to keep this setting off for short sound clips to ensure that they load completely before they play. Because the imported clips are short sound effects, you should leave Load In Background unchecked.

Finally, the most important settings are Load Type and Compression Format. Compression Format controls the formatting of the audio data that's stored. As discussed in the previous section, music should be compressed, so choose Vorbis (it's the name of a compressed audio format) in that case. Short sound clips don't need to be compressed, so choose PCM (pulse code modulation, the technical term for the raw, sampled sound wave) for these clips. The third setting, ADPCM, is a variation on PCM and occasionally results in slightly better sound quality.

Load Type controls how the data from the file will be loaded by the computer. Because computers have limited memory and audio files can be large, sometimes you want the audio to play while it's streaming into memory, saving the computer from needing to have the entire file loaded. But a bit of computing overhead is required when streaming audio like this, so audio plays fastest when it's loaded into memory first. Even then, you can choose whether the loaded audio data will be in compressed form or will be decompressed for faster playback. Because these sound clips are short, they don't need to stream and can be set to Decompress On Load.

The last option is Sample Rate Setting; leave this at Preserve Sample Rate so Unity won't change the samples in the imported file. At this point, the sound effects are all imported and ready to use.

11.2   *Playing sound effects*

Now that you have sound files added to the project, you naturally want to play the sounds. The code for triggering sound effects isn't terribly hard to understand, but the audio system in Unity does have multiple parts that must work in concert.

11.2.1   *Explaining what's involved: Audio clip vs. source vs. listener*

Although you might expect playing a sound to be simply a matter of telling Unity which clip to play, it turns out that you must define three parts in order to play sounds in Unity: `AudioClip`, `AudioSource`, and `AudioListener`. The reason for breaking the sound system into multiple components has to do with Unity's support for 3D sounds: the different components tell Unity positional information that it uses for manipulating 3D sounds.

2D vs. 3D sound

Sounds in games can be either 2D or 3D. 2D sounds are what you're already familiar with: standard audio that plays normally. The moniker *2D sound* mostly means *not 3D sound.*

3D sounds are specific to 3D simulations and may not already be familiar to you; these are sounds that have a specific location within the simulation. Their volume and pitch are influenced by the movement of the listener. A sound effect triggered in the distance will sound faint, for example.

Unity supports both kinds of audio, and you decide whether an audio source should play audio as 2D sounds or 3D sounds. Things like music should be 2D sounds, but using 3D sounds for most sound effects will create immersive audio in the scene.

As an analogy, imagine a room in the real world. The room has a stereo playing a CD. If a man comes into the room, he hears it clearly. When he leaves the room, he hears it less clearly, and eventually not at all. Similarly, if we move the stereo around the room, he'll hear the music changing volume as it moves. As figure 11.2 illustrates, in this analogy the CD is an `AudioClip`, the stereo is an `AudioSource`, and the man is the `AudioListener`.

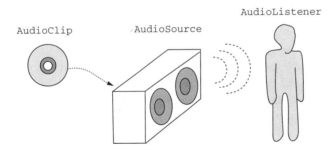

Figure 11.2   The three things you control in Unity's audio system

The first of the three parts is an *audio clip.* This is the sound file that we imported in the preceding section. This raw waveform data is the foundation for everything else the audio system does, but audio clips don't do anything by themselves.

The next kind of object is an *audio source.* This is the object that plays audio clips. This is an abstraction over what the audio system is actually doing, but it's a useful abstraction that makes 3D sounds easier to understand. A 3D sound played from a specific audio source is located at the position of that audio source; 2D sounds must also be played from an audio source, but the location doesn't matter.

The third kind of object involved in Unity's audio system is an *audio listener*. As the name indicates, this is the object that hears sounds projected from the audio sources. This is another abstraction on top of what the audio system is doing (obviously, the actual listener is the player of the game!), but—much as the position of the audio source gives the position that the sound is projected from—the position of the audio listener gives the position that the sound is heard from.

Advanced sound control using audio mixers

Audio mixers are an advanced alternative way to control audio in Unity. Rather than playing audio clips directly, audio mixers enable you to process audio signals and apply various effects to your clips. Learn more about `AudioMixer` in Unity's documentation. You can watch a Unity tutorial video, for example: http://mng.bz/Mlp3.

Although both the audio clips and the `AudioSource` components have to be assigned, an `AudioListener` component is already on the default camera when you create a new scene. Typically, you want 3D sounds to react to the position of the viewer.

11.2.2 Assigning a looping sound

All right, now let's set our first sound in Unity! The audio clips were already imported, and the default camera has an `AudioListener` component, so we need to assign only an `AudioSource` component. We're going to put a crackling fire sound on the Enemy prefab, the enemy character that wanders around.

> **NOTE** Because the enemy will sound like it's on fire, you might want to give it a particle system so that it looks like it's on fire. You can copy over the particle system created in chapter 4 by making the particle object into a prefab and then choosing Export Package from the Asset menu. Alternatively, you could redo the steps from chapter 4 here (after first double-clicking the Enemy prefab to open it for editing, rather than editing the scene) to create a new particle object from scratch.

Usually, you need to open a prefab into the scene to edit it, but just adding a component onto the object can be done without double-clicking the prefab to open it. Select the Enemy prefab so that its properties appear in the Inspector. Now add a new component: choose Audio > Audio Source. An `AudioSource` component will appear in the Inspector.

Tell the audio source what sound clip to play. Drag an audio file from the Project view up to the Audio Clip slot in the Inspector; we're going to use the "fireplace" sound effect for this example (refer to figure 11.3).

Skip down a bit in the settings and select both Play On Awake and Loop (of course, make sure that Mute isn't checked). Play On Awake tells the audio source to begin playing as soon as the scene starts (in the next section, you'll learn how to trigger

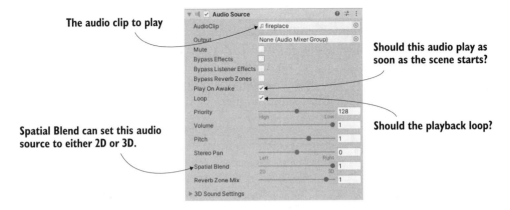

The audio clip to play

Should this audio play as soon as the scene starts?

Should the playback loop?

Spatial Blend can set this audio source to either 2D or 3D.

Figure 11.3   Settings for the `AudioSource` component

sounds manually while the scene is running). Loop tells the audio source to keep playing continuously, repeating the audio clip when playback is over.

You want this audio source to project 3D sounds. As explained earlier, 3D sounds have a distinct position within the scene. That aspect of the audio source is adjusted using the Spatial Blend setting, which is a slider from 2D to 3D. Set it to 3D for this audio source.

Now play the game and make sure your speakers are turned on. You can hear a crackling fire coming from the enemy, and the sound becomes faint if you move away because you used a 3D audio source.

11.2.3 *Triggering sound effects from code*

Setting the `AudioSource` component to play automatically is handy for some looping sounds, but for the majority of sound effects, you'll want to trigger the sound with code commands. That approach still requires an `AudioSource` component, but now the audio source will play sound clips only when told to by the program, instead of automatically all the time.

Add an `AudioSource` component to the player object (not the camera object). You don't have to link in a specific audio clip because the audio clips will be defined in code. You can turn off Play On Awake because sounds from this source will be triggered in code. Also, adjust Spatial Blend to 3D because this sound is located in the scene. Now make the additions shown in the next listing to `RayShooter`, the script that handles shooting.

Listing 11.1   Sound effects added in the `RayShooter` script

```
...
[SerializeField] AudioSource soundSource;
[SerializeField] AudioClip hitWallSound;
[SerializeField] AudioClip hitEnemySound;
```
References the two sound files you want to play

```
...
if (target != null) {
    target.ReactToHit();
    soundSource.PlayOneShot(hitEnemySound);
} else {
    StartCoroutine(SphereIndicator(hit.point));
    soundSource.PlayOneShot(hitWallSound);
}
...
```

If target is not null, the player has hit an enemy, so . . .

. . . call PlayOneShot() to play the Hit An Enemy sound, or . . .

. . . call PlayOneShot() to play the Hit A Wall sound if the player missed.

The new code includes several serialized variables at the top of the script. Drag the player object (the object with an `AudioSource` component) to the `soundSource` slot in the Inspector. Then drag the audio clips to play onto the sound slots; "swish" is for hitting the wall, and "ding" is for hitting the enemy.

The other two lines added are `PlayOneShot()` methods. `PlayOneShot()` causes an audio source to play a given audio clip. Add those methods inside the `target` conditional to play sounds when various objects are hit.

> **NOTE** You could set the clip in the `AudioSource` and call `Play()` to play the clip. Multiple sounds would cut one another off, though, so we used `PlayOneShot()` instead. Replace `PlayOneShot()` with this code and shoot a bunch rapidly to see (er, hear) the problem: `soundSource.clip=hitEnemySound; soundSource.Play();`.

All right, play the game and shoot around. You now have several sound effects in the game. These same basic steps can be used to add all sorts of sound effects. A robust sound system in a game requires a lot more than a bunch of disconnected sounds, though; at a minimum, all games should offer volume control. You'll implement that control next through a central audio module.

11.3 Using the audio control interface

Continuing the code architecture established in previous chapters, you're going to create an `AudioManager`. Recall that the `Managers` object has a master list of the various code modules used by the game, such as a manager for the player's inventory. This time, you'll create an audio manager to stick into the list. This central audio module will allow you to modulate the volume of audio in the game and even mute it. Initially, you'll worry about only sound effects, but in later sections you'll extend the `AudioManager` to handle music as well.

11.3.1 Setting up the central AudioManager

The first step in setting up `AudioManager` is to put in place the `Managers` code framework. From the chapter 10 project, copy over `IGameManager`, `ManagerStatus`, and `NetworkService`; we won't change them. (Remember that `IGameManager` is the interface that all managers must implement, whereas `ManagerStatus` is an enum that

IGameManager uses. NetworkService provides calls to the internet and won't be used in this chapter.)

> **NOTE** Unity will probably issue a warning because NetworkService is assigned but not used. You can ignore Unity's warning; we want to enable the code framework to access the internet, even though we don't use that functionality in this chapter.

Also copy over the Managers file, which will be adjusted for the new AudioManager. Leave it as is for now (or comment out the erroneous sections if the sight of compiler errors drives you crazy!). Create a new script called AudioManager that the Managers code can refer to.

Listing 11.2 Skeleton code for AudioManager

```
using System.Collections;
using System.Collections.Generic;
using UnityEngine;

public class AudioManager : MonoBehaviour, IGameManager {
    public ManagerStatus status {get; private set;}

    private NetworkService network;

    // Add volume controls here (listing 11.4)

    public void Startup(NetworkService service) {
        Debug.Log("Audio manager starting...");

        network = service;

        // Initialize music sources here (listing 11.11)   ◁── Any long-running startup tasks go here.

        status = ManagerStatus.Started;   ◁── Set status to Initializing if there are long-running startup tasks.
    }
}
```

This initial code looks like managers from previous chapters; this is the minimum amount that IGameManager requires the class to implement. The Managers script can now be adjusted with the new manager.

Listing 11.3 Managers script adjusted with AudioManager

```
using System.Collections;
using System.Collections.Generic;
using UnityEngine;

[RequireComponent(typeof(AudioManager))]

public class Managers : MonoBehaviour {
    public static AudioManager Audio {get; private set;}
```

```
       private List<IGameManager> startSequence;

       void Awake() {
          Audio = GetComponent<AudioManager>();       ◁─┐  List only AudioManager
                                                          in this project, instead of
          startSequence = new List<IGameManager>();       PlayerManager, and so on.
          startSequence.Add(Audio);

          StartCoroutine(StartupManagers());
       }

       private IEnumerator StartupManagers() {
          NetworkService network = new NetworkService();

          foreach (IGameManager manager in startSequence) {
             manager.Startup(network);
          }

          yield return null;

          int numModules = startSequence.Count;
          int numReady = 0;

          while (numReady < numModules) {
             int lastReady = numReady;
             numReady = 0;

             foreach (IGameManager manager in startSequence) {
                if (manager.status == ManagerStatus.Started) {
                   numReady++;
                }
             }

             if (numReady > lastReady)
                Debug.Log($"Progress: {numReady}/{numModules}");

             yield return null;
          }

          Debug.Log("All managers started up");
       }
    }
```

As you have in previous chapters, create the Game Managers object in the scene and then attach both `Managers` and `AudioManager` to the empty object. Playing the game will show the managers' startup messages in the console, but the audio manager doesn't do anything yet.

11.3.2 *Volume control UI*

With the bare-bones `AudioManager` set up, it's time to give it volume control functionality. These volume control methods will then be used by UI displays to mute the sound effects or adjust the volume.

You'll use the UI tools that were the focus of chapter 7. Specifically, you're going to create a pop-up window with a button and a slider to control volume settings (see figure 11.4). I'll list the steps involved without going into detail; if you need a refresher, refer to chapter 7. If needed, install the TextMeshPro and 2D Sprite packages (refer back to chapters 5 and 6 for these) before starting:

1. Import popup.png as a sprite (set Texture Type to Sprite).
2. In the Sprite Editor, set a 12-pixel border on all sides (remember to apply changes).
3. Create a canvas in the scene (GameObject > UI > Canvas).
4. Turn on the Pixel Perfect setting for the canvas.
5. (Optional) Name the object HUD Canvas and switch to 2D view mode.
6. Create an image connected to that canvas (GameObject > UI > Image).
7. Name the new object Settings Popup.
8. Assign the popup sprite to the image's Source Image.
9. Set Image Type to Sliced and turn on Fill Center.
10. Position the pop-up image at 0, 0 to center it.
11. Scale the pop-up to 250 width and 150 height.
12. Create a button (GameObject > UI > Button - TextMeshPro).
13. Parent the button to the pop-up (drag it in the Hierarchy).
14. Position the button at 0, 40.
15. Expand the button's hierarchy to select its text label.
16. Change the text to Toggle Sound.
17. Create a slider (GameObject > UI > Slider).
18. Parent the slider to the pop-up and position it at 0, 15.
19. Set the slider's Value (at the bottom of the Inspector) to 1.

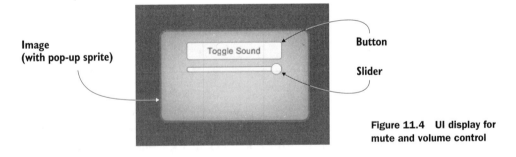

Figure 11.4   **UI display for mute and volume control**

Those are all the steps to create the settings pop-up! Now that the pop-up has been created, let's write code that it'll work with. This will involve a script on the pop-up object itself as well as the volume control functionality that the pop-up script calls. First, adjust the code in AudioManager according to this listing.

Listing 11.4   Volume control added to `AudioManager`

```
...
public float soundVolume {        ←——    Property with getter
   get {return AudioListener.volume;}      and setter for volume
   set {AudioListener.volume = value;}    Implement the getter/setter
}                                          using AudioListener.


public bool soundMute {           ←——— Add a similar property to mute.
   get {return AudioListener.pause;}
   set {AudioListener.pause = value;}
}
                                                Italicized code was already in
public void Startup(NetworkService service) {  ←——  script, shown here for reference.
   Debug.Log("Audio manager starting...");

   network = service;
                                   Initialize the value (0 to 1
   soundVolume = 1f;      ←——      range; 1 is full volume).

   status = ManagerStatus.Started;
}
...
```

Properties for `soundVolume` and `soundMute` were added to `AudioManager`. For both properties, the `get` and `set` functions were implemented using global values on `Audio-Listener`. The `AudioListener` class can modulate the volume of all sounds received by all `AudioListener` instances. Setting `AudioManager`'s `soundVolume` property has the same effect as setting the volume on `AudioListener`. The advantage here is encapsulation: everything having to do with audio is being handled in a single manager, without code outside the manager needing to know the details of the implementation.

With those methods added to `AudioManager`, you can now write a script for the pop-up. Create a script called `SettingsPopup` and add the contents of this listing.

Listing 11.5   `SettingsPopup` script with controls for adjusting the volume

```
using System.Collections;
using System.Collections.Generic;
using UnityEngine;

public class SettingsPopup : MonoBehaviour {
   public void OnSoundToggle() {         ←——   Button will toggle the mute
      Managers.Audio.soundMute = !Managers.Audio.soundMute;   property of AudioManager.
   }

   public void OnSoundValue(float volume) {   ←——
      Managers.Audio.soundVolume = volume;    Slider will adjust the volume
   }                                          property of AudioManager.
}
```

This script has two methods that affect the properties of AudioManager: OnSound-Toggle() sets the soundMute property, and OnSoundValue() sets the soundVolume property. As usual, link in the SettingsPopup script by dragging it onto the Settings Popup object in the UI.

Then, to call the functions from the button and slider, link the pop-up object to interaction events in those controls. In the Inspector for the button, look for the panel labeled On Click. Click the + button to add a new entry to this event. Drag Settings Popup to the object slot in the new entry and then look for SettingsPopup in the menu; select OnSoundToggle() to make the button call that function.

Now select the slider and link a function, just as you did with the button. First look for the interaction event in a panel of the slider's settings; in this case, the panel is called OnValueChanged. Click the + button to add a new entry and then drag Settings Popup to the object slot. In the function menu, find the SettingsPopup script and then choose OnSoundValue() under Dynamic Float.

> **WARNING** Remember to choose the function under Dynamic Float and not Static Parameter! Although the method appears in both sections of the list, in the latter case it will receive only a single value typed in ahead of time.

The settings controls are now working, but we need to address one more script—the pop-up is currently always covering up the screen. A simple fix is to make the pop-up open only when you press the M key. Create a new script called UIController, link that script to the controller object in the scene, and write this code.

Listing 11.6 `UIController` that toggles the settings pop-up

```
using System.Collections;
using System.Collections.Generic;
using UnityEngine;

public class UIController : MonoBehaviour {            References the pop-up
   [SerializeField] SettingsPopup popup;         ◁─┘  object in the scene

   void Start() {
      popup.gameObject.SetActive(false);    ◁────── Initializes the hidden pop-up
   }
                                                  Toggles the pop-up
   void Update() {                                with the M key
      if (Input.GetKeyDown(KeyCode.M)) {   ◁─┘
         bool isShowing = popup.gameObject.activeSelf;
         popup.gameObject.SetActive(!isShowing);

         if (isShowing) {
            Cursor.lockState = CursorLockMode.Locked;
            Cursor.visible = false;
         } else {                                      Also toggles the cursor
            Cursor.lockState = CursorLockMode.None;    along with the pop-up
            Cursor.visible = true;
         }
```

```
          }
      }
  }
```

To wire up this object reference, drag the settings pop-up to the slot on this script. Play now and try changing the slider (remember to activate the UI by pressing the M key) while shooting around to hear the sound effects; you'll hear the sound effects change volume according to the slider.

11.3.3 *Playing UI sounds*

You're going to make another addition to `AudioManager` now to allow the UI to play sounds when buttons are clicked. This task is more involved than it seems at first, owing to Unity's need for an `AudioSource`. When sound effects were issued from objects in the scene, it was fairly obvious where to attach the `AudioSource`. But UI sound effects aren't part of the scene, so you'll set up a special `AudioSource` for `AudioManager` to use when there isn't any other audio source.

Create a new empty `GameObject` and attach it as a child of the main Game Managers object; this new object is going to have an `AudioSource` used by `AudioManager`, so call the new object `Audio`. Add an `AudioSource` component to this object (leave the Spatial Blend setting at 2D this time, because the UI doesn't have a specific position in the scene) and then add this code to use this source in `AudioManager`.

Listing 11.7 Playing sound effects in `AudioManager`

```
...
[SerializeField] AudioSource soundSource;          ◁——— Variable slot in the Inspector to
...                                                      reference the new audio source
public void PlaySound(AudioClip clip) {            ◁———┐ Play sounds that don't
    soundSource.PlayOneShot(clip);                      │ have any other source.
}
...
```

A new variable slot will appear in the manager's Inspector; drag the `Audio` object onto this slot. Now modify the pop-up script (as shown in the following listing) to add the UI sound effect.

Listing 11.8 Adding sound effects to `SettingsPopup`

```
...
[SerializeField] AudioClip sound;                       ◁———┐ Inspector slot to reference
...                                                          │ the sound clip
public void OnSoundToggle() {
    Managers.Audio.soundMute = !Managers.Audio.soundMute;
    Managers.Audio.PlaySound(sound);                    ◁———┐ Play the sound effect when
}                                                            │ the button is clicked.
...
```

Drag the UI sound effect onto the variable slot; I used the 2D sound "thump." When you click the UI button, that sound effect plays at the same time (when the sound isn't muted, of course!). Even though the UI doesn't have an audio source itself, Audio-Manager has an audio source that plays the sound effect.

Great, we've set up all our sound effects! Now let's turn our attention to music.

11.4   Adding background music

You're going to add background music to the game, and you'll do that by adding music to AudioManager. As explained in the chapter introduction, music clips aren't fundamentally different from sound effects. The way digital audio functions through waveforms is the same, and the commands for playing the audio are largely the same. The main difference is the length of the audio, but that difference cascades out into numerous consequences.

For starters, music tracks tend to consume a large amount of memory on the computer, and that memory consumption must be optimized. You must watch out for two areas of memory issues: having the music loaded into memory before it's needed, and consuming too much memory when loaded.

Optimizing *when* music loads is done using the Resources.Load() command introduced in chapter 9. As you learned, this command allows you to load assets by name. Though that's certainly one handy feature, that's not the only reason to load assets from the Resources folder. Another key consideration is delaying loading: normally, Unity loads all assets in a scene as soon as the scene loads, but assets from Resources aren't loaded until the code manually fetches them. In this case, we want to *lazy-load* the audio clips for music. Otherwise, the music could consume a lot of memory even when it isn't being used.

> **DEFINITION**   With *lazy loading*, a file isn't loaded ahead of time but rather is delayed until it's needed. Typically, data responds faster (for example, the sound plays immediately) if it's loaded in advance of use, but lazy loading can save a lot of memory when responsiveness doesn't matter as much.

The second memory consideration is dealt with by streaming music off the disc. As explained in section 11.1.2, streaming the audio saves the computer from ever needing to have the entire file loaded at once. The style of loading was a setting in the Inspector of the imported audio clip. Ultimately, playing background music requires several steps, including steps to cover these memory optimizations.

11.4.1   Playing music loops

The process of playing music involves the same series of steps as UI sound effects did (background music is also 2D sound without a source within the scene), so we're going to go through all those steps again:

1. Importing audio clips.
2. Setting up an AudioSource for AudioManager to use.

3. Writing code to play the audio clips in `AudioManager`.

4. Adding music controls to the UI.

Each step will be modified slightly to work with music instead of sound effects. Let's look at the first step.

STEP 1: IMPORTING AUDIO CLIPS

Obtain some music by downloading or recording tracks. For the sample project, I went to www.freesound.org and downloaded the following public domain music loops:

- "loop" by Xythe/Ville Nousiainen
- "Intro Synth" by noirenex

Drag the files into Unity to import them and then adjust their import settings in the Inspector. As explained earlier, audio clips for music generally have different settings than audio clips for sound effects. First, the audio format should be set to Vorbis, for compressed audio. Remember, compressed audio will have a significantly smaller file size. Compression also degrades the audio quality slightly, but that slight degradation is an acceptable trade-off for long music clips; set Quality to 50% in the slider that appears.

The next import setting to adjust is Load Type. Again, music should stream from the disc rather than being loaded completely. Choose Streaming from the Load Type menu. Similarly, turn on Load In Background so that the game won't pause or slow down while music is loading.

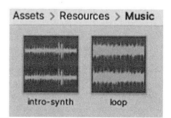

Even after you adjust all the import settings, the asset files must be moved to the correct location in order to load correctly. Remember that the `Resources.Load()` command requires the assets to be in the Resources folder. Create a new folder called `Resources`, create a folder within that called `Music`, and drag the audio files into the Music folder (see figure 11.5). That takes care of step 1.

Figure 11.5   Music audio clips placed inside the Resources folder

STEP 2: SETTING UP AN AUDIOSOURCE FOR AUDIOMANAGER TO USE

Step 2 is to create a new `AudioSource` for music playback. Create another empty `Game-Object`, name this object `Music 1` (instead of `Music` because we'll add `Music 2` later in the chapter), and attach it as a child of the Audio object.

Add an `AudioSource` component to `Music 1` and then adjust the settings in the component. Deselect Play On Awake but turn on the Loop option this time; whereas sound effects usually play only once, music plays over and over in a loop. Leave the Spatial Blend setting at 2D, because music doesn't have any specific position in the scene.

You may want to reduce the Priority value too. For sound effects, this value didn't matter, so we left the value at the default 128. But for music, you probably want to lower this value, so I set the music source to 60. This value tells Unity which sounds are most important when layering multiple sounds; somewhat counterintuitively, lower values are higher priority. When too many sounds are playing simultaneously, the audio system will start discarding sounds; by making music higher priority than sound effects, you ensure that the music will keep playing when too many sound effects trigger at the same time.

STEP 3: WRITING CODE TO PLAY THE AUDIO CLIPS IN AUDIOMANAGER

The Music audio source has been set up, so add the following listing to AudioManager.

Listing 11.9 Playing music in `AudioManager`

```
...
[SerializeField] AudioSource music1Source;

[SerializeField] string introBGMusic;          Write music names in these strings.
[SerializeField] string levelBGMusic;
...                                             Load intro music from Resources.
public void PlayIntroMusic() {
    PlayMusic(Resources.Load($"Music/{introBGMusic}") as AudioClip);
}                                               Load main music from Resources.
public void PlayLevelMusic() {
    PlayMusic(Resources.Load($"Music/{levelBGMusic}") as AudioClip);
}

private void PlayMusic(AudioClip clip) {        Play music by setting AudioSource.clip.
    music1Source.clip = clip;
    music1Source.Play();
}

public void StopMusic() {
    music1Source.Stop();
}
...
```

As usual, the new serialized variables will be visible in the Inspector when you select the Game Managers object. Drag Music 1 into the audio source slot. Then type in the names of the music files in the two string variables: intro-synth and loop.

The remainder of the added code calls commands for loading and playing music (or, in the last added method, stopping the music). The Resources.Load() command loads the named asset from the Resources folder (taking into account that the files are placed in the Music subfolder within Resources). A generic object is returned by that command, but the object can be converted to a more specific type (in this case, an AudioClip) by using the as keyword.

The loaded audio clip is then passed into the PlayMusic() method. This function sets the clip in the AudioSource and then calls Play(). As I explained earlier, sound effects are better implemented using `PlayOneShot()`, but setting the clip in the `AudioSource` is a more robust approach for music, allowing you to stop or pause the playing music.

STEP 4: ADDING MUSIC CONTROLS TO THE UI

The new music playback methods in `AudioManager` won't do anything unless they're called from elsewhere. Let's add more buttons to the audio UI that will play different music when clicked. Here are the steps again, enumerated with little explanation (refer to chapter 7 if needed):

1. Change the pop-up's width to 350 (to fit more buttons).
2. Create a new UI button and attach it to the pop-up.
3. Set the button's width to 100 and position to 0, –20.
4. Expand the button's hierarchy to select the text label and set that to Level Music.
5. Repeat these steps twice more to create two additional buttons.
6. Position one at –105, –20 and the other at 105, –20 (so they appear on either side).
7. Change the first text label to Intro Music and the last text label to No Music.

Now the pop-up has three buttons for playing different music. Write a method in `SettingsPopup` that will be linked to each button.

Listing 11.10 Adding music controls to `SettingsPopup`

```
...
public void OnPlayMusic(int selector) {        This method gets a number
    Managers.Audio.PlaySound(sound);           parameter from the button.

    switch (selector) {                        Call a different music function in
        case 1:                                AudioManager for each button.
            Managers.Audio.PlayIntroMusic();
            break;
        case 2:
            Managers.Audio.PlayLevelMusic();
            break;
        default:
            Managers.Audio.StopMusic();
            break;
    }
}
...
```

Note that the function takes an `int` parameter this time; normally, button methods don't have a parameter and are simply triggered by the button. In this case, we need to distinguish between the three buttons, so each button will send a different number.

Go through the typical steps to connect a button to this code: add an entry to the On Click panel in the Inspector, drag the pop-up to the object slot, and choose the appropriate function from the menu. This time, a text box for typing in a number is displayed, because `OnPlayMusic()` takes a number for a parameter. Type 1 for Intro Music, 2 for Level Music, and anything else for No Music (I went with 0). The `switch` statement in `OnMusic()` plays intro music or level music, depending on the number, or stops the music as a default if the number isn't 1 or 2.

When you click the music buttons while the game is playing, you'll hear the music. Great! The code is loading the audio clips from the Resources folder. Music plays efficiently, although we still have two bits of polish to add: separate music volume control and cross-fading when changing the music.

11.4.2 *Controlling music volume separately*

The game already has volume control, and currently that affects the music too. Most games have separate volume controls for sound effects and music, though, so let's tackle that now.

The first step is to tell the music `AudioSource` to ignore the settings on `Audio-Listener`. We want volume and mute on the global `AudioListener` to continue to affect all sound effects, but we don't want this volume to apply to music. Listing 11.10 includes code to tell the music source to ignore the volume on `AudioListener`. The following listing also adds volume control and mute for music, so add it to `AudioManager`.

> **Listing 11.11 Controlling music volume separately in `AudioManager`**

```
...
private float _musicVolume;          ◁──┐   Private variable that won't be
public float musicVolume {              │   accessed directly, only through
    get {                               │   the property's getter
        return _musicVolume;
    }
    set {
        _musicVolume = value;

        if (music1Source != null) {     ◁────┐  Adjust volume of the
            music1Source.volume = _musicVolume;  │  AudioSource directly.
        }
    }
}
...
public bool musicMute {
    get {
        if (music1Source != null) {
            return music1Source.mute;
        }
        return false;                ◁────┐  Default value in case the
    }                                      │  AudioSource is missing
    set {
        if (music1Source != null) {
            music1Source.mute = value;
        }
    }
```

```
}

public void Startup(NetworkService service) {        ⟵
    Debug.Log("Audio manager starting...");

    network = service;

    music1Source.ignoreListenerVolume = true;
    music1Source.ignoreListenerPause = true;

    soundVolume = 1f;
    musicVolume = 1f;

    status = ManagerStatus.Started;
}
...
```

Italicized code was already in script, shown here for reference.

These properties tell the AudioSource to ignore the AudioListener volume.

The key to this code is realizing you can adjust the volume of an AudioSource directly, even though that audio source is ignoring the global volume defined in AudioListener. Properties for both volume and mute manipulate the individual music source.

The Startup() method initializes the music source with both ignoreListener-Volume and ignoreListenerPause turned on. As the names suggest, those properties cause the audio source to ignore the global volume setting on AudioListener.

You can click Play now to verify that the music is no longer affected by the existing volume control. Let's add a second UI control for the music volume; start by adjusting SettingsPopup.

> **Listing 11.12 Music volume controls in SettingsPopup**

```
...
public void OnMusicToggle() {
    Managers.Audio.musicMute = !Managers.Audio.musicMute;      ⟵
    Managers.Audio.PlaySound(sound);
}

public void OnMusicValue(float volume) {
    Managers.Audio.musicVolume = volume;      ⟵
}
...
```

Repeat the mute control, but use musicMute instead.

Repeat the volume control, but use musicVolume instead.

This code doesn't need a lot of explaining—it's mostly repeating the sound volume controls. Obviously, the AudioManager properties used have changed from soundMute/soundVolume to musicMute/musicVolume.

In the editor, create a button and slider, as you did before. Here are those steps again:

1. Change the pop-up's height to 225 (to fit more controls).
2. Create a UI button.
3. Parent the button to the pop-up.

4. Position the button at 0, –60.

5. Expand the button's hierarchy to select its text label.

6. Change the text to `Toggle Music`.

7. Create a slider (from the same UI menu).

8. Parent the slider to the pop-up and position it at 0, –85.

9. Set the slider's Value (at the bottom of the Inspector) to 1.

Link these UI controls to the code in `SettingsPopup`. Find the On Click/OnValue-Changed panel in the UI element's settings, click the + button to add an entry, drag the pop-up object to the object slot, and select the function from the menu. The functions you need to pick are `OnMusicToggle()` and `OnMusicValue()` from the Dynamic Float section of the menu.

Run this code and you'll see that the controls affect sound effects and music separately. This is getting pretty sophisticated, but one more bit of polish remains: cross-fade between music tracks.

11.4.3 *Fading between songs*

As a final bit of polish, let's make `AudioManager` fade in and out between different background tunes. Currently, the switch between music tracks is pretty jarring, with the sound suddenly cutting off and changing to the new track. We can smooth out that transition by having the volume of the previous track quickly dwindle away while the volume quickly rises from 0 on the new track. This is a simple but clever bit of code that combines both the volume control methods you just saw, along with a coroutine to change the volume incrementally over time.

Listing 11.13 adds a lot of bits to `AudioManager`, but most revolve around a simple concept: now that we have two separate audio sources, we'll play separate music tracks on separate audio sources, and incrementally increase the volume of one source while simultaneously decreasing the volume of the other. (As usual, italicized code was already in the script and is shown here for reference.)

Listing 11.13   Cross-fading between music in `AudioManager`

```
...
[SerializeField] AudioSource music2Source;    ◁——  Second AudioSource
                                                    (keep the first, too)

private AudioSource activeMusic;    ◁——┐
private AudioSource inactiveMusic;          Keep track of which source
                                            is active vs. inactive.

public float crossFadeRate = 1.5f;
private bool crossFading;    ◁——┐
...                                 A toggle to avoid bugs while
public float musicVolume {          a cross-fade is happening
    ...
    set {
        _musicVolume = value;
```

```
        if (music1Source != null && !crossFading) {
            music1Source.volume = _musicVolume;
            music2Source.volume = _musicVolume;
        }
    }
}
...
public bool musicMute {
    ...
    set {
        if (music1Source != null) {
            music1Source.mute = value;
            music2Source.mute = value;
        }
    }
}

public void Startup(NetworkService service) {
    Debug.Log("Audio manager starting...");

    network = service;

    music1Source.ignoreListenerVolume = true;
    music2Source.ignoreListenerVolume = true;
    music1Source.ignoreListenerPause = true;
    music2Source.ignoreListenerPause = true;

    soundVolume = 1f;
    musicVolume = 1f;

    activeMusic = music1Source;
    inactiveMusic = music2Source;

    status = ManagerStatus.Started;
}
...
private void PlayMusic(AudioClip clip) {
    if (crossFading) {return;}
    StartCoroutine(CrossFadeMusic(clip));
}
private IEnumerator CrossFadeMusic(AudioClip clip) {
    crossFading = true;

    inactiveMusic.clip = clip;
    inactiveMusic.volume = 0;
    inactiveMusic.Play();

    float scaledRate = crossFadeRate * musicVolume;
    while (activeMusic.volume > 0) {
        activeMusic.volume -= scaledRate * Time.deltaTime;
        inactiveMusic.volume += scaledRate * Time.deltaTime;

        yield return null;
    }
```

Adjust the volume on both music sources.

Initialize one as the active AudioSource.

Call a coroutine when changing music.

Yield statement pauses for one frame.

```
        AudioSource temp = activeMusic;        ◁────┐  Temporary variable to use
                                                     │  while swapping active and
        activeMusic = inactiveMusic;                 │  inactive
        activeMusic.volume = musicVolume;

        inactiveMusic = temp;
        inactiveMusic.Stop();

        crossFading = false;
    }

    public void StopMusic() {
        activeMusic.Stop();
        inactiveMusic.Stop();
    }
    ...
```

The first addition is a variable for the second music source. While keeping the first
`AudioSource` object, duplicate that object (make sure the settings are the same—
select Loop) and then drag the new object into this Inspector slot. The code also
defines the `AudioSource` variables `activeMusic` and `inactiveMusic`, but those are private variables used within the code and not exposed in the Inspector. Specifically,
those variables define which of the two audio sources is considered active or inactive
at any given time.

The code now calls a coroutine when playing new music. This coroutine sets the
new music playing on one `AudioSource` while the old music keeps playing on the old
`AudioSource`. Then, the coroutine incrementally increases the volume of the new
music while incrementally decreasing the volume of the old music. Once the cross-
fading is complete (that is, the volumes have completely exchanged places), the function swaps which audio source is considered active and inactive.

Great! We've completed the background music for our game's audio system.

Advanced game audio plugins for FMOD and Wwise

The audio system in Unity is powered by FMOD, a popular audio programming library.
Unity has integrated many features of FMOD, but more advanced audio features are
accessible through FMOD Studio, with a plugin offered at www.fmod.com/unity/.
Alternatively, Wwise is a different audio system that also offers a Unity plugin:
http://mng.bz/6mvD.

The examples in this chapter stick to the functionality built into Unity, because that
core functionality comprises the most important features for a game's audio system.
Most game developers have their audio needs served quite well by this core functionality, but these plugins are useful for those wishing to get even more intricate with
their game's audio.

Summary

- Sound effects should be uncompressed audio, and music should be compressed, but use the WAV format for both because Unity applies compression to imported audio.
- Audio clips can be 2D sounds that always play the same, or 3D sounds that react to the listener's position.
- The volume of sound effects is easily adjusted globally using Unity's `AudioListener`.
- You can set the volume on individual audio sources that play music.
- You can fade background music in and out by setting the volume on individual audio sources.

Putting the parts together into a complete game

This chapter covers

- Assembling objects and code from other projects
- Programming point-and-click controls
- Upgrading the UI from the old to a new system
- Loading new levels in response to objectives
- Setting up win/loss conditions
- Saving and loading the player's progress

The project in this chapter will tie together everything from previous chapters. Most chapters have been pretty self-contained, and we haven't taken an end-to-end look at the entire game. I'll walk you through pulling together pieces that have been introduced separately so that you know how to build a complete game from all of those pieces.

I'll also discuss the encompassing structure of the game, including switching levels and ending the game (displaying Game Over when you die, and Success when you reach the exit). And I'll show you how to save the game, because saving the player's progress becomes increasingly important as the game grows in size.

> **WARNING** Much of this chapter uses tasks that were explained in detail in pre-
> vious chapters, so I'll move through the steps quickly. If certain steps confuse
> you, refer to the relevant chapter (for example, chapter 7 about the UI) for a
> more detailed explanation.

This chapter's project is a demo of an action role-playing game (RPG). In this sort of
game, the camera is placed high and looks down sharply (see figure 12.1), and the
character is controlled by clicking the mouse where you want to go. You may be familiar with the game *Diablo*, which is an action RPG like this. I'm switching to yet another
game genre so that we can squeeze in one more genre before the end of the book!

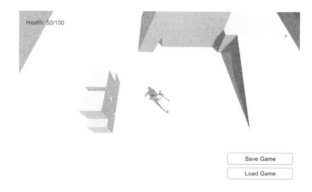

**Figure 12.1   Screenshot of
the top-down viewpoint**

In full, the project in this chapter will be the biggest game yet. It'll have these features:

- A top-down view with point-and-click movement
- The ability to click devices to operate them
- Scattered items you can collect
- Inventory that's displayed in a UI window
- Enemies wandering around the level
- The ability to save the game and restore your progress
- Three levels that must be completed in sequence

Whew, that's a lot to pack in; good thing this is almost the last chapter!

12.1   *Building an action RPG by repurposing projects*

We'll develop the action RPG demo by building on the project from chapter 9. Copy
that project's folder and open the copy in Unity to start working. Or, if you skipped
directly to this chapter, download the sample project for chapter 9 to build on that.

The reason we're building on the chapter 9 project is that it's the closest to our
goal for this chapter and thus will require the least modification (compared to other
projects). Ultimately, we'll pull together assets from several chapters, so technically it's
not that different than if we started with one of those projects and pulled in assets
from chapter 9.

Here's a recap of what's in the project from chapter 9:

- A character with an animation controller already set up
- A third-person camera that follows the character around
- A level with floors, walls, and ramps
- Lights and shadows all placed
- Operable devices, including a color-changing monitor
- Collectible inventory items
- Backend managers code framework

This hefty list of features covers quite a bit of the action in the RPG demo already, but we'll either need to modify or add a bit more.

12.1.1 *Assembling assets and code from multiple projects*

The first two modifications will be to update the managers framework and to bring in computer-controlled enemies. For the former task, recall that updates to the framework were made in chapter 10, which means those updates aren't in the project from chapter 9. For the latter task, recall that you programmed an enemy in chapter 3.

UPDATING THE MANAGERS FRAMEWORK

Updating the managers is a fairly simple task, so let's get that out of the way first. The `IGameManager` interface was modified in chapter 10.

Listing 12.1   Adjusted `IGameManager`

```
public interface IGameManager {
   ManagerStatus status {get;}

   void Startup(NetworkService service);
}
```

The code in this listing adds a reference to `NetworkService`, so also be sure to copy over that additional script; drag the file from its location in the chapter 10 project (remember, a Unity project is a folder on your disc, so get the file from there), and drop it in the new project. Now modify `Managers` to work with the changed interface.

Listing 12.2   Changing a bit of code in the `Managers` script

```
. . .
private IEnumerator StartupManagers() {          ⊲───┐   The adjustments are at the
   NetworkService network = new NetworkService();    │   beginning of this method.
                                                      ┘
   foreach (IGameManager manager in startSequence) {
      manager.Startup(network);
   }
   . . .
```

Finally, adjust both `InventoryManager` and `PlayerManager` to reflect the changed interface. The next listing shows the modified code from `InventoryManager`; `Player-Manager` needs the same code modifications but with different names.

Listing 12.3 Adjusting `InventoryManager` to reflect `IGameManager`

```
...
private NetworkService network;

public void Startup(NetworkService service) {
   Debug.Log("Inventory manager starting...");      ◁──┐  Same adjustments in both
                                                        │  managers, but change names
   network = service;

   items = new Dictionary<string, int>();
   ...
```

Once all the minor code changes are in, everything should still act as before. This update should work invisibly, and the game will still work the same. That adjustment was easy, but the next one will be harder.

BRINGING OVER THE AI ENEMY

Besides the `NetworkServices` adjustments from chapter 10, you also need the AI enemy from chapter 3. Implementing enemy characters involved a bunch of scripts and art assets, so you need to import all those assets.

First, copy over these scripts (remember, `WanderingAI` and `ReactiveTarget` were behaviors for the AI enemy, `Fireball` was the projectile fired, the enemy attacks the `PlayerCharacter` component, and `SceneController` handles spawning enemies):

- `PlayerCharacter`
- `SceneController`
- `WanderingAI`
- `ReactiveTarget`
- `Fireball`

Similarly, get the Flame material, Fireball prefab, and Enemy prefab by dragging in those files. If you got the enemy from chapter 11 instead of 3, you may also need the added fire particle material.

After copying over all the required assets, the links between assets will probably be broken, so you'll need to relink the referenced objects in broken assets to get them to work. In particular, check the scripts on all prefabs because they probably disconnected. For example, the Enemy prefab has two missing scripts in the Inspector, so click the circle button (indicated in figure 12.2) to choose `WanderingAI` and `ReactiveTarget` from the list of scripts. Similarly, check the Fireball prefab and relink that script if needed. Once you're through with the scripts, check the links to materials and textures.

Now add `SceneController` to the controller object and drag the Enemy prefab onto that component's Enemy slot in the Inspector. You may need to drag the Fireball

Figure 12.2   Linking a script to a component

prefab onto the Enemy's script component (select the Enemy prefab and look at `WanderingAI` in the Inspector). Also attach `PlayerCharacter` to the player object so that enemies will attack the player.

Play the game and you'll see the enemy wandering around. The enemy shoots fireballs at the player, although they won't do much damage; select the Fireball prefab and set its Damage value to `10`.

> **NOTE**   Currently, the enemy isn't particularly good at tracking down and hitting the player. In this case, I'd start by giving the enemy a wider field of vision (using the dot product approach from chapter 9). Ultimately, you'll spend a lot of time polishing a game, and that includes iterating on the behavior of enemies. Polishing a game to make it more fun, though crucial for a game to be released, isn't something you'll do in this book.

The other issue is that when you wrote this code in chapter 3, the player's health was an ad hoc addition, written for testing. Now the game has a `PlayerManager`, so modify `PlayerCharacter` according to the next listing in order to work with health in that manager.

Listing 12.4   Adjusting `PlayerCharacter` to use health in `PlayerManager`

```
using System.Collections;
using System.Collections.Generic;
using UnityEngine;

public class PlayerCharacter : MonoBehaviour {
    public void Hurt(int damage) {
        Managers.Player.ChangeHealth(-damage);        ⟵┐ Use the value in PlayerManager
    }                                                      instead of the variable in
}                                                          PlayerCharacter.
```

At this point, you have a game demo with pieces assembled from multiple previous projects. An enemy character has been added to the scene, making the game more threatening. But the controls and viewpoint are still from the third-person movement demo, so let's implement point-and-click controls for an action RPG.

12.1.2   *Programming point-and-click controls: Movement and devices*

This demo needs a top-down view and mouse control of the player's movement (refer to figure 12.1). Currently, the camera responds to the mouse, whereas the player responds to the keyboard (as programmed in chapter 8), which is the reverse of what you want in this chapter. In addition, you'll modify the color-changing monitor so that devices are operated by clicking them. In both cases, the existing code isn't terribly far from what you need; you'll make adjustments to both the movement and device scripts.

SETTING UP THE TOP-DOWN VIEW OF THE SCENE

First, you'll raise the camera to 8 Y to position it for an overhead view. You'll also adjust `OrbitCamera` to remove mouse controls from the camera and use only arrow keys.

Listing 12.5 Adjusting `OrbitCamera` to remove mouse controls

```
...
void LateUpdate() {
    rotY -= Input.GetAxis("Horizontal") * rotSpeed;          ⟵  Reverse the direction
    Quaternion rotation = Quaternion.Euler(0, rotY, 0);          from before.
    transform.position = target.position - (rotation * offset);
    transform.LookAt(target);
}
...
```

The camera's Near/Far clipping planes

While you're adjusting the camera, I want to point out the Near/Far clipping planes. These settings never came up before because the defaults are fine, but you may need to adjust these in a future project.

If you need to adjust these values, select the camera in the scene and look for the Clipping Planes section in the Inspector; both Near and Far are numbers you'll type here. These values define near and far boundaries within which meshes are rendered. Polygons closer than the Near clipping plane or farther than the Far clipping plane aren't drawn.

You want the Near/Far clipping planes as close together as possible, while still being far enough apart to render everything in your scene. When those planes are too far apart (Near is too close, or Far is too far), the rendering algorithm can no longer tell which polygons are closer. This results in a characteristic rendering error called *z-fighting* (as in the z-axis for depth), where polygons flicker on top of each other.

With the camera raised even higher, the view when you play the game will be top-down. At the moment, though, the movement controls still use the keyboard, so let's write a script for point-and-click movement.

WRITING THE MOVEMENT CODE

The general idea for this code will be to automatically move the player toward its target position (as illustrated in figure 12.3). This position is set by clicking in the scene. In this way, the code that moves the player isn't directly reacting to the mouse, but the player's movement is being controlled indirectly by clicking.

Every frame, the following sequence of steps is run:

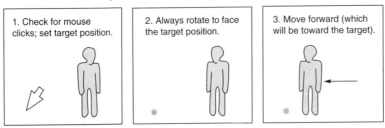

Figure 12.3   How point-and-click controls work

NOTE This movement algorithm is useful for AI characters as well. Rather than using mouse clicks, the target position could be on a path that the character follows.

To implement this, create a new script called PointClickMovement and replace the RelativeMovement component on the player. Start coding PointClickMovement by pasting in the entirety of RelativeMovement (because you still want most of that script for handling falling and animations). Then, adjust the code according to this listing.

Listing 12.6   New movement code in PointClickMovement script

```
...
public class PointClickMovement : MonoBehaviour {          Correct the name
...                                                        after pasting scripts.
public float deceleration = 25.0f;
public float targetBuffer = 1.5f;

private float curSpeed = 0f;            Define this value as "nullable"
private Vector3? targetPos;             with the ? symbol.
...
void Update() {
    Vector3 movement = Vector3.zero;
                                           Set the target position
                                           when the mouse clicks.
        if (Input.GetMouseButton(0)) {
Raycast at      Ray ray = Camera.main.ScreenPointToRay(Input.mousePosition);
the mouse       RaycastHit mouseHit;
position.       if (Physics.Raycast(ray, out mouseHit)) {     Set target to the
                    targetPos = mouseHit.point;               position that was hit.
                    curSpeed = moveSpeed;
            }
        }
                                        Move if the target
                                        position is set.      Rotate toward the target
        if (targetPos != null) {                             only while moving quickly.
            if (curSpeed > moveSpeed * .5f) {
                Vector3 adjustedPos = new Vector3(targetPos.Value.x,
                    transform.position.y, targetPos.Value.z);
                Quaternion targetRot = Quaternion.LookRotation(
                    adjustedPos - transform.position);
```

```
        transform.rotation = Quaternion.Slerp(transform.rotation,
            targetRot, rotSpeed * Time.deltaTime);
    }

    movement = curSpeed * Vector3.forward;
    movement = transform.TransformDirection(movement);

    if (Vector3.Distance(targetPos.Value, transform.position) <
    ➥ targetBuffer) {
        curSpeed -= deceleration * Time.deltaTime;      ◁──┐ Decelerate to 0 when
        if (curSpeed <= 0) {                                │ close to the target.
            targetPos = null;
        }
    }
}
animator.SetFloat("Speed", movement.sqrMagnitude);  ◁──┐ Everything stays the
...                                                     │ same from here down.
```

Almost everything at the beginning of the Update() method was gutted, because that code was handling keyboard movement. Notice that this new code has two main if statements: one that runs when the mouse clicks, and one that runs when a target is set.

> **TIP** *Nullable values* are a handy programming trick used in this script. Notice that the target position value is defined as Vector3? instead of just Vector3; this is C# syntax for declaring a nullable value. Some value types (such as Vector3) cannot normally be set to null, but you may encounter a situation where it is useful to have a null state that means "no value is set." In that case, you can make it a nullable value, allowing you to set the value to null, and then access the underlying Vector3 (or whatever) by typing targetPos.Value.

When the mouse clicks, set the target according to where the mouse clicked. Here's yet another great use for raycasting: to determine which point in the scene is under the mouse cursor. The target position is set to where the mouse hits.

As for the second conditional, first rotate to face the target. Quaternion.Slerp() rotates smoothly to face the target, rather than immediately snapping to that rotation; also lock rotation while slowing down (otherwise, the player can rotate oddly when at the target) by rotating only when over half-speed. Then, transform the forward direction from the player's local coordinates to global coordinates (to move forward). Finally, check the distance between the player and the target: if the player has almost reached the target, decrement the movement speed and eventually end the movement by removing the target position.

Exercise: Turn off jump control

Currently, this script still has the jump control from RelativeMovement. The player still jumps when the spacebar is pressed, but there shouldn't be a jump button with point-and-click movement. Here's a hint: adjust the code inside the 'if (hitGround)' conditional branch.

This takes care of moving the player by using mouse controls. Play the game to test it out. Next, let's make devices operate when clicked.

> ### Pathfinding with A* and NavMesh
> The movement code we just wrote directs the player straight toward the target. However, characters in a game often must find their way around obstacles, rather than moving in a straight line. Navigating characters around obstacles is referred to as *pathfinding*. Because this is such a common situation in games, Unity provides a built-in pathfinding solution, called NavMesh. Learn more at the following links:
>
> - http://mng.bz/o8Mr
> - http://mng.bz/nryg
>
> Meanwhile, although NavMesh is free and works well, many developers prefer A* Pathfinding Project, available from https://arongranberg.com/astar/.

OPERATING DEVICES BY USING THE MOUSE

In chapter 9 (and here, until we adjust the code), devices were operated by pressing a key. Instead, they should operate when clicked. To do this, you'll first create a base script that all devices will inherit from; the base script will have the mouse control, and devices will inherit that. Create a new script called BaseDevice and write the code shown in the following listing.

Listing 12.7   BaseDevice script that operates when clicked

```
using System.Collections;
using System.Collections.Generic;
using UnityEngine;

public class BaseDevice : MonoBehaviour {
    public float radius = 3.5f;                          Function that runs
                                                         when clicked
    void OnMouseUp() {
        Transform player = GameObject.FindWithTag("Player").transform;
        Vector3 playerPosition = player.position;
                                                         Correction to
                                                         vertical position
        playerPosition.y = transform.position.y;
        if (Vector3.Distance(transform.position, playerPosition) < radius) {
            Vector3 direction = transform.position - playerPosition;
            if (Vector3.Dot(player.forward, direction) > .5f) {
                Operate();                               Call Operate() if the player
            }                                            is nearby and facing.
        }
    }

    public virtual void Operate() {                      virtual marks a method that
        // behavior of the specific device              inheritance can override.
    }
}
```

Most of this code happens inside OnMouseDown because MonoBehaviour calls that method when the object is clicked. First, it checks the distance to the player (with a vertical position correction, just as in chapter 9) and then it uses the dot product to see whether the player is facing the device. Operate() is an empty shell to be filled in by devices that inherit this script.

> **NOTE** This code looks in the scene for an object with the Player tag, so assign this tag to the player object. Tag is a drop-down menu at the top of the Inspector; you can define custom tags as well, but several tags are defined by default, including Player. Select the player object to edit it and then select the Player tag.

Now that BaseDevice is programmed, you can modify ColorChangeDevice to inherit from that script. This is the new code.

Listing 12.8 Adjusting `ColorChangeDevice` to inherit from `BaseDevice`

```
using System.Collections;
using System.Collections.Generic;
using UnityEngine;

public class ColorChangeDevice : BaseDevice {          ⟵  Inherit BaseDevice instead
    public override void Operate() {                        of MonoBehaviour.
        Color random = new Color(Random.Range(0f,1f),  ⟵  Override this method
            Random.Range(0f,1f), Random.Range(0f,1f));      from the base class.
        GetComponent<Renderer>().material.color = random;
    }
}
```

Because this script inherits from BaseDevice instead of MonoBehaviour, it gets the mouse control functionality. Then it overrides the empty Operate() method to program the color-changing behavior.

Make the same changes (inherit from BaseDevice instead of MonoBehaviour, and add override to the Operate method) to DoorOpenDevice. Now these devices will operate when you click them. Also remove the player's DeviceOperator script component, because that script operates devices by pressing the key.

This new device input brings up an issue with the movement controls: currently, the movement target is set anytime the mouse clicks, but you don't want to set the movement target when clicking devices. You can fix this issue by using layers; similar to the way a tag was set on the player, objects can be set to different layers, and the code can check for that. Adjust PointClickMovement to check for the object's layer.

Listing 12.9 Adjusting mouse-click code in `PointClickMovement`

```
...
Ray ray = Camera.main.ScreenPointToRay(Input.mousePosition);
RaycastHit mouseHit;
```

```
if (Physics.Raycast(ray, out mouseHit)) {
    GameObject hitObject = mouseHit.transform.gameObject;
    if (hitObject.layer == LayerMask.NameToLayer("Ground")) {
        targetPos = mouseHit.point;
        curSpeed = moveSpeed;
    }
}
...
```

Added code; the rest is reference.

This listing adds a conditional inside the mouse-click code to see whether the clicked object is on the Ground layer. Layers (like Tags) is a drop-down menu at the top of the Inspector; click it to see the options. Also, like tags, several layers are already defined by default. You want to create a new layer, so choose Edit Layers in the menu. Type `Ground` in an empty layer slot (probably slot 8; `NameToLayer()` in the code converts names into layer numbers so that you can use the name instead of the number).

Now that the Ground layer has been added to the menu, set ground objects to the Ground layer—that means the floor of the building, along with the ramps and platforms that the player can walk on. Select those objects, and then select Ground in the Layers menu.

Play the game and you won't move when clicking the color-changing monitor. Great, the point-and-click controls are complete! One more thing to bring into this project from previous projects is the UI.

12.1.3 *Replacing the old GUI with a new interface*

Chapter 9 used Unity's old immediate-mode GUI because that approach was simpler to code. But the UI from chapter 9 doesn't look as nice as the one from chapter 7, so let's bring over that interface system. The newer UI is more visually polished than the old GUI; figure 12.4 shows the interface you're going to create.

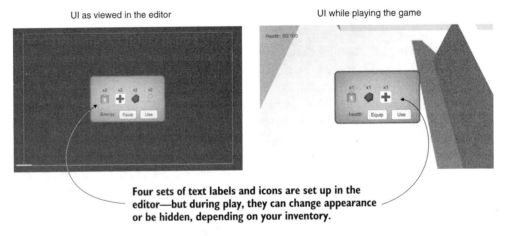

Four sets of text labels and icons are set up in the editor—but during play, they can change appearance or be hidden, depending on your inventory.

Figure 12.4   The UI for this chapter's project

First, you'll set up the UI graphics. Once the UI images are all in the scene, you can attach scripts to the UI objects. I'll list the steps involved without going into detail; if you need a refresher, refer to chapter 7. If needed, install the TextMeshPro and 2D Sprite packages (refer back to chapters 5 and 6 for these) before starting:

1. Import popup.png as a sprite (choose Texture Type).
2. In the Sprite Editor, set a 12-pixel border on all sides (remember to apply changes).
3. Create a canvas in the scene (GameObject > UI > Canvas).
4. Choose the Pixel Perfect setting of the canvas.
5. (Optional) Name the object HUD Canvas and switch to 2D view mode.
6. Create a Text object connected to that canvas (GameObject > UI > Text - Text-MeshPro).
7. Set the Text object's anchor to top left and the object's position to 120, -50.
8. Set the label's Vertex Color to black, set Font Size to 16, and type Health: as the text.
9. Create an image connected to that canvas (GameObject > UI > Image).
10. Name the new object Inventory Popup.
11. Assign the pop-up sprite to the image's Source Image.
12. Set Image Type to Sliced and select Fill Center.
13. Position the pop-up image at 0, 0 and scale the pop-up to 250 for width and 150 for height.

> **NOTE** Recall how to switch between viewing the 3D scene and the 2D inter-face: toggle 2D view mode and double-click either the Canvas or the Building to zoom in on that object.

Now you have the Health label in the corner and the large blue pop-up window in the center. Let's program these parts first before getting deeper into the UI functionality. The interface code will use the same Messenger system from chapter 7, so copy over the Messenger script. Then create a GameEvent script.

Listing 12.10   GameEvent script to use with this Messenger system

```
public static class GameEvent {
    public const string HEALTH_UPDATED = "HEALTH_UPDATED";
}
```

For now, only one event is defined; over the course of this chapter, you'll add a few more events. Broadcast this event from PlayerManager.

Listing 12.11   Broadcasting the health event from PlayerManager

```
...
public void ChangeHealth(int value) {
    health += value;
```

```
if (health > maxHealth) {
    health = maxHealth;
} else if (health < 0) {
    health = 0;
}

Messenger.Broadcast(GameEvent.HEALTH_UPDATED);
}
...
```

Add a line to the end of this function.

The event is broadcast every time `ChangeHealth()` finishes to tell the rest of the program that the health has changed. You want to adjust the health label in response to this event, so create a `UIController` script.

Listing 12.12   The script `UIController`, which handles the interface

```
using System.Collections;
using System.Collections.Generic;
using UnityEngine;
using TMPro;

public class UIController : MonoBehaviour {
    [SerializeField] TMP_Text healthLabel;
    [SerializeField] InventoryPopup popup;

    void OnEnable() {
        Messenger.AddListener(GameEvent.HEALTH_UPDATED, OnHealthUpdated);
    }
    void OnDisable() {
        Messenger.RemoveListener(GameEvent.HEALTH_UPDATED, OnHealthUpdated);
    }

    void Start() {
        OnHealthUpdated();

        popup.gameObject.SetActive(false);
    }

    void Update() {
        if (Input.GetKeyDown(KeyCode.M)) {
            bool isShowing = popup.gameObject.activeSelf;
            popup.gameObject.SetActive(!isShowing);
            popup.Refresh();
        }
    }

    private void OnHealthUpdated() {
        string message = $"Health:
    {Managers.Player.health}/{Managers.Player.maxHealth}";
        healthLabel.text = message;
    }
}
```

Reference the UI object in the scene.

Set the listener for the health update event.

Call the function manually at startup.

Initialize the pop-up to be hidden.

Toggle the pop-up with the M key.

Event listener calls the function to update the health label.

Remove `BasicUI` from the `Controller` object, and attach this new script to the `Canvas` (notably *not* the `Controller` object, which should have only `SceneController` now). Also, create an `InventoryPopup` script (add an empty public `Refresh()` method for now; the rest will be filled in later) and attach it to the `Inventory Popup` object. Now you can drag the pop-up to the reference slot in the `Canvas` object's `UIController` component (and then do the same for the health label).

The health label changes when you get hurt or use health packs, and pressing the M key toggles the pop-up window. One last detail to adjust is that clicking the pop-up window currently causes the player to move; as with devices, you don't want to set the target position when the UI has been clicked. Make the adjustment to `PointClickMovement`.

Listing 12.13 Checking the UI in `PointClickMovement`

```
using UnityEngine.EventSystems;
...
void Update() {
  Vector3 movement = Vector3.zero;
  if (Input.GetMouseButton(0) &&
    !EventSystem.current.IsPointerOverGameObject()) {
  ...
```

Note that the conditional checks whether or not the mouse is on the UI. That completes the overall structure of the interface, so now let's deal with the inventory pop-up specifically.

IMPLEMENTING THE INVENTORY POP-UP

The pop-up window is currently blank, but it should display the player's inventory (depicted in figure 12.5). These steps will create the UI objects:

1. Create four images and parent them to the pop-up (that is, drag objects in the Hierarchy).
2. Create four text labels and parent them to the pop-up.
3. Position all the images at 0 Y and set X values to -75, -25, 25, and 75.

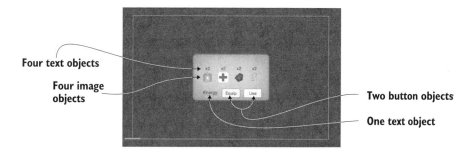

Figure 12.5 Diagram of the inventory UI

4. Position the text labels at 45 Y and set X values to -75, -25, 25, and 75.

5. Set the text (not the anchor!) to Center alignment, Bottom vertical align, and Height 60.

6. Enter x2 for all the text labels, set Vertex Color black, and Font Size to 16.

7. In Resources, set all inventory icons as Sprite (instead of Textures).

8. Drag these sprites to the Source Image slot of the Image objects (also set Native Size).

9. Add another text label and two buttons, all parented to the pop-up.

10. Position this text label at -140, -45 with Right alignment and Middle vertical align.

11. Type Energy: for the text on this label, set Vertex Color to black, and set Font Size to 14.

12. Set both buttons to Width 60. For Position, set Y to -50 and X to 0 or 70.

13. Expand the two buttons in the Hierarchy and type Equip on one button and Use on the other.

These are the visual elements for the inventory pop-up; next is the code. Write the contents of the following into the InventoryPopup script.

Listing 12.14 Full script for InventoryPopup

```
using System.Collections;
using System.Collections.Generic;
using UnityEngine;
using UnityEngine.UI;
using UnityEngine.EventSystems;
using TMPro;

public class InventoryPopup : MonoBehaviour {
    [SerializeField] Image[] itemIcons;              Arrays to reference four
    [SerializeField] TMP_Text[] itemLabels;          images and text labels

    [SerializeField] TMP_Text curItemLabel;
    [SerializeField] Button equipButton;
    [SerializeField] Button useButton;

    private string curItem;

    public void Refresh() {
        List<string> itemList = Managers.Inventory.GetItemList();

        int len = itemIcons.Length;                    Check the inventory list while
        for (int i = 0; i < len; i++) {                looping through all UI images.
            if (i < itemList.Count) {          ◁
                itemIcons[i].gameObject.SetActive(true);
                itemLabels[i].gameObject.SetActive(true);

                string item = itemList[i];                       Load the sprite from
                                                                          Resources.
                Sprite sprite = Resources.Load<Sprite>($"Icons/{item}");   ◁
```

Resize the image to the native size of the sprite.

```
        itemIcons[i].sprite = sprite;
        itemIcons[i].SetNativeSize();

        int count = Managers.Inventory.GetItemCount(item);
        string message = $"x{count}";
        if (item == Managers.Inventory.equippedItem) {
            message = "Equipped\n" + message;
        }
        itemLabels[i].text = message;
```

Label may say "Equipped" in addition to item count.

Enable clicking icons.

```
        EventTrigger.Entry entry = new EventTrigger.Entry();
        entry.eventID = EventTriggerType.PointerClick;
        entry.callback.AddListener((BaseEventData data) => {
            OnItem(item);
        });
```

Lambda function to trigger differently for each item

Add this listener function to EventTrigger.

```
        EventTrigger trigger = itemIcons[i].GetComponent<EventTrigger>();
        trigger.triggers.Clear();
        trigger.triggers.Add(entry);
    }
    else {
        itemIcons[i].gameObject.SetActive(false);
        itemLabels[i].gameObject.SetActive(false);
    }
}
```

Clear the listener to refresh from the clean slate.

Hide this image/text if there's no item to display.

```
    if (!itemList.Contains(curItem)) {
        curItem = null;
    }
    if (curItem == null) {
        curItemLabel.gameObject.SetActive(false);
        equipButton.gameObject.SetActive(false);
        useButton.gameObject.SetActive(false);
    }
```

Hide buttons if no item is selected.

Display currently selected item.

```
    else {
        curItemLabel.gameObject.SetActive(true);
        equipButton.gameObject.SetActive(true);
        if (curItem == "health") {
            useButton.gameObject.SetActive(true);
        } else {
            useButton.gameObject.SetActive(false);
        }

        curItemLabel.text = $"{curItem}:";
    }
}
```

Use button only for health item.

```
public void OnItem(string item) {
    curItem = item;
    Refresh();
}
```

Function called by mouse click listener

Refresh the inventory display after making changes.

```
public void OnEquip() {
    Managers.Inventory.EquipItem(curItem);
    Refresh();
```

```
    }

    public void OnUse() {
        Managers.Inventory.ConsumeItem(curItem);
        if (curItem == "health") {
            Managers.Player.ChangeHealth(25);
        }
        Refresh();
    }
}
```

Whew, that was a long script! With this programmed, it's time to link everything in the interface. The script component on the pop-up object now has the various object references, including the two arrays; expand both arrays and set to a length of 4 (see figure 12.6). Drag the four images to the icons array, and drag the four text labels to the labels array.

An array defined by the script component. Expand the array by clicking the arrow.

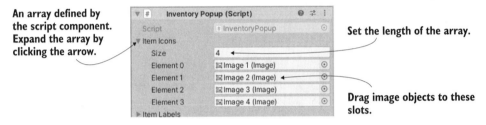

Set the length of the array.

Drag image objects to these slots.

Figure 12.6   Arrays displayed in the Inspector

NOTE   If you aren't sure which object was dragged where (they all look the same), click the slot in the Inspector to see that object highlighted in the Hierarchy view.

Similarly, slots in the component reference the text label and buttons at the bottom of the pop-up. After linking those objects, you'll add OnClick listeners for both buttons. Link these events to the pop-up object, and choose either OnEquip() or OnUse() as appropriate.

Finally, add an EventTrigger component to all four of the item images. The InventoryPopup script modifies this component on each icon, so they better have this component! You'll find EventTrigger under Add Component > Event. (It may be more convenient to copy/paste the component by clicking the little gear button in the top corner of the component, select Copy Component from one object, and then Paste As New on the other.) Add this component but don't assign event listeners, because that's done in the InventoryPopup code.

That completes the inventory UI! Play the game to watch the inventory pop-up respond when you collect items and click buttons. We're now finished assembling parts from previous projects; next I'll explain how to build a more expansive game from this beginning.

12.2 Developing the overarching game structure

Now that you have a functioning action RPG demo, we're going to build the overarching structure of this game. By that, I mean the overall flow of the game through multiple levels and progressing through the game by beating levels. What we got from chapter 9's project was a single level, but the road map for this chapter specified three levels.

Doing this will involve decoupling the scene even further from the Managers backend, so you'll broadcast messages about the managers (just as PlayerManager broadcasts health updates). Create a new script called StartupEvent (listing 12.15); define these events in a separate script because these events go with the reusable Managers system, whereas GameEvent is specific to the game.

Listing 12.15 The `StartupEvent` script

```
public static class StartupEvent {
    public const string MANAGERS_STARTED = "MANAGERS_STARTED";
    public const string MANAGERS_PROGRESS = "MANAGERS_PROGRESS";
}
```

Now it's time to start adjusting Managers, including broadcasting these new events!

12.2.1 Controlling mission flow and multiple levels

Currently, the project has only one scene, and the Game Managers object is in that scene. The problem with that is that every scene will have its own set of game managers, whereas you want a single set of game managers shared by all scenes. To do that, you'll create a separate Startup scene that initializes the managers and then shares that object with the other scenes of the game.

We're also going to need a new manager to handle progress through the game. Create a new script called MissionManager.

Listing 12.16 Creating `MissionManager`

```
using System.Collections;
using System.Collections.Generic;
using UnityEngine;
using UnityEngine.SceneManagement;

public class MissionManager : MonoBehaviour, IGameManager {
    public ManagerStatus status {get; private set;}

    public int curLevel {get; private set;}
    public int maxLevel {get; private set;}

    private NetworkService network;

    public void Startup(NetworkService service) {
        Debug.Log("Mission manager starting...");
```

```
        network = service;

        curLevel = 0;
        maxLevel = 1;

        status = ManagerStatus.Started;
    }

    public void GoToNext() {
        if (curLevel < maxLevel) {    ⟵──── Check if last level reached.
            curLevel++;
            string name = $"Level{curLevel}";
            Debug.Log($"Loading {name}");
            SceneManager.LoadScene(name);    ⟵─┐ Unity's command
        } else {                              │ to load a scene
            Debug.Log("Last level");
        }
    }
}
```

For the most part, nothing unusual is going on in this listing, but note the Load-Scene() method near the end. Although I mentioned this method before (in chapter 5), it's more important now. That's Unity's method for loading a scene file; in chapter 5, you used it to reload the one scene in the game, but you can load any scene by passing in the name of the scene file.

Attach this script to the Game Managers object in the scene. Also add the new component to the Managers script.

Listing 12.17 Adding a new component to the Managers script

```
...
[RequireComponent(typeof(MissionManager))]

public class Managers : MonoBehaviour {
    public static PlayerManager Player {get; private set;}
    public static InventoryManager Inventory {get; private set;}
    public static MissionManager Mission {get; private set;}
    ...
    void Awake() {                              │ Unity's command to persist
        DontDestroyOnLoad(gameObject);    ⟵──┘ an object between scenes

        Player = GetComponent<PlayerManager>();
        Inventory = GetComponent<InventoryManager>();
        Mission = GetComponent<MissionManager>();

        startSequence = new List<IGameManager>();
        startSequence.Add(Player);
        startSequence.Add(Inventory);
        startSequence.Add(Mission);
```

```
    StartCoroutine(StartupManagers());
}

private IEnumerator StartupManagers() {
  ...
    if (numReady > lastReady) {
      Debug.Log($"Progress: {numReady}/{numModules}");
      Messenger<int, int>.Broadcast(
        StartupEvent.MANAGERS_PROGRESS, numReady, numModules);
    }

    yield return null;
  }

  Debug.Log("All managers started up");
  Messenger.Broadcast(StartupEvent.MANAGERS_STARTED);
}
...
```

> **Startup event broadcast with data related to the event.**

> **Startup event broadcast without parameters.**

Most of this code should already be familiar to you (adding `MissionManager` is like adding other managers), but there are two new parts. One is the event that sends two integer values; you saw both generic valueless events and messages with a single number before, but you can send an arbitrary number of values with the same syntax.

The other new bit of code is the `DontDestroyOnLoad()` method. It's a method provided by Unity for persisting an object between scenes. Normally, all objects in a scene are purged when a new scene loads, but by using `DontDestroyOnLoad()` on an object, you ensure that object will still be there in the new scene.

SEPARATE SCENES FOR STARTUP AND LEVEL

Because the Game Managers object will persist in all scenes, you must separate the managers from individual levels of the game. In Project view, duplicate the scene file (Edit > Duplicate) and then rename the two files appropriately: one `Startup` and the other `Level1`. Open Level1 and delete the Game Managers object (it'll be provided by Startup). Open Startup and delete everything other than Game Managers, Controller, Main Camera, HUD Canvas, and EventSystem. Adjust the camera by removing the `OrbitCamera` component, and changing the Clear Flags menu from Skybox to Solid Color. Remove the script components on Controller, and delete the UI objects (health label and `Inventory Popup`) parented to the `Canvas`.

The UI is currently empty, so create a new slider (see figure 12.7) and then turn off its Interactable setting. The Controller object no longer has any script components, so create a new `StartupController` script (listing 12.18) and attach that to the Controller object.

Remaining objects:
Game Managers
Controller
HUD Canvas
EventSystem
Main Camera

Set the slider to
noninteractive

Replace everything on
Canvas with a Slider.

Figure 12.7   The Startup scene with everything unnecessary removed

```
Listing 12.18   The new StartupController script
```
```csharp
using System.Collections;
using System.Collections.Generic;
using UnityEngine;
using UnityEngine.UI;

public class StartupController : MonoBehaviour {
   [SerializeField] Slider progressBar;

   void OnEnable() {
      Messenger<int, int>.AddListener(StartupEvent.MANAGERS_PROGRESS,
         OnManagersProgress);
      Messenger.AddListener(StartupEvent.MANAGERS_STARTED,
         OnManagersStarted);
   }
   void OnDisable() {
      Messenger<int, int>.RemoveListener(StartupEvent.MANAGERS_PROGRESS,
         OnManagersProgress);
      Messenger.RemoveListener(StartupEvent.MANAGERS_STARTED,
         OnManagersStarted);
   }

   private void OnManagersProgress(int numReady, int numModules) {
      float progress = (float)numReady / numModules;
      progressBar.value = progress;          ◁──┐  Update the slider to
   }                                              show loading progress.

   private void OnManagersStarted() {
      Managers.Mission.GoToNext();    ◁──┐  Load the next scene after
   }                                        managers have started.
}
```

Next, link the Slider object to the slot in the Inspector. One last thing to do in preparation is add the two scenes to Build Settings. Building the app will be the topic of the next chapter, so for now choose File > Build Settings to see and adjust the list of scenes. Click the Add Open Scenes button to add a scene to the list (load both scenes and do this for each).

NOTE You need to add the scenes to Build Settings so that they can be loaded. If you don't, Unity won't know what scenes are available. You didn't need to do this in chapter 5 because you weren't actually switching levels— you were just reloading the current scene.

Now you can launch the game by clicking Play from the Startup scene. The Game Managers object will be shared in both scenes.

WARNING Because the managers are loaded in the Startup scene, you always need to launch the game from that scene. You could remember to always open that scene before clicking Play, but this editor script will automatically switch to a set scene when you click Play: https://github.com/jhocking/from-unity-wiki/blob/main/SceneAutoLoader.cs.

TIP By default, the lighting system regenerates the lightmaps when the level is loaded. But this works only while you are editing the level; lightmaps won't be generated when loading levels while the game is running. As you did in chapter 10, you can turn off Auto lighting in the lighting window (Window > Rendering > Lighting) and then click the button to manually bake lightmaps (remember, don't touch the lighting data that's created).

This structural change handles the sharing of game managers between different scenes, but you still don't have any success or failure conditions within the level.

12.2.2 *Completing a level by reaching the exit*

To handle level completion, you'll put an object in the scene for the player to touch, and that object will inform `MissionManager` when the player reaches the objective. This will involve the UI responding to a message about level completion, so add another entry to `GameEvent`.

Listing 12.19 Level Complete added to `GameEvent`

```
public static class GameEvent {
    public const string HEALTH_UPDATED = "HEALTH_UPDATED";
    public const string LEVEL_COMPLETE = "LEVEL_COMPLETE";
}
```

Now add a new method to `MissionManager` to keep track of mission objectives and broadcast the new event message.

Listing 12.20 Objective method in `MissionManager`

```
...
public void ReachObjective() {
    // could have logic to handle multiple objectives
    Messenger.Broadcast(GameEvent.LEVEL_COMPLETE);
}
...
```

Adjust the `UIController` script to respond to that event.

Listing 12.21 New event listener in `UIController`

```
...
[SerializeField] TMP_Text levelEnding;
...
void OnEnable() {
    Messenger.AddListener(GameEvent.HEALTH_UPDATED, OnHealthUpdated);
    Messenger.AddListener(GameEvent.LEVEL_COMPLETE, OnLevelComplete);
}
void OnDisable() {
    Messenger.RemoveListener(GameEvent.HEALTH_UPDATED, OnHealthUpdated);
    Messenger.RemoveListener(GameEvent.LEVEL_COMPLETE, OnLevelComplete);
}
...
void Start() {
    OnHealthUpdated();

    levelEnding.gameObject.SetActive(false);
    popup.gameObject.SetActive(false);
}
...
private void OnLevelComplete() {
    StartCoroutine(CompleteLevel());
}
private IEnumerator CompleteLevel() {
    levelEnding.gameObject.SetActive(true);
    levelEnding.text = "Level Complete!";

    yield return new WaitForSeconds(2);    ◁──┐ Show the message for two seconds
                                                and then go to next level.
    Managers.Mission.GoToNext();
}
...
```

You'll notice that this listing has a reference to a text label. Open the Level1 scene to edit it, and create a new UI text object. This label will be a level completion message that appears in the middle of the screen. Set this text to Width 240, Height 60, Center for both Align and Vertical-align, Vertex Color black, and Font Size 22. Type Level Complete! in the text area and then link this text object to the `levelEnding` reference of `UIController`.

Finally, we'll create an object that the player touches to complete the level (figure 12.8 shows what the objective looks like). This will be similar to collectible items: it needs a material and a script, and you'll make the entire thing a prefab.

Create a cube object at Position 18, 1, 0. Select the Is Trigger option of the Box Collider, turn off both Cast and Receive Shadows in Mesh Renderer, and set the object to the Ignore Raycast layer. Create a new material called `objective`; make it bright

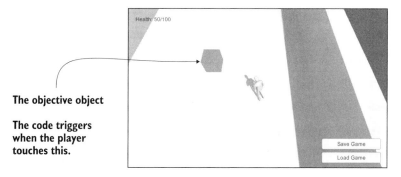

The objective object

The code triggers when the player touches this.

Figure 12.8   Objective object that the player touches to complete the level

green and set the shader to Unlit > Color for a flat, bright look. Next, create the `ObjectiveTrigger` script and attach that script to the cube object.

Listing 12.22   Code for `ObjectiveTrigger` to put on objective objects

```
using System.Collections;
using System.Collections.Generic;
using UnityEngine;

public class ObjectiveTrigger : MonoBehaviour {        Call the new objective
    void OnTriggerEnter(Collider other) {              method in MissionManager.
        Managers.Mission.ReachObjective();    ◁
    }
}
```

Drag this object from the Hierarchy into Project view to turn it into a prefab; in future levels, you could put the prefab in the scene. Now play the game and go reach the objective. The completion message shows when you beat the level. Next, let's have a failure message to show when you lose.

12.2.3   Losing the level when caught by enemies

The failure condition will be when the player runs out of health (because of the enemy attacking). First, add another entry in `GameEvent`:

```
public const string LEVEL_FAILED = "LEVEL_FAILED";
```

Now adjust `PlayerManager` to broadcast this message when the player's health drops to 0.

Listing 12.23   Broadcast level failed from `PlayerManager`

```
...
public void Startup(NetworkService service) {
    Debug.Log("Player manager starting...");
```

```
   network = service;                     Call the update method instead
                                          of setting variables directly.
   UpdateData(50, 100);        ←─┘

   status = ManagerStatus.Started;
}

public void UpdateData(int health, int maxHealth) {
   this.health = health;
   this.maxHealth = maxHealth;
}

public void ChangeHealth(int value) {
   health += value;
   if (health > maxHealth) {
      health = maxHealth;
   } else if (health < 0) {
      health = 0;
   }

   if (health == 0) {
      Messenger.Broadcast(GameEvent.LEVEL_FAILED);
   }
   Messenger.Broadcast(GameEvent.HEALTH_UPDATED);
}
                                     Reset the player to
                                     the initial state.
public void Respawn() {      ←─┘
   UpdateData(50, 100);
}
...
```

Add a method to `MissionManager` for restarting the level.

Listing 12.24   `MissionManager`, which can restart the current level

```
...
public void RestartCurrent() {
   string name = $"Level{curLevel}";
   Debug.Log($"Loading {name}");
   SceneManager.LoadScene(name);
}
...
```

With that in place, add another event listener to `UIController`.

Listing 12.25   Responding to failed level in `UIController`

```
...
Messenger.AddListener(GameEvent.LEVEL_FAILED, OnLevelFailed);
...
Messenger.RemoveListener(GameEvent.LEVEL_FAILED, OnLevelFailed);
...
```

```
private void OnLevelFailed() {
   StartCoroutine(FailLevel());
}
private IEnumerator FailLevel() {
   levelEnding.gameObject.SetActive(true);
   levelEnding.text = "Level Failed";          ◁─── Reuse the same text label,
                                                    but set a different message.
   yield return new WaitForSeconds(2);

   Managers.Player.Respawn();                        Restart the current level
   Managers.Mission.RestartCurrent();    ◁───        after a two-second pause.
}
...
```

Play the game and let the enemy shoot you several times; the level failure message will appear. Great job—the player can now complete and fail levels! Building off that, the game must keep track of the player's progress.

12.3 Handling the player's progression through the game

Right now, the individual level operates independently, without any relation to the overall game. You'll add two things that will make progress through the game feel more complete: saving the player's progress and detecting when the game (not just the level) is complete.

12.3.1 Saving and loading the player's progress

Saving and loading the game is an important part of most games. Unity and Mono provide I/O functionality that you can use for this purpose. Before you can start using that, though, you must add UpdateData() for both MissionManager and Inventory-Manager. That method will work as it does in PlayerManager and will enable code outside the manager to update data within the manager. Listing 12.26 and listing 12.27 show the changed managers.

Listing 12.26 UpdateData() method in MissionManager

```
...
public void Startup(NetworkService service) {
   Debug.Log("Mission manager starting...");

   network = service;                          Modify this line by using
   UpdateData(0, 1);          ◁───            the new method.

   status = ManagerStatus.Started;
}

public void UpdateData(int curLevel, int maxLevel) {
   this.curLevel = curLevel;
   this.maxLevel = maxLevel;
}
...
```

Listing 12.27 UpdateData() method in InventoryManager

```
...
public void Startup(NetworkService service) {
   Debug.Log("Inventory manager starting...");

   network = service;

   UpdateData(new Dictionary<string, int>());   ⟵─── Initialize an empty list.

   status = ManagerStatus.Started;
}

public void UpdateData(Dictionary<string, int> items) {
   this.items = items;
}
                                              ┌─── Need getter for save game
public Dictionary<string, int> GetData() {   ⟵─┘    code to access the data.
   return items;
}
...
```

Now that the various managers all have UpdateData() methods, the data can be saved from a new code module. Saving the data will involve a procedure referred to as *serializing* the data.

> **DEFINITION** *Serialize* means to encode a batch of data into a form that can be stored.

You'll save the game as binary data, but note that C# is also fully capable of saving text files. For example, the JSON strings you worked with in chapter 10 were data serialized as text. Previous chapters used PlayerPrefs, but in this project, you're going to save a local file; PlayerPrefs is intended to save only a handful of values, like settings, not an entire game. Create the DataManager script (listing 12.28).

> **WARNING** You can't directly access the filesystem in a web game. This is a security feature of web browsers. To save data for web games, you may need to write a plugin as described in the next chapter, or post the data to your server.

Listing 12.28 New script for DataManager

```
using System.Collections;
using System.Collections.Generic;
using System.Runtime.Serialization.Formatters.Binary;
using System.IO;
using UnityEngine;

public class DataManager : MonoBehaviour, IGameManager {
   public ManagerStatus status {get; private set;}

   private string filename;
```

```
    private NetworkService network;

    public void Startup(NetworkService service) {
        Debug.Log("Data manager starting...");

        network = service;

        filename = Path.Combine(                                    Construct full path
                Application.persistentDataPath, "game.dat");   ◁─┘  to the game.dat file.

        status = ManagerStatus.Started;
    }

    public void SaveGameState() {
        Dictionary<string, object> gamestate =        │  Dictionary that
            new Dictionary<string, object>();    ◁─────┘  will be serialized
        gamestate.Add("inventory", Managers.Inventory.GetData());
        gamestate.Add("health", Managers.Player.health);
        gamestate.Add("maxHealth", Managers.Player.maxHealth);
        gamestate.Add("curLevel", Managers.Mission.curLevel);
        gamestate.Add("maxLevel", Managers.Mission.maxLevel);
                                                          │  Create a file at
        using (FileStream stream = File.Create(filename)) {  ◁─┘  the file path.
            BinaryFormatter formatter = new BinaryFormatter();
            formatter.Serialize(stream, gamestate);  ◁─────┐
        }                                           Serialize the Dictionary as
    }                                               contents of the created file.

    public void LoadGameState() {          │  Continue to load only
        if (!File.Exists(filename)) {   ◁──┘  if the file exists.
            Debug.Log("No saved game");
            return;
        }
                                                  │  Dictionary to put
        Dictionary<string, object> gamestate;  ◁──┘  loaded data in

        using (FileStream stream = File.Open(filename, FileMode.Open)) {
            BinaryFormatter formatter = new BinaryFormatter();
            gamestate = formatter.Deserialize(stream) as Dictionary<string,
            ➡ object>;
        }
                                                              │  Update managers
        Managers.Inventory.UpdateData((Dictionary<string,     │  with deserialized
        ➡ int>)gamestate["inventory"]);                  ◁────┘  data.
        Managers.Player.UpdateData((int)gamestate["health"],
        ➡ (int)gamestate["maxHealth"]);
        Managers.Mission.UpdateData((int)gamestate["curLevel"],
        ➡ (int)gamestate["maxLevel"]);
        Managers.Mission.RestartCurrent();
    }
}
```

During `Startup()`, the full file path is constructed using `Application.persistent-DataPath`, a location Unity provides to store data in. The exact file path differs on different platforms, but Unity abstracts it behind this static variable. The `File.Create()` method will create a binary file; call `File.CreateText()` if you want a text file.

> **WARNING**   When constructing file paths, the path separator is different on different computer platforms. C# has `Path.DirectorySeparatorChar` to account for this.

Open the Startup scene to find Game Managers. Add the `DataManager` script component to the Game Managers object, and then add the new manager to the `Managers` script.

Listing 12.29   Adding `DataManager` to `Managers`

```
...
[RequireComponent(typeof(DataManager))]
...
public static DataManager Data {get; private set;}
...
void Awake() {
   DontDestroyOnLoad(gameObject);

   Data = GetComponent<DataManager>();
   Player = GetComponent<PlayerManager>();
   Inventory = GetComponent<InventoryManager>();
   Mission = GetComponent<MissionManager>();            Managers start
                                                        in this order.
   startSequence = new List<IGameManager>();    ⟵
   startSequence.Add(Player);
   startSequence.Add(Inventory);
   startSequence.Add(Mission);
   startSequence.Add(Data);

   StartCoroutine(StartupManagers());
}
...
```

> **WARNING**   Because `DataManager` uses other managers (to update them), you should make sure that the other managers appear earlier in the startup sequence.

Finally, in `Level1`, add buttons to use functions in `DataManager` (figure 12.9 shows the buttons). Create two buttons parented to the HUD Canvas (not in the Inventory pop-up). Call them (set the attached text objects) `Save Game` and `Load Game`, set the Anchor button to bottom right, and position them at `-100,65`, and `-100,30`.

These buttons will link to functions in `UIController`, so write those methods.

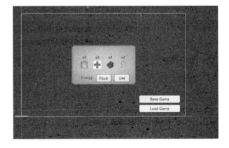

Figure 12.9   Save and Load buttons on the bottom right of the screen

---

Listing 12.30   Save and load methods in `UIController`

```
...
public void SaveGame() {
   Managers.Data.SaveGameState();
}

public void LoadGame() {
   Managers.Data.LoadGameState();
}
...
```

Link these functions to `OnClick` listeners in the buttons (add a listing in the `OnClick` setting, drag in the `UIController` object, and select functions from the menu). Now play the game, pick up a few items, use a health pack to increase your health, and then save the game. Restart the game and check your inventory to verify that it's empty. Click Load; you now have the health and items you had when you saved the game!

12.3.2 Beating the game by completing three levels

As implied by our saving of the player's progress, this game can have multiple levels, not just the one level you've been testing. To properly handle multiple levels, the game must detect the completion of not only a single level, but also the entire game. First, add yet another GameEvent:

```
public const string GAME_COMPLETE = "GAME_COMPLETE";
```

Now modify `MissionManager` to broadcast that message after the last level.

Listing 12.31   Broadcasting Game Complete from `MissionManager`

```
...
public void GoToNext() {
   ...
   } else {
      Debug.Log("Last level");
      Messenger.Broadcast(GameEvent.GAME_COMPLETE);
   }
}
```

Respond to that message in `UIController`.

Listing 12.32   Adding an event listener to `UIController`

```
...
Messenger.AddListener(GameEvent.GAME_COMPLETE, OnGameComplete);
...
Messenger.RemoveListener(GameEvent.GAME_COMPLETE, OnGameComplete);
...
private void OnGameComplete() {
```

```
    levelEnding.gameObject.SetActive(true);
    levelEnding.text = "You Finished the Game!";
}
...
```

Try completing the level to see what happens: move the player to the level objective to complete the level as before. You'll first see the Level Complete message, but after a couple of seconds, it'll change to a message about completing the game.

ADDING MORE LEVELS

At this point, you can add an arbitrary number of additional levels, and `MissionManager` will watch for the last level. The final thing you'll do in this chapter is add a few more levels to the project to demonstrate the game progressing through multiple levels.

Duplicate the `Level1` scene file twice, make sure the names are `Level2` and `Level3`, and add the new levels to Build Settings (so that they can be loaded during gameplay; remember to generate the lighting). Modify each scene so that you can tell the difference between levels; feel free to rearrange most of the scene, but you must keep several essential game elements: the player object that's tagged Player, the floor object set to the Ground layer, and the objective object, Controller, HUD Canvas, and EventSystem.

> ### Architecting a shared HUD
>
> The UI was duplicated along with the rest of the level, resulting in three identical UI setups. That's fine for this small learning project but would be unwieldy for a polished game with many levels. Instead, you should move the UI to a central place that's shared among the levels.
>
> Much as you did with the Startup scene, you could put the UI (both HUD Canvas and EventSystem) in a separate scene to load in addition to the levels. Unlike the Startup scene, however, you will probably want to control the loading of the UI more deliberately than simply using the `DontDestroyOnLoad()` function. That function causes objects to persist in *all* scenes, but the UI is not identical in every scene of a game. For example, a game's starting menu scene usually has a different UI than all the levels.
>
> Unity solves this problem with the Additive scene loading mode. Scenes loaded in this mode are added on to what's already loaded, rather than replacing it. For example, modifying this project's code to use a shared UI scene would simply entail adding a line of code like `SceneManager.LoadScene( "HUDScene", LoadSceneMode.Additive);` immediately after every standard `LoadScene()` call in `MissionManager`. Read the documentation about this optional scene loading mode at http://mng.bz/v4GJ.

You also need to adjust `MissionManager` to load the new levels. Change `maxLevel` to 3 by changing the `UpdateData(0, 1)` call to `UpdateData(0, 3)`. Now play the game and you'll start on `Level1` initially; reach the level objective and you'll move on to the next level! Incidentally, you can also save on a later level to see that the game will restore that progress.

You now know how to create a full game with multiple levels. The obvious next task is the final chapter: getting your game into the hands of players.

> **Exercise: Integrating audio into the full game**
>
> Chapter 11 was all about implementing audio in Unity. I didn't explain how to integrate that into this chapter's project, but at this point you should understand how. I encourage you to practice your skills by integrating the audio functionality from the previous chapter into this chapter's project. Here's a hint: change the key to toggle the audio settings pop-up so that it doesn't interfere with the inventory pop-up.

Summary

- Unity makes it easy to repurpose assets and code from a project in a different game genre.
- Another great use for raycasting is to determine where in the scene the player is clicking.
- Unity has simple methods for both loading levels and persisting certain objects between levels.
- You progress through levels in response to various events within the game.
- You can use the I/O methods that come with C# to store data at `Application` `.persistentDataPath`.

Deploying your game to players' devices

This chapter covers

- Building an application package for various platforms
- Assigning build settings, such as the app icon or name
- Interacting with the web page for web games
- Developing plugins for apps on mobile platforms

Throughout this book, you've learned how to program various games within Unity, but the crucial last step has been missing so far: deploying those games to players. Until a game is playable outside the Unity editor, it's of little interest to anyone other than the developer. Unity shines at this last step, with the ability to build applications for a huge variety of gaming platforms. This final chapter covers how to build games for these various platforms.

When I speak of "building" for a platform, I'm referring to generating an application package that will run on that platform. On each platform (Windows, iOS, and so on), the exact form of a built application differs, but once the executable has been generated, that app package can be played without Unity and can be distributed to players. A single Unity project can be deployed to any platform without needing to be redone for each one.

This "build once, deploy anywhere" capability applies to the vast majority of features in your games, but not to everything. I would estimate that 95% of the code written in Unity (for example, almost everything we've done so far in this book) is platform-agnostic and will work just as well across all platforms. But a few specific tasks differ for different platforms, so we'll go over those platform-specific areas of development.

Unity is capable of building apps for the following platforms:

- Windows PC
- macOS
- Linux
- WebGL
- Android
- iOS
- tvOS
- Oculus VR
- VIVE VR
- Windows Mixed Reality
- Microsoft HoloLens
- Magic Leap

In addition, by contacting the platform owners for access, Unity can even build for game consoles like these:

- Xbox One
- Xbox Series X
- PlayStation 4
- PlayStation 5
- Nintendo Switch

Whew, that full list is really long! Frankly, that's almost comically long, and way more than the supported platforms of most other game development tools out there. This chapter focuses especially on the first six platforms listed, because those platforms are of primary interest to the majority of people exploring Unity, but keep in mind how many options are available to you.

To see all these platforms, open the Build Settings window. That's the window you used in the previous chapter to add scenes to be loaded; to access it, choose File > Build Settings. In chapter 12, you cared only about the list at the top, but now you want to pay attention to the buttons at the bottom (see figure 13.1). You'll notice a lot of space taken up by the list of platforms; the currently active platform is indicated with the Unity icon.

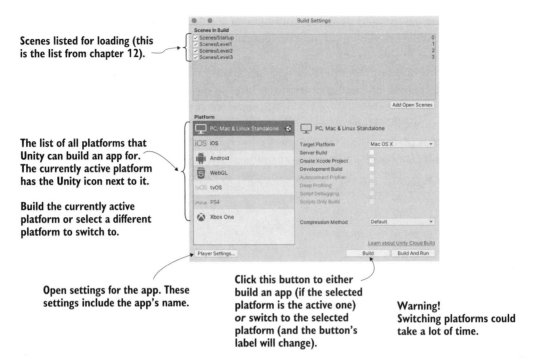

Scenes listed for loading (this is the list from chapter 12).

The list of all platforms that Unity can build an app for. The currently active platform has the Unity icon next to it.

Build the currently active platform or select a different platform to switch to.

Open settings for the app. These settings include the app's name.

Click this button to either build an app (if the selected platform is the active one) or switch to the selected platform (and the button's label will change).

Warning! Switching platforms could take a lot of time.

Figure 13.1   The Build Settings window

NOTE When installing Unity, Unity Hub asks which export modules you want, and you can build only the selected modules. If you later want to install a module you hadn't selected initially, go to Installs in Unity Hub, click the three dots for the Unity version you want to modify, and then select Add Modules in the menu.

Also across the bottom of this window are the Player Settings and Build/Switch Platform buttons. Click Player Settings to view settings for the app in the Inspector, such as the name and icon for the app. The other button changes its label depending on which platform you select in the list of platforms. If you have the active platform selected, clicking Build launches the build process. For any other platform, clicking Switch Platform makes that the active platform that Unity is currently dealing with.

WARNING When in a big project, switching platforms often takes quite a bit of time to complete; make sure you're ready to wait. This is because Unity recompresses all assets (such as textures) in an optimal way for each platform.

TIP Build And Run does the same thing as Build, plus it automatically runs the built application. I usually want to do that part manually, so I rarely use Build And Run.

When you click Build, the first thing that comes up is a file selector so that you can tell Unity where to generate the app package. Once you select a file location, the build process starts. Unity creates an executable app package for the currently active platform. Let's go over the build process for the most popular platforms: desktop, web, and mobile.

13.1 Start by building for the desktop: Windows, Mac, and Linux

The simplest place to start when first learning to build Unity games is by deploying to desktop computers—Windows PC, macOS, or Linux. Because Unity runs on desktop computers, that means you'll build an app for the computer you're already using.

> **NOTE** Open up any project to work with in this section. Seriously, any Unity project will work. In fact, I strongly suggest using a different project in every section to drive home the fact that Unity can build any project to any platform!

13.1.1 Building the application

First choose File > Build Settings to open the Build Settings window. By default, the current platform will be set to PC, Mac, and Linux, but if that isn't current, select the correct platform from the list and click Switch Platform.

On the right-hand side of the window, you'll notice the Target Platform menu. This menu lets you choose between Windows PC, macOS, and Linux. All three are treated as one platform in the list on the left-hand side, but these are very different platforms, so choose the correct one.

Once you've chosen your desktop platform, click Build. As explained previously, a file dialog pops up, allowing you to choose where the built application will go. Then the build process starts; this could take a while for a big project, but the build process should be fast for the tiny demos you've been making.

> **Custom post-build script**
>
> Although the basic build process works fine in most situations, you may want a series of steps to be taken (such as moving help files into the same directory as the application) every time you build your game. You can easily automate such tasks by programming them in a script that will execute after the build process completes.
>
> First, create a new folder in the Project view and name that folder `Editor`; any scripts that affect Unity's editor (and that includes the build process) must go in a folder named Editor. Create a new script named `TestPostBuild` in that folder and write the following code in it:

(continued)

```
using UnityEngine;
using UnityEditor;
using UnityEditor.Callbacks;

public static class TestPostBuild {

    [PostProcessBuild]
    public static void OnPostprocessBuild(BuildTarget target, string
    ➥ pathToBuiltProject) {
        Debug.Log($"build location: {pathToBuiltProject}");
    }
}
```

The [PostProcessBuild] directive tells the script to run the function that's immediately after it. That function will receive the location of the built app; you could then use that location with the various filesystem commands provided by C#.

The application will appear in the location you chose; double-click it to run it, like any other program. Congrats, that was easy! Building applications is a snap, but the process can be customized in various ways; let's look at how to adjust the build.

TIP Quit full-screen games with Alt-F4 on Windows or Cmd-Q on Mac. Finished games should have a button that calls Application.Quit().

13.1.2 Adjusting player settings: Setting the game's name and icon

Go back to the Build Settings window, but this time click Player Settings instead of Build. A huge list of settings will appear in the Inspector (see figure 13.2); these settings control multiple aspects of the built application.

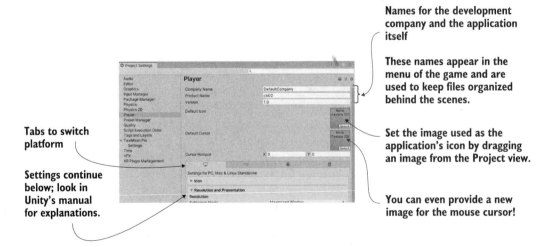

Names for the development company and the application itself

These names appear in the menu of the game and are used to keep files organized behind the scenes.

Tabs to switch platform

Settings continue below; look in Unity's manual for explanations.

Set the image used as the application's icon by dragging an image from the Project view.

You can even provide a new image for the mouse cursor!

Figure 13.2   Player settings displayed in the Inspector

Because of the large number of settings, you'll probably want to look them up in Unity's manual. The relevant doc page is http://mng.bz/4Koa.

The first several settings at the top are easiest to understand: Company Name, Product Name, Version, and Default Icon. Type in values for the first three: Company Name is the name for your development studio, Product Name is the name of this specific game, and Version is a number designation to increase as you update the game. Then drag an image from the Project view (import an image into the project if needed) to set that image as the icon; when the app is built, this image will appear as the application's icon.

Customizing the icon and name of the application is important for giving it a finished appearance. Another useful way of customizing the behavior of built applications is with platform-dependent code.

13.1.3 *Platform-dependent compilation*

By default, all the code you write will run the same way on all platforms. But Unity provides compiler directives (known as *platform defines*) that cause different code to run on different platforms. You'll find the full list of platform defines in the manual at http://mng.bz/Qq4w.

As that page indicates, directives are available for every platform that Unity supports, allowing you to run separate code on every platform. Usually, the majority of your code doesn't have to be inside platform directives, but occasionally small bits of the code need to run differently on different platforms. For example, some code assemblies exist on only one platform, so you need to have platform compiler directives around those commands. The following listing shows how to write such code.

> **Listing 13.1 `PlatformTest` script showing how to write platform-dependent code**

```
using System.Collections;
using System.Collections.Generic;
using UnityEngine;

public class PlatformTest : MonoBehaviour {          This section runs only
    void OnGUI() {                                   within the editor.
#if UNITY_EDITOR                              ◁──┘
        GUI.Label(new Rect(10, 10, 200, 20), "Running in Editor");
#elif UNITY_STANDALONE                                              ◁──────────
        GUI.Label(new Rect(10, 10, 200, 20), "Running on Desktop");
#else
        GUI.Label(new Rect(10, 10, 200, 20), "Running on other platform");
#endif                                        Only in desktop/standalone
    }                                                         applications
}
```

Create a script called `PlatformTest` and write the code from this listing in it. Attach that script to an object in the scene (any object will do for testing), and a small message will appear in the top-left of the screen. When you play the game within Unity's editor, the message will say Running in Editor, but if you build the game and run the built application, the message will say Running on Desktop. Different code is being run in each case!

For this test, you used the platform define that treats all desktop platforms as one, but as indicated on that doc page, separate platform defines are available for Windows, Mac, and Linux. In fact, there are platform defines for all the platforms supported by Unity so that you can run different code on each. Let's move on to the next important platform: the web.

Quality settings

The built application is also affected by project settings located under the Edit menu. In particular, the visual quality of the final app can be tuned there. Go to Project Settings in the Edit menu to open that window, and then choose Quality from the menu along the left side.

Quality settings appear in the right side of the window, and the most important settings are the grid of check marks at the top. The different platforms that Unity can target are listed as icons across the top, and the possible quality settings are listed along the side. The boxes are checked for quality settings available for that platform, and the check box is highlighted green for the setting being used. Most of the time, these settings default to Very Low, but you can change to Ultra quality if things look bad; if you click the down arrow underneath a platform's column, a pop-up menu will appear.

It seems a bit redundant that this UI has both check boxes and the Default menu, but there you have it. Different platforms often have different graphical capabilities, so Unity allows you to set different quality levels for different build targets (such as highest quality on desktop and lower quality on mobile).

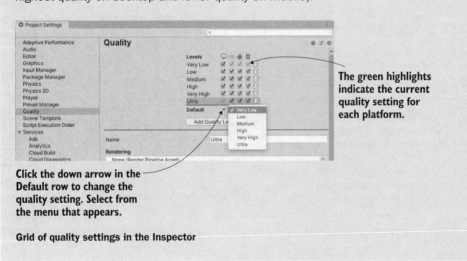

The green highlights indicate the current quality setting for each platform.

Click the down arrow in the Default row to change the quality setting. Select from the menu that appears.

Grid of quality settings in the Inspector

13.2 Building for the web

Although desktop platforms are the most basic targets to build for, another important platform for Unity games is the web. Games deployed to the web run within a web browser and can thus be played over the internet.

Unity Web Player vs. HTML5/WebGL

Initially, Unity had to deploy web builds in a form that played within a custom browser plugin. This had long been necessary because 3D graphics weren't built into web browsers. Eventually, however, most browsers adopted WebGL, a standard for 3D graphics on the web. Technically, WebGL is separate from HTML5, but the two terms are related and are often used interchangeably when talking about 3D on the web.

For version 5, Unity added WebGL to the build platforms list, and a few versions later the browser plugin was dropped, making WebGL the sole avenue for web builds. In part, these changes in Unity's web build were being driven by strategic decisions made within Unity (the company). But these changes were also being driven by pushes from browser makers, who are moving away from custom plugins and embracing HTML5/WebGL as the way to develop interactive web applications, including games.

13.2.1 Building the game embedded in a web page

Open a different project (again, this is to emphasize that any project will work) and open the Build Settings window. Switch the platform to WebGL and then click the Build button. A file selector will come up; type in the name `WebTest` for this application, and change to a safe location (a location not within the Unity project) if necessary.

The build process will now create a folder containing an index.html web page, as well as subfolders with all the game's code and other assets. Open this web page, and the game should be embedded in the middle of the otherwise blank page. You will need to run the game from a web server, rather than simply opening index.html as a local file. Just as in chapter 10, you could use an existing web server if you already have a website, or you could test on http://localhost/ with something like XAMPP.

> **NOTE** You may need to adjust the settings of your web server for correct handling of compressed archives in the WebGL build. Unity's manual (http://mng.bz/XreG) explains these server settings, but if you can't adjust these for some reason (for example, the game will be on a third-party site that you cannot configure), you can also tell Unity to include a decompressor in the build. Turn on Decompressor Fallback in the Publishing Settings section of the WebGL player settings. This setting is off by default, because the browser's decompression is better. Be warned though, because with this setting on, you won't notice an improperly configured server.

There's nothing particularly special about this web page; it's just an example to test your game with. It's possible to customize the code on that page or even provide your own web page (discussed later). One of the most important customizations to make is enabling communication between Unity and the browser, so let's go over that next.

13.2.2   *Communicating with JavaScript in the browser*

A Unity web game can communicate with the browser (or rather with JavaScript running in the browser), and these messages can go in both directions: from Unity to the browser, and from the browser to Unity. To send messages to the browser, you write JavaScript code into a code library, and then Unity has special commands to use functions in that library.

Meanwhile, for messages from the browser, JavaScript in the browser identifies an object by name, and then Unity passes the message to the named object in the scene. Thus, you must have an object in the scene that will receive communications from the browser.

To demonstrate these tasks, create a new script in Unity called `WebTestObject`. Also create an empty object in the active scene called `JSListener` (the object in the scene must have that exact name, because that's the name used by the JavaScript code in listing 13.4). Attach the new script to that object and then write in the code from this listing.

> **Listing 13.2   `WebTestObject` script for testing communication with the browser**

```
using System.Runtime.InteropServices;
using UnityEngine;

public class WebTestObject : MonoBehaviour {
   private string message;

   [DllImport("__Internal")]                            ⟵  Import the function
   private static extern void ShowAlert(string msg);        from the JS library.

   void Start() {
      message = "No message yet";
   }

   void Update() {                                      On mouse click, call the
      if (Input.GetMouseButtonDown(0)) {   ⟵           imported function.
         ShowAlert("Hello out there!");
      }
   }

   void OnGUI() {                                       Display the message in
      GUI.Label(new Rect(10, 10, 200, 20), message);  ⟵  top left of the screen.
   }
                                                       Function for the
   public void RespondToBrowser(string message) {  ⟵  browser to call
      this.message = message;
   }
}
```

The main new bit is the `DllImport` command. That imports a function from the Java-Script library to use in C# code. That obviously implies you *have* a JavaScript library, so write that next.

First create the special folder to contain it: create a folder called `Plugins`, and within that create a folder called `WebGL`. Now put a file called `WebTest` that has the extension jslib (so WebTest.jslib) in the WebGL folder; the simplest way is to create a text file outside Unity, rename it, and then drag the file in. Unity will recognize that file as a JavaScript library, so write this code in it.

Listing 13.3 WebTest JavaScript library

```
mergeInto(LibraryManager.library, {          The function imported
                                             and called from C#
  ShowAlert: function(msg) {
    window.alert(Pointer_stringify(msg));
  },

});
```

The jslib file contains both a JavaScript object containing functions and the command to merge the custom object into Unity's library manager. Note that the function written includes `Pointer_stringify()` besides standard JavaScript commands; when passing a string from Unity, it's turned into a numeric identifier, so Unity provides that function to look up the string pointed to.

Now build for the web again to see the new code in action. The `WebTestObject` in Unity calls a function in the JavaScript code when you click within the Unity game part of the web page; try clicking a few times, and you'll see an alert box appear in the browser!

> **NOTE** Unity also has `Application.ExternalEval()` for running code in the browser; `ExternalEval` runs arbitrary snippets of JavaScript, rather than calling defined functions. This method is deprecated and should be avoided, but sometimes its simplicity is useful, like reloading the page with just `Application.ExternalEval("location.reload();")`.

All right, you have tested communication from the Unity game to JavaScript in the web page, but the web page can also send a message back to Unity, so let's do that too. This will involve new code and buttons on the page; fortunately, Unity provides an easy way to customize the web page. Specifically, Unity fills in a web page *template* when it builds to WebGL, and you can choose a custom template instead of the default one.

The default templates can be found in the Unity installation folder (usually C:\Program Files\Unity\Editor\Data on Windows, or /Applications/Unity/Editor on Mac) under /WebGLSupport/BuildTools/WebGLTemplates. Open a template page in a text editor and you'll see that a template is largely standard HTML and JavaScript, plus some special tags that Unity replaces with generated information. Although it's best for you to leave Unity's built-in templates alone, they (especially the *minimal* one) make a good base on which to build your own. You'll copy the minimal template web page into the custom template you make.

In Unity's Project view, create a folder called `WebGLTemplates` (no space) directly under Assets; that's where custom templates go. Now create a subfolder within it named `WebTest`; that folder is for your new template. Put an index.html file in here (you can copy in the web page from the minimal template), open that in a text editor, and write this code in it.

Listing 13.4   WebGL template to enable browser–Unity communication

```
<!DOCTYPE html>
<html lang="en-us">
  <head>
    <meta charset="utf-8">
    <meta http-equiv="Content-Type" content="text/html; charset=utf-8">
    <title>Unity WebGL Player | {{{ PRODUCT_NAME }}}</title>
    <style>body { background-color: #333; }</style>          ◁┐  Making the page dark
  </head>                                                        │  instead of white
  <body style="text-align: center">
    <canvas id="unity-canvas" width={{{ WIDTH }}} height={{{ HEIGHT }}}
     style="width: {{{ WIDTH }}}px; height: {{{ HEIGHT }}}px; background: {{{
     BACKGROUND_FILENAME ? 'url(\'Build/' + BACKGROUND_FILENAME.replace(/'/g,
     '%27') + '\') center / cover' : BACKGROUND_COLOR }}}"></canvas>
    <br><input type="button" value="Send to Unity" onclick="SendToUnity();" /> ◁┐
                                                                    Button that calls
    <script src="Build/{{{ LOADER_FILENAME }}}"></script>         the JavaScript
    <script>                                                          function
      var unityInstance = null;

      createUnityInstance(document.querySelector("#unity-canvas"), {
        dataUrl: "Build/{{{ DATA_FILENAME }}}",
        frameworkUrl: "Build/{{{ FRAMEWORK_FILENAME }}}",
        codeUrl: "Build/{{{ CODE_FILENAME }}}",
#if MEMORY_FILENAME
        memoryUrl: "Build/{{{ MEMORY_FILENAME }}}",
#endif
#if SYMBOLS_FILENAME
        symbolsUrl: "Build/{{{ SYMBOLS_FILENAME }}}",
#endif
        streamingAssetsUrl: "StreamingAssets",
        companyName: "{{{ COMPANY_NAME }}}",
        productName: "{{{ PRODUCT_NAME }}}",
        productVersion: "{{{ PRODUCT_VERSION }}}",
      }).then((createdInstance) => {
        unityInstance = createdInstance;
      });
                                                    SendMessage() points to
      function SendToUnity() {                       the named object in Unity.
        unityInstance.SendMessage("JSListener",   ◁┘
          "RespondToBrowser", "Hello from the browser!");
      }
```

```
    </script>
  </body>
</html>
```

If you copied the minimal template, you'll see that listing 13.4 simply adds a few lines there. The two important additions are a function in the script tag and an input button on the page; the added style changes the color of the page to make it easier to see the embedded game. The button's HTML tag links to a JavaScript function, and that function calls `SendMessage()` on the Unity instance. This method calls a function on a named object within Unity; the first parameter is the name of the object, the second parameter is the name of the method, and the third parameter is a string to pass in while calling the method.

You've made your custom template, but you still have to tell Unity to use this template instead of the default. Open the Player Settings again (remember, click Player Settings in the Build Settings window) and find WebGL Template in the web settings (shown in figure 13.3). You'll see that Default is currently selected, but WebTest (the template folder you created) is also on the list; click that one instead.

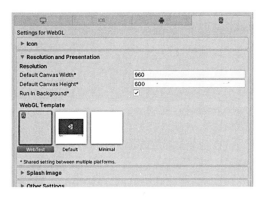

Figure 13.3   WebGL Template setting

With the custom template selected, build to WebGL again. Open the generated web page, and this time a button is at the bottom of the page. Click the button and you'll see the changed message displayed in Unity!

That wraps up browser communication for web builds. On to the next important platform (or rather, set of platforms) for building apps: mobile.

13.3   *Building for mobile: iOS and Android*

Mobile apps are another important build target for Unity. My gut impression (totally unscientific) is that most commercial games created using Unity are mobile games.

> **DEFINITION** *Mobile* is a category of handheld computing devices. The designation started with smartphones but now includes tablets. The two most widely used mobile computing platforms are iOS (from Apple) and Android (from Google).

Setting up the build process for mobile apps is more complicated than either desktop or web builds, so this is another optional section—optional as in only read through it, without actually following the steps. I'll still write as if you're working along, but you'd have to buy a developer license for iOS and install all the developer tools for Android.

> **WARNING** Mobile devices undergo so much rapid change that the exact build process is likely to be slightly different by the time you read this. The high-level concepts are probably still true, but you should look at up-to-date documentation online for an exact rundown of the commands to execute and buttons to push. For starters, here are the doc pages from Apple (https://developer .apple.com/documentation/xcode) and Google (https://developer.android .com/studio/build).

Touch input

Input on mobile devices works differently than on desktop or the web. Mobile input is done by touching the screen, rather than with the mouse and keyboard. Unity has input functionality for handling touches, including code like `Input.touchCount` and `Input.GetTouch()`.

You may want to use these commands to write platform-specific code on mobile devices. Handling input that way can be a hassle, though, so code frameworks are available to streamline the use of touch input. For example, search on Unity's Asset Store for Fingers or Lean Touch.

All right, with those caveats out of the way, I'll explain the overall build process for both iOS and Android. Keep in mind that these platforms occasionally change the details of the build process.

13.3.1 *Setting up the build tools*

Mobile devices are all separate from the computer you're developing on, and that separateness makes the process of building and deploying to devices slightly more complex. You'll need to set up a variety of specialized tools before you can click Build.

SETTING UP IOS BUILD TOOLS

At a high level, the process of deploying a Unity game on iOS requires first building an Xcode project from Unity and then building the Xcode project into an iOS application package (IPA) using Xcode. Unity can't build the final IPA directly because all iOS apps have to go through Apple's build tools. That means you need to install Xcode (Apple's programming IDE), including the iOS SDK.

> **WARNING** You have to be working on a Mac when deploying an iOS game— Xcode runs only on macOS. Developing a game within Unity can be done on either Windows or Mac, but building the iOS app must be done on a Mac.

Get Xcode from Apple's website, in the developer section: https://developer.apple .com/xcode/.

> **NOTE** You need membership in the Apple Developer Program in order to sell your iOS game on the App Store. Apple's developer program costs $99/year; enroll at https://developer.apple.com/programs/.

Once Xcode is installed, launch it and open Preferences to add your developer account. You need to be logged in when Xcode accesses your account while building an app.

Now go back to Unity and switch to iOS. You need to adjust the Player settings for the iOS app (remember, open Build Settings and click Player Settings). You should already be on the iOS tab of the Player settings, but click the tab with an iOS icon if needed. Scroll down to Other Settings and then look for Identification. Bundle Identifier needs to be adjusted so that Apple will correctly identify the app.

> **NOTE** iOS calls it Bundle Identifier, and Android calls it Package Name, but naming otherwise works the same way on both platforms. The identifier should follow the same convention as that for any code package: all lowercase in the form `com.companyname.productname`.

Another important setting that applies to both iOS and Android is Version (this is the version number of the app). Most of the settings beyond that are platform-specific; for example, iOS added an additional build number, separate from the main version number. There's also a setting for Scripting Backend; Mono was always used in the past, but the newer IL2CPP backend supports iOS updates, like 64-bit binaries.

> **NOTE** iOS builds from Unity don't work with both real devices (iPhones and iPads) and iOS simulators. By default, iOS builds from Unity work only on real devices, but you can switch to building for simulators by scrolling down to Target SDK in Player settings. In practice, I've never had to do this, because all my "testing outside real device" work is done within Unity itself, and if I'm doing an iOS build, then I want to run it on an actual phone.

Now click Build in the Build Settings window. Select the location for the built files, and that'll generate an Xcode project in that location; you probably want to click the button to create a new folder and then choose that newly created folder.

The Xcode project that results can be modified directly if you want (simple modifications could be part of the post-build script). Regardless, open the Xcode project; the built folder has many files, but double-click the .xcodeproj file (it has an icon of a blueprint). Xcode will open with this project loaded. Unity already took care of most of the settings needed in the project, but you do need to adjust the provisioning profiles being used.

Xcode will attempt to set up the signing profiles automatically, so this is why you added your account in Preferences earlier. Select your app in the project list on the left-hand side of Xcode, and several tabs relevant to the selected project will appear. Click the tab for Signing & Capabilities and click the Team menu to select the team

iOS provisioning profiles

Of all the aspects of iOS development, provisioning profiles are the most unusual. In short, these are files used for identification and authorization. Apple tightly controls what apps can run on what devices; apps submitted to Apple for approval use special provisioning profiles that allow them to work through the App Store, whereas apps in development use provisioning profiles that are specific to registered devices.

You'll need to add both your iPhone's UDID (an ID specific to your device) and the app's ID (the Bundle Identifier in Unity) to your account on Apple's website for iOS developers. For a complete explanation of this process, visit https://developer .apple.com/support/code-signing/.

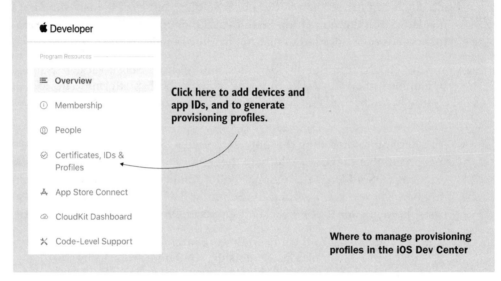

Where to manage provisioning profiles in the iOS Dev Center

registered with Apple's developer program (see figure 13.4). If for some reason you don't want Xcode to automatically manage signing, provisioning profiles can be adjusted manually by scrolling down to Signing in the Build Settings tab.

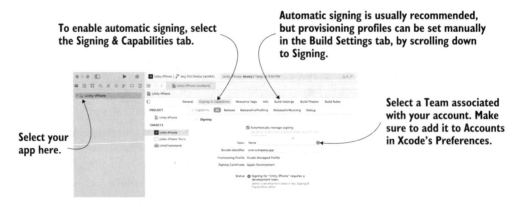

Figure 13.4 Provisioning/signing settings in Xcode

Once the provisioning profiles are set, you're ready to build the app. From the Product menu, choose either Run or Archive. The Product menu has a lot of options, including the tantalizingly named Build, but for our purposes, the two options that are useful are Run and Archive. Build generates executable files but doesn't bundle them for iOS, whereas this is what Run and Archive do:

- Run will test the application on an iPhone connected to the computer with a USB cable.
- Archive will create an application package that can be sent to other registered devices (either for release, or testing via what Apple refers to as *ad hoc distribution*).

Archive doesn't create the app package directly but rather creates a bundle in an intermediate stage between the raw code files and an IPA. The created archive will be listed in Xcode's Organizer window; in that window, select the generated archive and click Distribute App on the right-hand side. After you click that, you'll be asked if you want to distribute the app on the store or ad hoc.

If you choose ad hoc distribution, you'll end up with an IPA file that can be sent to testers. You could send the file directly for them to install through iTunes, but it's more convenient to set up a website to handle distributing and installing test builds. Alternatively, use TestFlight (https://developer.apple.com/testflight/) on builds that have been uploaded to the store but not submitted yet.

SETTING UP ANDROID BUILD TOOLS

Unlike iOS apps, Unity can generate the final Android application (either an APK, for Android application package, or AAB, for Android app bundle) directly. This requires pointing Unity to the Android SDK, which includes the necessary compiler. You could install the Android SDK along with the Android build module for Unity, or you could install it from within Android Studio and point to that file location in Unity's preferences (see figure 13.5). You can download the Android build tools from https://developer.android.com/studio.

You can add the Android SDK (and associated build tools) along with the Android module when managing installs in Unity Hub.

Uncheck this setting if you downloaded the Android SDK yourself, not through Unity Hub.

This button's label will change to Browse if the check box is turned off, so click it to find where the SDK is located.

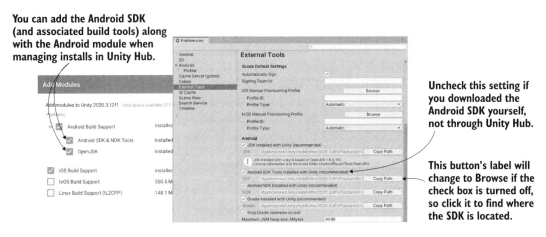

Figure 13.5   Unity preference setting to point to Android SDK

After setting the Android SDK in Unity's preferences, you need to specify the app's identifier just as you did for iOS. You'll find Package Name in Player Settings; set it to com.companyname.productname (as explained previously when setting the Bundle Identifier for iOS). Then click Build to start the process. As with all builds, Unity will first ask where to save the file. Then it'll create an APK file in that location.

Now that you have the app package, you must install it on a device. You can get the APK file onto an Android phone by downloading the file from the web (cloud storage like Google Drive is useful for this purpose) or by transferring the file via a USB cable connected to your computer (an approach referred to as *sideloading*). The details of how to transfer files via USB vary for every device, but once there, the files can be installed using a file manager app. I don't know why file managers aren't built into Android, but you can install one for free from the Google Play Store. Navigate to your APK file within the file manager and then install the app.

APK vs. AAB for Android builds

Since the inception of Android, applications have been distributed as APK (Android application package) files. However, Google has supported AAB (Android app bundle, an alternative kind of application file) for a little while now, and has started requiring that format for apps submitted to the Play Store. Instead of having support for every device baked into the single application package, app bundles allow the Play Store to instead generate a smaller application package designed just for the specific user to download, resulting in smaller files.

Unity supports both formats in the Build Settings window. When you have the Android platform selected, look for the Build App Bundle check box; leave that off for APK, or turn that on for AAB. It's generally better to build APK files while testing (since those are easier to install on testing devices) and then build AAB for the final version to submit to the Play Store.

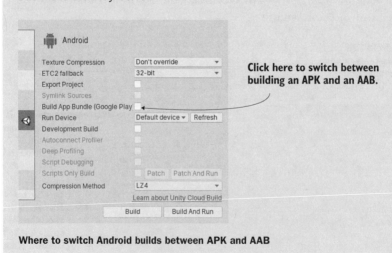

Where to switch Android builds between APK and AAB

As you can see, the basic build process for Android is a lot simpler than the build process for iOS. Unfortunately, the process of customizing the build and implementing plugins is more complicated than with iOS; you'll learn how in a bit. But before that, let's talk about texture compression.

13.3.2 Texture compression

Assets can eat up a lot of memory, and this especially includes textures. To reduce their file size, you can compress assets in various ways, with pros and cons to each method. Because of these pros and cons, you may need to adjust how Unity compresses textures.

Managing texture compression on mobile devices is essential, though technically, textures are often compressed on other platforms too. But you don't have to pay as much attention to compression on other platforms for various reasons—the chief one being that the platform is more technologically mature. On mobile devices, you need to pay closer attention to texture compression because the devices are touchier about this detail.

Unity automatically compresses textures for you. In most development tools, you need to compress images yourself, but in Unity, you generally import uncompressed images, and then it applies image compression in the import settings for the image (see figure 13.6).

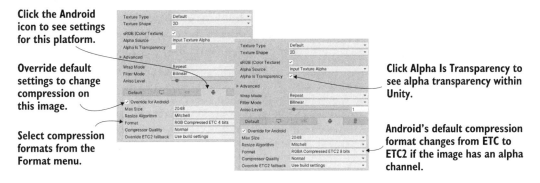

Figure 13.6　Texture compression settings in the Inspector

The compression settings are different on different platforms, so Unity recompresses images when you switch platforms. Initially, the settings are default values, and you may need to adjust them for specific images and specific platforms. In particular, image compression is trickier on Android. This is mostly due to the fragmentation of Android devices: because all iOS devices use pretty much the same video hardware, iOS apps can have texture compression optimized for their graphics chips (the GPU). Android apps don't enjoy the same uniformity of hardware, so their texture compression has to aim for the lowest common denominator.

To be more specific, all iOS devices use (or rather used to use, and still maintain compatibility with) PowerVR GPUs. Thus, iOS apps can use optimized PowerVR Texture Compression (PVRTC) on all iOS devices, or even the newer ASTC format that is supported on all iPhones since version 6. Some Android devices also use PowerVR chips, but they just as frequently use Adreno chips from Qualcomm, Mali GPUs from ARM, or other options. As a result, Android apps generally rely on Ericsson Texture Compression (ETC), a more generic compression algorithm supported by all Android devices. Unity defaults to ETC2 (the more advanced second version) for textures with an alpha channel, since the original ETC compression format doesn't have an alpha channel, but note that older Android devices may not support ETC2.

This default works fairly well most of the time, but if you need to adjust compression on a texture, adjust the settings shown in figure 13.6. Click the Android icon tab to override the default settings for that platform, and then use the Format menu to pick specific compression formats. In particular, you may find that certain key images need to be uncompressed; although their file size will be much larger, the image quality will be better. As long as you compress the majority of textures and choose uncompressed only on a case-by-case basis, the increased file size probably won't be too bad. With that discussion out of the way, the final topic for mobile development is developing native plugins.

13.3.3 *Developing plugins*

Unity has a huge amount of functionality built in, but that functionality is mostly limited to features common across all platforms. Taking advantage of platform-specific toolkits (such as Play Game Services on Android) often requires add-on plugins for Unity.

> **TIP** A variety of premade mobile plugins are available for iOS- and Android-specific features; appendix D lists a few places to get mobile plugins. These plugins operate in the manner described here, except that the plugin code is already written for you.

The process of communicating with mobile plugins is similar to the process of communicating with the browser. On the Unity side of things, special commands call functions within the plugin. On the plugin's side, the plugin can use `SendMessage()` to send a message to an object in Unity's scene. The exact code looks different on different platforms, but the general idea is always the same.

> **WARNING** Just as with the initial build process, the process for native development on mobile tends to change frequently—not so much the Unity end of the process, but the native code part. I'll cover things at a high level, but you should look for up-to-date documentation online.

Plugins for both platforms are put in the same place within Unity. If needed, create a folder in the Project view called `Plugins`; then, inside Plugins create a folder each for

Android and iOS. Once they're put into Unity, plugin files also have settings for the platforms they apply to. Normally, Unity figures this out automatically (iOS plugins are set to iOS, Android plugins are set to Android, and so on), but if necessary, look for these settings in the Inspector.

iOS PLUGINS

The plugin is really just some native code that gets called by Unity. First, create a script in Unity to handle the native code; call this script TestPlugin (see the next listing).

Listing 13.5 `TestPlugin` script that calls iOS native code from Unity

```
using System;
using System.Collections;
using System.Runtime.InteropServices;
using UnityEngine;

public class TestPlugin : MonoBehaviour {
   private static TestPlugin _instance;

   public static void Initialize() {
      if (_instance != null) {
         Debug.Log("TestPlugin instance was found. Already initialized");
         return;
      }
      Debug.Log("TestPlugin instance not found. Initializing...");

      GameObject owner = new GameObject("TestPlugin_instance");
      _instance = owner.AddComponent<TestPlugin>();
      DontDestroyOnLoad(_instance);
   }

   #region iOS
   [DllImport("__Internal")]
   private static extern float _TestNumber();

   [DllImport("__Internal")]
   private static extern string _TestString(string test);
   #endregion iOS

   public static float TestNumber() {
      float val = 0f;
      if (Application.platform == RuntimePlatform.IPhonePlayer)
         val = _TestNumber();
      return val;
   }

   public static string TestString(string test) {
      string val = "";
      if (Application.platform == RuntimePlatform.IPhonePlayer)
         val = _TestString(test);
      return val;
   }
}
```

The object is created in this static function, so you don't have to create it in the editor.

Tag that identifies section of code; the tag doesn't do anything by itself.

Refer to the function in the iOS code.

Call this if the platform is IPhonePlayer.

First, note that the static `Initialize()` function creates a permanent object in the scene so that you don't have to do it manually in the editor. You haven't previously seen code to create an object from scratch because using a prefab is a lot simpler in most cases, but in this case, it's cleaner to create the object in code (so that you can use the plugin script without editing the scene).

The main wizardry going on here involves the `DllImport` and `static extern` commands. Those commands tell Unity to link up to functions in the native code you provide. Then you can use those referenced functions in this script's methods (with a check to make sure the code is running on iPhone/iOS).

Next, you'll use these plugin functions to test them. Create a new script called `MobileTestObject`, create an empty object in the scene, and then attach the script to the object.

Listing 13.6   Using the plugin from `MobileTestObject`

```
using System.Collections;
using System.Collections.Generic;
using UnityEngine;

public class MobileTestObject : MonoBehaviour {
   private string message;

   void Awake() {                          Initialize the plugin
      TestPlugin.Initialize();      ◁──┘  at the beginning.
   }

   // Use this for initialization
   void Start() {
      message = "START: " + TestPlugin.TestString("ThIs Is A tEsT");
   }

   // Update is called once per frame
   void Update() {

      // Make sure the user touched the screen
      if (Input.touchCount==0){return;}

      Touch touch = Input.GetTouch(0);     ◁────── Respond to touch input.
      if (touch.phase == TouchPhase.Began) {
         message = "TOUCH: " + TestPlugin.TestNumber();
      }
   }

   void OnGUI() {                                        Display a message in the
      GUI.Label(new Rect(10, 10, 200, 20), message);  ◁──┘ corner of the screen.
   }
}
```

The script in this listing initializes the plugin object and then calls plugin methods in response to touch input. Once this is running on the device, you'll see the test message in the corner change whenever you tap the screen.

The final thing left to do is to write the native code that `TestPlugin` references. Code on iOS devices is written using Objective C and/or C (or Swift, but we won't be using that language), so you need both a .h header file and a .mm implementation file. As described earlier, they need to go in the Plugins/iOS/ folder in the Project view. Create `TestPlugin.h` and `TestPlugin.mm` there; in the .h file, write this code.

Listing 13.7 TestPlugin.h header for iOS code

```
#import <Foundation/Foundation.h>

@interface TestObject : NSObject {
NSString* status;
}

@end
```

Look for an explanation about iOS programming to understand what this header is doing; explaining iOS programming is beyond the scope of this book. Write the code from this listing in the .mm file.

Listing 13.8 TestPlugin.mm implementation

```
#import "TestPlugin.h"

@implementation TestObject
@end

NSString* CreateNSString (const char* string)
{
if (string)
return [NSString stringWithUTF8String: string];
else
return [NSString stringWithUTF8String: ""];
}

char* MakeStringCopy (const char* string)
{
if (string == NULL)
return NULL;

char* res = (char*)malloc(strlen(string) + 1);
strcpy(res, string);
return res;
}
```

```
extern "C" {
    const char* _TestString(const char* string) {
        NSString* oldString = CreateNSString(string);
        NSString* newString = [oldString lowercaseString];
        return MakeStringCopy([newString UTF8String]);
    }

    float _TestNumber() {
        return (arc4random() % 100)/100.0f;
    }
}
```

Again, a detailed explanation of this code is a bit beyond this book's scope. Note that many of the `string` functions are there to convert Unity's representation of string data into the native code.

> **TIP** This sample communicates in only one direction, from Unity to the plugin. But the native code could also communicate to Unity by using the `UnitySendMessage()` method. You can send a message to a named object in the scene; during initialization, the plugin created `TestPlugin_instance` to send messages to.

With the native code in place, you can build the iOS app and test it on a device. The message in the corner will initially be all lowercase; then tap the screen to watch the numbers displayed. Very cool!

For more information, visit https://docs.unity3d.com/Manual/PluginsForIOS.html. That's how to make an iOS plugin, so let's look at Android too.

ANDROID PLUGINS

To create an Android plugin, the Unity side of things is almost exactly the same. You don't need to change `MobileTestObject` at all. Make the additions shown here in `TestPlugin`.

Listing 13.9   Modifying `TestPlugin` to use the Android plugin

```
...
    #region iOS
    [DllImport("__Internal")]
    private static extern float _TestNumber();

    [DllImport("__Internal")]
    private static extern string _TestString(string test);
    #endregion iOS

#if UNITY_ANDROID
    private static Exception _pluginError;
    private static AndroidJavaClass _pluginClass;
    private static AndroidJavaClass GetPluginClass() {
        if (_pluginClass == null && _pluginError == null) {
            AndroidJNI.AttachCurrentThread();
```

AndroidJNI functionality provided by Unity

```
        try {
            _pluginClass = new
    AndroidJavaClass("com.testcompany.testplugin.TestPlugin");
        } catch (Exception e) {
            _pluginError = e;
        }
      }
      return _pluginClass;
    }

  private static AndroidJavaObject _unityActivity;
  private static AndroidJavaObject GetUnityActivity() {
      if (_unityActivity == null) {
          AndroidJavaClass unityPlayer = new
    AndroidJavaClass("com.unity3d.player.UnityPlayer");
          _unityActivity =
    unityPlayer.GetStatic<AndroidJavaObject>("currentActivity");
      }
      return _unityActivity;
  }
#endif

  public static float TestNumber() {
      float val = 0f;
      if (Application.platform == RuntimePlatform.IPhonePlayer)
          val = _TestNumber();
#if UNITY_ANDROID
      if (!Application.isEditor && _pluginError == null)
          val = GetPluginClass().CallStatic<int>("getNumber");
#endif
      return val;
  }

  public static string TestString(string test) {
      string val = "";
      if (Application.platform == RuntimePlatform.IPhonePlayer)
          val = _TestString(test);
#if UNITY_ANDROID
      if (!Application.isEditor && _pluginError == null)
          val = GetPluginClass().CallStatic<string>("getString", test);
#endif
      return val;
  }
}
```

> Name of the class you programmed; change this name as needed.

> Unity creates an activity for the Android app.

> Call to functions in plugin .jar

You'll notice that most of the additions happen inside UNITY_ANDROID platform defines. As explained earlier in the chapter, these compiler directives cause code to apply only to certain platforms and are omitted on other platforms. Whereas the iOS code wasn't doing anything that would break on other platforms (it won't do anything, but it won't cause errors, either), the code for Android plugins will compile only when Unity is set to the Android platform.

In particular, note the calls to AndroidJNI. That's the system within Unity for connecting to native Android. The other possibly confusing word that appears is Activity; in Android apps, an *activity* is an app process. The Unity game is an activity of the Android app, so the plugin code needs access to that activity to pass it around when needed.

Finally, you need the native Android code. Whereas iOS code is written in languages like Objective C and C, Android is programmed in Java (or Kotlin, but we'll use Java). But you can't simply provide the raw Java code for the plugin; the plugin must be a JAR packaged from the Java code. Here, again, the details of Android programming are out of scope for an introduction to Unity, but we'll go over the basics briefly. First off, you should install Android Studio if you didn't do so as part of downloading the Android SDK.

Figure 13.7 illustrates the steps to set up a plugin project in Android Studio (with screenshots from version 4.2.1):

1. Create a New Project by either selecting that in the startup window or going to File > New > New Project.

2. In the New Project window that appears, select the No Activity template (since this is a plugin, not a standalone Android app) and click Next.

3. Now name it TestPluginProj; for this test, it doesn't matter what the Min SDK is, but leave Language as Java and take note of the project location because you'll need to find it later. Click Finish to create the new project, and if there is a brief wait for loading, then click Finish again to dismiss the window.

4. Once the editor view appears, choose File > New > New Module to add a library.

5. Select Android Library, name it testplugin, change Package Name to com.testcompany.testplugin, and then click Finish.

6. With that module added, choose Build > Select Build Variant; in the panel that opens, click the Active Build Variant for TestPluginProj.testplugin and select Release.

7. Now expand testplugin > java in the upper Project panel, right-click com.testcompany.testplugin, and choose New > Java Class.

8. A tiny window opens to configure the new class, so type the name TestPlugin and press Enter.

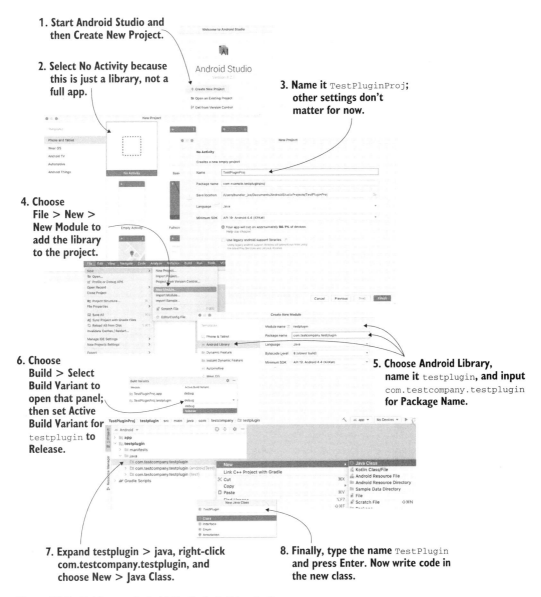

1. **Start Android Studio and then Create New Project.**

2. **Select No Activity because this is just a library, not a full app.**

3. **Name it** `TestPluginProj`; **other settings don't matter for now.**

4. **Choose File > New > New Module to add the library to the project.**

5. **Choose Android Library, name it** `testplugin`, **and input** `com.testcompany.testplugin` **for Package Name.**

6. **Choose Build > Select Build Variant to open that panel; then set Active Build Variant for** `testplugin` **to Release.**

7. **Expand testplugin > java, right-click com.testcompany.testplugin, and choose New > Java Class.**

8. **Finally, type the name** `TestPlugin` **and press Enter. Now write code in the new class.**

Figure 13.7   Setting up Android Studio to build a plugin

`TestPlugin` is currently empty, so write the plugin functions in it. Listing 13.10 shows the Java code for the plugin.

Listing 13.10   TestPlugin.java that compiles into a JAR

```
package com.testcompany.testplugin;

public class TestPlugin {
```

```
    private static int number = 0;

    public static int getNumber() {
        number++;
        return number;
    }

    public static String getString(String message) {
        return message.toLowerCase();
    }
}
```

All right, now you can package this code into a JAR (or rather an Android Archive file, which contains the JAR). In the top menu, choose Build > Make Project. Once the build is complete, go to the project on your computer and find testplugin-release.aar in *<project location>*/testplugin/build/outputs/aar/. Drag the archive file into Unity's Android plugins folder to import it.

Android's manifest and resources folder

It wasn't required for this simple test plugin, but Android plugins often must edit the manifest file. All Android apps are controlled by a main configuration file called AndroidManifest.xml; Unity creates a basic manifest file if you don't provide one, but you could provide one manually by putting it in Plugins/Android/ alongside the plugin.

Unity adds a Temp folder to the project while it runs, and Unity puts the generated manifest file in there (StagingArea/UnityManifest.xml) when an Android app is built. Copy that file to manually edit it; this chapter's code download includes a sample manifest file.

Similarly, there's a folder called *res* where you can put resources like custom icons. To replace this generated folder with your own resources, you could create a res folder in the Android plug-ins folder.

With the archive file in Plugins/Android, build the game and install it on a device, and the message will change whenever you tap the screen. Also, like the iOS plugin, an Android plugin could use `UnityPlayer.UnitySendMessage()` to communicate with the object in the scene. The Java code would need to import Unity's Android Player library, which is contained in the Unity installation folder (again, usually C:\Program Files\ Unity\Editor\Data on Windows or /Applications/Unity/Editor on Mac) as /PlaybackEngines/AndroidPlayer/Variations/mono/Release/Classes/classes.jar.

I know I glossed over a lot in developing Android libraries, but that's because the process is both complicated and changes frequently. If you become advanced enough to develop plugins for your Android games, you're going to have to look up documentation on Android's developer website, as well as refer to Unity's documentation at http://mng.bz/yJKG.

13.4 Developing XR (both VR and AR)

NOTE The initials *XR* stand for *extended reality*, a term that encompasses both *virtual reality* (VR) and *augmented reality* (AR). VR refers to immersing the user in a completely synthetic environment, while AR refers to adding computer graphics to the natural environment, but both fall under the umbrella of technologies that mediate the environment surrounding the user.

XR is the last "platform" covered in this chapter. "Platform" is in quotes because XR isn't technically considered a separate platform when building the application. Instead, XR support comes from plugin packages that can be added to the relevant build platforms, such as desktop VR or mobile AR. Let's go over how this works, first for VR and then AR.

13.4.1 Supporting virtual reality headsets

The major VR devices on the market right now are Oculus Quest, HTC VIVE, Valve Index, and PlayStation VR. Ignoring PlayStation VR (since this book doesn't cover console development), all the other devices are supported by adding a VR SDK to either Unity's PC build target, or (in the case of Oculus Quest) to Android.

A variety of such SDKs are available, distributed through Unity's Package Manager. For example, browse the Unity Registry to find options like Oculus XR or Windows XR. Meanwhile, another attractive option offered to Unity developers is XR Interaction Toolkit, but that package is slightly harder to find. Because that package is still not considered complete (mostly incomplete in AR support, though; the VR support is pretty solid), it is considered a preview package. Packages designated as *preview* aren't shown by default, but you can adjust the settings of the Package Manager window to show preview packages (see figure 13.8).

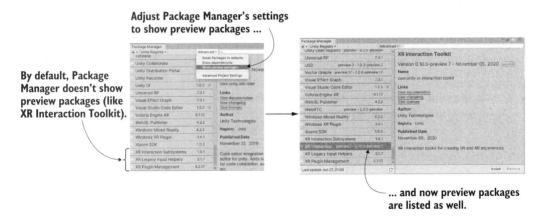

Figure 13.8 How to see preview packages in Package Manager

Once an XR package is installed, you must enable it in Project Settings (remember, that's Edit > Project Settings) under XR Plug-in Management (shown in figure 13.9).

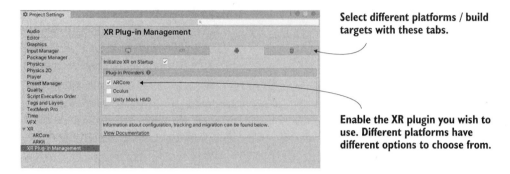

Figure 13.9   XR Plugin Management in Project Settings

NOTE XR Plug-in Management is *itself* a package, although that should have been installed along with whatever other XR package you chose. If those settings aren't appearing, though, you may need to install the package manually.

We're not going to go over code for any specific VR device, because there are just too many options to cover. Instead, I encourage you visit the documentation for the relevant XR plugin:

- XR Interaction Toolkit: http://mng.bz/Mv67
- Oculus XR: http://mng.bz/aZjz
- Windows XR: http://mng.bz/g16l
- OpenXR: http://mng.bz/ePNz

We *are*, however, going to implement a simple example to help explain AR.

13.4.2 AR Foundation for mobile Augmented Reality

Unlike VR, augmented reality doesn't necessarily imply a head-mounted display (HMD). It certainly *can* involve an HMD, and Unity supports devices like the HoloLens and Magic Leap. However, AR also is provided through mobile phones, what's sometimes referred to as *handheld AR*.

Both Apple and Google provide SDKs for handheld AR on iOS and Android, respectively. Apple's SDK is called ARKit, while Google provides ARCore. These libraries are specific to those platforms however, so Unity provides a cross-platform wrapper called *AR Foundation*. As a developer, it's important to understand that you are working with ARKit or ARCore under the hood, but you code against the API of AR Foundation.

To start with, create a new Unity project. In this new project, go to Package Manager and install AR Foundation, along with either ARKit XR or ARCore XR (or both!), depending on which mobile platform you are developing for. Then enable ARKit or ARCore in XR Plug-in Management (shown back in figure 13.9).

> **NOTE** The face-tracking bit of ARKit has a separate package from the rest of ARKit. That's because Apple will reject submitted apps that have code for face-tracking but aren't actually doing facial AR. Thus, install only the main ARKit XR plug-in package if you aren't doing facial AR, and install both packages if you are.

ARKit and ARCore have requirements that must be met in the Player settings for the iOS and Android platforms (see figure 13.10a and b). On Android, first remove Vulkan from the list of Graphics APIs (select Vulkan and then click the minus button), then scroll down and change the Minimum API Level to 24. On iOS, set the Minimum iOS Version to 11, make sure Architecture is set to ARM64, turn on the Requires ARKit setting, and enter a camera usage description (something like `Camera required for AR`).

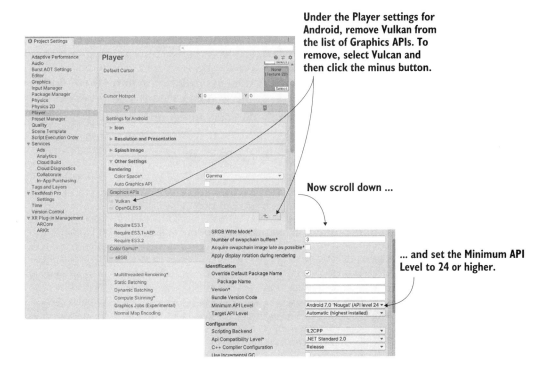

Figure 13.10a   Adjust Android settings to support AR

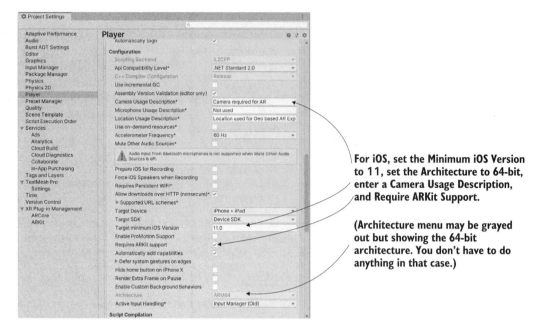

Figure 13.10b   Adjust iOS settings to support AR

ARKit requires those iOS settings to function, and ARCore requires those Android settings. Having made all the necessary adjustments in Player settings, next set up the various objects needed in the scene. As depicted in figure 13.11, the steps to take are as follows:

1. From the GameObject menu, choose XR > AR Session.
2. Choose GameObject > XR > AR Session Origin.
3. Choose GameObject > XR > AR Default Plane.
4. Delete Main Camera (since Session Origin includes a camera set up for AR).
5. Create an empty GameObject and name it `Controllers`.

Next, create a new C# script called `PlaneTrackingController`, and write listing 13.11 into it.

Listing 13.11   `PlaneTrackingController` script that uses AR Foundation

```
using System.Collections;
using System.Collections.Generic;
using UnityEngine;
using UnityEngine.XR.ARFoundation;
using UnityEngine.XR.ARSubsystems;

public class PlaneTrackingController : MonoBehaviour {
    [SerializeField] ARSessionOrigin arOrigin = null;
    [SerializeField] GameObject planePrefab = null;
```

This should be the plane prefab from XR objects, not just any game object.

```
    private ARPlaneManager planeManager;

    void Start() {
        planeManager = arOrigin.gameObject.AddComponent<ARPlaneManager>();  ◁┐
        planeManager.detectionMode = PlaneDetectionMode.Horizontal;
        planeManager.planePrefab = planePrefab;
    }
}
```

**It would also work to add this
component in the editor, but
we'll add it in code.**

This script adds a component called `ARPlaneManager` to the session origin and then assigns a couple of settings to the plane manager, including which object to use for visualizing the detected plane. This component could have been added in the editor, but adding it in code affords more flexibility in controlling the AR.

Drag this script onto the Controllers object to link it as a component. Now (as figure 13.11 shows), drag AR Session Origin and AR Default Plane onto their component slots in the Inspector.

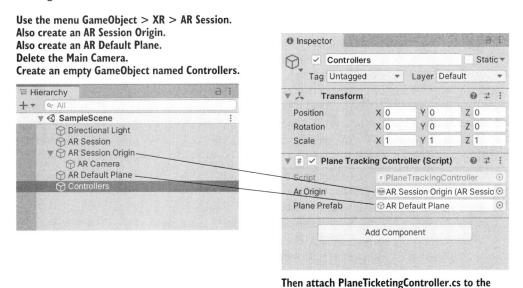

Starting with a default scene:

**Use the menu GameObject > XR > AR Session.
Also create an AR Session Origin.
Also create an AR Default Plane.
Delete the Main Camera.
Create an empty GameObject named Controllers.**

**Then attach PlaneTicketingController.cs to the
Controllers object, and drag in AR Session Origin
and AR Default Plane to the script component's slots.**

Figure 13.11   Setting up objects in the scene for simple AR

With everything in place, build the mobile app in order to see plane tracking functioning. Because `PlaneTrackingController` uses AR Foundation (rather than either ARKit or ARCore directly), the project should work on both iOS and Android. Once the app is running on your device, you should see something like figure 13.12 when moving the camera around.

Figure 13.12   AR plane detection in action

Great, planar surfaces are being detected in the environment! However, right now nothing is going on other than that the computer detects surfaces. That is, nothing is being placed *on* the detected surface. AR Foundation provides several useful bits of functionality, not just plane tracking, and another useful feature is raycasting against detected AR surfaces. Follow listing 13.12 to add code for doing AR raycasting.

Listing 13.12   Adding raycasting to `PlaneTrackingController`

```
...
    private ARPlaneManager planeManager;            Add the new fields just under
    private ARRaycastManager raycastManager;   ⬁── the existing manager.
    private GameObject prim;
...                                                              Create an
    void Start() {                                               object to
        prim = GameObject.CreatePrimitive(PrimitiveType.Cube);  ⬁── place on
        prim.SetActive(false);                                   detected
                                                                 surfaces.
        raycastManager =
    arOrigin.gameObject.AddComponent<ARRaycastManager>();

        planeManager = arOrigin.gameObject.AddComponent<ARPlaneManager>();
        ...
    }

    void Update() {
        if (Input.GetMouseButtonDown(0)) {          Call the Raycast method in
            var hits = new List<ARRaycastHit>();      response to user input.
            if (raycastManager.Raycast(Input.mousePosition, hits,   ⬁──┘
                TrackableType.PlaneWithinPolygon)) {
                prim.SetActive(true);
                prim.transform.localScale = new Vector3(.1f, .1f, .1f);

                var pose = hits[0].pose;
                prim.transform.localPosition = pose.position;
                prim.transform.localRotation = pose.rotation;
            }
```

```
        }
    }
...
```

Deploy the app again onto your mobile device. This time, tap the detected plane, and a cube should appear, just like figure 13.13. In this way, you are placing virtual objects around your real environment.

Figure 13.13   A cube placed on the tracked plane

This example touches on only the very basics of AR Foundation. For more in-depth uses, refer to Unity's manual (http://mng.bz/p9aG) as well as the sample projects Unity has on GitHub (http://mng.bz/YwpN).

Unity as a Library

Ordinarily, Unity projects are deployed as self-contained apps, a configuration that makes perfect sense for games. However, Unity is increasingly being used for non-game XR development, and those users may want to integrate their Unity projects with an external app.

For that reason, Unity now has the ability to deploy projects as a library to use in a larger app. The Unity as a Library capability supports both iOS and Android, enabling mobile developers to add augmented reality content (powered by AR Foundation) to their apps. For more information, follow these links:

- https://unity.com/features/unity-as-a-library
- http://mng.bz/OQnn

CONGRATULATIONS, YOU'VE REACHED THE END!

Congratulations, you now know the steps for deploying a Unity game on most major platforms. The basic build process for all platforms is simple (just a single button), but customizing the app on various platforms can get complicated. Now you're ready to get out there and build your own games!

Summary

- Unity can build executable applications for a huge variety of platforms, including desktop computers, mobile devices, and websites.
- A host of settings can be applied to builds, including details like the icon for the app and the name that appears.
- Web games can interact with the web page they're embedded in, allowing for all kinds of interesting web apps.
- Unity supports custom plugins in order to extend its functionality.

afterword

At this point, you know everything you need to know to build a complete game using Unity—everything from a programming standpoint, that is; a top-notch game needs fantastic art and sound too. But success as a game developer involves a lot more than technical skills. Let's face it—learning Unity isn't your end goal. Your goal is to create successful games, and Unity is just a tool (granted, a very good tool) to get you to that goal.

Beyond the technical skills to implement everything in the game, you need an additional intangible attribute: grit. I'm talking about the doggedness and confidence to keep working on a challenging project and see it through to the end—what I sometimes refer to as "finishing ability." There's only one way to build up your finishing ability, and that's to complete lots of projects. That seems like a catch-22 (to gain the ability to complete projects, you first need to complete a lot of projects), but the key point to recognize is that small projects are way easier to complete than large ones.

Therefore, the path forward is to first build a lot of small projects—because those are easy to complete—and work up to larger projects. Many new game developers make the mistake of tackling a project that's too large for two main reasons: they want to copy their favorite (big) game, and everyone underestimates how much work it takes to make a game. The project seemingly starts off fine but quickly gets bogged down in too many challenges, and eventually the developer gets dejected and quits.

Instead, someone new to game development should start small. Start with projects so small that they seem trivial. The projects in this book are the sort of "small, almost to the point of trivial" projects that you should start with. If you've done all the projects in this book, you've already gotten a lot of these starter projects out of the way. Try something bigger for your next project, but be wary of making too big a jump. You'll build up your skills and confidence, so you can get a little more ambitious each time.

You'll hear this same advice almost anytime you ask how to start developing games. For example, Unity asked the web series *Extra Credits* (a great series about game development) to make some videos about starting in game dev, and you'll find them at http://mng.bz/GOjq.

Game design

The entire *Extra Credits* series goes way beyond this handful of videos sponsored by Unity. It covers a lot of ground but mostly focuses on the discipline of game design.

> **DEFINITION** *Game design* is the process of defining a game by creating its goals, rules, and challenges. It is not to be confused with *visual design*, which is designing appearance, not function. This is a common mistake because the average person is most familiar with "design" in the context of "graphic design."

> **DEFINITION** One of the most central parts of game design is crafting game *mechanics*—the individual actions (or systems of actions) within a game. The mechanics in a game are often set up by its rules, whereas the challenges in a game generally come from applying the mechanics to specific situations. For example, walking around the game is a mechanic; a maze is a kind of challenge based on that mechanic.

Thinking about game design can be tricky for newcomers to game development. The most successful (and satisfying to create!) games are built with interesting and innovative game mechanics. Conversely, worrying too much about the design of your first game can distract you from other aspects of game development, like learning how to program it. You're better off starting out by aping the design of existing games. (Remember, I'm only talking about *starting out*; cloning existing games is great for initial practice, but eventually you'll have enough skills and experience to branch out further.)

That said, any successful game developer should be curious about game design. There are lots of ways to learn more about game design—you already know about the *Extra Credits* videos, but here are some other websites:

- www.gamedeveloper.com—Offers jobs, games updates, good news/bad news about games; everything you want/need to know about the art and business of making games.
- https://lostgarden.home.blog/worth-reading/—Readable, thoughtful essays on game design theory, art, and the business of design.
- http://sloperama.com—Click School-a-rama for the game biz advice page.

Great books on the subject are also available, such as the following:

- *The Art of Game Design*, Third Edition, by Jesse Schell (A K Peters/CRC Press, 2019)
- *Game Design Workshop*, Fourth Edition, by Tracy Fullerton (A K Peters/CRC Press, 2018)
- *A Theory of Fun for Game Design*, Second Edition, by Raph Koster (O'Reilly Media, 2013)

Marketing your game

In the *Extra Credits* videos, the fourth video is about marketing your game. Sometimes game developers put off thinking about marketing. They want to think only about building the game and not marketing it, but that attitude will probably result in a failed game. The best game in the world still won't be successful if nobody knows about it!

The word *marketing* often evokes thoughts of ads, and if you have the budget, then running ads for your game is certainly one way to market it. But you can get the word out about your game in lots of low cost or even free ways. Specifics tend to change over time, but overall strategies mentioned in that video include tweeting about your game (or posting on social media in general, not just Twitter) and creating a trailer video to share on YouTube with reviewers, bloggers, and so on. Be persistent and get creative!

Now go and create some great games. Unity is an excellent tool for doing just that, and you've learned how to use it. Good luck on your journey!

appendix A
Scene navigation
and keyboard shortcuts

Operating Unity is done through the mouse and keyboard, but it isn't obvious to a newcomer *how* the mouse and keyboard are used in Unity. In particular, the most basic sort of mouse and keyboard input is navigating around the scene and looking around the 3D objects. Unity also has keyboard commands for commonly used operations.

I'll explain the input controls here, but you also can refer to a couple of web pages (these are the relevant pages in Unity's online manual):

- http://mng.bz/01Ex
- http://mng.bz/KoNK

A.1   Scene navigation using the mouse

Scene navigation is primarily done with three main navigation maneuvers: Move, Orbit, and Zoom. The three movements involve clicking and dragging while holding down a combination of Alt (or Option on the Mac) and Ctrl (Command on a Mac). The exact controls vary for one-, two-, and three-button mice; table A.1 lists all the controls.

Table A.1   Scene navigation controls for various kinds of mice

Navigation action	Three-button mouse	Two-button mouse	One-button mouse
Move	Middle-button click/drag	Alt-Command + left-click/drag	Alt-Command + click/drag
Orbit	Hold Alt + left-click/drag	Alt + left-click/drag	Alt + click/drag
Zoom	Hold Alt + right-click/drag	Alt + right-click/drag	Alt-Ctrl + click/drag

NOTE Although Unity can be used with one- or two-button mice, I highly recommend getting a three-button mouse (and yes, a three-button mouse works fine on a Mac).

Besides the navigation maneuvers done using the mouse, some view controls are based on the keyboard. If you hold down the right button on the mouse, the W, A, S, D keys on the keyboard can be used to walk around in the manner common to most first-person games. Hold Shift during any other control to move faster.

But most important, if you press F while an object is selected, the Scene view will pan and zoom to focus on that object. If you get lost while navigating your scene, a common "escape hatch" is to select an object listed in the Hierarchy, move the mouse over the Scene view (this shortcut works only while in that view), and then press F.

A.2 *Commonly used keyboard shortcuts*

Unity has keyboard commands to quickly access important functions. The most important keyboard shortcuts are W, E, R, and T: those keys activate the transform tools Translate, Rotate, and Scale (refer to chapter 1 if you don't recall what the transform tools do), as well as the 2D Rect tool. Because those keys are right next to each other, it's common to leave your left hand on those keys while your right hand operates the mouse.

In addition to the transform tools, you can use keyboard shortcuts. Table A.2 lists many useful keyboard shortcuts in Unity.

Table A.2 Useful keyboard shortcuts

Keystroke	Function
W	Translate (move the selected object)
E	Rotate (rotate the selected object)
R	Scale (resize the selected object)
T	Rect tool (manipulate 2D objects)
F	Focus view on the selected object
V	Snap to vertices
Ctrl/Command-Shift-N	New GameObject
Ctrl/Command-P	Play game
Ctrl/Command-R	Refresh project
Ctrl/ Command-1	Set current window to Scene view
Ctrl/Command-2	Set to Game view
Ctrl/Command-3	Set to Inspector view
Ctrl/Command-4	Set to Hierarchy view

Table A.2 Useful keyboard shortcuts

Keystroke	Function
Ctrl/Command-5	Set to Project view
Ctrl/Command-6	Set to Animation view

Unity responds to other keyboard shortcuts as well, but they get increasingly obscure the further down the list we get.

appendix B
External tools
used alongside Unity

Developing a game using Unity relies on a variety of external software tools for taking care of various tasks. In chapter 1, we discussed one external tool: Visual Studio, which is technically a separate application, even though it's bundled along with Unity. In a similar manner, developers rely on an array of external tools to do work not internal to Unity.

This isn't to say that Unity is lacking capabilities that it ought to have. Rather, the game development process is so complex and multifaceted that any well-designed piece of software with a clear focus and clean separation of concerns will inevitably limit itself to being good at a limited subset of the process. In this case, Unity concentrates on being the glue and the engine that brings together all the content of a game and makes it function. Creating all that content is done with other tools; let's take a look at several categories of software that could be useful to you.

B.1 Programming tools

We've already looked at Visual Studio, the most significant programming tool used alongside Unity. But you should be aware of other programming tools, as you'll see in this section.

B.1.1 Rider

As mentioned in chapter 1, although Unity comes with one flavor of Visual Studio, you could choose to use a different IDE instead. The most common alternatives are either Visual Studio Code or JetBrains Rider. Rider (www.jetbrains.com/lp/dotnet-unity/) is a powerful C# programming environment with Unity integration.

B.1.2 Xcode

Xcode is the programming environment provided by Apple (in particular, an IDE, but also including SDKs for Apple platforms). Although you'd still be doing the vast majority of the work within Unity, you need to use Xcode (https://developer.apple .com/xcode/) to deploy a game to iOS. That work often involves debugging or profiling your app by using the tools in Xcode.

B.1.3 Android SDK

Just as you need to install Xcode to deploy to iOS, you need to download the Android SDK to deploy to Android. Usually, you'll want to download the SDK along with the Android module in Unity Hub. Alternatively, the Android SDK is provided along with Android Studio at https://developer.android.com/studio. Unlike when building an iOS game, you don't need to fire up any development tools outside of Unity—you simply have to set preferences in Unity that point to the Android SDK.

B.1.4 Version control (Git, SVN)

Any decent-sized software development project will involve a lot of complex revisions to code files, so programmers have developed a class of software called a *version-control system* (*VCS*) to handle this problem. A couple of the most popular free systems are Git (https://git-scm.com) and Apache Subversion (also known as SVN, https://subversion .apache.org).

   If you don't already use a VCS, I highly recommend starting to use one. Unity fills the project folder with temp files and workspace settings, but the only folders that need to be in version control are Assets (make sure your version control is picking up the meta files generated by Unity), Packages, and ProjectSettings.

B.2 3D art applications

Although Unity is perfectly capable of handling 2D graphics (chapters 5 and 6 focus on 2D graphics), it originated as a 3D game engine and continues to have strong 3D graphics features. Many 3D artists work with at least one of the software packages described in this section.

B.2.1 Maya

Autodesk Maya (www.autodesk.com/products/maya/overview) is a 3D art and animation package with deep roots in moviemaking. Maya's feature set covers almost every task that comes up for 3D artists, from crafting beautiful cinematic animations to making efficient game-ready models. 3D animation done in Maya (such as a character walking) can be exported over to Unity.

B.2.2 3ds Max

Another widely used 3D art and animation package, Autodesk 3ds Max (www.autodesk .com/products/3ds-max/overview) offers an almost identical feature set and is quite comparable in workflow to Maya. 3ds Max runs only on Windows (whereas other tools, including Maya, are cross-platform), but it's used just as often in the game industry.

B.2.3   Blender

Though not as commonly used in the game industry as either 3ds Max or Maya, Blender (www.blender.org) is comparable to those other applications. Blender also covers almost all 3D art tasks and, best of all, Blender is open source! Given that it's available for free on all platforms, Blender is the only 3D art application that's assumed to be available by this book.

B.2.4   SketchUp

This simple-to-use modeling tool is especially well-suited for buildings and architectural elements. Unlike the previous tools, SketchUp (www.sketchup.com) does not cover all or even most 3D art tasks; instead, it focuses on making it easy to model buildings and other simple shapes. This tool is useful in game development for whiteboxing and level editing.

B.3   2D image editors

2D images are crucial to all games, whether they're displayed directly for 2D games or as textures on the surface of 3D models. Several 2D graphics tools come up often in game development, as you'll see in this section.

B.3.1   Photoshop

Adobe Photoshop (www.adobe.com/products/photoshop.html) is easily the most widely used 2D image application there is. The tools in Photoshop can be used to touch up existing images, apply image filters, or even paint pictures from scratch. Photoshop supports dozens of file formats, including all image formats used in Unity.

B.3.2   GIMP

An acronym for *GNU Image Manipulation Program*, GIMP (www.gimp.org) is the best-known open source 2D graphics application. GIMP trails Photoshop in both features and usability, but it's still a useful image editor, and you can't beat the price!

B.3.3   TexturePacker

Whereas the previously mentioned tools are all used beyond the field of game development, TexturePacker is useful only for game development. But it's very good at the task it was designed for: assembling sprite sheets to use in 2D games. If you're developing a 2D game, you probably want to try out TexturePacker (www.codeandweb.com/texturepacker).

B.3.4   Aseprite, Pyxel Edit

Pixel art is one of the most recognizable 2D gaming art styles, and Aseprite (www.aseprite.org) and Pyxel Edit (www.pyxeledit.com) are good pixel art tools. Photoshop can technically be used for pixel art as well, but it's not focused on that task. Furthermore, the animation features are more front-and-center at Aseprite and Pyxel Edit.

B.4 Audio software

A dizzying array of audio production tools is available, including both sound editors (which work with raw waveforms) and sequencers (which compose music using a sequence of notes). To give a taste of the audio software available, this section looks at two major sound-editing tools. Other examples beyond this list include Logic, Ableton, and Reason.

B.4.1 Pro Tools

Pro Tools audio software (www.avid.com/en/pro-tools) boasts many useful features and is considered the industry standard by countless music producers and audio engineers. It's frequently used for all sorts of professional audio work, including game development.

B.4.2 Audacity

Although it is nowhere near as useful for professional audio work, Audacity (www.audacityteam.org) is a handy sound editor for small-scale audio work, like preparing short sound files to use as sound effects in a game. This is a popular choice for those looking for open source sound-editing software.

appendix C
Modeling
a bench in Blender

In chapters 2 and 4, we looked at creating levels with large flat walls and floors. But what about more detailed objects? What if you want, say, interesting furniture in the room? You can accomplish that by building 3D models in external 3D art apps. Recall the definition from the introduction to chapter 4: 3D models are the mesh objects in the game (the 3D shapes). In this appendix, I'll show you how to create a mesh object of a simple bench (figure C.1).

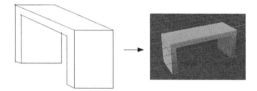

Figure C.1   Diagram of the simple bench you're going to model.

Although appendix B lists several 3D art tools, we'll use Blender for this exercise because it's open source and thus accessible to all readers. You'll create a mesh object in Blender and export that to an art asset that works with Unity.

> **TIP** Modeling is a huge topic, but we'll cover only a handful of modeling functions that will allow you to create the bench. If you want to keep learning more about modeling after this chapter, look at some of the many books and tutorials on the subject (to start with, look at the learning resources at www.blender.org).

WARNING I used Blender 2.91, so the explanations and screenshots come from that version of the software. Newer versions of Blender are released frequently, and changes may occur to the placement of buttons or names of commands.

C.1 *Building the mesh geometry*

Launch Blender and click outside the splash screen to dismiss it; the initial default screen looks like figure C.2, with a cube in the middle of the scene. Use the middle mouse button to manipulate the camera view: click and drag to tumble, Shift with click-drag to pan, and Ctrl with click-drag to zoom. Left-click the camera to select it, hold Shift while clicking the light to select it too, and then press X to delete both.

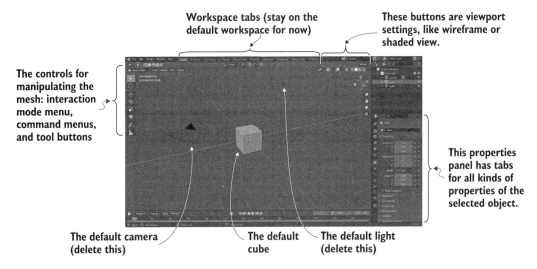

Workspace tabs (stay on the default workspace for now)

These buttons are viewport settings, like wireframe or shaded view.

The controls for manipulating the mesh: interaction mode menu, command menus, and tool buttons

This properties panel has tabs for all kinds of properties of the selected object.

The default camera (delete this)

The default cube

The default light (delete this)

Figure C.2 The initial default screen in Blender

Blender starts out in Object mode, which, as the name implies, enables you to manipulate entire objects, moving them around the scene. To edit a single mesh object in detail, you must select it and switch to Edit mode; figure C.3 shows the menu you use.

WARNING Many parts of Blender's interface are context sensitive, and this menu is one. The menu items listed vary depending on which object is selected, be it a mesh, a camera, or something else.

When you first switch to Edit mode, Blender is set to Vertex Selection mode, but buttons let you switch between Vertex, Edge, and Face Selection modes (refer to figure C.4). The various selection modes allow you to select different mesh elements.

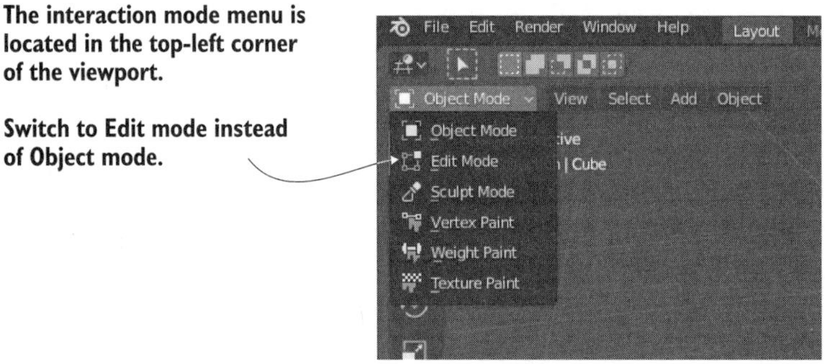
The interaction mode menu is located in the top-left corner of the viewport.
Switch to Edit mode instead of Object mode.
File
Edit
Render
Window
Help
Layout
Object Mode
View
Select
Add
Object
Object Mode
Edit Mode
Sculpt Mode
Vertex Paint
Weight Paint
Texture Paint

Figure C.3 Menu for switching from Object to Edit mode

> **DEFINITION** *Mesh elements* are the vertices, edges, and faces that make up the geometry of the mesh—in other words, the individual corner points, the lines connecting the points, and the shapes filled in between connected lines.

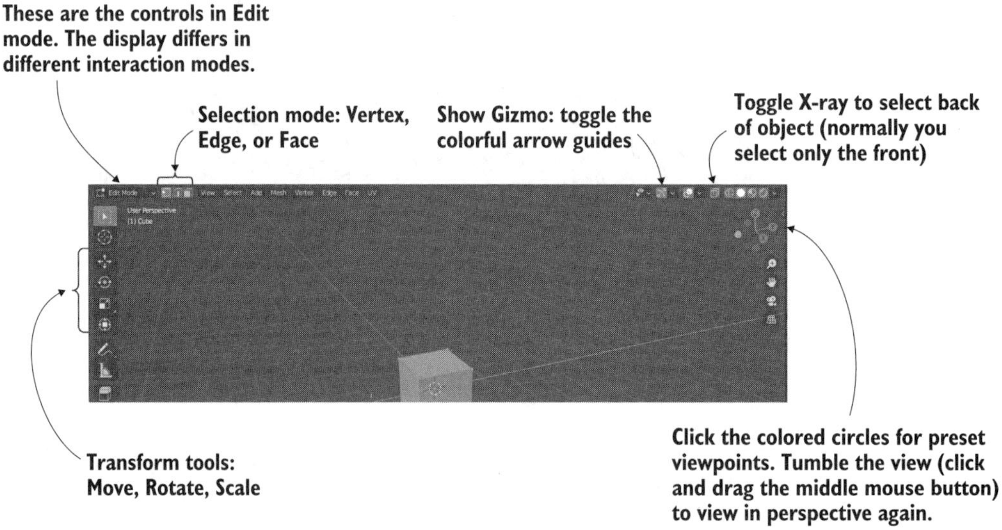
These are the controls in Edit mode. The display differs in different interaction modes.
Selection mode: Vertex, Edge, or Face
Show Gizmo: toggle the colorful arrow guides
Toggle X-ray to select back of object (normally you select only the front)
Transform tools: Move, Rotate, Scale
Click the colored circles for preset viewpoints. Tumble the view (click and drag the middle mouse button) to view in perspective again.

Figure C.4 Controls along the sides of the viewport

> **Fundamental mouse and keyboard shortcuts in Blender**
>
> Also depicted in figure C.4 are the transform tools. As in Unity, the transforms are Move, Rotate, and Scale. Toward the top right of the viewport is a button to toggle Show Gizmo (the arrows in the scene) on and off; I recommend leaving that gizmo on, because otherwise you can access the transform tools only via keyboard shortcuts. The keyboard shortcuts in Blender are difficult to use, and the main reason Blender's UI has a bad reputation.

Blender also used to force rather nonstandard mouse functionality. Though the use of the middle mouse button to manipulate the camera always made sense, selecting elements in the scene was done with the right mouse button (in most applications, the left mouse button selects things). Left-click is now the default for selecting, but the old functionality is why the splash screen shows this setting (accessible in Edit > Preferences after the first launch) when you first launch Blender:

Blender mouse settings

Similarly, both box selection and deselecting used to be pretty odd, although now you simply click and drag or click empty space, respectively. Incidentally, you can hold Shift while something is already selected to add to the selection, and simply press A (for All) to select everything.

These are the basic controls for using Blender, so now we'll see some functions for editing the model. To start, scale the cube into a long, thin plank. Select every vertex of the model (be sure to also select vertices on the side of the object facing away; press A to select all) and then switch to the Scale tool. Click-drag the blue arm to scale down vertically, and then click-drag the green arrow to scale out sideways (see figure C.5).

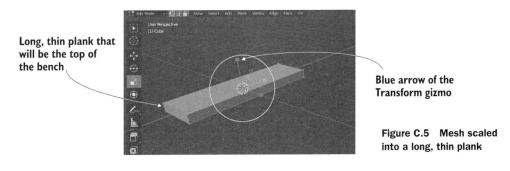

Long, thin plank that will be the top of the bench

Blue arrow of the Transform gizmo

Figure C.5 Mesh scaled into a long, thin plank

Switch to Face Selection mode (use the button indicated in figure C.4) and select both small ends of the plank. You can click faces individually, and remember to hold Shift when adding to the selection. Now click the Mesh menu at the top of the viewport and choose Extrude > Extrude Individual Faces (see figure C.6). As you move the mouse, you'll see additional sections added to the ends of the plank; move them out slightly and then left-click to confirm. Make this additional section only the width of the bench legs, giving yourself a little additional geometry to work with.

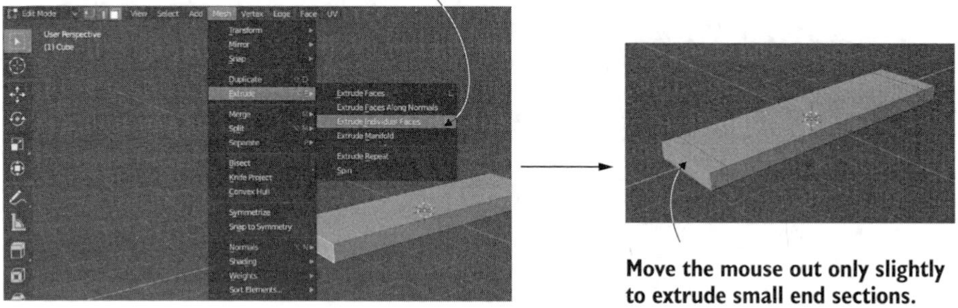

Select the thin polygons on either end of the bench; then choose Extrude Individual Faces in the Mesh menu.

Move the mouse out only slightly to extrude small end sections.

Figure C.6   In the Mesh menu, use Extrude Individual Faces to pull out extra sections.

DEFINITION   *Extrude* pushes out new geometry with a cross section in the shape of the selected faces. The different extrude commands define what to do when multiple elements are selected: Extrude Individual Faces treats each face as a separate piece to extrude, whereas the standard Extrude Faces command treats the entire selection as a single piece.

Now look at the bottom of the plank and select the two thin faces on each end. Use the Extrude Individual Faces command again to pull down legs for the bench (refer to figure C.7).

Select thin faces underneath and Extrude them down to make legs.

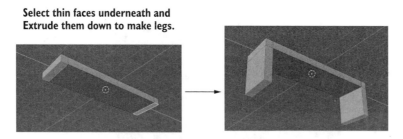

Figure C.7   Select the thin faces underneath the bench and pull down legs.

The shape is complete! But before you export the model over to Unity, you want to take care of texturing the model.

C.2   *Texture-mapping the model*

3D models can have 2D images (referred to as *textures*) displayed on their surface. How exactly the 2D images relate to the 3D surface is straightforward for a large, flat surface like a wall: simply stretch the image across the flat surface. But what about an oddly shaped surface, like the sides of the bench? This is where it becomes important to understand the concept of texture coordinates.

Texture coordinates define how parts of the texture relate to parts of the mesh. These coordinates assign mesh elements to areas of the texture. Think about it like wrapping paper (see figure C.8); the 3D model is the box being wrapped, the texture is the wrapping paper, and the texture coordinates represent the points on the box where the wrapping paper will go. The texture coordinates define points and shapes on the 2D image; those shapes correlate to polygons on the mesh, and that part of the image appears on that part of the mesh.

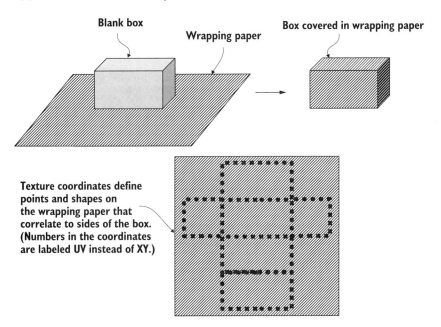

Figure C.8   Wrapping paper makes a good analogy for how texture coordinates work.

> **TIP**   Another name for texture coordinates is *UV coordinates*. This is because texture coordinates are defined using the letters U and V, just as coordinates on the 3D model are defined using X, Y, and Z.

The technical term for correlating part of one thing to part of another is *mapping*—hence the term *texture mapping* for the process of creating texture coordinates. Coming from the wrapping paper analogy, another name for the process is *unwrapping*. And still more terms are created by mashing up the other terminology, like *UV unwrapping*; a lot of essentially synonymous terms surrounding texture mapping exist, so try not to get confused.

Traditionally, the process of texture mapping has been wickedly complicated, but fortunately, Blender provides tools to make the process fairly simple. First you define seams on the model; if you think further about wrapping around a box (or better yet, think about the other direction, unfolding a box), you'll realize that not every part of a 3D shape can remain seamless when unfolded into two dimensions. There will have to be seams in the 3D form where the sides come apart. Blender enables you to select edges and declare them as seams.

Switch to Edge Selection mode (see the buttons in figure C.4) and select the edges along the outside of the bottom of the bench. Now choose Edge > Mark Seam (see figure C.9). This tells Blender to separate the bottom of the bench for the purposes of texture mapping. Do the same thing for the sides of the bench, but don't separate the sides entirely. Instead, seam only the edges running up the legs of the bench; this way, the sides will remain connected to the bench while spreading out like wings.

Select the bottom edges.

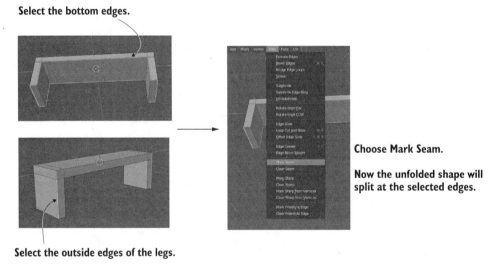

Choose Mark Seam.

Now the unfolded shape will split at the selected edges.

Select the outside edges of the legs.

Figure C.9   Seam edges along the bottom of the bench and along the legs

Once all the seams are marked, run the texture unwrap command. First, select the entire mesh (just press A to select everything, or box select and don't forget the side of the object facing away). Next, choose UV > Unwrap to create the texture coordinates. But you can't see the texture coordinates in this view; Blender defaults to a 3D view of the scene. Switch to the UV Editing workspace to see the texture coordinates, using the workspace tabs at the top of the screen (see figure C.10).

Now you can see the texture coordinates. You can see the polygons of the bench laid out flat, separated, and unfolded according to the seams you marked. To paint a texture, you have to see these UV coordinates in your image-editing program. Referring

Select the UV Editing
workspace at the top.

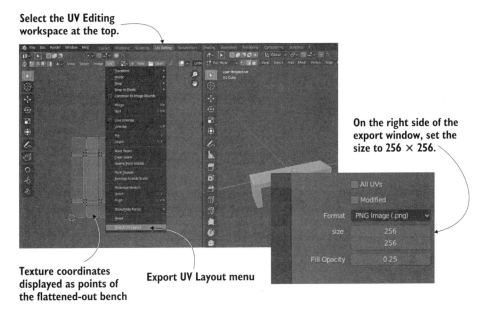

On the right side of the
export window, set the
size to 256 × 256.

Texture coordinates
displayed as points of
the flattened-out bench

Export UV Layout menu

Figure C.10   Switch to UV Editing, then Export UV Layout.

again to figure C.10, choose Export UV Layout under the UV menu in the texture coordinates viewport; save the image as bench.png (this name will also be used later when
importing into Unity) with a size of 256.

Open this image in your image editor and paint colors for the various parts of your
texture. Painting different colors for different UVs will put different colors on those
faces. For example, figure C.11 shows darker blue where the bottom of the bench was
unfolded on the top of the UV layout, and red was painted on the sides of the bench. Now
the image can be brought back into Blender to texture the model; choose Image > Open.

UV Editor after choosing
Open in the Image menu

Texture image painted

Exported UV layout

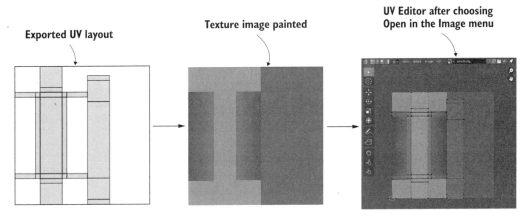

Figure C.11   Paint colors over the exported UVs and then bring the texture into Blender.

Even though the texture image is open in the UV editing view, you still can't see the texture on the model in the 3D view. That requires a couple more steps: assign the image to the object's material and then turn on textures in the viewport (see figure C.12). Now you can see the finished bench, with texture applied!

4. Look at the buttons along the top of the main viewport and find the down arrow all the way to the right. Click this button to open shading settings, and select Texture for the Color setting.

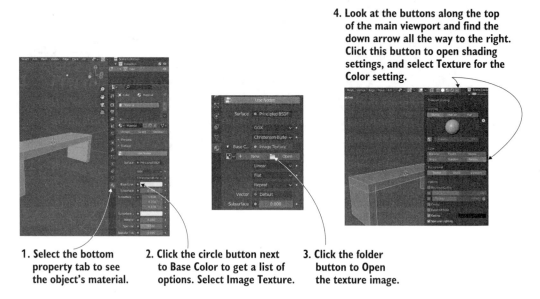

1. Select the bottom property tab to see the object's material.

2. Click the circle button next to Base Color to get a list of options. Select Image Texture.

3. Click the folder button to Open the texture image.

Figure C.12   Set the image on the object's material to view the texture on the model.

Save the model now. Blender will save the file with the .blend extension, using the native file format for Blender. Work in the native file format so that all the features of Blender will be preserved correctly, but later you'll have to export the model to a different file format (FBX is recommended in chapter 4) to import it into Unity. Note that the texture image isn't saved in the model file; what's saved is a reference to the image, but you still need the image file that's being referenced.

appendix D
Online learning resources

This book is a complete introduction to game development in Unity, but there's much more to learn beyond this introduction. You'll find lots of great resources online that you can use to go further after finishing this book.

D.1 Additional tutorials

Many sites provide directed information on a variety of topics within Unity. Several of these are even provided officially by the company behind Unity.

UNITY MANUAL

Unity provides a comprehensive user manual. Not only is it useful for looking up information, but the list of topics is useful by itself for providing a full idea of what Unity is capable of. You can find the manual at http://docs.unity3d.com/Manual/index.html.

SCRIPTING REFERENCE

Unity programmers end up reading the scripting reference more than any other resource (at least, I do!). The user manual covers the capabilities of the engine and use of the editor, but the scripting reference is a thorough reference to Unity's programming API. Every command is listed at http://docs.unity3d.com/ScriptReference/index.html.

UNITY LEARN TUTORIALS

Unity's official website includes several comprehensive tutorials, found in the Learn section. Most importantly, the tutorials are all videos. This may be good or bad, depending on your perspective; if you are someone who likes to watch video tutorials, https://learn.unity.com is a good site to check out.

CATLIKE CODING

Rather than walking learners through a complete game, Catlike Coding offers a grab bag of useful and interesting topics. The topics aren't even necessarily about game development specifically, but are a great way to build up programming skills in Unity. The tutorials can be found at catlikecoding.com/unity/tutorials/.

GAME DEVELOPMENT AT STACK EXCHANGE

Stack Exchange is another great information site with a different format from the previous ones listed. Rather than a series of self-contained tutorials, Stack Exchange presents a mostly text QA that encourages searching. It has sections about a huge array of topics, and https://gamedev.stackexchange.com is the area of the site focused on game development. For what it's worth, I look for Unity information there almost as often as I use the script reference.

MAYA LT GUIDE

As described in appendix B, external art applications are a crucial part of creating visually stunning games. Many resources that teach about Maya, 3ds Max, Blender, or any of the other 3D art applications are available. Appendix C offers a tutorial about Blender. One online guide about using Maya LT (a game development–oriented and less expensive version of Maya) is at https://steamcommunity.com/sharedfiles/filedetails/?id=242847724.

D.2   *Code libraries*

Although the previously listed resources provide tutorials and/or learning information about Unity, the sites in this section provide code that can be used in your projects. Libraries and plugins are another kind of resource that can be useful for new developers, not only for using directly but also for learning from (by reading their code).

UNITY COMMUNITY LIBRARY

The Unity Library is a central database of code contributions from many developers, and the scripts hosted there cover a wide range of functionality. The Resources section of that page links to additional script collections. You can browse the content at https://github.com/UnityCommunity/UnityLibrary.

DOTWEEN AND LEANTWEEN

As mentioned briefly in chapter 3, a kind of motion effect commonly used in games is referred to as a *tween*. In this type of movement, a single code command can set an object moving to a target over a certain amount of time. Tweening functionality can be added using libraries like DOTween (http://dotween.demigiant.com) or Lean-Tween (https://github.com/dentedpixel/LeanTween).

POST-PROCESSING STACK

The Post-Processing Stack is an easy way to add a bunch of visual effects like depth of field and motion blur to your games. Many of these effects have been integrated into one über component. This package is described at http://mng.bz/9aXl.

MOBILE NOTIFICATIONS PACKAGE

While the core of Unity already covers all sorts of features across all gaming platforms, for mobile games you may want to install packages with additional features. The Unity Mobile Notifications package (http://mng.bz/jjvx) focuses on notifications, the little alerts generated by apps on your phone.

FIREBASE CLOUD MESSAGING

While the Unity package just mentioned handles local notifications for both Android and iOS, it supports remote notifications (also called *push notifications*) on iOS only. Push notifications on Android work through a service called Firebase Cloud Messaging, and the developer pages for Firebase (http://mng.bz/WBg0) explain how to use its Unity SDK.

PLAY GAMES SERVICES FROM GOOGLE

On iOS, Unity has GameCenter integration built in so that your games can have platform-native leaderboards and achievements. The equivalent system on Android is called Google Play Games; although it isn't built into Unity, Google maintains a plugin at http://mng.bz/80QP.

FMOD STUDIO

The audio functionality built into Unity works well for playing back recordings, but can be limited for advanced sound design work. FMOD Studio is an advanced sound design tool that has a Unity plugin. Find it at www.fmod.com/studio.

index

Numerics

2D game demo 127
 building card object and making it react to
   clicks 110–112
  building object out of sprites 110
  mouse input code 111–112
  revealing card on click 112
 displaying various card images 113–119
  instantiating grid of cards 116–117
  loading images programmatically 113–114
  setting image from invisible
    SceneController 114–116
  shuffling cards 118–119
 making and scoring matches 119–123
  hiding mismatched cards 120–121
  storing and comparing revealed cards 120
  text display for score 121–123
 restart button 123–127
  calling LoadScene from
    SceneController 126–127
  programming UIButton component using
    SendMessage 124–126
 setting up for 2D graphics 104–110
  displaying 2D images 107–108
  preparing project 105
  switching camera to 2D mode 108–110
2D image editors 358–359
2D images, texturing scene with 82–87
 applying image 85–87
 choosing file format 83–84
 importing image file 84–85
2D interface, advanced 149–150
2D platformer 146
 additional features 140–146
  camera control 145–146

moving platforms 142–144
  slopes and one-way platforms 140–141
 jump ability, adding 137–140
  applying upward impulse 138–139
  detecting ground 139–140
  falling from gravity 137–138
 moving player left and right 132–134
  collision detection 134
  writing keyboard controls 133
 playing sprite's animation 134–137
  Mecanim animation system 134–136
  triggering animations from code 136–137
 setting up graphics 129–132
  importing sprite sheets 130–132
  placing scenery 129–130
3D art applications 357–358
3D demo 49, 74
 basic wandering AI 60–63
  diagramming how basic AI works 60–61
  tracking character's state 62–63
 keyboard input component 44–49
  adjusting components for walking 47–49
  moving CharacterController for collision
    detection 46–47
  responding to keypresses 44–45
  setting rate of movement independent of
    computer speed 45–46
 movement scripts 33–36
  local vs. global coordinate space 35–36
  visualizing how movement is programmed 33
  writing code to implement diagram 34–35
 placing objects in scene 27–33
  lights and cameras 30–32
  player's collider and viewpoint 32–33
  scenery 28–30
 planning project 24–25

3D demo *(continued)*
  script component for looking around 37–43
    horizontal and vertical rotation at same
        time 41–43
    horizontal rotation tracking mouse
        movement 38–39
    vertical rotation with limits 39–41
  scripting reactive targets 57–60
    alerting target that it was hit 58–60
    determining what was hit 57–58
  shooting by instantiating prefabs 68–74
    creating projectile prefab 68–69
    damaging player 73–74
    shooting projectile and colliding with
        target 70–72
  shooting via raycasts 51–57
    adding visual indicators for aiming and
        hits 54–57
    raycasting, defined 51–52
    ScreenPointToRay command 52–54
  spawning enemy prefabs 64–68
    creating enemy prefab 65
    instantiating from invisible
        SceneController 65–68
    prefabs, defined 64
  understanding 3D coordinate space 25–27
3D models, custom 90–94
  exporting and importing 92–94
  file formats 91–92
3D objects, attaching particle effects to 99–100
3ds Max 357–358

A

acceleration, in third-person 3D game 185–186
Action keyword 240
action role-playing game (RPG) demo 313
  building by repurposing projects 283–298
    assembling assets and code from multiple
        projects 284–286
    bringing over AI enemy 285–286
    implementing inventory pop-up 295–298
    operating devices by using mouse 290–292
    programming point-and-click controls
        286–292
    replacing old GUI with new interface
        292–298
    setting up top-down view of scene 287
    updating managers framework 284–285
    writing movement code 287–290
  developing overarching game structure
        299–307
    completing level by reaching exit 303–305

controlling mission flow and multiple
        levels 299–303
    losing level when caught by enemies 305–307
    separate scenes for Startup and Level
        301–303
  handling player progression through
        game 307–313
    adding more levels 312–313
    beating game by completing three levels
        311–313
    saving and loading progress 307–311
Action type 239
Activate() function 209
Activate() method 210
AddComponentMenu attribute 48
AddForce() command 139
AddItem() method 218
additive 98
advanced 2D interface 149–150
AI (artificial intelligence)
  basic wandering 60–63
    diagramming how basic AI works 60–61
    tracking character's state 62–63
  bringing enemies to action RPG demo 285–286
aiming, visual indicators for 54–57
alpha channel 83
anchors 156
Android
  plugins 336–340
  setting up build tools 329–331
Android SDK 357
animations
  on player character, in third-person 3D
        game 190–198
    creating animator controller 194–197
    defining animation clips in imported
        model 192–194
    writing code that operates animator 197–198
  sprite, in 2D platformer 134–137
    Mecanim animation system 134–136
    triggering animations from code 136–137
AR Foundation for mobile augmented
        reality 342–348
art assets 76–78
as keyword 274
Aseprite 358–359
assets 64
atmosphere controlled by code, setting up
        232–235
Audacity 359
audio 281
  audio control interface 265–272
    playing UI sounds 271–272
    setting up central AudioManager 265–267
    volume control UI 267–271

audio *(continued)*
  background music, adding 272–280
    controlling music volume separately
      276–278
    fading between songs 278–280
    playing music loops 272–276
  importing sound effects 258–261
    importing audio files 260–261
    supported file formats 258–260
  playing sound effects 261–265
    assigning looping sound 263–264
    audio system parts 261–263
    triggering sound effects from code 264–265
audio listener 263
Audio object 271
audio software 359
audio source 262
AudioListener class 269
AudioListener component 263
AudioManager
  setting up 265–267
  setting up AudioSource for 273–274
  writing code to play audio clips in 274–275
AudioManager property 277
AudioSource 273–274
AudioSource component 263
AudioSource object 280
AudioSource variable 280
augmented reality (AR), mobile 342–348
Awake() method 217

B

background music 272–280
  controlling music volume separately 276–278
  fading between songs 278–280
  playing music loops 272–276
    adding music controls to UI 275–276
    importing audio clips 273
    setting up AudioSource 273–274
    writing code to play audio clips in
      AudioManager 274–275
baking shadows 176
billboard, networked 247–253
  caching downloaded image for reuse 251–253
  displaying images on billboard 250–251
  loading images from internet 247–250
Blender
  general discussion 358
  modeling bench in 360–368
    building mesh geometry 361–364
    texture-mapping model 365–368
broadcast messenger system 166–170

broadcasting and listening for events from
  HUD 168–170
broadcasting and listening for events from
  scene 167–168
integrating event system 166–167
browser, communicating with JavaScript in
  322–325
build tools, for mobile games 326–331
buttons, in GUI 153–155

C

cache 251
caching downloaded image for reuse 251–253
callback 240
callback parameter 240
callback, understanding 240
Camera component 53
Camera object 30
camera-relative movement controls 180–184
  moving forward in that direction 183–184
  rotating character to face movement
    direction 180–183
cameras
  adjusting view for third-person 173–179
    adding shadows to scene 175–177
    importing character to look at 174–175
    orbiting camera around player
      character 177–179
  controlling in 2D platformer 145–146
  in 3D demo 30–32
  switching to 2D mode 108–110
Canvas object 295
canvas, creating for GUI 151–153
card_back sprite 110
CardRevealed() method 119
cards, Memory game demo
  building card object and making it react to
    clicks 110–112
    building object out of sprites 110
    mouse input code 111–112
    revealing card on click 112
  displaying various images 113–119
    instantiating grid of cards 116–117
    loading images programmatically 113–114
    setting image from invisible
      SceneController 114–116
    shuffling cards 118–119
  hiding mismatched cards 120–121
  storing and comparing revealed cards 120
Cartesian coordinate system 25
Catlike Coding 369–370
ChangeHealth() method 225
CharacterController 46–47

characters
  animations on, in third-person 3D game
      190–198
    creating animator controller 194–197
    defining animation clips in imported
        model 192–194
    writing code that operates animator 197–198
  importing for third-person game 174–175
  orbiting camera around 177–179
  rotating to face movement direction 180–183
  tracking state of 62–63
Clamp() method 40
click, revealing card on in Memory game 112
code libraries 370–371
CollectibleItem script 218
collecting items scattered around level 210–212
collection object, storing inventory in 217–220
collider, player, in 3D demo 32–33
colliding with target, in 3D demo 70–72
collision detection
  in 2D platformer 134
  moving CharacterController for 46–47
collision responses 206–212
  collecting items scattered around level 210–212
  colliding with physics-enabled obstacles
      206–207
  operating door with trigger object 207–210
Color object 206
color-changing monitor 205–206
components 5
computer speed, setting rate of movement
    independent of 45–46
console games developed in Unity 7–8
Console tab 16
console, printing to 19–21
ConsumeItem() method 225
ContainsKey() method 220
controller 212
Controller object 295
coordinates, 3D 25–27
coroutines, HTTP requests using 238–242
  callback 240
  coroutine methods cascading through each
      other 239–240
  making use of networking code 241–242
  writing code for 238–239
cross product 182
CSG (constructive solid geometry) 80
Cube object 30
culling mask 177
Cursor settings 157
custom 3D models 90–94
  exporting and importing 92–94
  file formats 91–92

D

damaging player, in first-person shooter game
    73–74
DataManager script 308
Deactivate() function 209
Deactivate() method 210
Debug statement 120
Debug.Log() command 21
dependencies block 244
deploying games to players 348
  building for desktop 317–320
    adjusting player settings 318–319
    building application 317–318
    platform-dependent compilation 319–320
  building for mobile 325–340
    developing plugins 332–340
    setting up build tools 326–331
    texture compression 331–332
  building for web 321–325
    communicating with JavaScript in
        browser 322–325
    game embedded in web page 321–322
  developing extended reality 341–348
    AR Foundation for mobile augmented
        reality 342–348
    supporting virtual reality headsets 341–342
deserialization 245
desktop games
  building for desktop 317–320
    adjusting player settings 318–319
    building application 317–318
    platform-dependent compilation 319–320
  built with Unity, examples of 7–8
Destroy()method 68
developer 4
DeviceOperator script 204, 250, 291
DeviceTrigger script 210
Dictionary, storing inventory in 217–220
directional lights 30
directive 318
distance property 62
DllImport command 323
DontDestroyOnLoad() function 312
DontDestroyOnLoad() method 127, 301
DoorOpenDevice script 209
doors
  checking distance and facing before
      opening 203–205
  equipping key to use on locked 223–224
  operating with trigger object 207–210
  that open and close on keypress, creating 201–
      203
dot product 190
DOTween 370

downloading weather data 235–247
    changing scene based on weather data 246–247
    parsing JSON 243–246
    parsing XML 242–243
    requesting HTTP data using coroutines 238–242
DrawLine() command 143
DrawRay() command 143
dynamic string 165

E

edges, handling in third-person 3D game 186–190
effects, creating using particle systems 95–100
    adjusting parameters on default effect 96
    applying new texture for fire 98–99
    attaching particle effects to 3D objects 99–100
enemies, adding to 3D game
    basic wandering AI 60–63
        diagramming how basic AI works 60–61
        tracking character's state 62–63
    scripting reactive targets 57–60
        alerting target that it was hit 58–60
        determining what was hit 57–58
    shooting by instantiating prefabs 68–74
        creating projectile prefab 68–69
        damaging player 73–74
        shooting projectile and colliding with target 70–72
    spawning enemy prefabs 64–68
        creating enemy prefab 65
        instantiating from invisible SceneController 65–68
        prefabs, defined 64
enemies, in action RPG demo
    bringing from 3D game 285–286
    losing level when caught by 305–307
EquipItem() method 223
equippedItem property 223
ETC (Ericsson Texture Compression) 332
events, updating game by responding to 166–170
    broadcasting and listening for events from HUD 168–170
    broadcasting and listening for events from scene 167–168
    integrating event system 166–167
EventTrigger component 298
exit, completing level by reaching 303–305
exporting custom 3D models 92–94
extended reality (XR), developing 341–348
    AR Foundation for mobile augmented reality 342–348
    supporting virtual reality headsets 341–342

external software tools 356–359
    2D image editors 358–359
    3D art applications 357–358
    audio software 359
    programming tools 356–357
extrude 364

F

fading between songs 278–280
file formats
    2D images 83–84
    custom 3D models 91–92
    supported for sound effects 258–260
File.Create() method 310
fire effect, creating using particle systems 95–100
    adjusting parameters on default effect 96
    applying new texture for fire 98–99
    attaching particle effects to 3D objects 99–100
Fireball object 69
Firebase Cloud Messaging 371
first-person controls, in 3D demo 44–49
    adjusting components for walking 47–49
    moving CharacterController for collision detection 46–47
    responding to keypresses 44–45
    setting rate of movement independent of computer speed 45–46
first-person shooter (FPS) game demo 74
    basic wandering AI 60–63
        diagramming how basic AI works 60–61
        tracking character's state 62–63
    scripting reactive targets 57–60
        alerting target that it was hit 58–60
        determining what was hit 57–58
    shooting by instantiating prefabs 68–74
        creating projectile prefab 68–69
        damaging player 73–74
        shooting projectile and colliding with target 70–72
    shooting via raycasts 51–57
        adding visual indicators for aiming and hits 54–57
        raycasting, defined 51–52
        ScreenPointToRay command 52–54
    spawning enemy prefabs 64–68
        creating enemy prefab 65
        instantiating from invisible SceneController 65–68
        prefabs, defined 64
Floor object 30
floor plan for level
    drawing 79–80
    laying out primitives according to 80–81
FMOD Studio 371

FPS (first-person shooter) 24
frame 17
frame-rate dependent 45
frame-rate independent 45
freezeRotation property 42
FSM (finite-state machine) 63

G

game state, managing 212–220
   programming game managers 214–217
   setting up player and inventory managers
      212–213
   storing inventory in collection object 217–220
Game view 12–14
GameEvent script 167, 293
GameObject type 67
get command 165
get function 269
GetAxis() method 39
GetButtonDown() function 186
GetComponent() method 58, 113
GetItemCount() method 221
GetItemList() method 221
GIMP 358
global coordinates 35–36
Google Play Games 371
graphics 100
   art assets 76–78
   custom 3D models 90–94
      exporting and importing 92–94
      file formats 91–92
   generating sky visuals by using texture
      images 87–90
      creating new skybox material 88–90
      skybox, defined 87–88
   importing UI images 151
   particle systems, creating effects using 95–100
      adjusting parameters on default effect 96
      applying new texture for fire 98–99
      attaching particle effects to 3D objects
         99–100
   texturing scene with 2D images 82–87
      applying image 85–87
      choosing file format 83–84
      importing image file 84–85
   whiteboxing 78–81
      drawing floor plan for level 79–80
      explained 79
      laying out primitives according to plan
         80–81
gravity variable 47
gravity, in 2D platformer 137–138
grid of cards, Memory game demo 116–117

ground detection
   in 2D platformer 139–140
   modifying in third-person 3D game 186–190
grounded variable 140
GUI (graphical user interface) 170
   action RPG demo 292–298
   adding music controls to 275–276
   defined 121
   immediate mode GUI vs. advanced 2D
      interface 149–150
   importing UI images 151
   planning layout 150
   playing UI sounds 271–272
   programming interactivity in 157–166
      creating pop-up window 160–163
      invisible UIController 158–160
      setting values using sliders and input
         fields 163–166
   setting up display 151–157
      buttons, images, and text labels 153–155
      controlling position of elements 156–157
      creating canvas for interface 151–153
   updating game by responding to events
      166–170
      broadcasting and listening for events from
         HUD 168–170
      broadcasting and listening for events from
         scene 167–168
      integrating event system 166–167
volume control 267–271

H

health, restoring player 224–225
Hello World! script 19–21
hiding mismatched cards, Memory game
   demo 120–121
Hierarchy tab 15
hits
   alerting target that it was hit 58–60
   determining what was hit 57–58
   visual indicators for 54–57
HMD (head-mounted display) 342
horizontal movement, in 2D platformer 132–134
   collision detection 134
   writing keyboard controls 133
horizontal rotation
   and vertical rotation at same time 41–43
   tracking mouse movement 38–39
HTTP (Hypertext Transfer Protocol) 230
HUD (heads-up display) 148
Hurt() method 73
Hypertext Transfer Protocol (HTTP) requests
   using coroutines 238–242
   callback 240

Hypertext Transfer Protocol (HTTP) requests
(*continued*)
coroutine methods cascading through each
other 239–240
making use of networking code 241–242
writing code for 238–239

I

icons array 298
IDE (integrated development environment) 5
if statement 67, 186, 224, 289
IGameManager interface 215, 284
image variable 113
images
2D, displaying 107–108
card, displaying various in Memory game
113–119
instantiating grid of cards 116–117
loading images programmatically 113–114
setting image from invisible
SceneController 114–116
shuffling cards 118–119
in GUI 153–155
networked billboard
caching downloaded image for reuse
251–253
displaying images on billboard 250–251
loading images from internet 247–250
immediate mode GUI 149–150
importing
audio clips 273
custom 3D models 92–94
sound effects 258–261
importing audio files 260–261
supported file formats 258–260
sprite sheets 130–132
UI images 151
impulse 139
Initialize() function 334
Input class 39
input fields, pop-up window 163–166
Input.GetMouseButtonDown() method 53
Inspector tab 15
instantiate 65
Instantiate() method 67, 116
instantiating grid of cards, Memory game
demo 116–117
instantiating prefabs
from invisible SceneController 65–68
shooting by 68–74
creating projectile prefab 68–69
damaging player 73–74

shooting projectile and colliding with
target 70–72
int parameter 275
interactive devices and items 226
collision responses 206–212
collecting items scattered around level
210–212
colliding with physics-enabled obstacles
206–207
operating door with trigger object 207–210
creating doors and other devices 201–206
checking distance and facing before opening
door 203–205
doors that open and close on keypress
201–203
operating color-changing monitor 205–206
inventory UI 220–225
displaying inventory items in UI 220–222
equipping key to use on locked doors
223–224
restoring player health 224–225
managing inventory data and game state
212–220
programming game managers 214–217
setting up player and inventory
managers 212–213
storing inventory in collection object
217–220
operating devices by using mouse 290–292
interactivity in GUI, programming 157–166
creating pop-up window 160–163
invisible UIController 158–160
setting values using sliders and input fields
163–166
internet, connecting game to 256
downloading weather data 235–247
changing scene based on weather data
246–247
HTTP requests using coroutines 238–242
parsing JSON 243–246
parsing XML 242–243
networked billboard, adding 247–253
caching downloaded image for reuse
251–253
displaying images on billboard 250–251
loading images from internet 247–250
outdoor scene, creating 231–235
generating sky visuals by using skybox
231–232
setting up atmosphere controlled by
code 232–235
posting data to web server 253–256
server-side code in PHP 255–256
tracking current weather 254–255

inventory data, managing 212–220
   programming game managers 214–217
   setting up player and inventory managers
     212–213
   storing inventory in collection object 217–220
inventory manager
   programming 214–217
   setting up 212–213
inventory pop-up, action RPG demo 295–298
Inventory Popup object 295
inventory UI 220–225
   displaying inventory items in 220–222
   equipping key to use on locked doors 223–224
   restoring player health 224–225
InventoryManager script 217
InventoryPopup script 295
iOS
   plugins 333–336
   setting up build tools 326–329
IPA (iOS application package) 326
isGrounded property 186

J

JavaScript, communicating with in browser 322–325
JSON (JavaScript Object Notation), parsing when
   downloading weather data 243–246
JSON Linq 245
JsonConvert.DeserializeObject command 245
JsonUtility class 244
jump ability, adding to 2D platformer 137–140
   applying upward impulse 138–139
   detecting ground 139–140
   falling from gravity 137–138
jump action, third-person 3D game 184–190
   applying vertical speed and acceleration
     185–186
   modifying ground detection to handle edges
     and slopes 186–190

K

key, to use on locked doors 223–224
keyboard controls, 2D platformer 133
keyboard input component, 3D demo 44–49
   adjusting components for walking 47–49
   moving CharacterController for collision
     detection 46–47
   responding to keypresses 44–45
   setting rate of movement independent of
     computer speed 45–46
keyboard shortcuts 354–355
keyboard use with Unity 14–15
Knuth shuffle algorithm 118

L

labels array 298
lambda function 252
LateUpdate() function 178
LateUpdate() method 145
layout, planning GUI 150
lazy loading 272
LeanTween 370
level design 79
level designer 79
levels
   action RPG demo
     adding more 312–313
     beating game by completing three 311–313
     completing by reaching exit 303–305
     controlling mission flow and 299–303
     losing when caught by enemies 305–307
     separate scenes for 301–303
   collecting items scattered around 210–212
   level design 79–80
lightmaps 176
lights, in 3D demo 30–32
linear interpolation 182
List object, storing inventory in 217–220
loading images programmatically 113–114
loading player progress 307–311
LoadScene method, calling from
   SceneController 126–127
LoadScene() method 300
local coordinates 35–36
locked doors, equipping key to use on 223–224
LookAt() method 179
looking around, script component for 37–43
   horizontal and vertical rotation at same
     time 41–43
   horizontal rotation tracking mouse
     movement 38–39
   vertical rotation with limits 39–41
LookRotation() value 182
looping sound, assigning 263–264
loops, defined 193
loops, playing music 272–276
   adding music controls to UI 275–276
   importing audio clips 273
   setting up AudioSource 273–274
   writing code to play audio clips in
     AudioManager 274–275
losing level when caught by enemies, action RPG
   demo 305–307

M

manager of managers 212
managers framework, updating for action RPG
   demo 284–285

Managers object 213, 265
Managers script 217, 266, 300
ManagerStatus script 214
material 69, 77
material, skybox 88–90
Maya 357, 370
Mecanim animation system 134–136
Memory game demo 127
　　building card object and making it react to
　　　　clicks 110–112
　　　　building object out of sprites 110
　　　　mouse input code 111–112
　　　　revealing card on click 112
　　displaying various card images 113–119
　　　　instantiating grid of cards 116–117
　　　　loading images programmatically 113–114
　　　　setting image from invisible
　　　　　　SceneController 114–116
　　　　shuffling cards 118–119
　　making and scoring matches 119–123
　　　　hiding mismatched cards 120–121
　　　　storing and comparing revealed cards 120
　　　　text display for score 121–123
　　restart button 123–127
　　　　calling LoadScene from
　　　　　　SceneController 126–127
　　　　programming UIButton component using
　　　　　　SendMessage 124–126
　　setting up for 2D graphics 104–110
　　　　displaying 2D images 107–108
　　　　preparing project 105
　　　　switching camera to 2D mode 108–110
MemoryCard script 113
mesh elements 362
mesh object 13
mesh object, creating in Blender 360–368
　　building mesh geometry 361–364
　　texture-mapping model 365–368
Messenger script 167, 293
mismatched cards, Memory game demo 120–121
mission flow, action RPG demo 299–303
MMO (massively multiplayer online) 229
MMORPGs (MMO role-playing games) 229
mobile 325
mobile augmented reality 342–348
mobile games
　　building for mobile 325–340
　　　　developing plugins 332–340
　　　　setting up build tools 326–331
　　　　texture compression 331–332
　　built with Unity, examples of 8–9
Mobile Notifications package 371
model 76
modeling bench in Blender 360–368
　　building mesh geometry 361–364

texture-mapping model 365–368
MonoBehaviour class 30
mouse
　　operating devices by using 290–292
　　scene navigation using 353–354
　　use with Unity 14–15
mouse input code, Memory game demo 111–112
mouse picking 52
MouseLook script 37–43
　　horizontal and vertical rotation at same
　　　　time 41–43
　　horizontal rotation tracking mouse
　　　　movement 38–39
　　vertical rotation with limits 39–41
Move() method 47
movement 33–36
　　action RPG demo 287–290
　　adjusting components for walking 47–49
　　local vs. global coordinate space 35–36
　　moving CharacterController for collision
　　　　detection 46–47
　　programming camera-relative controls 180–184
　　　　moving forward in that direction 183–184
　　　　rotating character to face movement
　　　　　　direction 180–183
　　responding to keypresses 44–45
　　setting rate of, independent of computer
　　　　speed 45–46
　　visualizing how movement is programmed 33
　　writing code to implement diagram 34–35
movement script 134
moving platforms, in 2D platformers 142–144
MovingPlatform script 143

N

navigation using mouse 353–354
networked billboard 247–253
　　caching downloaded image for reuse 251–253
　　displaying images on billboard 250–251
　　loading images from internet 247–250
networking code, making use of 241–242
NetworkService class 236
NetworkService object 235
NetworkService script 238
normal property 189
normalized vectors 204
normals 175
nullable values 289

O

Object type 67
ObjectiveTrigger script 305

objects, placing in scene 27–33
  lights and cameras 30–32
  player's collider and viewpoint 32–33
  scenery 28–30
OnControllerColliderHit() function 190
OnDisable() method 168
OnDrawGizmos() method 143
one-way platforms, in 2D platformers 140–141
OnEnable() method 168
OnGUI() method 57, 149, 222
online learning resources 369–371
  additional tutorials 369–370
  code libraries 370–371
OnMouseDown() function 112
OnMouseSomething function 125
OnSpeedValue() method 165
OnSubmitName() function 165
OnTriggerEnter() method 72, 209
OnTriggerExit() method 209
Operate function 206
Operate() method 202, 291
OrbitCamera component 301
orbiting camera around player character 177–179
orthographic, defined 109
outdoor scene, creating 231–235
  changing scene based on weather data 246–247
  generating sky visuals by using skybox 231–232
  setting up atmosphere controlled by code 232–235
OverlapSphere() method 204

P

parameters 136
parsing 242
  JSON when downloading weather data 243–246
  XML when downloading weather data 242–243
particle systems, creating effects using 95–100
  adjusting parameters on default effect 96
  applying new texture for fire 98–99
  attaching particle effects to 3D objects 99–100
PCM (pulse code modulation) 261
Photoshop 358
PHP, server-side code in 255–256
physics-enabled obstacles, colliding with 206–207
Physics.Raycast() method 52
Physics.SphereCast() method 62
pixel-perfect 109
platform-dependent compilation 319–320
PlatformerPlayer script 136
player manager
  programming 214–217
  setting up 212–213
Player object 30
Player Settings, Build Settings window 318–319

Player tag 291
PlayerCharacter script 73
PlayerManager script 217
players
  collider and viewpoint, in 3D demo 32–33
  damaging in first-person shooter game 73–74
  handling progression through action RPG 307–313
    adding more levels 312–313
    beating game by completing three levels 311–313
    saving and loading progress 307–311
  moving left and right in 2D platformer 132–134
    collision detection 134
    writing keyboard controls 133
playing music loops 272–276
  adding music controls to UI 275–276
  importing audio clips 273
  setting up AudioSource 273–274
  writing code to play audio clips in AudioManager 274–275
playing sound effects 261–265
  assigning looping sound 263–264
  audio system parts 261–263
  triggering sound effects from code 264–265
playing UI sounds 271–272
PlayMusic() method 274
PlayOneShot() method 265
plugins for mobile games 332–340
point lights 30
point-and-click controls for action RPG demo 286–292
pop-up window
  creating 160–163
  inventory, action RPG demo 295–298
  setting values using sliders and input fields 163–166
positioning objects on GUI 156–157
Post-Processing Stack 370
posting data to web server 253–256
  server-side code in PHP 255–256
  tracking current weather 254–255 318
prefabs
  shooting by instantiating 68–74
    creating projectile prefab 68–69
    damaging player 73–74
    shooting projectile and colliding with target 70–72
  spawning enemy 64–68
    creating enemy prefab 65
    instantiating from invisible SceneController 65–68
  prefabs, defined 64

primitives, laying out according to floor plan 80–81
printing to console 19–21
Pro Tools 359
programmer 4
programming 16–21
  external software tools 356–357
  of movement, visualizing 33
  printing to console 19–21
  script components 17–18
  using Visual Studio 18–19
Project tab 16
projectile prefab, creating 68–69
PVRTC (PowerVR Texture Compression) 332
Pyxel Edit 358–359

Q

Quaternion.Lerp() method 182

R

radius variable 204
Random.Range() method 62, 115
ray 52
Ray object 54
Raycast() method 54
raycasts 61–62
  shooting via 51–57
    adding visual indicators for aiming and hits 54–57
    raycasting, defined 51–52
    ScreenPointToRay command 52–54
RayShooter class 56
reactive targets, scripting 57–60
  alerting target that it was hit 58–60
  determining what was hit 57–58
ReactiveTarget script 59
ReactToHit()method 59
Rect tool 14
RelativeMovement component 288
RelativeMovement script 183, 203
rendering, defined 57
RequireComponent attribute 48, 184
requireKey Boolean 223
requireKey option 224
Resources.Load() command 272
Resources.Load() method 221
restart button, Memory game demo 123–127
  calling LoadScene from SceneController 126–127
  programming UIButton component using SendMessage 124–126
Restart() method 126

retained mode 149
revealed cards, Memory game demo 120
Rider 356
Rigidbody component 42, 133
root object 29
Rotate command 39
Rotate() method 35
rotating character to face movement direction 180–183
rotation, responding to mouse input 37–43
  horizontal and vertical rotation at same time 41–43
  horizontal rotation tracking mouse movement 38–39
  vertical rotation with limits 39–41
RPG (role-playing game) 283
running code in Unity 17–18

S

saving player progress 307–311
scene
  broadcasting and listening for events from 167–168
  for startup and levels in action RPG demo 301–303
  navigation using mouse 353–354
  top-down view in action RPG demo 287
Scene view 12–14
SceneController
  calling LoadScene from 126–127
  instantiating enemy prefab from 65–68
  setting card image from 114–116
SceneController component 113
SceneController object 126
SceneController script 67
scenery
  in 3D demo 28–30
  placing in 2D platformer 129–130
score variable 123
score, Memory game demo 121–123
scoreLabel variable 123
Screen Space—Camera setting 152
Screen Space—Overlay setting 152
ScreenPointToRay command 52–54
ScreenPointToRay() method 52
script components
  for looking around 37–43
    horizontal and vertical rotation at same time 41–43
    horizontal rotation tracking mouse movement 38–39
    vertical rotation with limits 39–41
  general discussion 17–18
scripting reference 369

scripts
  movement 33–36
    adjusting components for walking 47–49
    local vs. global coordinate space 35–36
    moving CharacterController for collision
      detection 46–47
    responding to keypresses 44–45
    setting rate of movement independent of
      computer speed 45–46
    visualizing how movement is programmed 33
    writing code to implement diagram 34–35
  reactive targets 57–60
    alerting target that it was hit 58–60
    determining what was hit 57–58
SendMessage, programming UIButton component
  using 124–126
SendMessage() method 126
serialization 245, 308
SerializeField attribute 66
server, posting data to 253–256
  server-side code in PHP 255–256
  tracking current weather 254–255
set function 269
SetActive() method 112
SetFloat() method 233
SetOvercast() method 246
SettingsPopup script 162, 270
shader 88
shadows, adding to third-person scene 175–177
shooting
  by instantiating prefabs 68–74
    creating projectile prefab 68–69
    damaging player 73–74
    shooting projectile and colliding with
      target 70–72
  via raycasts 51–57
    adding visual indicators for aiming and
      hits 54–57
    raycasting, defined 51–52
    ScreenPointToRay command 52–54
shortcuts, keyboard 354–355
shuffling cards, Memory game demo 118–119
skeletal animation 191
SketchUp 358
sky visuals
  generating by using texture images 87–90
    creating new skybox material 88–90
    skybox, defined 87–88
  generating using skybox 231–232
skyboxes
  creating new skybox material 88–90
  defined 87–88
  generating sky visuals using 231–232
slerp (spherical linear interpolation) 182
sliced image 160

sliders, pop-up window 163–166
slopes
  handling, in third-person 3D game 186–190
  in 2D platformers 140–141
SmoothDamp() function 146
software tools, external 356–359
  2D image editors 358–359
  3D art applications 357–358
  audio software 359
  programming tools 356–357
sound effects
  importing 258–261
    importing audio files 260–261
    supported file formats 258–260
  playing 261–265
    assigning looping sound 263–264
    audio system parts 261–263
    triggering sound effects from code 264–265
soundMute property 270
soundVolume property 269
spawning enemy prefabs 64–68
  creating enemy prefab 65
  instantiating from invisible
    SceneController 65–68
  prefabs, defined 64
speed parameter 136
Sphere object 30
SphereCast() method 61
Spin script 36
spot lights 30
sprite property 113
sprite sheets, importing 130–132
Sprite variable 113
SpriteRenderer component 113
SpriteRenderer object 113
sprites
  building card object out of 110
  displaying 107–108
  playing animation in 2D platformer 134–137
    Mecanim animation system 134–136
    triggering animations from code 136–137
SSAO (screen space ambient occlusion) 4
Stack Exchange 370
Start() method 17, 42, 57, 157
StartCoroutine() method 238
Startup() function 236
Startup() method 217, 277
StartupController script 301
state machine 134
state, tracking character's 62–63
states 135
static extern command 334
status property 214, 236
storing inventory in collection object 217–220
string function 336

string interpolation 73
switch statement 276
System namespace 239

T

T-pose 175
table_top sprite 107
target property 180
targets property 210
targets, reactive 57–60
    alerting target that it was hit 58–60
    determining what was hit 57–58
text display for score, Memory game demo 121–123
text labels, in GUI 153–155
texture 82
texture coordinates 93, 365
texture-mapping model in Blender 365–368
TexturePacker 358
textures
    compression for mobile games 331–332
    for fire effect 98–99
    generating sky visuals by using 87–90
        creating new skybox material 88–90
        skybox, defined 87–88
    texturing scene with 2D images 82–87
        applying image 85–87
        choosing file format 83–84
        importing image file 84–85
TGA file format 83
third-person 3D game 199
    adjusting camera view for third-person 173–179
        adding shadows to scene 175–177
        importing character to look at 174–175
        orbiting camera around player character 177–179
    implementing jump action 184–190
        applying vertical speed and acceleration 185–186
        modifying ground detection to handle edges and slopes 186–190
    programming camera-relative movement controls 180–184
        moving forward in that direction 183–184
        rotating character to face movement direction 180–183
    setting up animations on player character 190–198
        creating animator controller 194–197
        defining animation clips in imported model 192–194
        writing code that operates animator 197–198
tileable images 84
Time class 46

Toolbar 12–14
top-down view of scene, action RPG demo 287
tracking character's state 62–63
tracking current weather 254–255
transform 47
Transform class 35
Transform component 58, 113
TransformDirection() method 47
transforms, script applying 33–36
    local vs. global coordinate space 35–36
    visualizing how movement is programmed 33
    writing code to implement diagram 34–35
Translate() method 45, 62
trigger object, operating door with 207–210
triggering animations from code 136–137
triggering sound effects from code 264–265
triggers 209
tutorials, Unity 369–370

U

UI (user interface) 7–170
    action RPG demo 292–298
    adding music controls to 275–276
    immediate mode GUI vs. advanced 2D interface 149–150
    importing UI images 151
    inventory UI 220–225
        displaying inventory items in 220–222
        equipping key to use on locked doors 223–224
        restoring player health 224–225
    planning layout 150
    playing UI sounds 271–272
    programming interactivity in 157–166
        creating pop-up window 160–163
        invisible UIController 158–160
        setting values using sliders and input fields 163–166
    setting up display 151–157
        buttons, images, and text labels 153–155
        controlling position of elements 156–157
        creating canvas for interface 151–153
    updating game by responding to events 166–170
        broadcasting and listening for events from HUD 168–170
        broadcasting and listening for events from scene 167–168
        integrating event system 166–167
    volume control 267–271
UIButton component, programming using SendMessage 124–126
UIController component 295
UIController script 158–160, 294

Unity 22
   downsides of 6–7
   example games built with 7–10
   programming in 16–21
      printing to console 19–21
      script components 17–18
      using Visual Studio 18–19
   scripting reference 369
   strengths and advantages of 4–6
   tutorials 369
   use of 10–16
      Hierarchy and Inspector tabs 15
      mouse and keyboard use 14–15
      Project and Console tabs 16
      Scene view, Game view, and Toolbar 12–14
   user manual 369
Unity Library 370
UNITY_ANDROID platform 337
UnitySendMessage() method 336
UnityWebRequest class 238
UnityWebRequest object 247
unusual floors, in 2D platformers 140–141
unwrapping 365
Update() function 112, 181, 203
Update() method 17, 33, 55, 167, 190, 289
UpdateData() method 308
updating game by responding to events 166–170
   broadcasting and listening for events from
      HUD 168–170
   broadcasting and listening for events from
      scene 167–168
   integrating event system 166–167
UPM (Unity Package Manager) 244
user manual 369
using statement 239
UV unwrapping 366

V

VCS (version-control system) 357
Vector3 value 203
vertical movement
   in 2D platformer 137–140
      applying upward impulse 138–139
      detecting ground 139–140
      falling from gravity 137–138
   in third-person 3D game 185–186
vertical rotation
   and horizontal rotation at same time 41–43
   for MouseLook 39–41
viewpoint, player's, in 3D demo 32–33
visual indicators for aiming and hits 54–57
Visual Studio 18–19
volume control UI 267–271
volume, music, controlling separately 276–278

VR (virtual reality) games 9–10
VR (virtual reality) headsets 341–342

W

walking, adjusting components for 47–49
wandering AI, basic 60–63
   diagramming how basic AI works 60–61
   tracking character's state 62–63
WanderingAI script 63
weather data
   downloading 235–247
      changing scene based on weather data
         246–247
      parsing JSON 243–246
      parsing XML 242–243
      requesting HTTP data using coroutines
         238–242
   posting to web server 253–256
      server-side code in PHP 255–256
      tracking current weather 254–255
WeatherController script 246
WeatherManager class 235
web API 235
web server, posting data to 253–256
   server-side code in PHP 255–256
   tracking current weather 254–255
web service 235
web, building for 321–325
   communicating with JavaScript in browser
      322–325
   game embedded in web page 321–322
whiteboxing 78–81
   drawing floor plan for level 79–80
   explained 79
   laying out primitives according to plan 80–81
World Space setting 152
WWWForm object 254

X

Xcode 357
XML (Extensible Markup Language) 242
XR (extended reality) 5

Y

yield command 56, 121
yield keyword 56, 238
yield statement 239

Z

z-fighting 287